Contemporary State Terrorism

This volume aims to 'bring the state back into terrorism studies' and fill the notable gap that currently exists in our understanding of the ways in which states employ terrorism as a political strategy of internal governance or foreign policy.

Within this broader context, the volume has a number of specific aims. First, it aims to make the argument that state terrorism is a valid and analytically useful concept which can do much to illuminate our understanding of state repression and governance, and illustrate the varieties of actors, modalities, aims, forms, and outcomes of this form of contemporary political violence. Second, by discussing a rich and diverse set of empirical case studies of contemporary state terrorism this volume explores and tests theoretical notions, generates new questions and provides a resource for further research. Third, it contributes to a critical-normative approach to the study of terrorism more broadly and challenges dominant approaches and perspectives which assume that states, particularly Western states, are primarily victims and not perpetrators of terrorism. Given the scarceness of current and past research on state terrorism, this volume will make a genuine contribution to the wider field, particularly in terms of ongoing efforts to generate more critical approaches to the study of political terrorism.

This book will be of much interest to students of critical terrorism studies, critical security studies, terrorism and political violence and political theory in general.

Richard Jackson is Reader in International Politics at Aberystwyth University, UK. He is the founding editor of the Routledge journal, *Critical Studies on Terrorism* and the convenor of the BISA Critical Studies on Terrorism Working Group (CSTWG). **Eamon Murphy** is Professor of History and International Relations at Curtin University of Technology in Western Australia. **Scott Poynting** is Professor in Sociology at Manchester Metropolitan University.

Series: Critical Terrorism Studies
Series Editors: Richard Jackson, Marie Breen Smyth and Jeroen Gunning
Aberystwyth University, UK

This book series will publish rigorous and innovative studies on all aspects of terrorism, counter-terrorism and state terror. It seeks to advance a new generation of thinking on traditional subjects and investigate topics frequently overlooked in orthodox accounts of terrorism. Books in this series will typically adopt approaches informed by critical-normative theory, post-positivist methodologies and non-Western perspectives, as well as rigorous and reflective orthodox terrorism studies.

Terrorism and the Politics of Response
Edited by Angharad Closs Stephens and Nick Vaughan-Williams

Critical Terrorism Studies
Framing a New Research Agenda
Edited by Richard Jackson, Marie Breen Smyth and Jeroen Gunning

State Terrorism and Neoliberalism
The North in the South
Ruth Blakeley

Contemporary State Terrorism
Theory and practice
Edited by Richard Jackson, Eamon Murphy and Scott Poynting

State Violence and Genocide in Latin America
The Cold War Years
Edited by Marcia Esparza, Henry R. Huttenbach and Daniel Feierstein

Contemporary State Terrorism

Theory and practice

**Edited by Richard Jackson,
Eamon Murphy and Scott Poynting**

Routledge
Taylor & Francis Group

LONDON AND NEW YORK

First published 2010
by Routledge
2 Park Square, Milton Park, Abingdon, Oxon, OX14 4RN

Simultaneously published in the USA and Canada
by Routledge
711 Third Avenue, New York, NY 10017

Routledge is an imprint of the Taylor & Francis Group, an informa business

First issued in paperback 2011

Typeset in Times New Roman by Wearset Ltd, Boldon, Tyne and Wear

British Library Cataloguing in Publication Data
A catalogue record for this book is available from the British Library

Library of Congress Cataloging in Publication Data
Contemporary state terrorism : theory and practice / edited by Richard
Jackson, Eamon Murphy and Scott Poynting.
p. cm.
1. State-sponsored terrorism. 2. Terrorism. I. Jackson, Richard. II.
Murphy, Eamon. III. Poynting, Scott.
HV6431.C6536 2009
327.1'17-dc22

2009014983

ISBN10: 0-415-49801-5 (hbk)
ISBN10: 0-415-66447-0 (pbk)
ISBN10: 0-203-86835-8 (ebk)

ISBN13: 978-0-415-49801-2 (hbk)
ISBN13: 978-0-415-66447-9 (pbk)
ISBN13: 978-0-203-86835-5 (ebk)

Contents

Illustrations

Contributors

Ruth Blakeley is Lecturer in International Relations at the University of Kent, Canterbury, UK. She is the author of *State Terrorism and Neoliberalism: The North in the South* (Routledge, 2009) and has published several journal articles on state terrorism and torture.

Karine Hamilton completed her PhD about the politics of memory in the Israel–Palestine conflict in 2007 at Curtin University of Technology in Western Australia. She has lectured in international relations of the Middle East and the medieval history of the Crusades and Jihad.

Kristian Lasslett is Lecturer in Criminology at the University of Ulster, and has just submitted his PhD at the University of Westminster. His present research interests include conflict and development in Papua New Guinea, classical Marxism and critical criminology.

Richard Jackson is Reader in International Politics at Aberystwyth University. He is the founding editor of the Routledge journal, *Critical Studies on Terrorism* and the convenor of the BISA Critical Studies on Terrorism Working Group (CSTWG). He is the editor of *Critical Terrorism Studies: Framing a New Research Agenda* (co-edited with Marie Breen Smyth and Jeroen Gunning, Routledge, 2009), and the author of *Writing the War on Terrorism: Language, Politics and Counterterrorism* (Manchester University Press, 2005).

Jude McCulloch is Professor of Criminology at Monash University, Melbourne. Prior to taking up an academic career, she worked in community legal centres for many years where she was active on criminal justice issues. Her research interrogates institutionalized state violence. Her most recent book is *The Violence of Incarceration* (edited with Phil Scraton).

Victoria Mason is Lecturer in Politics and International Relations at Lancaster University in the UK. Her broad research areas are Middle East politics and human rights issues. She focuses particularly on the Palestinian question, conflict and conflict resolution in the Middle East and the treatment of refugees and minorities.

David Mickler teaches in Security, Terrorism and Counterterrorism Studies at Murdoch University, Western Australia, where he recently completed his PhD on the response of the UN Security Council to the crisis in Darfur. He has been appointed as a Lecturer in International Relations at the University of Melbourne, commencing in 2010.

Eamon Murphy is Professor of History and International Relations at Curtin University of Technology in Western Australia. He has recently published three articles on aspects of South Indian state terrorism and is currently writing a monograph on terrorism in Pakistan.

Sandra Nasr is completing her PhD in Politics at Curtin University of Technology where she teaches Middle East history and politics. She presented a paper, 'Barrier to Peace?' to the second World Congress of Middle Eastern Studies in Jordan in 2006.

Scott Poynting is Professor in Sociology, Manchester Metropolitan University. He is co-author of *Bin Laden in the Suburbs: Criminalising the Arab Other* (Sydney University Institute of Criminology, 2004) and *Kebabs, Kids, Cops and Crime: Youth, Ethnicity and Crime* (Pluto Australia, 2000).

Sam Raphael is Lecturer in Politics and International Relations at Kingston University. His work examines US coercive interventions in the global South, energy security, and 'counterterrorism'. He has also published on the exclusion of state terrorism from the orthodox 'terrorism studies' field.

Aazar Tamana is completing his PhD thesis on the United States–Pakistan security relationship, post 9/11, at Curtin University of Technology. His work deals with Pakistan's cooperation in the US war against global terrorism. He is the author of *United States–Pakistan Relations in the Post Cold War Era* (2004). The book reveals Pakistan's security concerns in the 1990s following the end of Soviet–Afghan war.

Joan Wardrop is Associate Professor of History at Curtin University of Technology, teaching and supervising undergraduate and higher degree students in the anthropology and history programmes. Trained as a medieval historian, she is co-editor of H-SAfrica, has researched and written on violence, trauma and dislocation in southern Africa and elsewhere, and now researches place, memories, identities and nostalgia through the practices of everyday life, and individual and collective senses of place and belonging. In particular, she is concerned with the intricate connections between displacement, cultural rupture, cultural sustainability, memory work and the shaping of identities in urban contexts.

Foreword

After the 9/11 atrocities in 2001, President George W. Bush declared a 'war on terror' and, as an immediate response, the Taliban regime was quickly terminated. Shortly afterwards, in the January 2002 State of the Union Address, President Bush then extended the war to an 'axis of evil' of states sponsoring terror while seeking weapons of mass destruction. The Iraqi regime of Saddam Hussein was the first to be terminated in a war that started in March 2003. US soldiers and marines involved in the conflict were convinced that they had dealt with a terrorist regime so that the subsequent and unexpected insurgency was essentially seen as a manifestation of this same terrorism.

Just over a year after the start of the war, the US armed forces were taking serious casualties, with scores of people being killed or critically wounded every week. Much of the conflict was centred on the city of Fallujah, west of Baghdad and known in Iraq as the 'city of mosques'. The reaction of local inhabitants to the US military presence was so heated that in one incident four US private security contractors were dragged from their vehicles and killed, and their bodies mutilated, burnt and hung from the supports of a bridge.

In another incident, in April 2004, a marines supply convoy was ambushed in the city, with 17 troops becoming isolated and taking cover, under heavy fire, in a group of buildings. A large force of marines moved in and succeeded in extricating their comrades after a three-hour intensive conflict, with some of the marines injured. What happened next is instructive and came into the public domain because a journalist with the *Washington Post* was embedded with the marines outside Fallujah. According to her report, before dawn the following day:

> AC-130 Spectre gunships launched a devastating punitive raid over a six-block area around where the convoy was attacked, firing dozens of artillery shells that shook the city and lit up the sky. Marine officials said the area was virtually destroyed and that no further insurgent activity has been seen there.
>
> (Constable 2004)

No indication was given of the civilians killed in the destruction of scores of houses in a crowded city, but it is clear that the response was a collective punishment, a form of terror intended to warn the citizens of Fallujah of the consequences of the insurgency. From the perspective of the marines, the Iraqi insurgents were terrorists, pure and simple, and this was a reasonable counterterrorism operation – using force to deter further action by people who in some manner threatened the security of the United States when it had already suffered an appalling attack. To people in Fallujah, however, the operation was an act of terror perpetrated by the military forces of a state that was occupying their country. For them it was a clear instance of state terrorism.

This book, *Contemporary State Terrorism*, extends much further than Iraq or Afghanistan, but one of its core concerns is the manner in which post-9/11 academic analysis has concentrated almost exclusively on sub-state terrorism, specifically al-Qaida but extending to the Taliban, Hezbollah, Hamas and other Islamic paramilitaries. Virtually no attention has been paid to state terrorism, either before or since 9/11, in spite of the fact that state terrorism has been massively more costly in terms of lives and human well-being. This book is one attempt to start the process of redressing that imbalance and does so by collecting together an impressive range of case studies, all drawing on experiences of state terrorism in recent years.

The editors do not pretend that it is comprehensive – indeed they make the point that state terrorism has a long and costly history. Some of the most appalling examples, including Stalin's Russia, Nazi Germany, and Mao's Great Leap Forward, have had extensive coverage, but others have not. These include the numerous examples of punitive raids, massacres and exemplary executions that marked many aspects of the colonial era, especially the brutal actions of the Belgians in Central Africa, but not excluding the British, French and others during their own conquests.

What is clear from this text is that state terror is a common feature of state behaviour, across all regions of the world, from autocracies to democracies. Very commonly it is a key part of the maintenance of control by an elite community against threats from a marginalized majority. *Contemporary State Terrorism* thus ranges widely over examples of recent years, and seeks to incorporate theoretical perspectives while arguing strongly for a much greater focus on the issue. In that sense it is a timely counter to the emphasis on sub-state groups, but it is also timely in relation to current world-wide trends.

In the past two decades it has become clear that there are two fundamental drivers of global insecurity. One is the widening divide between a trans-national elite community of more than a billion people that has well over 80 per cent of world wealth, and the other five billion people who are relatively marginalized. The second is the evolving phenomenon of environmental constraints, especially climate change, which will impact most strongly on that marginalized majority, quite probably with devastating effect. Such trends were expected, until recently, to produce increasingly resentful and angry communities over quite a long period, perhaps two to three decades, but the financial collapse of 2008–09 has brought that much further forward in a manner that is still not fully understood.

What is clear is that state authorities in many countries, not least China, India and many in Western Europe, now see a clear threat to their elite communities that is coming from the margins. The rapid development of expanded public order forces is an immediate part of the response to this trend, but there is every risk that much more extreme measures will become the order of the day. If that is the case, and if they even become the norm, then part of the reason will be a failure of academic communities across the world to address the worryingly common instances of repressive state control which all too often extend to the use of terror. The editors of this volume do not claim more than to start the process of redressing that imbalance. It is a task that is necessary at any time, but now has a much greater urgency.

Paul Rogers

Reference

Constable, Pamela (2004) 'A Wrong Turn, Chaos and a Rescue', *Washington Post*, 15 April.

Acknowledgements

Contemporary State Terrorism had its origins in lunchtime discussions in November 2006 between Eamon Murphy, his PhD student Sandra Nasr and PhD student David Mickler from Murdoch University. The commitment and support of David and Sandra were important throughout the production of the book. With the enthusiastic joining of the project by (in chronological order) Victoria Mason, Scott Poynting and Richard Jackson, and the contributors whom the latter two also invited, the volume grew to its present scope.

The production of the volume was remarkably smooth and problem-free. For this we thank Caryn Coatney, whose considerable journalistic experience informed the assiduous text-editing and compilation of the index, and who also managed the correspondence of the project. We thank the Faculty of Humanities at Curtin University of Technology for the three humanities publication grants which facilitated Caryn's employment on the project. We thank Andrew Humphrys at Routledge for his immediate enthusiasm about the volume, as well as the Routledge Editorial Assistant, Rebecca Brennan, and the team for their professionalism and their unruffled and polished production. We are grateful for the positive feedback and constructive criticism from the peer reviewers, and the careful attention from Routledge's editors.

We acknowledge the UN Office for the Coordination of Humanitarian Affairs for providing the map of Darfur. The UN Cartographic Section sent the maps of Papua New Guinea and Zimbabwe. Also Yale University Press provided copyright permission for the publication of the Pakistan map, and Routledge gave copyright permission for a section of Chapter 1 by Ruth Blakeley.

We accept the customary responsibility for deficiencies in our own chapters, and add to that our acknowledgement of some gaps in the collection as a whole. Circumstances prevented us from including a chapter on the history of British state terrorism in Northern Ireland, which was both the genesis of 'exceptionalist' arguments that have come to the fore in the War on Terror, and some of the terrifying techniques of incarceration and interrogation, from hooding to trophy photos, that are familiar in the contemporary context. As we worked on the book, in July 2008, the report of the bilateral Commission of Truth and Friendship (CTF) into crimes against humanity during East Timor's independence vote in 1999 was delivered, with its findings on state crimes perpetrated by the Indonesian military, police, and government, including participation in and encouragement of murder, forced displacement, illegal detention and rape. As we finalized the book in March 2009, the European Court of Human Rights handed down its judgment (*Musayev and Others* v. *Russia*) about certain acts of what must be considered Russian state terrorism in Grozny, Chechnya in 2000. During the production of the book, Sri Lanka saw the assassination of the editor of the *Sunday Leader*, Lasantha Wickrematunge, then the apparent culmination of the government's counter-insurgency campaign against the Liberation Tigers of Tamil Eelam, which bore many of the hallmarks of state terrorism. These cases, missing here, may be presented and argued in future collections, and perhaps only underline the need for further systematic study of state terrorism.

While two chapters in this book deal with the state terrorism of Israel, both in the West Bank and in its attacks on Lebanon in 2006, the book was completed too late to include substantive material on the Israeli state terrorism in its incursion into Gaza from December 2008 to January 2009. Bombing and shelling of universities, schools, hospitals, UN food and aid stores, deliberate targeting of civilians, including with white phosphorous and flechettes, prevention of medical treatment, and the rest of the atrocities already documented and still being investigated, must count as state terrorism as much as in the two chapters we do include, but could not be included in this volume.

We dedicate this book to those who have suffered state terrorism, and to those brave souls who stand up against it.

Introduction

Terrorism, the state and the study of political terror

Richard Jackson, Eamon Murphy and Scott Poynting

By all accounts, state terrorism has been one of the greatest sources of human suffering and destruction of the past five centuries. Employing extreme forms of exemplary violence against ordinary people and specific groups in order to engender political submission to newly formed nation states, transfer popula-tions, and generate labour in conquered colonial territories, imperial powers and early modern states killed literally tens of millions of people and destroyed entire civilizations and peoples across the Americas, the Asia-Pacific, the sub-continent, the Middle East, and Africa. Later, during the twentieth century, modern states were responsible for the deaths of 170 million to 200 million people outside of war (Rummel 1994), a great many of them murdered during notorious campaigns of state terrorism such as Stalin's great terror, Mao's Great Leap Forward, and Kampuchea's return to Year Zero, and the rule of various dictatorial regimes in Chile, Argentina, South Africa, Uganda, Somalia, Indone-sia, Iran, Iraq and dozens of other countries. During the great wars of the twenti-eth century, millions of civilians were killed in atomic attacks and 'terror bombing' campaigns designed specifically to undermine morale and intimidate into submission – a case of randomly killing some people in order to influence others, which is the essence of the terrorist strategy (Grosscup 2006).

Disturbingly, state terrorism remains as one of the single greatest threats to human and societal security and well-being today. Certainly, in comparison to the terrorism perpetrated by non-state insurgent groups, the few thousand deaths and injuries caused by 'terrorism from below' every year pales into rela-tive insignificance besides the hundreds of thousands of people killed, kid-napped, 'disappeared', injured, tortured, raped, abused, intimidated, and threatened by state agents and their proxies in dozens of countries across the globe in places like Chechnya, Kashmir, Palestine, Iraq, Colombia, Zimbabwe, Darfur, Congo, Somalia, Uzbekistan, China and elsewhere. Even more disturb-ingly, government-directed campaigns of counter-terrorism in the past few decades have frequently descended into state terrorism by failing to distinguish between the innocent and the guilty, responding highly disproportionately to acts of insurgent violence, and aiming to terrify or intimidate the wider population or particular communities into submission (Goodin 2006: 69–73). Consequently, the victims of state counter-terrorism have always vastly outnumbered the deaths caused by non-state or insurgent terrorism, including in the ongoing global war on terrorism.

Given that state terrorism is incontrovertibly far more prevalent and destructive than non-state or insurgent terrorism, it is surprising that it has not yet received the attention it deserves within the international relations (IR), security studies or terrorism studies fields (Jackson 2008; Blakeley 2008), even though human rights activists and scholars have studied state repression more broadly for several decades. In fact, despite the truly vast growth in terrorism-related research since 11 September 2001, the subject of state terrorism remains poorly understood, theoretically under-developed, lacking in the kind of rich empirical data needed for advancing knowledge, and largely neglected in terms of the wider study of the terrorism phenomenon.

It is in this context – the continuous and widespread suffering caused by persistent state terrorism and the relative lack of scholarly analysis of its nature, causes, and prevention – that we offer this collection of theoretical writings and case studies. Our aims are fairly modest but nonetheless important. First, we aim to provide a clear and unambiguous defence of the concept of state terrorism and to contribute to further theoretical development regarding the aims, nature, causes, and consequences of state uses of terrorism, both domestically and internationally. Second, we aim to provide a rich and diverse set of empirical case studies of contemporary state terrorism which can then be used to explore theoretical notions, generate new questions, and provide a resource for further research. Third, we aim to contribute to the growing critical-normative approach to the study of terrorism more broadly, and to challenge dominant approaches and perspectives which assume that states, particularly Western states, are primarily victims and not perpetrators of terrorism (Blakeley 2007). Last, the volume aims to broadly map out the current state of knowledge and suggest a future research agenda for the critically important study of state terrorism.

We believe that such a study is intellectually and politically timely for a number of reasons. In the first place, there is an emerging 'critical turn' taking place in the wider terrorism studies field which is calling for, among other things, a greater focus by scholars on the more serious problem of state terrorism (see Jackson *et al.* 2009). This volume is, in part, a direct response to this call. Second, there is growing public concern over the consequences and impact of the global War on Terror. In particular, there is increasing concern about whether Western forms of counter-terrorism sometimes cross the line into state terrorism (such as when they involve torture, rendition, and the 'targeted' killing of suspected terrorists), and whether some key Western allies, such as Pakistan, Israel, Egypt and others, are systematic perpetrators of state terrorism. Third, the legacy of colonialism continues to contribute to state terrorism currently taking place, from various parts of Africa, to Central America, to the Indian subcontinent, to South-East Asia and the Middle East. Last, in places like Chechnya and Tibet, we find contemporary state activities in many ways similar to the cases in this book. In this context, a volume devoted to the examination of state terrorism takes on particular significance.

Making the case for *state* terrorism

For the purposes of this volume, we understand state terrorism to be the intentional use or threat of violence by state agents or their proxies against individuals or groups who are victimized for the purpose of intimidating or frightening a broader audience. The direct victims of the violence are therefore not the main targets, but are instrumental to the primary goal of frightening the watching audience, who are intimidated through the communicative power of violence. The intended effects of the violence are the achievement of specific political or political-economic, as opposed to religious or criminal, goals.

We recognize that making the case to study *state* terrorism (as opposed to the almost axiomatic focus on non-state terrorism by most scholars) is a critical move, particularly in the current intellectual and political context where large numbers of terrorism researchers and government officials reject the idea that states employ terrorism or that there is any value in making it a subject of sustained analysis. Although the question of whether state terrorism is a valid concept for research is examined in some detail in Ruth Blakeley's contribution in Chapter 1, the core dimensions of the argument are worth briefly reprising here.

There appear to be five main objections to the use of the term 'state terrorism' in the wider terrorism studies field. First, it is argued by a surprising number of scholars that one of the core defining features of 'terrorism' is that it is a form of political violence practised solely by non-state actors, and that states cannot engage in terrorism because they have the legitimate right to use violence – in contradistinction to non-state actors who have no such right. This objection can be dismissed on several grounds. In the first place, it is obvious that terrorism is first and foremost a strategy of violence utilized to achieve political aims; it is akin to the strategies employed in insurgency and guerrilla warfare. To suggest that when state agents engage in the very same strategies as non-state terrorists, such as when they blow up civilian airliners (the Lockerbie bombing) or a protest ship (the *Rainbow Warrior* bombing) or plant a series of bombs in public places (the Lavon affair), it ceases to be terrorism is effectively the abandonment of scholarly research principles. As a phenomenon, terrorism can only be identified according to the conceptually defined characteristics of the violence, not the (politically or otherwise privileged) nature of the actor employing the violence: if the violence has all the necessary characteristics of terrorism, it must be included in the analytical category of terrorism, regardless of which actor perpetrates it.

Additionally, the suggestion that states have a legitimate right to use violence while non-state actors do not is not so clear-cut. In the first instance, it can be argued that although states have the legitimate right to use violence, this right is highly circumscribed and does not include the right to use extra-legal violence against randomly chosen civilian targets – or to commit genocide, ethnic cleansing, war crimes, and other such acts. Second, there is a long-standing moral principle that non-state actors may use violence against highly repressive and genocidal states when other methods have failed or other states fail to intervene. In reality, Western states and international organizations have a long history of recognizing and even supporting violent non-state groups, some of whom have practised terrorism, including: the resistance to Nazi occupation; the PLO, the ANC, SWAPO, and other UN-recognized movements; and the Contras, anti-Castro groups, UNITA, and other groups who received extensive military and political support from Western states.

A second objection to the concept of state terrorism revolves around the argument that state repressive violence is very different from non-state terrorism because its victims are not randomly chosen (they are all opponents of the state), and individuals know what they can do to avoid state violence (unlike in cases of non-state terrorism). The first answer to this argument is that the empirical facts of the matter, as already mentioned, are that state agents frequently do engage in random acts of violence (bombing civilian airliners, for example) and regularly provide material support to non-state proxy actors to do the same. Conversely, non-state terrorist groups frequently choose their victims very specifically, rather than randomly. Both ETA and the IRA for example, have long targeted soldiers, police officers, and state officials. The point is that terrorism is not defined by the choice of victims, but by the instrumentalization of the victims (however they are chosen, randomly or deliberately) in order to communicate a message to an audience. Second, states can never eliminate *all* of their opponents so they invariably target opponents randomly in order to intimidate both the wider opposition movement and the state's own supporters. Moreover, the state may have dual objectives to their terroristic violence: to eliminate opponents while simultaneously sending a message to other real or potential opponents. The reality is that in 'terror states' such as Nazi Germany, Stalin's Soviet Union, Pol Pot's Kampuchea, and Pinochet's Chile, for example, the entire population lived in fear precisely because no one was completely safe; even faithful party members could inadvertently or through no fault of their own, fall victim to state terror.

A third objection suggests that state repressive violence is not terrorism because state agents do not seek publicity but rather try to hide their involvement – unlike non-state terrorism which is aimed at maximizing publicity. This argument mistakes publicity for communication. It is communication to an audience which is one of the key elements of terrorist violence, not necessarily publicity (see Duvall and Stohl 1988: 239–40). For non-state actors lacking societal penetration, publicity is the easiest way to communicate, but this is not the case for states whose violence does not necessarily require publicity to reach its intended audience. In reality, when an individual in a terror state is kidnapped and then 'disappeared', returned following torture or their corpse is left mutilated in a public place, the local observers know exactly who the intended audience is, what the message is intended to convey, and who has sent it. The body with its physical marks of violence – or the absence of their bodily presence – serves as a direct reminder of the presence and power of the state and the need to acquiesce. The lack of publicity and denial by the state is usually for external audiences in order to maintain international assistance or for domestic constituents whom the state relies upon for support – such as the white community in South Africa who were largely unaware of the violence meted out to its non-white population.

A fourth objection is that what we have called 'state *terrorism*' is already covered by terms like 'repression' and 'human rights abuses', and that acts of state terrorism are already circumscribed in international law and do not require new legal or analytical concepts. This is a political or pragmatic argument which, as we have shown, ignores the fundamental scholarly principle of including all the cases that fit the criteria in order to retain analytical consistency. Moreover, it ignores the fact that the same situation applies to non-state 'terrorism': all the acts and activities performed by non-state terrorists are also already circumscribed in law and there exist a range of useful terms to describe their actions. It can also be argued that state (and non-state) actions are never solely 'terrorism', 'human rights abuses', or 'repression'. They can be – and by definition always are – both acts of 'terrorism' and 'human rights abuses' at the same time, and there is no contradiction in describing them using either term. In the end, we follow Robert Goodin and Ruth Blakeley in suggesting that terrorism, whether conducted by state or non-state actors, involves a number of specific moral wrongs (beyond unjustified killing and harm), such as the instrumentalization of human suffering, the intention to cause widespread fear, and the betrayal of the duty of care towards fellow citizens (see Goodin, 2006: 102; Blakeley this volume). For this and other reasons, we argue that the term 'state terrorism' should be retained as an analytical and political category.

A final related objection is that although states may engage in terrorism which is far more destructive than non-state terrorism, it is qualitatively different in aims, modes, and outcomes and there is therefore little analytical value in studying state violence and non-state violence under the same label. In response to this, we would argue that, given the aetiology of the term 'terrorism' as a descriptor of violent state consolidation, state terrorism represents the purest and original form of the terrorism phenomenon and therefore has much to tell us about its causes and effects. Certainly, state terrorism comes closest to generating real 'terror' among a population and this is what non-state groups also frequently aspire to achieve in their actions. In practice however, state and non-state actors actually employ many of the very same strategies – kidnap, extra-judicial killing, bombing, torture and the like – and have similar aims – intimidation of an audience to achieve political aims, either revolutionary or conservative. In essence, state and non-state terrorism utilizes violence instrumentally in identical ways and often for similar reasons.

As an addendum to this discussion, we would add that in addition to the analytical reasons we have mentioned above, there are important ethical-normative reasons for retaining the term 'state terrorism'. For example, due to the powerful connotations of the 'terrorism' label, its retention as a descriptor of certain forms of state violence could be an important means of advancing a progressive political project aimed at protecting marginalized and vulnerable populations from indiscriminate and oppressive forms of state violence, whether they occur under the rubric of war or counter-terrorism. That is, at the most basic level, employing the concept and identifying criteria of 'state terrorism' can have the effect of de-legitimizing any and all forms of violence that seek to instrumentalize human suffering for the purpose of sending a message to an audience. In the present context where state counter-terrorism is causing mass suffering around the world, and where states are oppressing groups and individuals in the name of counter-terrorism, making the case that 'states can be terrorists too' could have a powerful normative effect of constraining state excesses and promoting genuine human and societal security. In short, it is our assertion, following Robert Goodin, that the objections raised by certain scholars and state officials to the concept of state terrorism

> Cannot change any logical or deontological facts of the matter. If what [states] do is otherwise indistinguishable from what is done by non-state actors that we would deem to be terroristic, then the acts of the state officials doing the same thing would be morally wrong for just the same reasons.
>
> (Goodin 2006: 56)

Overview of the book

With the aims and context described above in mind, we invited a specially selected group of contributors from a variety of methodological and disciplinary perspectives – including international relations and politics, history, sociology, criminology, and human rights studies – to explore some of the most important dimensions and aspects of contemporary state terrorism in a wide-ranging set of theoretical reflections and case studies. The volume begins with an initial chapter devoted to setting out the key conceptual aspects of state terrorism, including its definition and main forms. On this foundation, the subsequent chapters each examine a specific case of contemporary state terrorism, employing a unique blend of empirical material and theoretical reflection. In a collected volume such as this, the choice of case studies is always limited, particularly when the potential number of relevant cases is so wide. Although there may be concerns over our specific choice of cases, we believe that the cases examined here more than fulfil our primary aims as set out above: adding other cases, while potentially interesting, would not alter the primary conclusions we are able to draw from this rich set of case studies and theoretical reflections about the aims, nature, causes, and outcomes of state terrorism.

In Chapter 1, 'State terrorism in the social sciences: theories, methods and concepts', Ruth Blakeley introduces the reader to the debates surrounding how terrorism generally, and state terrorism specifically, are defined. She argues that while these are highly contested terms, nevertheless there is now sufficient agreement among scholars on the key constitutive elements of terrorism. What distinguishes state terrorism from other forms of state repression is its instrumentality in that it involves the illegal targeting of individuals that the state has a duty to protect in order to instil fear in a target audience beyond the direct victims. Last, she discusses the main difficulties associated with identifying state terrorism which relate primarily to questions of agency.

In Chapter 2, 'Darfur's dread: contemporary state terror in the Sudan', David Mickler demonstrates how the Sudanese state has been guilty of committing terrorism against its own citizens since at least early 2003. Widespread brutal attacks by the Sudanese military and its allied militias in the Darfur region of western Sudan against rebel groups have left at least 200,000 civilians dead and more than 2.5 million people displaced from their homes and villages. Mickler argues that by deliberately targeting and killing, raping, and maiming innocent civilians, and destroying their crops, livestock, homes, villages, and wells as part of its strategy both to dissuade support or potential recruitment for the rebels and to effect 'ethnic cleansing', the Sudanese state is clearly guilty of acts of state terrorism. He further argues that strong Chinese interest in preserving its key economic relationship with the state, in conjunction with Sudan's valuable cooperation in US-led counter-terrorism operations, have hampered international intervention to protect vulnerable civilians against the oppression undertaken by their own state.

In Chapter 3, 'State terrorism and the military in Pakistan', Eamon Murphy and Aazar Tamana analyse the dominant role that the Pakistani armed forces have played in the political and economic development of the state since its formation in 1947. They demonstrate how the military, both as a corporate body and through the actions of individual military commanders, have resorted to state terrorism in order to protect and advance their economic and political interests. Military state terrorism in Pakistan has involved acts ranging from brutal widespread mass murder, through to the use of sexual assault, as a weapon of terror. The chapter discusses how state terrorism has been used against many groups and individuals within Pakistani society: regional separatist groups, political rivals of the military and its political allies, human rights activists and lawyers, minority religions and religious sects, and the women of Pakistan. The Pakistan military has also encouraged the emergence of religious extremism by sponsoring state terrorism in the disputed Indian state of Kashmir.

In Chapter 4, 'Israel's *other* terrorism challenge', Sandra Nasr argues that Israel has resorted to the use of state terrorism by deliberately targeting innocent civilians in response to suicide attacks and other forms of terrorism by Palestinians against Israeli civilian and military targets. During Israel's 43-year occupation of the West Bank, a number of policies have been enacted by the state whose intent has been to induce fear and submission through the use of violence. She argues that physical and psychological intimidation at checkpoints, arbitrary closures and curfews, harsh mobility restrictions, home demolitions, random detentions and the denial of a whole range of basic human rights contrive to keep Palestinians in a constant state of anxiety and trepidation and are clear examples of state terrorism.

In Chapter 5, '"We have no orders to save you": state terrorism, politics and communal violence in the Indian state of Gujarat, 2002', Eamon Murphy discusses the role of state terrorism in the violent communal riots between Hindus and Muslims that rocked the Western Indian state of Gujarat during 2002. Hindu mobs, encouraged by the state's ruling Hindu nationalist party, the Bharatiya Janata Party (BJP) and its chief minister, brutally assaulted, raped, and killed defenceless Muslim men, women, and children. State officials, including the police force, both encouraged and participated in the violence. The Gujarat riots were a classic example of politically motivated state terrorism, in that the primary motivation of the BJP's leaders in encouraging the riots was to send a clear, political message to the Hindu voters of Gujarat that the BJP was the only political party that would protect Hindus from the perceived threat posed by the state's Muslims.

In Chapter 6, 'The politics of convenient silence in southern Africa: relocating the terrorism of the state', Joan Wardrop argues that postcolonial Zimbabwe is frozen in a condition of continuous state terror, nurtured in the terror imposed by the colonial state through the violence of dispossession and the (re)creation of its indigenous inhabitants as illegitimate, and nourished by a postcolonial elite determined to maintain its position and power. Wardrop shows that the present difficulties in Zimbabwe do not stand isolated from the past; rather, they can only be understood in the context of their violent history, recovered through a collective memory of invasion, betrayal, and suffering in which terror from above is naturalized as both political technique and cultural practice. The collective memory of violence, vulnerability, and fear as a way of life has become the norm for Zimbabweans. Moreover, private memories of past terror make possible the terror of the present. Wardrop also suggests that examples from elsewhere of memories recuperated and reshaped into public narratives through truth (and reconciliation) commissions demonstrate the power of memory and narrative exercised in public spaces for healing the terrorized, a power which has not yet been felt but is sorely needed in Zimbabwe.

In Chapter 7, 'Revenge and terror: the destruction of the Palestinian community in Kuwait', Victoria Mason examines the Kuwaiti campaign of terror against its Palestinian community following the 1991 liberation of Kuwait from Iraqi occupation. Although most Palestinians in Kuwait opposed the Iraqi occupation, Kuwait argued that its Palestinian community had collaborated with the Iraqis. As a result brutal attacks against Palestinians were undertaken by Kuwaiti vigilantes. Once sovereign rule returned to Kuwait, however, a more systematic campaign of state terror was instituted. This included extra-judicial killings; humiliations, intimidations and beatings; mass arrests and detentions (with systematic torture and trials under martial-law courts without due process); large-scale deportations and sacking Palestinians from employment. While this campaign was driven to a certain extent by scapegoating and revenge, the chapter demonstrates that it was also driven by more sinister motives. Due to the size and influence of the Palestinian community in Kuwait, by the 1980s they were increasingly seen as a potential demographic threat. The 1990 Gulf crisis thus provided the necessary catalyst to justify a radical and enforced reduction in the number of Palestinians in Kuwait. The chapter explores how the actions taken against Palestinians following liberation were part of a more systematic process aimed at terrorizing the entire Palestinian civilian population to force them to leave Kuwait.

In Chapter 8, 'Winning hearts and mines: the Bougainville Crisis, 1988–90', Kristian Lasslett discusses how from 1988 to 1990, the Papua New Guinea security apparatus and Bougainville Copper Limited, propped up by the Australian state, undertook a campaign of terror against local communities in the North Solomons province of Papua New Guinea. The campaign was directed against militant landowners of the New Panguna Landowners Association, who, frustrated by the socio-economic consequences of mining in their region, engaged in a campaign of industrial sabotage against the lucrative Panguna copper and gold mine. Acts of state terrorism included the burning of villages, brutalizing and killing militant 'supporters', implementing a full blockade of the island, and the militarization of ethnic factions that opposed the protesting landowners and their supporters. The goal of the state terrorism was to coerce civilian communities to support landowner factions loyal to the government and the mining company. The chapter also analyses Bougainville Copper Limited's attempt to influence the geopolitical strategy of the Papua New Guinean state, and the instrumental logistical support they gave to the state's security apparatus when conducting terror operations on the island in 1989.

In Chapter 9, 'Paramilitarism and state terror in Colombia', Sam Raphael examines the systematic use of terrorism by the Colombian and, indirectly, US governments during the civil war in Colombia in order to contain any significant challenge to incumbent elites. The vast majority of terrorist acts were conducted by right-wing paramilitary groups closely linked to the state. The majority of these come under the umbrella of the United Self-Defence Forces (AUC), and the use of terror through collusion with these illegal, armed groups was, and is still, the primary strategy employed by the state to impose order on Colombian society. Raphael examines the nature and extent of collusion between state security forces and paramilitary groups, particularly in the post-9/11 era. Overall, the chapter charts the extensive use of terrorism by the state in Colombia, and the support it receives from the United States.

In Chapter 10, 'We are all in Guantánamo: state terror and the case of Mamdouh Habib', Scott Poynting provides a case study of how certain anti-terrorism measures practised by Western states and their allies since 9/11 have amounted to state terrorism. In examining the abduction, 'extraordinary rendition', torture, and incarceration without charge of the Australian citizen, Mamdouh Habib, Poynting argues that the United States, Australia, Egypt, and Pakistan are acting illegally in common purpose to terrify particular sections of civilian populations for political ends. From his kidnapping and interrogation under abuse and torture in Pakistan, to a torture cell in Cairo with data from Sydney and questions from Washington, to further such atrocities at the US base at Bagram in Afghanistan, to longer torture and detention under the infamous regime at the US base at Guantánamo Bay, a presumptively innocent Mamdouh Habib is victimized in a global web of state crime to send a message to the radical Muslim 'other'.

In Chapter 11, 'From garrison state to garrison planet: state terror, the War on Terror and the rise of a global carceral complex', Jude McCulloch explores the links between the US criminal justice system and violence and incarceration in the War on Terror. She describes the nature and extent of state terror that are part of the everyday reality of state violence and incarceration in the US domestic criminal justice system, and draws links between this and violence and incarceration in the US-led War on Terror. The chapter documents the way that the terror of the US criminal justice system is being exported under the banner of the War on Terror and the impact of the role of this trade in proliferating state terror. Issues considered include private profit and mass incarceration, racialized punishment, torture and sexual violence in incarceration, and the continuities evident in the 'war on crime', the 'war on drugs', and the War on Terror.

In Chapter 12, 'The deterrence logic of state warfare: Israel and the Second Lebanon War, 2006', Karine Hamilton examines the response of the Israeli government after the Lebanese group Hezbollah launched a series of rockets against northern Israeli towns and simultaneously attacked two Israeli army vehicles patrolling the Lebanese border. Using naval and aerial bombardments, as well as a ground offensive, the Israel Defence Forces (IDF) targeted the communal centres of Hezbollah's support in the mostly Shia localities of the Beqaa Valley, southern Lebanon, and Beirut. The IDF also targeted Lebanon's civilian infrastructure including main roads, bridges, water and sewage plants, petrol stations, and airports. The Israeli government policy of deterrence involved the use of massive military retaliation in order to prevent future attacks from enemy forces and included the deliberate bombing of civilian targets in order to dissuade Lebanese civilians, especially the Shia population, from supporting Hezbollah.

Finally, in the Conclusion, 'Contemporary state terrorism – towards a new research agenda', Richard Jackson summarizes some of the key findings of the volume, in particular, reflecting upon how the case studies contribute theoretically to our understanding of the aims, nature, causes, modalities, and consequences of state terrorism under different conditions. Second, by linking the findings of the volume with previous research, he provides a general summary of the current state of knowledge about state terrorism. Third, the conclusion explores some of the key questions and puzzles raised by the case studies which require further research, thereby sketching out a future research agenda. The volume ends with a brief reflection on some well-signposted dangers and challenges for the ongoing study of state terrorism.

References

Blakeley, R. (2007) 'Bringing the State Back into Terrorism Studies', *European Political Science*, 6 (3): 228–53.

—— (2008) 'The Elephant in the Room: A Response to John Horgan and Michael J. Boyle', *Critical Studies on Terrorism*, 1 (2): 151–65.

Duvall, R., and M. Stohl (1988) 'Governance by Terror', in M. Stohl (ed.) *The Politics of Terrorism*, 3rd edition, New York: Marce Dekker, Inc.

Goodin, R. (2006) *What's Wrong with Terrorism?* Cambridge: Polity Press.

Grosscup, B. (2006) *Strategic Terror: The Politics and Ethics of Aerial Bombardment.* London: Zed Books.

Jackson, R. (2008) 'The Ghosts of State Terror: Knowledge, Politics and Terrorism Studies', *Critical Studies on Terrorism*, 1 (3): 377–92.

Jackson, Richard, Marie Breen Smyth and Jeroen Gunning (eds) (2009) *Critical Terrorism Studies: A New Research Agenda*, Abingdon: Routledge.

Rummel, R.J. (1994) *Death by Government*, New Brunswick, NJ: Transaction Books.

1 State terrorism in the social sciences

Theories, methods and concepts

Ruth Blakeley[1]

Introduction

The governments of many countries have used repression against their own and external populations. This has included terrorism. Yet there has been relatively little research on state terrorism within the discipline of international relations and even less on state terrorism by liberal democratic states from the North (Blakeley 2008; 2009). Some scholars even argue that political violence by states should not be classified as 'terrorism'. I begin by exploring the core characteristics common to existing definitions of terrorism. I show that states should not be precluded as potential perpetrators of terrorism because those core characteristics are concerned with the actions involved in terrorism, rather than the nature of the perpetrators. I then set out the key elements that must be present for an act to constitute state terrorism. I show that a defining feature of state terrorism, and that which distinguishes it from other forms of state repression, is its instrumentality because it involves the illegal targeting of persons that the state has a duty to protect in order to instil fear in a target audience beyond the direct victim(s). In exploring state terrorism in relation to other forms of repression, I show that state terrorism always violates international law because of the methods used to instil terror. Last, I outline the main challenges involved in identifying state terrorism. These relate primarily to questions of agency and motive. Measures that can be taken to overcome these challenges are then proposed.

Defining state terrorism

For an act to be labelled 'state terrorism', its constitutive elements must be consistent with those of non-state terrorism. There is no consensus on how terrorism should be defined. Indeed, as Andrew Silke notes, most works on terrorism begin with a discussion of the various associated definitional problems of the term (Silke 2004: 2) and the failure of scholars to reach agreement (Badey 1998: 90–107; Barker 2003: 23; Cooper 2001: 881–93; Duggard 1974: 67–81; Jenkins 1980; Weinberg *et al.* 2004: 777–94). There are nevertheless a group of core characteristics that are common to competing definitions. They relate to the act of terrorism, rather than the nature of the perpetrator. State terrorism receives so little attention primarily because many scholars focus on terrorism by non-state rather than state actors. Some do not even accept that terrorism by states should be equated with terrorism by non-state actors. Walter Laqueur, for example, has argued: 'There are basic differences in motives, function and effect between oppression by the state (or society or religion) and political terrorism. To equate them, to obliterate them is to spread confusion' (Laqueur 1986: 89). He further argued that including state terror in the study of terrorism 'would have made the study of terrorism impossible, for it would have included not only US foreign policy, but also Hitler and Stalin' (Laqueur 2003: 140).

Laqueur's position shows that his analysis of terrorism is actor-based, rather than action-based. Even if the motives, functions, and effects of terrorism by states and non-state actors are different, the act of terrorism itself is not, because the core characteristics of terrorism are the same whether the perpetrator is a state or a non-state actor. Laqueur's argument also serves to entrench the supposed moral legitimacy of state violence. He claims that those who argue that state terrorism should be included in studies of terrorism ignore the fact that: 'the very existence of a state is based on its monopoly of power. If it were different, states would not have the right, nor be in a position, to maintain that minimum of order on which all civilised life rests' (Laqueur 2003: 237).

Bruce Hoffman has made similar claims. He argues that failing to differentiate between state and non-state violence, and equating the innocents killed by states and non-state actors would 'ignore the fact that, even while national armed forces have been responsible for far more death and destruction than terrorists might ever aspire to bring about, there nonetheless is a fundamental qualitative difference between the two types of violence'. He argues that this difference is based upon the historical emergence of 'rules and accepted norms of behaviour that prohibit the use of certain types of weapons' and 'proscribe various tactics and outlaw attacks on specific categories of targets'. He adds that 'terrorists' had by contrast 'violated all these rules' (Hoffman 1998: 34).[2] This argument would only stand if it could be shown that states did not violate these rules, as set out in the Geneva Convention. The reality is that they do. Any monopoly of violence that the state has is neither a justification for excluding state terrorism from studies of terrorism, nor, more importantly, for affording states the right to use violence in any way they choose (Stohl 2006: 4–5). Indeed, even in situations where, according to international law and norms, states have the legitimate right to use violence (*jus ad bellum*), it is not always the case that their conduct (*jus in bello*) is necessarily legitimate.

A helpful starting point in identifying the core characteristics of terrorism is the definition offered by Eugene Victor Walter (1969), for whom terrorism involves three key features: first, threatened or perpetrated violence directed at some victim; second, the violent actor intends that violence to induce terror in some witness who is generally distinct from the victim, in other words, the victim is instrumental; and third, the violent actor intends or expects that the terrorized witness to the violence will alter his or her behaviour. Paul Wilkinson's widely quoted definition echoes Walter's. Wilkinson argues that terrorism has five main characteristics:

> It is premeditated and aims to create a climate of extreme fear or terror; it is directed at a wider audience or target than the immediate victims of the violence; it inherently involves attacks on random and symbolic targets, including civilians; the acts of violence committed are seen by the society in which they occur as extra-normal, in the literal sense that they breach the social norms, thus causing a sense of outrage; and terrorism is used to try to influence political behaviour in some way.
>
> (Wilkinson 1992: 228–9)

The emphasis here on the random nature of the terrorist attack may give rise to the assumption that states do not commit terrorism and instead can only commit acts of repression. Such arguments posit that states often try to suppress their opponents; if individuals oppose the government and are victims of state repression as a result, they are not really random targets. People know what they need to do to avoid state violence and need not, therefore, be terrorized if they are compliant. This argument is easily dismissed because it is implied that states can and will repress every single one of their opponents, precluding the possibility that their attacks are random. The reality is that even targets of state terrorism are selected fairly randomly from among all opponents, with the purpose of making an example of them to others. When states target opponents, the intention is not simply to terrify other opponents but to ensure that compliant citizens remain compliant. This highlights the importance of the distinction between state terrorism and repression. The difference lies in the instrumentality of state terrorism. There is a specific logic of not only harming the direct victim, but exploiting the opportunity afforded by the harm to terrorize others. That this instrumentality was captured by Wilkinson meant his definition contained all the core characteristics outlined by Walter. Equally important, in line with Walter, terrorism is defined according to the actions carried out, rather than who the actors are, meaning that the state is not precluded as a potential perpetrator of terrorism.

In an attempt to establish an agenda for research on state terrorism in the 1980s, Christopher Mitchell, Michael Stohl, David Carleton, and George Lopez, incorporated Walter's core characteristics into their definition of state terrorism. They argued:

> Terrorism by the state (or non-state actors) involves deliberate coercion and violence (or the threat thereof) directed at some victim, with the intention of inducing extreme fear in some target observers who identify with that victim in such a way that they perceive themselves as potential future victims. In this way they are forced to consider altering their behaviour in some manner desired by the actor.
>
> (Mitchell *et al.* 1986: 5)

While this argument is not far removed from Wilkinson's definition of terrorism, it retains one of the elements established by Walter that is missing from sub-sequent definitions (for example, Barker 2003: 23; Ganor 1998); namely, that the threat of violence is sufficient for a state to be perpetrating terror. I would add the caveat that a threat would only be sufficient in a pre-existing climate of fear induced by prior acts of state terrorism. As Ted Robert Gurr argues, a threat would not be adequate unless it was part of a pattern of activity 'in which instru-mental violence occurs often enough that threats of similar violence, made then or later, have their intended effects' (Gurr 1986: 46).

Drawing on existing definitions, and specifically Walter, I propose that state terrorism involves the following four key elements: (*a*) there must be a deliber-ate act of violence against individuals that the state has a duty to protect, or a threat of such an act if a climate of fear has already been established through preceding acts of state violence; (*b*) the act must be perpetrated by actors on behalf of or in conjunction with the state, including paramilitaries and private security agents; (*c*) the act or threat of violence is intended to induce extreme fear in some target observers who identify with that victim; and (*d*) the target audience is forced to consider changing their behaviour in some way. With the exception of Walter's definition, the definitions discussed argued that the change in behaviour in the target audience was to be political. In line with Walter, I do not make the same claim because states have frequently used violence to terror-ize a wider audience so that they subordinate themselves to the wishes of the state. Those wishes may, of course, include lending political support to the state, but those wishes may also involve citizens labouring in the interests of elites. This was frequently the case in colonial states, where imperialists used terror to coerce citizens into working, often as slaves, to extract resources (Blakeley 2009). The strength of Walter's criteria, therefore, is that changes in behaviour other than political behaviour are not precluded. As already implied, the key ingredient that distinguishes state terrorism from other forms of state repression is its instrumentality.

International law and state terrorism

Before discussing the importance of the target audience in more detail, a few words on state terrorism in relation to international law are warranted. State ter-rorism has not been codified in international law as an illegal act. It nevertheless involves acts which violate international law, with the aim of terrorizing others through those illegal acts. A case of state terrorism, as such, was never put to the legal test, although acts that violated international law and were intended to ter-rorize were tried as war crimes. In this regard, state terrorism can be defined with reference to the illegality of the acts it involves, even though we cannot argue that state terrorism itself is illegal.

State terrorism involves the deliberate targeting of individuals that the state has a duty to protect to invoke terror in a wider audience. The deliberate target-ing of civilians, either in armed conflict or in peace-time, violates principles enshrined in the two bodies of international law that deal with the protection of human rights: international humanitarian law (IHL) and international human rights law (IHRL). Human rights are those rights which all citizens share under international law, both in peace-time and during armed conflict. The most fundamental of these liberties are: the right to life; the prohibition of torture or degrading treatment or punishment; the prohibition of slavery and servitude; and the prohibition of retroactive criminal laws (ICRC 2003). Targeting armed, enemy combatants is legitimate in warfare, but certain acts are nevertheless prohibited. These prohibited acts include: killing prisoners of war; subjecting them to torture; and other degrading treatment or punishment (ICRC 1949). Where the laws prohibiting such acts are violated, states may also be guilty of state terrorism, as I will show. IHL also deals with the thorny question of which acts are permissible in warfare where civilian casualties are likely to ensue. The targeting of civilians is prohibited, both by IHL and IHRL, in times of war and peace. It is acknowledged in IHL, however, that civilian casualties are likely to be a secondary effect of certain actions deemed to be legitimate in armed conflict. IHL is therefore concerned with ensuring that maximum effort is made to protect civilians when such operations take place, and with ensuring that any risks taken with civilian life are proportional to the acts being carried out. This is far from straightforward, as the use of strategic aerial bombardment shows.

Military planners will argue that the aim of aerial bombardment is to attack strategically significant targets. This can, but does not always, include the targeting of a civilian population with the intention of terrorizing to provoke a political response. Terrorizing the civilian population is not necessarily always the primary objective of an air campaign, but it can be a welcome secondary effect. For example in Operation Desert Storm, the US-led campaign against Iraq in 1990–91, civilians were never intended as direct targets. According to the Gulf War Air Power Surveys (an analysis carried out by the US Air Force following the Gulf War), 'there was widespread agreement from the outset of the planning process that directly attacking the people of Iraq or their food supply was neither compatible with US objectives nor morally acceptable to the American people' (Keaney and Cohen 1993: 3, chapter 6). The target categories drawn up by the planners also indicated that civilians were not intended as direct targets (Keaney and Cohen 1993: 3, chapter 6). The authors of the Gulf War Air Power Surveys claim the air campaign had not only been 'precise, efficient and legal, but had resulted in very few civilian casualties' (Keaney and Cohen 1993: 3, chapter 6). A Greenpeace International study estimated between 5,000 and 15,000 civilians were killed as a direct result of sorties flown against strategic targets in the war (Arkin *et al.* 1991: 46–7). The Greenpeace report highlights the catastrophic human impact of the air campaign, caused by the devastation of the Iraqi infrastructure and the intense environmental degradation caused by the bombing (Arkin *et al.* 1991: 5). This destruction was a result of the intensity of the air campaign. As Greenpeace reported: 'In one day of the Gulf War, there were as many combat missions flown against Iraq as Saddam Hussein experienced in the entire Iran–Iraq war' (Arkin *et al.* 1991: 6).

There was, however, no indication in the Gulf War Air Power Surveys that measures were taken to minimize the secondary effect of terrorizing the population, which would undoubtedly ensue from aerial bombardment of targets deemed to be legitimate, especially given the extensive nature of the bombing campaign. The opposite was true. There was a view among a number of those involved in the planning of the air campaign that harming the morale of the civilian population would be a welcome secondary effect of the targeting of Iraq's electricity generating capacity. For example:

> As for civilian morale, some of the air planners, including General Glosson, felt that 'putting the lights out on Baghdad' would have psychological effects on the average Iraqi ... By demonstrating that Saddam Hussein could not even keep the electricity flowing in Baghdad, it was hoped the Ba'th Party's grip on the Iraqi population could be loosened, thereby helping to bring about a change in the regime.
>
> (Keaney and Cohen 1993, vol. ii, part ii, chapter 6:19)

Aerial bombardments that killed between 5,000 and 15,000 civilians, and that were sufficient to cripple the entire electricity-generation capacity of modern cities such as Baghdad and Basra, were likely to have resulted in considerable levels of fear among the civilian population. This was not seen by the planners as an illegitimate secondary effect, but instead as a welcome means by which to undermine the regime. Indeed, it was hoped that the population would be sufficiently 'psychologically affected' (a euphemism for 'terrorized') that opposition to the regime would increase. Rather than try to prevent the terrorizing of the population, those involved in planning the air campaign actively encouraged it, even though this was illegitimate, according to IHRL.

Some IHRL treaties permit governments to derogate from certain rights in situations of public emergency threatening the life of the nation, but there are some rights that are never to be violated:

> Derogations must, however, be proportional to the crisis at hand, must not be introduced on a discriminatory basis and must not contravene other rules of international law – including rules of IHL. Certain human rights are never derogable. Among them are the right to life, freedom from torture, or inhuman or degrading treatment or punishment, prohibition of slavery and servitude and prohibition of retroactive criminal laws.
>
> (ICRC 2003)

State terrorism involves the derogation from one or more of these against an individual or group to invoke fear in a wider audience. The illegally targeted individual may be a civilian or an enemy combatant who has been disarmed and is being detained. The law is clear that there should be no derogations at all from the provisions of IHL that uphold the right to life and the right to freedom from degrading treatment or punishment. State terrorism, then, only exists through the illegal targeting of individuals that states have a duty to protect. In this regard, as with other forms of state repression, a key ingredient of state terrorism is that it involves acts that are illegal under international law. It is deemed illegal and inhuman when non-state actors commit those acts, and it is no more humane if the perpetrator is a state.

The importance of the target audience

What differentiates state terrorism from other forms of repression is the intent of the actor to create extreme fear among an audience beyond the direct victim of the violence. That audience may be a domestic audience and it may be a limited one, consisting of only the immediate acquaintances of the actual victim. The number of victims is significant because it helps us to make an important distinction between isolated incidents of what we might determine to be repression or criminal activity on the one hand, and state terrorism on the other. The case of torture is helpful for exploring the significance of the target audience.

Many victims of state repression are subjected to torture. In some cases, torture is carried out covertly and is aimed primarily at tormenting the victim. Of course, it violates international law. For torture to constitute state terrorism it must be aimed at, or have the effect of, terrorizing an audience beyond the direct victim. Torture was used in history, very publicly, as a form of punishment, but also as a means of deterring criminal behaviour (Beccaria 1995 [1764]; Foucault 1977; Peters 1985; Vidal-Naquet 1963). Torture continues to be used as a means of terrorizing other, incarcerated detainees to compel certain behaviour by ensuring that they hear the torture occurring, or see the physical harm inflicted on their fellow captives. Torture is often intended to alter behaviour among a much wider audience well beyond the prison walls. It was used in this way by the Guatemalan state during the counterinsurgency war of the 1970s and 1980s, during which, as Amnesty International reported, newspapers were permitted to publish photographs of dead torture victims. Amnesty International reported:

> Guatemalan counterinsurgency operations in the early 1980s ... included the terrorisation of targeted rural populations in an effort to ensure that they did not provide support for guerrillas. Tortured, dying villagers were displayed to relatives and neighbours who were prevented from helping them. Newspapers in urban areas during this period were allowed to publish photographs of mutilated bodies, ostensibly as an aid to families seeking their missing relatives, but also as a warning to all citizens not to oppose the government.
>
> (AI 1976)

The publication of the photographs in the Guatemalan case clearly indicates that the target of the terrorism was a very general audience. Indeed, the intention was to terrorize the populations of entire cities. In some cases, a much more specific organization or set of individuals will be the intended audience. Had the victims in the Guatemalan case been members of a specific political group that the government opposed, and had the victims' bodies been returned to the group's headquarters, the target of the terrorism would have been that political group, although others in the community may also have been terrorized if they came to know of the torture and murder of those individuals.

If torture occurs in complete secrecy and there is no audience to witness it, then it is difficult to argue that this constitutes state terrorism. For example, if an isolated individual or group of prison guards or members of the armed forces used torture secretly, went to great lengths to ensure that no one else knew of it, and there was no evidence that higher authorities had sanctioned the torture, we might conclude that this was the criminal act of an individual or group, rather than an act of state terrorism. In practice, most torture committed by state agents is part of a wider pattern of state repression and in many cases, state terrorism. Nevertheless, it is important to make this distinction between criminal activities by individuals on the one hand, and state terrorism on the other, thereby reserving the label of state terrorism for those acts which are condoned at some level by the state. I will discuss in more detail below how we might determine when individual acts are part of a wider policy of state terrorism and when they are simply isolated, illegitimate incidents.

Forms of state terrorism

Terrorism is used by states internally and across state boundaries against their own populations as a means of maintaining order and quelling political opposition. This involves a range of activities, including disappearances, illegal detention, torture, and assassinations. Terrorism was used in this way by, among others, the Latin American national security states during the Cold War. They targeted civilians at home to instil fear among a much wider population and they targeted their own citizens living abroad, in collaboration with other states, through programmes such as Operation Condor. This entailed intelligence-gathering and sharing and the kidnap, interrogation, torture, and assassinations of nationals of one Condor state – Argentina, Brazil, Uruguay, Paraguay and Chile – by its own agents or agents of other Condor states (Dinges 2004; McClintock 2001; McSherry 2002). States also use terrorism externally in pursuit of specific foreign policy objectives, either by undertaking limited campaigns of terror against specific individuals or groups, often officials of that state, using acts such as assassinations and bombing campaigns, or by engaging in much more generalized campaigns of terror which are intended to destabilize whole societies. More generalized state terrorism involves the following: acts of war that violate the Geneva Convention, including the torture and killing of enemy combatants that have been disarmed and the illegal targeting of civilians; hijackings; kidnappings; illegal detentions; torture and other degrading treatment. In both cases, there are varying degrees to which states are involved in terrorism. At times, they are the main perpetrators, deploying their own agents, such as armed forces or secret services, to engage in acts of terrorism (Stohl 2006: 7). States may also be sponsors of terrorism by other entities. Domestically, sponsorship tends to involve covert support for paramilitary or vigilante groups, or pro-government extremists involved in acts of terrorism against the citizens of the state. Externally, this involves any or all of the following: lending ideological support to, providing financial or military support to, or collaborating and cooperating with, an external terrorist organization or state involved in terrorism against individuals or groups within its own or another population (Martin 2003: 81–111; Stohl 2006: 7). Such terrorism may include acts of war that violate the Geneva Convention, including: the torture and killing of enemy combatants who have been disarmed; the illegal targeting of civilians; disappearances; assassinations; hijackings; kidnappings; illegal detentions; torture; other degrading treatment; and terrorist attacks, such as the bombing of civilian targets.

The difficulties of identifying state terrorism

Central to determining whether a specific act constitutes state terrorism depends on establishing that the intimidation of a target audience beyond the direct victim was the intention of the state agents involved. Determining the intentions of state actors is not easy. Often their purposes will, at best, be ambiguous. This is largely because in most cases, governments seek to conceal the extent to which they use terrorism and when such activities are exposed, they tend to be justified as 'necessary measures' or more benignly as 'police action' (Mitchell *et al.* 1986: 2–3; Nicholson 1986: 31). Obtaining data on acts of terrorism committed by states is extremely difficult because they tend not to advertise their terrorist activities or intent (Chambliss 1989: 203–4; Gibbs 1989: 330; Mitchell *et al.* 1986: 2; Nicholson 1986: 31). When such activities are exposed, considerable analytical effort is required to determine whether such an act constitutes state terrorism, because they are unlikely to be included in the major data sets of terrorist incidents. This also means that drawing concrete conclusions about whether certain acts constitute state terrorism may not always be possible and instead we might need to make inferences from other, context-specific evidence. I will explore some of the difficulties involved in identifying state terrorism. They relate primarily to problems of agency and motive.

The problem of agency: when are state representatives acting on behalf of the state?

As discussed above, before concluding that a violent act by a state representative is an act of state terrorism, we are confronted with a number of challenges relating to agency and motive. We must first rule out the possibility that the act was simply an isolated criminal act by an individual with no sanction from the state. Even then, however, the state still holds a degree of responsibility for the actions of its representatives. Whether we conclude that a state sanctioned the act, and therefore was complicit in state terrorism through its agents, often depends on how the state responds afterwards. If the state fails to prosecute the individual to the full extent of the law and fails to compensate the victims, and if the state attempts to excuse the actions in some way, the state is condoning the actions of that individual. We can argue, therefore, that the state was complicit. With reference to the use of torture at Abu Ghraib, I will demonstrate the importance of context-specific evidence in determining first, whether violent acts by state agents are acts of state terrorism, and second, whether those acts are part of an institutionalized policy of state terrorism.

To differentiate between the odd, isolated criminal act of a prison officer or member of the armed forces and an act of state terrorism, it is important to examine the reaction of the relevant officials and the state. If measures are taken swiftly to try to punish the perpetrator(s) through proper legal and disciplinary channels, and if there is no evidence of a broader pattern of such incidents, nor of the state sanctioning such activities, we might conclude that this is a criminal act by an individual or group and not an act deliberately enacted by the state to terrorize. This was indeed what the Pentagon and the administration of President George W. Bush claimed, once the photographs emerged in 2004, revealing that detainees at the Abu Ghraib prison in Iraq had been tortured by US personnel. Nevertheless, this claim could not be sustained because there were very few prosecutions, sentences were light and punitive measures were limited to lower-ranking soldiers, rather than the senior officers involved, or indeed the officials in the Bush administration who fought to ensure that methods tantamount to torture be permitted against terror suspects. In a speech on Iraq on 24 May 2004, shortly after the public had learned of the torture, President Bush declared 'under the dictator [Saddam Hussein], prisons like Abu Ghraib were symbols of death and torture. That same prison became a symbol of disgraceful conduct by a few American troops who dishonored our country and disregarded our values' (Bush, cited in Milbank 2004). The same conclusions were drawn by Major General Antonio Tabuga in his initial inquiry. He concluded that the torture was the work of a few bad apples in need of improved training (Taguba 2004: 37).

Yet the record of events uncovered through various leaked documents, traced by Seymour Hersh (2004) and compiled by Karen Greenberg and Joshua Dratel (2005), shows that despite the public statement condemning torture, the administration had been behind numerous attempts to allow torture of detainees in the War on Terror. Policies outlined in the various memos that passed between the upper echelons of the administration, including the White House, the Department of Justice, and the senior counsel to the president, were enacted. These policies included: not affording protection under the Geneva Convention to detainees and allowing torture, such as: the use of stress positions; extremes of temperature and light; hooding; interrogations for 20 hours; forced grooming and removal of clothing; water boarding; and the use of scenarios designed to persuade the detainee that death or severe pain were imminent, as advocated in a memo from Major General Dunlavey, dated 11 October 2002, requesting approval for such techniques (Dunlavey 2002). These techniques subsequently were sanctioned by Defense Secretary Donald Rumsfeld on 2 December 2002 (Haynes 2002).

The response of the administration to the abuses at Abu Ghraib involved proceedings in military courts against nine reservists involved in the abuses, three of whom were convicted; the other six made plea bargain deals (Gutierrez 2005). None of the senior officers implicated was brought to trial and there was no attempt to hold to account those in the Bush administration who had been involved in efforts to legitimize the torture. Without examining the wider context of the Abu Ghraib case, it would be possible to conclude that this was an isolated incident committed by a small number of miscreants, and this was certainly the message that the administration attempted to convey. The reality is that there have been many cases of abuse in the 'War on Terror' at numerous camps in Iraq and Afghanistan, as well as at Guantánamo Bay, at the hands of US and allied forces. Furthermore, the policy of extraordinary rendition has resulted in torture and abuse, sanctioned by the United States and various liberal democratic allies and carried out by security agents from many countries with appalling, human rights abuses (Blakeley 2009). Abu Ghraib, therefore, was not an isolated incident, but part of a much bigger pattern of terrorism sanctioned by the United States.

The case of Abu Ghraib underlines the importance of the wider context when considering whether acts of violence by state agents constitute state terrorism. Without evidence of intentions, we have to look to the broader context. In the case of disappearances, it would be helpful to determine whether there were disappearances of other individuals critical of the state during the same period. Certainly, in the Latin American states during the Cold War, initially a small number of people assumed to be a threat to the regime disappeared, but these occurred in sufficient numbers to imply a pattern. In many cases, there was nothing terribly secretive about the means by which individuals were taken. In Argentina and Chile, for example, it was not uncommon for individuals to be taken by government agents in broad daylight. This would imply that the disappearances were as much a part of an attempt by the governments to intimidate their associates as an effort to remove political opponents. Examining the context of specific acts, therefore, can also help to indicate whether there was an intention on the part of the state to terrorize.

A further indicator of intention concerns the reasonably anticipated likely consequence of an act. For example, if a state chooses to bomb civilian areas of a city, knowing that this is almost certainly going to result in civilian casualties, it cannot claim that no harm is meant to civilians. Similarly, if state agents are in the business of kidnapping political activists, the state cannot claim that it does not intend to terrorize other political activists. If such acts are carried out repeatedly, despite the state having already seen that civilians are killed and terrorized by the bombing and that political activists are fearful, we can conclude that this is the intended outcome of those acts and that the state, therefore, is committing acts of terrorism against civilians.

Unintended consequence as state terrorism

In some cases, groups within a society may be terrorized as a consequence of other repressive acts. This raises the question of whether we can argue that state terrorism has occurred if it is not the primary or only outcome of an action. According to Mitchell *et al.*, if the terror was unintentional, we could not argue that this was 'true' terrorism. But this assumes that we can determine that the terror is not intentional, rather than one of a number of intentions of the act. If we apply this condition, an act of repression cannot be defined as state terrorism if it is primarily aimed at harming the victim, a secondary effect of which is to terrorize other groups within a population. Mitchell *et al.* illustrate their argument with the example of the policies of the Khmer Rouge that were aimed at the destruction of a particular sector of society and which therefore constituted genocide. While this will have instilled terror throughout society, this was not the primary intention. By contrast, they argue, policies such as US Operation Phoenix in South Vietnam, which involved terrorizing people associated with members of the National Liberation Front by publicly rounding them up, torturing, and assassinating them, did constitute state terrorism because terrorizing the target audience was the primary objective (Mitchell *et al.* 1986: 6).

Such a sharp distinction should not be made between terror as a secondary effect and terror as the primary objective of an act, particularly in cases where the act itself is illegitimate. A parallel can be drawn with Michael Walzer's work on the legitimacy of acts in war which are likely to have evil consequences. He argues that, in line with the *jus in bello* principles, such an act was only permissible providing it met the following four conditions:

> That the act is good in itself or at least indifferent, which means ... that it is a legitimate act of war; that the direct effect is morally acceptable ... that the intention of the actor is good, that is, he aims only at the acceptable effect; the evil effect is not one of his ends, nor is it a means to an ends; that the good effect is sufficiently good to compensate for allowing the evil effect; it must be justifiable under the proportionality rule.
>
> (Walzer 2000: 153)

With regard to intentions, Walzer restates the third condition as follows:

> The intention of the actor is good, that is, he aims narrowly at the acceptable effect; the evil effect is not one of his ends, nor is it a means to his ends, and, aware of the evil involved, he seeks to minimise it, accepting costs to himself.
>
> (Walzer 2000: 155)

These conditions can be usefully applied to state terrorism, where it appears to be a secondary effect of some other act. State terrorism in such cases is not the unintended secondary effect of some good or indifferent act. It is a consequence of a policy which is illegitimate, repressive, and on Walzer's terms, evil. Furthermore, if the state seeks to commit genocide, for example, against a specific group, are they not assisted because others outside of that group are sufficiently fearful of the consequences for themselves if they are to intervene in an attempt to prevent the genocide? Can the terror that arises among other groups not be an intended effect, whether primary or secondary? In the case of the genocide by Nazi Germany against Jews, gypsies, and homosexuals, individuals outside of those groups might not have intervened because they had been sufficiently terrorized by the increasing intensity of efforts by the Nazis to single these groups out, round them up, and transport them to unknown places and subsequently by the rumours they had heard of concentration camps, and of others outside of those groups who had attempted to protect the vulnerable, themselves disappearing. Indeed, as Gurr notes, Adolf Hitler, while in power, was explicit about the fact that his genocidal policies served as a tool of terror to deter opposition. Hitler stated:

> I shall spread terror through the surprising application of all means. The sudden shock of a terrible fear of death is what matters. Why should I deal otherwise with all my political opponents? These so-called atrocities save me hundreds of thousands of individual actions against the protestors and discontents. Each one of them will think twice to oppose me when he learns what is [awaiting] him in the [concentration] camp.
>
> (Adolf Hitler, cited in Gurr 1986: 46–7)

Even when the terror is not a secondary objective, it may prove expedient to the state and should be labelled state terrorism. Walzer argues that to conclude that a secondary effect was unintentional, there would have to be evidence that the actors involved sought to minimize the secondary effect. It is difficult to envisage that a state involved in a genocidal policy would be too concerned about minimizing the ensuing terror among others outside of the targeted group, particularly where the terror may be instrumental to its overall objectives.

As with various phenomena in the social sciences, identifying state terrorism and determining whether it is used instrumentally in pursuit of a state's objectives requires that we make judgements concerning the agency and motives behind specific acts. To label legitimately violent incidents by state representatives as state terrorism, those incidents should not be analysed in isolation but with reference to the wider context. This helps to overcome some of the ambiguities we face when seeking to determine the degree of sanction from the state for those acts of violence, and the purpose that they are intended to serve. In some cases, it simply may not be possible to make a decisive judgement and it may only be through the passage of time that sufficient evidence comes to light to confirm that an act of state terrorism has been committed and to confirm that it is part of a wider, institutionalized policy of terrorism.

Conclusion

Existing definitions of terrorism adequately encompass acts by state agents. I have shown that state terrorism involves a deliberate threat or act of violence against a victim by state representatives, or a threat of such when a climate of fear already exists through prior acts of state terrorism, which is intended to induce fear in some target observers who identify with the victim, so that the target audience is forced to consider changing their behaviour in some way. This can be, but is not limited to, their political behaviour. The key ingredients identified are entirely consistent with existing definitions of terrorism. It is the intent of the actor to create extreme fear among a target audience that differentiates state terrorism from other forms of state repression, as well as from criminal acts on the part of state agents who are not part of a broader strategy of state terrorism. The audience can be a very specific audience or a much broader one. Where widespread state terrorism takes place, it may emerge from the use of other forms of repression, where the main objective is not to terrorize but where this is a secondary, and often welcome consequence. With reference to the 'just war' tradition, I have argued that where state terrorism appears to be a secondary effect (albeit an instrumental one) rather than the primary motive of some other act of repression, it still constitutes state terrorism. While state terrorism has not been deemed illegal in international law, the acts it involves are criminal because they involve the illegal targeting of individuals that the state has a duty to protect.

Neither definitions of terrorism nor international law pertaining to human rights present significant obstacles to scholars of state terrorism. On the contrary, they provide helpful criteria by which to identify and oppose state terrorism. The challenge for scholars, however, is determining whether violent acts by state representatives can be labelled state terrorism, and when acts of state terrorism are part of a wider, institutionalized policy. As with other atrocities, there is a scarcity of evidence that shows explicitly such acts to have been sanctioned by the state. We are therefore faced with considerable challenges in identifying agency and intent when atrocities are committed. We can overcome some of these challenges by situating specific acts of state violence within a much broader context. This involves analysing the circumstances surrounding the events in question, both at the local level, and in relation to other events and broader policies and strategies.

Notes

1 This chapter draws on material published in Blakeley (2009), chapter two. We are grateful to the publishers for granting permission for use of this material.
2 A more detailed critique of the work of these scholars can be found in Raphael (2007).

References

AI (Amnesty International) (1976) 'Guatemala', *Amnesty International Briefing Papers*, 8, London: Amnesty International.

Arkin, W., Durrant, D., and Cherni, M. (1991) 'On Impact: Modern Warfare and the Environment – A Case Study of the Gulf War'. Online, available at: www.greenpeace. org/raw/content/international/press/reports/on-impact-modern-warfare-and.pdf (accessed 6 October 2008).

Badey, T. (1998) 'Defining International Terrorism: A Pragmatic Approach', *Terrorism and Political Violence*, 10 (1): 90–107.

Barker, J. (2003) *The No-nonsense Guide to Terrorism*, London: Verso.

Beccaria, C. (1995 [1764]) *On Crimes and Punishments and Other Writings*, R. Bellamy (ed.), R. Davies (trans.), Cambridge, UK: Cambridge University Press.

Blakeley, R. (2008) 'The Elephant in the Room: A Response to John Horgan and Michael Boyle', *Critical Studies on Terrorism*, 1 (2): 151–65.

—— (2009) *State Terrorism and Neoliberalism: The North in the South*, London: Routledge.

Chambliss, W. (1989) 'State-organized Crime – The American Society of Criminology, 1988 Presidential Address', *Criminology*, 27 (2): 183–208.

Cooper, H. (2001) 'Terrorism: The Problem of Definition Revisited', *American Behavioral Scientist*, 44: 881–93.

Dinges, J. (2004) *The Condor Years*, New York: The New Press.

Duggard, J. (1974) 'International Terrorism: Problems of Definition', *International Affairs*, 50 (1): 67–81.

Dunlavey, M. (2002) 'Counter-resistance Strategies (Memorandum for Commander, US Southern Command)', 11 October. Online, available at: www.torturingdemocracy.org/documents/20021011.pdf (accessed 18 October 2008).

Foucault, M. (1977) *Discipline and Punish: The Birth of the Prison*, A. Sheridan (trans.), London: Penguin Books.

Ganor, B. (1998) 'Defining Terrorism: Is One Man's Terrorist Another Man's Freedom Fighter?'. Online, available at: www.ict.org.il/ (accessed 17 July 2008).

Gibbs, J. (1989) 'Conceptualization of Terrorism', *American Sociological Review*, 54 (3): 329–40.

Greenberg, K. and Dratel, J. (eds) (2005) *The Torture Papers: The Road to Abu Ghraib*, Cambridge, UK: Cambridge University Press.

Gurr, T.R. (1986) 'The Political Origins of State Violence and Terror: A Theoretical Analysis', in Michael Stohl and George Lopez (eds) *Government Violence and Repression: An Agenda for Research*, New York: Greenwood Press: 45–71.

Gutierrez, T. (2005) 'Lynndie England Convicted in Abu Ghraib Trial', *USA Today*, 26 September 2005.

Haynes, W.J. (2002) 'Counter-resistance Techniques (Action Memo from William J. Haynes, General Counsel, to Secretary of State for Defense Donald Rumsfeld)', 27 November. Online, available at: www.torturingdemocracy.org/documents/20021127–1.pdf (accessed 18 October 2008).

Hersh, S. (2004) *Chain of Command: The Road from 9/11 to Abu Ghraib*, London: Penguin Books.

Hoffman, B. (1998) *Inside Terrorism*, New York: Columbia University Press.

International Committee of the Red Cross (ICRC) (1949) 'Convention (III) Relative to the Treatment of Prisoners of War'. Online, available at: www.icrc.org/ihl.nsf/7c4d08d

9b287a42141256739003e636b/6fef854a3517b75ac125641e004a9e68 (accessed 2 May 2005).

——— (2003) 'International Humanitarian Law and International Human Rights Law: Similarities and Differences'. Online, available at: www.icrc.org/Web/Eng/siteeng0. nsf/htmlall/57JR8L/$FILE/IHL_and_IHRL.pdf?OpenElement (accessed 6 June 2005).

Jenkins, B. (1980) 'The Study of Terrorism: Definitional Problems', Santa Monica: The RAND Corporation.

Keaney, T. and Cohen, E. (1993) 'Gulf War Air Power Surveys (vol. II, part II, chapters 6 and 7), Washington, DC: John Hopkins University Press and the US Air Force.

Laqueur, W. (1986) 'Reflections on Terrorism', *Foreign Affairs*, 65: 86–100.

——— (2003) *No End to War: Terrorism in the Twenty-first Century*, New York: Continuum.

McClintock, M. (2001) 'The United States and Operation Condor: Military Doctrine in an Unconventional War', *Latin American Studies Association Conference*, Washington, DC.

McSherry, J.P. (2002) 'Tracking the Origins of a State Terror Network: Operation Condor', *Latin American Perspectives*, 29 (1): 38–60.

Martin, G. (2003) *Understanding Terrorism: Challenges, Perspectives, and Issues*, London: Sage Publications.

Milbank, D. (2004) 'Bush Seeks to Reassure Nation on Iraq', *Washington Post*, 25 May 2004.

Mitchell, C., Stohl, M., Carleton, D., Lopez, G. (1986) 'State Terrorism: Issues of Concept and Measurement', in Michael Stohl and George Lopez (eds) *Government Violence and Repression: An Agenda for Research*, New York: Greenwood Press: 1–26.

Nicholson, M. (1986) 'Conceptual Problems of Studying State Terrorism', in Michael Stohl and George Lopez (eds) *Government Violence and Repression: An Agenda for Research*, New York: Greenwood Press: 27–44.

Peters, E. (1985) *Torture*, New York: Basil Blackwell.

Raphael, S. (2007) 'Putting the State Back In: The Orthodox Definition of Terrorism and the Critical Need to Address State Terrorism', paper given at British International Studies Association Annual Conference, Cambridge, UK.

Silke, A. (2004) *Research on Terrorism: Trends, Achievements and Failures*, London: Frank Cass.

Stohl, M. (2006) 'The State as Terrorist: Insights and Implications', *Democracy and Security*, 2: 1–25.

Taguba, M.G.A. (2004) 'Article 15–6 Investigation of the 800th Military Police Brigade', Washington, DC: US Department of Defence.

Vidal-Naquet, P. (1963) *Torture: Cancer of Democracy*, Middlesex: Penguin Books.

Walter, E.V. (1969) *Terror and Resistance*, Oxford: Oxford University Press.

Walzer, M. (2000) *Just and Unjust Wars* 3rd edition, New York: Basic Books.

Weinberg, L., Pedahzur, A., and Hirsch-Hoefler, S. (2004) 'The Challenges of Conceptualizing Terrorism', *Terrorism and Political Violence*, 16 (4): 777–94.

Wilkinson, P. (1992) 'International Terrorism: New Risks to World Order', in John Baylis and Nick Rengger (eds) *Dilemmas of World Politics: International Issues in a Changing World*, London: Clarenden Press: 228–57.

2 Darfur's dread

Contemporary state terrorism in the Sudan

David Mickler

Introduction

Ostensibly a response to a local armed rebellion, the systematic destruction of civilian lives and livelihoods in Sudan's western region of Darfur by the national military and state-sponsored militias since 2003 has constituted a campaign of terrorism by the Sudanese government. As a result, out of Darfur's population of six million, it has been estimated that 300,000 people died directly from violence or indirectly from ensuing disease and malnutrition, while more than four million have been 'seriously affected' by the conflict and severe humanitarian crisis. Furthermore, the powerful psychological terrorization caused by this violence was evident in the 2.7 million Darfurians who fled from their homes and villages to arrive in despondent refugee camps in neighbouring Chad or to remain displaced, and vulnerable to further attacks, elsewhere inside Sudan (see Figure 1) (United Nations 2008).

The Darfur case demonstrates vividly that regimes of terror are not only phenomena of history. In their daily lives, millions of ordinary people across the globe continue to experience politically motivated repression, violence and terrorism. Such instances are particularly concerning when it is in fact the institutions of the state which are the source of acute – and indeed intentional – human suffering. In addition to the basic immorality of such violence, this is a matter of fundamental social, political, and intellectual importance because of the powerfully destructive capabilities of modern states, the violation of the posited social contract between citizens and their governments, and also because of an emerging international consensus that states which abuse the fundamental human rights or security of their populations should incur a suspension of their assumed sovereign legitimacy and immunity (ICISS 2001). Using Darfur as a case study, this chapter argues that in addition to more commonly used legal designations such as genocide, war crimes, and crimes against humanity, we can characterize certain forms of state violence as 'terrorism' if those acts conform to the following constitutive criteria: they are politically motivated, intentional and pre-determined, and they intend to cause fear and intimidate a wider audience than just the immediate targets, which are primarily (but not only) civilians (Jackson 2008: 29–30).

In a context in which 'no word in the contemporary American and international political lexicon is more frequently invoked or more emotionally charged

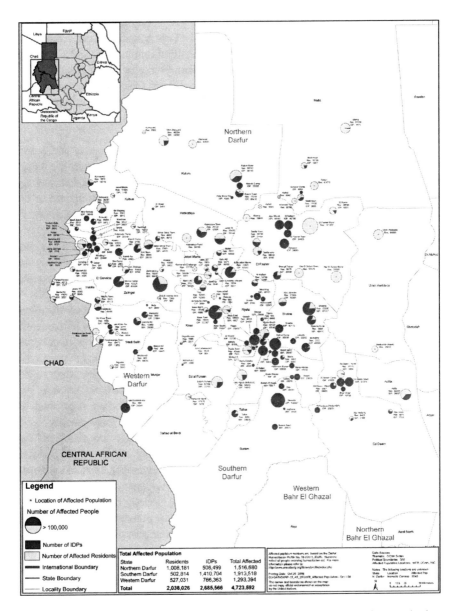

The legend and data table within the figure read:

Legend

× Location of Affected Population

Number of Affected People

⬤ > 100,000

◼ Number of IDPs

◻ Number of Affected Residents

▬▬ International Boundary

——— State Boundary

········· Locality Boundary

Total Affected Population			
State	Residents	IDPs	Total Affected
Northern Darfur	1,008,181	508,499	1,516,680
Southern Darfur	502,814	1,410,704	1,913,518
Western Darfur	527,031	766,363	1,293,394
Total	2,038,026	2,685,566	4,723,592

Figure 1 Darfur, Sudan, 2008 (source: UN Office for the Coordination of Humanitarian Affairs).

Note

The boundaries and names shown and the designations used on this map do not imply official endorsement or acceptance by the United Nations.

than "terrorist"' (Selden and So 2004: 3), however, critics highlight the intellectual anomaly of how – historically and at present – such 'state terrorism' has been collectively responsible for a vast number of civilian deaths per annum but is generally de-emphasized, ignored, or even justified in much of the burgeoning contemporary discourse and analysis of terrorism (Blakeley 2007; Booth 2008). Indeed, one observation is that 'mainstream social scientists have failed to recognise the possibility that states ... can and do carry out acts of terrorism' (Selden and So 2004: 4). Yet, as Sluka has argued convincingly:

> If we allow the definition [of terrorism] to include violence by states and agents of states, then we find that the major form of terrorism in the world today is that practiced by states and their agents and allies, and that, quantitatively, antistate terrorism pales into relative insignificance compared to it.
>
> (Sluka 2000: 1)

In fact an influential recent study concluded that 'although the focus of enormous attention', terrorism by non-state actors 'has killed fewer than 1,000 people a year, on average, over the past 30 years' (Human Security Centre 2005: 6), comparable, for example, to only one-tenth of the estimated death toll in Darfur since 2003.

Despite such quantitative data, opposition to the concept and label of 'state terrorism' remains. According to Sluka, 'while there is now a massive literature on antistate terrorism, state terror has been neglected by academics, the media and governments', for reasons which have been 'more political and ideological than empirical' (2000: 1). For example, after 9/11 the administration of President George W. Bush had 'taken on the mantle of leading a worldwide antiterrorist crusade, the scope of which is defined in such a way as to conceive of terrorism as confined to antistate violence' (Falk 2004: 48). Similarly, in noting that governments 'have shown themselves to be very keen to keep the idea of "state terrorism" off the agenda', Booth argued that 'there is no logical reason (only self-interested political arguments) for keeping state terrorism off the academic agenda' (2008: 76). Importantly, the political consequences of such discursive framing are that:

> This distorting control of language and of media presentations of terrorism has a profoundly misleading effect, obscuring the primary reality of terrorism, namely, that states rather than antistate actors are responsible for the great majority of civilian deaths over the course of the past several decades, as well as throughout modern history. As a consequence, the lesser antistate violence is demonized, while the greater state violence is virtually immunised from criticism.
>
> (Falk 2004: 48)

Additionally, in observing that consensus in international political debates over defining terrorism was obstructed, *inter alia*, by 'the argument that any definition should include States' use of armed forces against civilians' a 2004 UN panel of experts did not find compelling the label of 'state terrorism', because the 'legal and normative framework against State violations is far stronger than in the case of non-State actors' (United Nations 2004: 51). Former UN Secretary-General Kofi Annan endorsed this view, arguing that 'it is time to set aside debates on so-called "State terrorism" [because the] use of force by States is already thoroughly regulated under international law' (Annan 2005: 35). This line of argument, centred upon how 'state terrorism' had the potential to create conceptual confusion instead of clarity, was not unexpected from an organization constituted primarily by states and their interests. Yet it does raise the important issue of why certain state acts should be identified as 'terrorism' when other designations may have already been applied.

First, accepting certain acts of state violence as 'terrorism' could help us to better understand the nature of state power, both in a physical sense relative to unarmed civilians, and, as Falk has suggested above, in a discursive sense pertaining to the ways in which governments have been able to frame state interests. Second, the additional de-legitimation that comes with the label of 'terrorism', particularly in an era defined by the US-led 'War on Terror', could generate important political pressure for action to halt acts of state terrorism where other rhetorical and moral appeals have failed (such as in Darfur). Third, it could enable new perspectives on, and solutions to, cycles of state repression, injustice, and violent resistance: it is 'only by recognising the terrorism of states [that makes it] possible to understand, and deal with, acts of terrorism by groups and individuals which, however horrific, are tiny by comparison' (Pilger 2004).

The Darfur crisis, after initially attracting little international attention, developed into one of the most discussed conflicts and humanitarian emergencies in modern times. The orchestration and commission of atrocities by the Sudanese government has been investigated, documented, and variously determined to constitute war crimes, crimes against humanity, and genocide. Yet, Sudan's actions have rarely been also characterized as 'state terrorism' in official discourse or by the mainstream media. In this context, the central analytical aim of this chapter is to demonstrate how Khartoum's intentions and actions conform to the above constitutive elements of terrorism. To do this, it will explain how the regime deliberately targeted, killed, and terrorized Darfur's non-Arab civilian population for the dual political purpose of punishing the ethnic groups with which the rebels identified, and dissuading, through pervasive fear, any further support to the insurgency against the Arab-controlled Sudanese state.

The remainder of the chapter will be divided into three main parts. First, it will briefly background the eruption of armed conflict in Darfur in 2003 in order to contextualize the civilian victims' position in relation to powerful central state institutions and to highlight the cynicism with which Khartoum has governed Sudan's peripheries. Second, it will examine in greater detail the Sudanese government's violent response to the armed rebellion in the country's west: (*a*) by identifying the tactics and results of Sudan's counter-insurgency campaign to illustrate the nature and magnitude of this example of contemporary state terrorism; and (*b*) by explaining the regime's political and psychological motives to establish its deliberate intent to terrorize the wider population. In light of such pervasive violence, the chapter will conclude by arguing that a lack of coercive UN intervention in Sudan to protect vulnerable civilians has been a direct product of extensive Chinese and Russian economic interests in Sudan, and, tellingly, valuable post-9/11 intelligence cooperation by Khartoum in Western-led regional 'counter-terrorism' operations.

Darfur and the Sudanese state: from exclusion to rebellion

Darfur, meaning homeland of the local *Fur* ethnic group, is a vast and mostly arid region comprising the western portion of the modern state of Sudan. It emerged in the mid-seventeenth century as an independent Islamic sultanate ruled by indigenous (non-Arab) tribes, but was forcibly annexed to the colonial Anglo-Egyptian Condominium in Sudan in 1916. Indeed, 'grossly neglected in the "Nilocentric" historiography of Sudan' (de Waal 2005: 183), Darfur has been described as a 'backwater, a prisoner of geography' (Flint and de Waal 2005: 16) and, until the recent crisis, as 'one of the least known places in the world. Poor, remote, landlocked, and sparsely populated, it was obscure even to the rest of Sudan' (Daly 2007: 1).

However, in early 2003 disaffection with Darfur's perpetual national political marginalization and severe economic underdevelopment, combined with increasing resource scarcity and inter-ethnic tension, led members of the two most prominent of the newly organizing rebel groups in the region – the secular Sudan Liberation Movement/Army (SLM/A) and the Islamist-leaning Justice and Equality Movement (JEM) – to attack local organs of the Sudanese state, including most notably the military garrison at El Fasher, capital of North Darfur state, on 25 April. According to one account, the seven-hour attack left a number of government Antonov aircraft and helicopter gunships destroyed, and led to 75 Sudanese military personnel killed and 32 captured, including the local commander (Flint and de Waal 2005: 99).

The Darfur rebels' grievances were in part a product of the colonial 'native administration' system, under which local tribal leaders were afforded a degree of self-rule as long as they remained compliant. Critics argued that this was a 'recipe for stagnation and for building a two-tiered society in which the natives, on the pretext of cultural integrity, were marginalized from the benefits of the modern world which the colonialists could monopolize for their own advantage' (Prunier 2005: 29). As a result, Darfur was sorely neglected and underdeveloped during British rule, receiving scant investment in healthcare, education, infrastructure or agricultural production. Yet, little changed after Sudanese independence in 1956, as successive national governments – both civilian and military – remained under the control of a clique of Arab tribes from north of the capital, who reserved development, investment, and services for Khartoum and its surrounds (Flint and de Waal 2005: 17–18; Kasfir 2005: 198–9).

In addition, cynical leaders have often attempted to redefine multiethnic and multicultural Sudanese identity in exclusive Arab and Islamic terms. Most notably, much of the country's post-independence history involved civil war between Khartoum and non-Arab and Christian/animist southern Sudan. This was compounded after the 1989 military coup, led by (now President) Omar al-Bashir, brought to power the National Islamic Front (NIF) regime, characterized by its radical Islamism and Arab supremacist tendencies. In Darfur, too, political constructions of inherently antagonistic Arab/African identities, particularly those promoted by Khartoum to shore up its own Arab constituencies, have fuelled ethnic conflict.

Ethnic identities in Darfur are complex. Commonly, distinctions are made between 'Arabs' and 'Africans' (or non-Arabs), but most Darfurians are similarly dark-skinned, while nearly all of the population adheres to Islam (Prunier 2005: 4–5). Indigenous groups claiming black African heritage, such as the *Fur*, *Massalit* and *Zaghawa*, were joined in the region over time by migrating Arab groups, but centuries of intermarriage and cohabitation blurred sharp differences. As such, 'rather than by skin colour or other physical traits, Darfurians, like other Sudanese, have always identified themselves in ethnocultural or tribal terms' (Mahmoud 2004: 3).

The ethnic dimension of the recent conflict does have an origin in historical land ownership claims, whereby Darfur sultans distributed allotments to groups on the basis of ethnicity and mode of livelihood. Those that were sedentary farmers – generally non-Arabs – mostly received *hawakir* ('enclosures', or land titles), obtaining ownership over specific lands, while others, particularly nomadic Arab pastoralists, were often excluded due to their transient lifestyles (Tubiana 2007: 73–5). This was less conflictual in the past, when arable land and water were more abundant, as a traditional system of land sharing evolved in which herders were permitted to seasonally traverse cultivated property. However, over time, climate change and desertification resulted in diminishing natural resources, creating tension between different types of land users (Ban 2007). In this context, the cynical manipulation of ethnic identities by political elites exacerbated recent hostilities in Darfur.

Indeed, in Darfur ethnic identities were generally not a salient cause of conflict. It is only relatively recently that Darfurians have been 'polarised into Arab versus African identifications in response to deep political and ideological disputes in which state repression and economic under-development of the country's marginal regions have played a significant role' (Mahmoud 2004: 3). Similarly, Darfur 'best represents a case of neglected and protracted conflict over resources, which took the form of identity conflict'; however, importantly 'not all resource conflicts are based on a situation of resource scarcity, rather they are political in nature and have to do with the workings of the Sudanese state' (Assal 2006: 101–2). More generally, in post-independence Sudan:

> Successive regimes have manipulated administrative structures to undermine the control of local people and authorities over resources. Identity and ideology, particular Arab nationalism and political Islamism, have been used to mobilize support to compensate for the governance and development

failings of state policies. Elites have mastered the divide-and-rule tactics inherited from the colonial era through their territorial organization of the modern Sudanese state. The result has been underdevelopment, exclusion, and violent conflict.

(el-Battahani 2006: 10)

While appreciating this historical context, this chapter does not seek to obfuscate or apologize for the actions of the Darfur rebels in their insurgency against the state. Indeed, although not conducted on a 'systematic or widespread' basis, a UN investigation found:

Credible evidence that rebel forces, namely members of the SLA and JEM ... are responsible for serious violations of international human rights and humanitarian law which may amount to war crimes. In particular, these violations include cases of murder of civilians and pillage.

(United Nations 2005: 4)

Instead, this chapter illustrates how and explains why the Sudanese government, in response to this armed insurgency in the country's west, enacted a strategy of state terrorism targeting the non-Arab civilian population of Darfur.

Terrorize Darfur: Khartoum's counter-insurgency strategy

It is not uncommon for governments to defend themselves and state institutions militarily against armed insurgencies, and this reaction may often be accepted as a necessary, legal, and legitimate exercise of national power and authority: this is exactly what the Sudanese government has claimed as its justification for taking military action in response to the Darfur rebellion since 2003. According to a number of authoritative accounts elaborated below, however, Khartoum's counter-insurgency strategy went far beyond a defensive military operation; instead, Darfur's non-Arab civilian population was the target of a regime of murder, rape and destruction orchestrated and implemented by their own state. As the UN-established International Commission of Inquiry on Darfur (COI) concluded, the 'most significant element of the conflict has been the attacks on civilians, which has led to the destruction and burning of entire villages, and the displacement of large parts of the civilian population' (United Nations 2005: 25).

Conforming to Jackson's (2008: 29–30) constitutive criteria, the Sudanese government's strategy and actions in Darfur since 2003 have constituted 'terrorism' by the state. To substantiate this argument, the chapter will illustrate the nature and extent of violence against Darfurians, demonstrating that civilians were indeed the targets of coordinated attacks by the Sudanese military and government-sponsored militias. According to international investigations, these attacks should be prosecuted under existing international humanitarian law as war crimes and crimes against humanity. It will also demonstrate that deliberate state violence against Darfur's civilian population was part of a dual strategy, consisting of genocidal motivations to 'ethnically cleanse' Darfur of its non-Arab citizens, and psychological tactics aimed at instilling fear in the wider population. The overall political objective was to dissuade further support for the rebels and thus retain and strengthen Arabist Khartoum's control over the state.

The Sudanese government's plan for dealing with the Darfur rebellion involved instituting, as a first step, a 'campaign of repression' in which a 'state of emergency was declared as hundreds of alleged rebel sympathisers were arrested. The governors of Northern and Western Darfur were dismissed. President Bashir appointed a "special task force" of loyalists and old Darfur hands' (Daly 2007: 282). Then, in a move 'first viewed as conciliatory but in retrospect ominous of the reign of terror about to be unleashed', the government abolished the special courts of summary justice in Darfur (ibid.: 282). In addition, the 'Darfur Security' desk, headed by Interior Minister Ahmed Harun, was created as a powerful position to coordinate the regime's plan of attack against the rebels and, importantly, against ordinary Sudanese citizens in Darfur. These initial bureaucratic measures were soon complemented by violent acts of state terrorism.

Next, Khartoum employed, armed, financed, and directed groups of nomadic Arab-identifying militias from across western Sudan to attack the rebels and to destroy the non-Arab towns and villages in Darfur that were alleged to be the basis of SLA and JEM support. These local militias – popularly referred to as *Janjaweed* ('devil-horsemen') – held sympathies towards Arabist Khartoum and had their own interests in local land and population redistribution, particularly those nomadic groups who remained outside the traditional land ownership system (Tubiana 2007: 71–5). Others were simply concerned with their own enrichment and exhibited an unconscionable disregard for the lives of their fellow Sudanese. This was a deliberate and calculated move by Khartoum: because the government was militarily unprepared and initially incapable of meeting the rebel threat in Darfur with national forces, it 'exploited the existing tensions between different tribes' by employing local Arab militias to engage the rebels (United Nations 2005: 24).

Describing this divide-and-rule strategy, Collins has argued that as the 'most unpopular regime in the history of independent Sudan', al-Bashir's government 'was now able to weaken any potential opposition by exploiting ethnic divisions [and] branding the insurgency as an African attempt to rid Darfur of the "Arab race", whose dominance was the very foundation of the Islamist government and its extremist groups' (2006: 11). As a result, the conflict in Darfur quickly morphed from a centre-periphery rebellion to one imbued with the dangerous characteristics of ethnic violence that had been witnessed previously in other African countries and in the Balkans during the 1990s, for example. Indeed, the *Janjaweed* did not primarily engage the rebels; civilians were targeted in attacks aimed at the purging of Darfur's non-Arab population:

> the mounted *Janjaweed* commandos, usually comprised of one hundred warriors, would sweep down on a village just before dawn. The pattern of destruction was the same. The men were killed, often mutilated, the women

raped, and the children sometimes abducted. The village was burnt, the live-stock seized, the fields torched, and the infrastructure – wells, irrigation works, schools, clinics – methodologically destroyed in a systematic scheme to drive the African population from their ancestral holdings.

(Collins 2006: 11–12)

While it was soon evident to the international community that the militias were responsible for committing such atrocities on the ground in Darfur, it was not until later that their direct relationship to the Sudanese government and its counter-insurgency strategy in Darfur became widely acknowledged, represent-ing a clear example of a state sponsoring militias to commit violence and terror-ism against civilians on its behalf. What added weight to the argument that the Darfur case became an example of state terrorism, however, was that in addition to their concealed support for the *Janjaweed*, the Sudanese military, paramili-tary, intelligence, and 'security' services also participated directly in attacks on civilians. According to the COI, Sudan's National Security and Intelligence Service played a 'central role and is responsible for the design, planning and implementation of policies associated with the conflict … its influence appears to reach the highest levels of authority' (United Nations 2005: 27). Indeed, the Sudan Armed Forces (SAF) and *Janjaweed* operated in a close and brutally effective partnership against Darfur's non-Arab population:

Improvised bombs of 'explosives and metallic debris' dumped out of the doors of Russian transport aircraft were followed closely by successive raids by attack helicopters and fighter-bombers. Janjaweed militia on camel and horseback, sometimes assisted by army units, swept in to finish the job, by burning villages, killing principally young men, and forcing survivors to flee. The displaced fled to areas sometimes protected by the Sudanese police. Janjaweed patrolled the perimeters, however, attacking women and girls who left.

(Feinstein 2007: 38)

This cooperative relationship between organs of the SAF and proxies of the Sudanese state brought terror to Darfurian civilians by land and by air. Reaching similar conclusions, the commission of inquiry found that in Darfur 'several of the attacks on villages were carried out with the support of Government of the Sudan including the air force, involving air bombardments and regular aerial surveillance'. As such, there was:

Credible evidence of the use of Mi-8 helicopters, Mi-24 helicopters and Antonov aircraft during air attacks on villages. Ground attacks frequently were preceded by the presence of aircraft near or directly above the villages, which would either bomb the village or surrounding areas, or circle over the village and then retreat.

(United Nations 2005: 65)

According to another account by Reeves:

> Following early morning bombing attacks on targeted villages, attacks which dispersed the terrified inhabitants, the *Janjaweed* would sweep in, shooting all in their sight. Very often they would be accompanied by regular SAF forces in trucks, armoured personnel carriers, and other vehicles.
>
> (Reeves 2007: 3)

After this 'deadly helicopter gunships would also be deployed, killing fleeing civilians and any who might chose to resist' (ibid.: 3). Indeed, the improvised use of the national air force illustrates in vivid terms Khartoum's indiscriminate killing of Sudanese civilians in Darfur:

> Attacks on African villages typically began with aerial attacks by Antonov 'bombers'. In fact, the Antonov is not a bomber by design, but rather a ret-rofitted Russian cargo plane from which crude barrel bombs are simply rolled out the back cargo bay ... Bombs dropped from Antonovs are far too imprecise to be used against military targets. To avoid ground fire, Antonovs typically fly at altitudes over 15,000 feet. But such bombs are exquisitely suited as instruments of civilian terror.
>
> (Reeves 2007: 3)

As many as 2.7 million Darfurians who were not killed or severely maimed in such attacks by their own government fled to neighbouring settlements, camps, or into the wilderness, often to find themselves victims of follow-up raids. Others wandered for days before reaching internally displaced person (IDP) or refugee camps, only to then fall victim to disease or hunger in desperate conditions. Others still were prey for *Janjaweed* patrols while roaming the outskirts of such camps in search of firewood. Compellingly, the testimonies of victims and witnesses to such attacks revealed the nature and magnitude of these experiences of violence and terror. In May 2004, Amnesty International interviewed a number of Darfurian refugees living in camps inside Chad. Describing one attack, the following testimony was given by 'N', a 30-year-old Darfurian woman from Um Baru, living in the Konoungou camp:

> The attack took place at 8am on 29 February 2004 when soldiers arrived by car, camels and horses. The Janjawid [*sic*] were inside the houses and the soldiers outside. Some 15 women and girls who had not fled quickly enough were raped in different huts in the village. The Janjawid broke the limbs ... of some women and girls to prevent them from escaping. The Janjawid remained in the village for six or seven days. After the rapes, the Janjawid looted the houses.
>
> (Amnesty International USA n.d.a)

Recounted in another Amnesty International interview in the Mile refugee camp in Chad, an unnamed 25-year-old Darfurian woman from Abu Jidad village, in the Abu Gamra region, explained how her village was attacked on 28 June 2003:

> Men on horses and camels and in cars came in and surrounded the village at midday. The Janjawid [*sic*] were accompanied by soldiers of the government, the latter using cars. Two hours later, an Antonov plane and two helicopters flew over the village and shot rockets. The attackers came into the houses and shot my mother and grandfather, without any word. Most of the inhabitants had stayed in their houses. The attack lasted for two hours and everything was burnt down in the village.
>
> (Amnesty International USA n.d.b)

The Coalition for International Justice and the US State Department's Atrocities Documentation Project collected further harrowing testimonies, including, for example:

> A Massalit woman in West Darfur (near El Geneina) in February 2004 saw [Sudanese government] soldiers catch sixteen women with babies. They broke the baby boys' necks in front of the mothers and beat mothers with their own babies like whips until the babies died.
>
> (cited in Askin 2006: 146)

As a result of evidence of attacks like these, the commission of inquiry concluded in its authoritative and revealing January 2005 report that both the Sudanese government and the *Janjaweed* were 'responsible for serious violations of international human rights and humanitarian law amounting to crimes under international law' (United Nations 2005: 3). More specifically, noting that the majority of victims of such violence were from the *Fur, Zaghawa, Massalit, Jebel, Aranga* and 'other so-called "African" tribes', the commission found that Sudanese government forces and their allied militias conducted:

> Indiscriminate attacks, including killing of civilians, torture, enforced disappearances, destruction of villages, rape and other forms of sexual violence, pillaging and forced displacement, throughout Darfur. These acts were conducted on a widespread and systematic basis, and therefore may amount to crimes against humanity. The extensive destruction and displacement have resulted in a loss of livelihood and means of survival for countless women, men and children. In addition to the large scale attacks, many people have been arrested and detained, and many have been held *incommunicado* for prolonged periods and tortured.
>
> (United Nations 2005: 3)

Such 'indiscriminate attacks', in which civilians are killed, are prohibited under the Fourth Geneva Convention, which requires belligerents to distinguish between combatants and non-combatants during armed conflict and to protect the latter group from harm. Indeed, confirming earlier reports, innocent Darfurian civilians were not merely 'collateral damage' or unintended victims of the conflict: while Sudanese government officials had protested to the COI that their use of force was for legitimate military purposes as part of what they claimed to be a necessary counter-insurgency campaign against the SLA and JEM rebels, the Commission instead made it clear that 'most attacks were deliberately and indiscriminately directed against civilians' (United Nations 2005: 3).

Furthermore, in February 2007, the chief prosecutor of the International Criminal Court (ICC) publicly presented evidence of crimes committed during the Darfur conflict. The findings unambiguously demonstrated the Sudanese government's role in orchestrating violence against civilians in Darfur, including Khartoum's sponsoring of the *Janjaweed*, and led to the May 2007 issuing of arrest warrants (as yet unsuccessfully executed) for Ahmed Harun, the former interior minister, and Ali Kushayb, a *Janjaweed* leader, upon evidence that they had:

> Jointly committed crimes against the civilian population in Darfur [and] bear criminal responsibility in relation to 51 counts of alleged crimes against humanity and war crimes. The evidence shows they acted together, and with others, with the common purpose of carrying out attacks against the civilian populations.
>
> (ICC 2007)

Because violence targeting civilians is one of the central constitutive criteria of terrorism, the COI and ICC findings that Darfurian civilians had been deliberately killed by the Sudan Armed Forces and government-sponsored *Janjaweed* militias gave a solid basis to the claim that the Sudanese state committed terrorism against its own citizens. While this is a necessary condition, however, it is not on its own a sufficient one to justify a designation of 'state terrorism'. Such a characterization would require us to also establish that such violence was politically motivated and that the targeted killing of civilians was designed to engender fear in a wider audience than only the immediate victims.

Yet establishing Khartoum's intent and motivation for killing Sudanese civilians en masse is more difficult than illustrating the nature and scale of such violence. The debate in official and academic circles generally pertained to whether Khartoum had pursued in Darfur a policy of genocide – based upon underlying ethnic animosity – or whether it was instead more interested in 'regime survival'. Put differently, the question has been whether the Sudanese government has 'adopted a policy of cultural annihilation [or] decided to crush a rebellion to protect its dominance' (Kasfir 2005: 200).

For example, according to Patrick the actions and intentions of the *Janjaweed* were genocidal in nature because the militias had done 'everything possible not only to force civilians to flee their land and villages, but to prevent them from being able to come home any time soon and to rebuild their lives even upon return' (2005: 413). Due to this:

Not only have villages been attacked, looted and burned to the ground, but the Janjaweed have thrown dead bodies into wells to poison them and systematically destroyed fields, seeds and agricultural implements – elements critical to the survival of a population dependent on farming for its livelihood. Men have been killed and women raped and branded to ostracise them from society.

(Patrick 2005: 413)

Power has argued that both the Sudanese government and *Janjaweed* committed genocide by: 'systematically expelling Darfur's non-Arab population, murdering tens of thousands and permitting widespread gang-rape – to make sure what they say will be lighter-skinned babies and ensure that the non-Arab tribes will be too degraded to return to their homes' (Power 2004). Reeves has similarly contended that Khartoum's 'comprehensive destruction, clearly animated by a desire to destroy the Fur, Massaleit, and Zaghawa people as such, constituted genocide – as did the direct, ethnically-targeted murder of these people' (2007: 3).

These arguments are supported by a number of official findings. Notably, after a US State Department investigation, then Secretary of State Colin Powell testified before the US Congress in September 2004 that: 'we concluded – I concluded – that genocide has been committed in Darfur and that the government of Sudan and the Janjaweed bear responsibility and that genocide may still be occurring' (Powell 2004). President Bush publicly endorsed the genocide charge, the first time a US president had done so while that particular crime was ongoing (although the administration claimed that such a designation did not legally compel it to act) (Power 2004). Then, in a potentially more effective act, the ICC chief prosecutor presented evidence in July 2008 that President Bashir himself 'bears criminal responsibility in relation to 10 counts of genocide, crimes against humanity and war crimes' because he had:

Masterminded and implemented a plan to destroy in substantial part the Fur, Masalit and Zaghawa groups, on account of their ethnicity. Members of the three groups, historically influential in Darfur, were challenging the marginalization of the province; they engaged in a rebellion. [Bashir] failed to defeat the armed movements, so he went after the people.

(ICC 2008)

These arguments supporting the finding of genocide to characterize the Sudanese government's motivations are compelling. But if the act of genocide in Darfur was based upon underlying elements of ethnic animosity, it was also highly political in nature, pertaining, fundamentally, to power and control over the state. The ICC prosecutor alleged that in attacking Darfur's non-Arab population, the Sudanese president's 'motives were largely political. His alibi was a "counterinsurgency." His intent was a genocide' (ICC 2008). According to another analysis, the government of Sudan 'used its policy of Arabization in an effort to bolster or restore its hegemony' (Kasfir 2005: 199). In this sense, Khartoum attempted to ' "drain the swamp" by driving civilians from their villages, thereby denying the rebels sanctuary in much of Darfur' (Grono 2006: 624). Similarly, according to the UN Human Rights Council, 'villages have been razed, livestock stolen or killed, and crops destroyed, and whole populations forcefully displaced, in part in an attempt to deprive rebel groups of support and resources' (United Nations 2007: 12).

Furthermore the COI, which had earlier concluded that the Sudanese government had 'not pursued a policy of genocide' because the 'crucial element of genocidal intent appears to be missing, as least as far as the central Government authorities are concerned' (United Nations 2005: 4), supported the analysis that Khartoum's motives for attacking Darfurian civilians were based on strategic political interests. In a 'vast majority of cases, victims of the attacks belonged to African tribes, in particular the Fur, Masaalit and Zaghawa tribes, who were systematically targeted on political grounds in the context of the counter-insurgency policy of the Government' (United Nations 2005: 160) while 'it would seem that those who planned and organized attacks on villages pursued the intent to drive the victims from their homes, primarily for purposes of counter-insurgency warfare' (ibid.: 4).

Khartoum, therefore, while supporting the interests of local Arab groups in the region – a key government constituency – pursued a campaign of violence against non-Arab civilians in Darfur to assert the control, and maintain the historical domination, of Arabist regimes in Sudan. As such, in addition to the deliberate targeting and killing of civilians, the political motivations behind Khartoum's strategy in Darfur satisfy a second constitutive criterion of terrorism.

This political objective of 'regime security' was achieved through the communicative act of instilling pervasive fear in a wider audience than only the immediate targets of the violence, a third key constitutive criterion of terrorism. Indeed, while targeting non-Arab Darfurians directly, the broader psychological aim of such violence was to terrorize the general population to deter further support for the rebels and thus strengthen Khartoum's control. The Sudanese government was aware of its tenuous claims to legitimacy and fragile hold on national power: 'having only recently entered into power-sharing talks with its long-term enemy [South Sudan rebels] and aware of the unrest brewing in many other of its so-called "peripheral" areas', Khartoum 'feared that being anything less than harsh with the Darfur rebels would invite similar uprisings in other restive regions' (Patrick 2005: 411). As such, in order to 'prevent the emergence of simultaneous rebellions', Khartoum was 'sending a message to potential guerrillas everywhere that if they rebel, civilians in their region will face atrocities on a scale similar to those in Darfur' (Kasfir 2005: 201).

The tactic of diffusing dread was indeed central to the Sudanese government's strategy in Darfur:

> [The] effect of the repeated attacks on villages and the manner in which they were carried out, including regular aerial surveillance at dawn, hovering of

helicopter gun-ships and frequent bombing, was to terrorise civilians and force them to flee the villages.

(United Nations 2005: 65)

In one sense, this state terrorism was successful, as those people who were fortunate to survive the initial attacks and find refuge in camps 'often refused to return to their villages out of fear of further attacks' (United Nations 2005: 65). Overall, however, at the time of writing, the Darfur rebels had not been militarily defeated and, as evidenced by the JEM's attempted attack on the Sudanese capital in May 2008, they became emboldened (an attack which prompted Khartoum to label the JEM as a 'terrorist organization'). This suggests that, at great human cost to the citizens of Darfur, a strategy of terrorism by the Sudanese government had succeeded only in creating further foundations for insurgency against the state.

Enabling state terrorism: protecting international interests in Sudan

Due to the nature and scale of crimes committed in Darfur, extensive public evidence of Sudanese government orchestration and participation in such atrocities, and the failure of the peace process, calls for external actors to intervene militarily in Sudan emerged and coalesced on the argument that Darfur represented a quintessential case for the nascent 'responsibility to protect' doctrine. While states have the primary responsibility to protect their populations from genocide, war crimes, crimes against humanity or ethnic cleansing ('state terrorism' is not listed), if a government is either unable or unwilling to do so, then its sovereignty can be 'suspended' and a UN military intervention may become a necessary and legitimate means of providing security for civilians on the ground (ICISS 2001).

This doctrine was formally and unanimously endorsed, in principle, by states at the 2005 UN World Summit, and by the UN Security Council the following year. Yet, despite a persuasive moral and normative case for coercive UN intervention to protect ordinary Darfurians from being killed or further terrorized by the Sudanese government and *Janjaweed*, such an intervention did not occur because powerful members of the Security Council had an interest in maintaining their cooperative relationships with the incumbent regime in Khartoum.

China and, to a lesser extent, Russia, have established lucrative bilateral trade and investment deals with Sudan. Most significantly, China has been Sudan's largest foreign investor, buying increasing quantities of oil from an emerging local petroleum industry which China has itself largely developed. Sudan, awash with petrodollars, has then purchased Chinese- and Russian-made military equipment to use against dissenting Sudanese in the outlying regions of the country. In return, both Beijing and Moscow 'continue to oppose sanctions against Sudan, largely because of their own economic and political interests. Russia is a major supplier of weapons to Sudan, and China is a major consumer of oil from the country' (Udombana 2007: 109–10). Similarly, Belloni suggested that China and Russia, 'wanting to maintain their privileged access to Sudanese oil reserves, have made known their decision to veto any proposal for military action' (2006: 338–9). This has perhaps been the most significant obstacle to international intervention in Sudan and cannot be overstated.

In addition, and more revealingly for a study of 'terrorism', Western powers, particularly the United States, while using harsh public rhetoric against the Sudanese government over Darfur, have had their own reasons for wanting to keep President Bashir onside: significant Sudanese cooperation in regional US 'counter-terrorism' operations since 9/11. In a general context, Stohl has argued that the relationship between Washington's strategic and tactical choices in the 'War on Terror' and repression in US-allied states 'has not been examined closely':

> Because scholars of terrorism have seen state violence and terrorism as outside the bounds of terrorism studies they do not consider how the choices in the Bush administration's counterterrorism strategy enable, acquiesce to or ignore the violence of the recruited states and this has deleterious effects not only for the populations that are repressed but also the counterterrorism efforts of the United States.
>
> (Stohl 2008: 5)

Indeed, for the US government, Sudan since 9/11 was viewed and treated as a key ally in the 'War on Terror', a dramatic about-face from the 1990s when the country was placed on the US 'state sponsors of terrorism' list and under US sanctions due to its hosting of Osama bin Laden and other radical Islamists (Prendergast and Roessler 2004). With the Bush administration's post-9/11 policy of 'preventive war' and the invasions of Afghanistan and Iraq, Khartoum made the prudent decision to accelerate cooperation with US counter-terrorism operations to stave off any potential intervention in Sudan (ICG 2006). In particular, the United States was keen to use unique Sudanese sources and capabilities to gain intelligence on the Iraqi insurgency and other foreign militants operating under the US occupation, as well as on the Islamist movement in anarchic Somalia (Miller and Meyer 2007).

Sudanese cooperation proved to be highly valuable in these theatres in which US intelligence capabilities were limited and constrained (Goldberg 2005). This cooperative intelligence relationship was most vividly symbolized by the hosting of Sudanese chief of national security and intelligence, Salah Abdallah Gosh, by the CIA for counter-terrorism talks in April 2005 (shortly after the release of the damning COI report) (Prendergast 2006). Members of the US Congress had accused Gosh of being involved in orchestrating atrocities in Darfur (Silverstein 2005).

What is clear from this relationship is that Washington's 'counter-terrorism' strategy has actually involved, *inter alia*, obstructing more coercive international action against a regime that had been committing state terrorism against its own citizens: the intelligence cooperation 'blunted any US response' to the violence in Darfur because 'access to Gosh's information would be jeopardized if the Bush administration confronted Khartoum' (Prendergast 2006). Such circumstances illustrate how 'terrorism' has been constructed by governments to refer primarily to certain actions of non-state groups, while greater state acts of terrorism are often ignored or even accepted. This is not to assert that the major powers played an active role in killing Darfurians; rather, that their national interests and cooperative relationships with Khartoum have enabled the Sudanese government to continue to terrorize its own citizens. Indeed, such ties between powerful interests and Sudan underscore the claim that we can 'better understand state terrorism when we examine the collaborations that are established between elites across state boundaries' (Blakeley 2007: 234).

Conclusion

Following a history of underdevelopment and marginalization by successive colonial and national governments in Khartoum, the people of the remote Darfur region have since 2003 been forced to endure a campaign of terror orchestrated and conducted by the Sudanese state. President Bashir has deliberately employed local militias and 'mobilised the entire state apparatus, including the armed forces, the intelligence services, the diplomatic and public information bureaucracies, and the justice system' (ICC 2008) to terrorize non-Arab Sudanese citizens to maintain and extend the power and control of his regime and of Arab interests in the Sudan. As such, it has been demonstrated that the actions of the Sudanese state in Darfur since 2003 meet the criteria for terrorism.

Acknowledging and characterizing Khartoum's actions as 'state terrorism' enables a better understanding of the nature of the violence committed and can build new forms of pressure for political action to halt atrocities in Darfur and elsewhere. However, the failure of coercive international action to protect Sudanese citizens from their own government illustrates that state terrorism will be allowed to continue as long as powerful states privilege their own national interests over the security of some of the world's most marginalized, vulnerable, and terrorized people.

References

Annan, K. (2005) *In Larger Freedom: towards development, security and human rights for all*, report of the United Nations Secretary-General, New York: United Nations.

Amnesty International USA (n.d.a) 'Darfur in crisis: speaking out on violence against women in Darfur'. Online, available at: www.amnestyusa.org/Reports_and_Background/Testimony_Women_in_Darfur/page.do?id=1101971&n1=3&n2=52&n3=1172 (accessed 3 February 2009).

—— (n.d.b) 'From the ground: Darfuri refugees in Chad speak out'. Online, available at: www.amnestyusa.org/Reports_and_Background/Testimony_Darfuri_Refugees_in_Chad/page.do?id=1101970&n1=3&n2=52&n3=1172 (accessed 3 February 2009).

Askin, K.D. (2006) 'Prosecuting gender crimes committed in Darfur: holding leaders accountable for sexual violence', in S. Totten and E. Markusen (eds) *Genocide in Darfur: investigating the atrocities in the Sudan*, New York and UK: Routledge.

Assal, M.A.M. (2006) 'Sudan: identity and conflict over natural resources', *Development*, 49 (3): 101–5.

Ban, K. (2007) 'A climate culprit in Darfur', *Washington Post*, 16 June. Online, available at: www.washingtonpost.com/wp-dyn/content/article/2007/06/15/AR2007061501857. html (accessed 3 February 2009).

El-Battahani, A. (2006) 'A complex web: politics and conflict in Sudan', in M. Simmons and P. Dixon (eds) *Peace by piece: addressing Sudan's conflicts*, London: Conciliation Resources.

Belloni, R. (2006) 'The tragedy of Darfur and the limits of the "responsibility to Protect"', *Ethnopolitics*, 5 (4): 327–46.

Blakeley, R. (2007) 'Bringing the state back into terrorism studies', *European Political Science*, 6 (3): 228–35.

Booth, K. (2008) 'The human faces of terror: reflections in a cracked looking-glass', *Critical Studies on Terrorism*, 1 (1): 65–79.

Collins, R.O. (2006) 'Disaster in Darfur: historical overview', in S. Totten and E. Markusen (eds) *Genocide in Darfur: investigating the atrocities in the Sudan*, New York and UK: Routledge.

Daly, M.W. (2007) *Darfur's sorrow: a history of destruction and genocide*, New York: Cambridge University Press.

Falk, R. (2004) 'State terror versus humanitarian law', in M. Selden and A.Y. So (eds) *War and state terrorism: the United States, Japan, and the Asia Pacific in the long twentieth century*, Lanham, MD: Rowman & Littlefield.

Feinstein, L. (2007) 'Darfur and beyond: what is needed to prevent mass atrocities', Council Special Report no. 22, New York: Council on Foreign Relations.

Flint, J. and de Waal, A. (2005) *Darfur: a short history of a long war*, London and New York: Zed Books.

Goldberg, S. (2005) 'Sudan becomes US ally in "war on terror"', *Guardian*, 30 April. Online, available at: www.guardian.co.uk/world/2005/apr/30/sudan.usa (accessed 3 February 2009).

Grono, N. (2006) 'Briefing – Darfur: the international community's failure to protect', *African Affairs*, 105/421: 621–31.

Human Security Centre (2005) *Human Security Report 2005: war and peace in the 21st century*, New York and Oxford: Oxford University Press.

International Criminal Court (ICC) (2007) 'ICC prosecutor presents evidence on Darfur crimes', press release, The Hague: International Criminal Court, 27 February. Online, available at: www.icc-cpi.int/menus/icc/press%20and%20media/press%20releases/2007/ icc%20prosecutor%20presents%20evidence%20on%20darfur%20crimes (accessed 17 February 2007).

—— (2008) 'ICC prosecutor presents case against Sudanese President, Hassan Ahmad Al Bashir, for genocide, crimes against humanity and war crimes in Darfur', press release, The Hague: International Criminal Court, 14 July. Online, available at: www. icc-cpi.int/menus/icc/press%20and%20media/press%20releases/press%20releases%20 (2008)/a (accessed 17 February 2009).

International Commission on Intervention and State Sovereignty (ICISS) (2001) *The responsibility to protect*, report of the International Commission on Intervention and State Sovereignty (ICISS), Canada, International Development Research Centre.

International Crisis Group (ICG) (2006) 'Getting the UN into Darfur', Africa Briefing,

43, Brussels: International Crisis Group. Online, available at: www.crisisgroup.org/home/index.cfm?id=4442 (accessed 3 February 2009).

Jackson, R. (2008) 'An argument for terrorism', *Perspectives on Terrorism* 2 (2). Online, available at: www.terrorismanalysts.com/pt/index.php?option=com_rokzine&view=article&id=28 (accessed 3 February 2009).

Kasfir, N. (2005) 'Sudan's Darfur: is it genocide?', *Current History*, 104 (682): 195–202.

Mahmoud, M.E. (2004) 'Inside Darfur: ethnic genocide by a governance crisis', *Comparative Studies of South Asia, Africa and the Middle East*, 24 (2): 3–17.

Miller, G. and Meyer, J. (2007) 'US relies on Sudan despite condemning it', *Los Angeles Times*, 11 June. Online, available at: articles.latimes.com/2007/jun/11/world/fg-ussudan11 (accessed 3 February 2009).

Patrick, E. (2005) 'Intent to destroy: the genocidal impact of forced migration in Darfur, Sudan', *Journal of Refugee Studies*, 18 (4): 410–29.

Pilger, J. (2004) 'Time to recognise state terror', Antiwar.com., 17 September. Online, available at: www.antiwar.com/orig/pilger.php?articleid=3592 (accessed 3 February 2009).

Powell, C.L. (2004) 'The crisis in Darfur', Testimony before the Senate Foreign Relations Committee, Washington, DC, 9 September 2004. Online, available at: http://2001–2009.state.gov/secretary/former/powell/remarks/36042.htm (accessed 3 February 2009).

Power, S. (2004) 'It's not enough to call it genocide', *Time* 164 (14), 4 October. Online, available at: www.time.com/time/magazine/article/0,9171,995282,00.html (accessed 3 February 2009).

Prendergast, J. (2006) 'So how come we haven't stopped it yet?', *Washington Post*, 19 November. Online, available at: www.washingtonpost.com/wp-dyn/content/article/2006/11/17/AR2006111701480.html (accessed 3 February 2009).

Prendergast, J. and Roessler, P. (2004) 'Can a leopard change its spots? Sudan's evolving relationship with terrorism', in United States Institute of Peace *Terrorism in the Horn of Africa*, Special Report 113, Washington, DC: United States Institute of Peace. Online, available at: www.usip.org/pubs/specialreports/sr113.html (accessed 3 February 2009).

Prunier, G. (2005) *Darfur: the ambiguous genocide*, Ithaca, New York: Cornell University Press.

Reeves, E. (2007) *A long day's dying: critical moments in the Darfur genocide*, Toronto: Key Publishing House.

Selden, M. and So, A.Y. (2004) 'Introduction: war and state terrorism', in M. Selden and A.Y. So (eds) *War and state terrorism: the United States, Japan, and the Asia Pacific in the long twentieth century*, Lanham, MD: Rowman & Littlefield.

Silverstein, K. (2005) 'Official pariah Sudan valuable to America's war on terrorism', *Los Angeles Times*, 29 April. Online, available at: www.articles.latimes.com/2005/apr/29/world/fg-sudan29 (accessed 3 February 2009).

Sluka, J. (2000) 'Introduction: state terror and anthropology', in J. Sluka (ed.) *Death squad: the anthropology of state terror*, Philadelphia: University of Philadelphia Press.

Stohl, M. (2008) 'The global war on terror and state terrorism', *Perspectives on Terrorism*, Special issue: under-investigated topics in terrorism research, June: 4–10. Online, available at: www.terrorismanalysts.com/pt/index.php?option=com_rokzine&view=article&id=56&Itemid=54 (accessed 3 February 2009).

Tubiana, J. (2007) 'Darfur: a conflict for land?', in A. de Waal (ed.) *War in Darfur and the search for peace*, London and Boston: Justice Africa and Harvard University Global Equity Initiative.

Udombana, N.J. (2007) 'Still playing dice with lives: Darfur and Security Council Resolution 1706', *Third World Quarterly* 28 (1): 97–116.

United Nations (2004) *A more secure world: our shared responsibility*, Report of the high-level panel on Threats, Challenges and Change, New York: United Nations. Online, available at: www.un.org/secureworld (accessed 3 February 2009).

—— (2005) Report of the International Commission of Inquiry on Darfur to the United Nations Secretary-General, Geneva: United Nations, 21 January. Online, available at: www.un.org/news/dh/sudan/com_inq_darfur.pdf (accessed 3 February 2009).

—— (2007) 'Report of the High-Level Mission on the situation of human rights in Darfur pursuant to Human Rights Council decision S-4/101', United Nations, 7 March. Online, available at: www2.ohchr.org/english/bodies/hrcouncil/specialsession/4/index.htm (accessed 3 February 2009).

—— (2008) 'Security Council told still no lasting solution to suffering in Darfur, difficult for UNAMID to implement mandate, protect civilians if there is no peace to keep', Security Council SC/9304, 22 April. Online, available at: www.un.org/News/Press/docs//2008/sc9304.doc.htm (accessed 3 February 2009).

Waal, A. de (2005) 'Who are the Darfurians? Arab and African identities, violence, and external engagement', *African Affairs*, 104 (415): 181–205.

3 State terrorism and the military in Pakistan

Eamon Murphy and Aazar Tamana

Introduction

The Pakistani military, particularly the army, has been the single most important political force in Pakistan since the formation of the state in 1947. Through its nexus with bureaucratic, landed feudal and business elites, the military has dominated Pakistani politics either by directly seizing power or by strongly interfering in the political process. In retirement, army officers have been provided with key positions in government, the universities, and other state institutions. The armed forces also control a large number of lucrative economic enterprises.

Many in Pakistan and in the West have regarded the military as a disciplined, professional force that has been forced to rule Pakistan because of the corruption and ineptitude of politicians. Western governments, especially the United States, have regarded the military as close allies initially in the fight against communism and more recently, in the global war on religious terrorism. For many analysts, the armed forces, with their discipline and organization, make much better rulers than politicians. The military has also played a crucial role in holding Pakistan together in the face of ethnic separatist movements.

Over time, however, allegations of the abuse of power and business-related corruption have tarnished the reputation of the military, particularly within Pakistan itself, but increasingly in the outside world. The military has been criticized at home and abroad for its arrogant abuse of power and use of excessive force. In particular, the main intelligence service, the Inter-Services Intelligence (ISI), has consistently meddled in politics.

The tragedy for Pakistan, and indeed for the armed forces itself, is that over time the military has become the main instrument of state terrorism in Pakistan. The dominant role of the military in the political and economic life of Pakistan has, in a large part, subverted the development of democracy, encouraged religious terrorism, and contributed to the current political, economic, and social crises facing Pakistan. To understand how this happened, it is necessary to analyse the historical factors that have both forced and encouraged the armed forces to intervene in the political process and, at times, to resort to state terrorism at home and state-sponsored terrorism abroad.

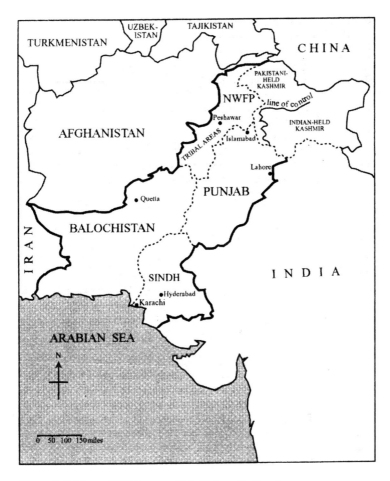

Figure 2 Pakistan, 2001 (source: Yale University Press).

Martin provides a very useful definition of state terrorism – terrorism from above – committed by governments, government agencies and personnel. He states: 'Terrorism by states is characterized by official government support for policies of violence, repression and intimidation' (2007: 66). In analysing whether certain actions of the military in Pakistan constitute state terrorism, I will call upon the definition of Jackson (2008) that state terrorism is a specific form of political violence with the following four main characteristics. First, it is a pre-determined strategy of political violence employed in the pursuit of strategic goals. Thus, it implies political motivation rather than random acts of violence or the unintended consequences of such violence. Spontaneous communal riots, therefore, would be excluded from such a definition because they were not deliberately planned (Jackson 2008: 7). Second, it is a form of political communication whose primary audience is not the victims of terrorism. Thus, terrorism is a deliberate act of communicating a political message. For example, terrorist actions such as kidnapping, the use of torture, and the use of disappearance send out a clear message to all citizens that the state is all-powerful and will ruthlessly crush any opposition. Third, by definition, the central purpose of terrorism is to deliberately cause fear and intimidation. Last, terrorism is directed primarily, although not necessarily exclusively, against civilians (Jackson 2008: 8).

The Pakistani military

The Pakistan armed forces, comprising army, air force, and navy, is a professional voluntary service of 650,000 men and women, making it about the seventh largest military force in the world. By far the most numerically important service is the army of approximately 550,000 people. In addition, the army controls Pakistan's paramilitary forces of approximately 300,000 personnel, who are largely responsible for internal security. About 75 per cent of army personnel are recruited from three districts of the Punjab while another 20 per cent are recruited from three or four districts in the North West Frontier Province.[1] The army, therefore, is almost entirely dominated by Punjabis and Pathans, who are the dominant ethnic groups in these regions (Siddiqa 2007: 59).

This fact makes the army a very homogeneous organization with a strong sense of corporate ethos, especially among the officers. This homogeneity has created major problems, however, especially when the army has to deal with unrest in the other provinces, Sindh and Baluchistan. Linguistic, cultural, and ethnic differences between the Punjabi-dominated army and the people of Sindh and Baluchistan are an ongoing cause of tensions and bitterness, which have accentuated regional identity and separatist movements in both provinces. Army actions against dissidents in Baluchistan, in particular, are regarded by the Baluchis as state terrorism by the foreign Punjabi-dominated state and its army (Siddiqa 2007: 60).

Army power is accentuated by its control of the secretive and very powerful Inter-Services Intelligence (ISI), which is under the control of the army chief. The ISI is feared and resented by many civilians and by some among the armed forces itself for what is perceived as its independence, lack of accountability, and its surveillance of both citizens and the military. For some, the ISI is regarded almost as an independent state, as it has been difficult, even for the higher command, to discipline and control the actions of individual officers (Chazan 2002). As we shall see, many ISI officers have had – and still have – sympathy with, and give support to, religious extremists, despite attempts by the government and military since 11 September 2001 (hereafter known as 9/11) to fight religious terrorism.

A further source of the military's power is its lucrative business interests. Military-owned businesses are involved in a wide range of enterprises including textiles, cereals, sugar, oil, gas, fertilizer, construction, and trucking. For example, the military-controlled National Logistic Cell is the largest goods transport company in Pakistan. Normally under the control of the Department of the

Ministry of Planning, it is in effect controlled by the army and staffed by army officers (Chazan 2002: 115).

The military is one of the largest landowners in Pakistan, controlling about 12 per cent of state land. Senior officers have become large landowners, both in the city and in the countryside. It is said that the best housing estates and clubs belong to the military, while even junior officers on retirement build very lavish houses in the most expensive suburbs (Chazan 2002: 174). The launch of Ayesha Siddique's controversial book *Military Inc* in 2007,[2] which exposed the extent of the military's economic resources and lack of financial accountability, caused great consternation. The launch of the book at the exclusive Islamabad Club was cancelled, and the author's life was threatened. President Musharraf himself branded the author as a traitor (Rankin-Reid 2008: 1). In attempting to analyse and to understand the rule of the military and its involvement in state terrorism, it is essential, therefore, to take into consideration the military's need to protect its extensive business interests. The military's economic interests directly contributed to state terrorism and to the corruption, unaccountability to civilian control, and the arrogance among army personnel that helped precipitate acts of irresponsible violence.

The military and the formation of Pakistan

The problems that face the armed forces and Pakistan itself have their origins in the formation of the state in 1947. From its origins, Pakistan has been a fragile state, its very survival threatened by ethnic, regional, and religious divisions. The very formation of the state was highly traumatic. The partition of India into Hindu-dominated India and Muslim-dominated Pakistan was accompanied by massive communal violence and mass migration. The structure of the new state was bizarre, being made up of eastern and western wings, separated by 1,600 km of territory controlled by the hostile state of India. The new state had to cope with the massive influx of refugees from Hindu-dominated India, which put huge strains upon the infrastructure and, in addition, created tensions between the indigenous inhabitants and the migrants, which has remained a factor in Pakistani politics ever since.[3]

Pakistan has faced the problem of ineffectual, weak leadership in combination with a very corrupt political culture. Unfortunately for Pakistan, the single most important political figure, Mohamed Ali Jinnah, known as Quaid-e-Azam or Great Leader, who almost single-handedly was the prime instigator for an independent Muslim state, died in September 1948.[4] Pakistan was left without a strong, central political party or a political leader who could dominate politics and begin to develop a tradition of democratic rule. The regions that comprised Pakistan had little experience of political movements and of the workings of democracy. Pakistani politics ever since has been riddled with factionalism, corruption, and inefficiency, which have hampered good government and led to the usurpation of power by the military. As Pervez Musharraf, former chief of army staff and president of Pakistan stated in his autobiography, *In the Line of Fire*:

'Sadly, a functioning democracy is exactly what has eluded Pakistan ever since its birth on August 14, 1947. This weakness lies at the root of most of our ills' (2006: 154).

Pakistan has faced the serious threat of regional separatist movements. The strongest demands for independence came initially from East Pakistan, which had little in common with western Pakistan, except that they both had a Muslim majority. East Pakistan, now the independent state of Bangladesh, was ethnically, linguistically, and culturally very different from western Pakistan. In what used to be known as West Pakistan, now Pakistan, there were also powerful separatist movements. Minority ethnic and linguistic groups, dominant in the provinces of Sind and Baluchistan, have resented the dominance of the Punjabis, who comprise the most numerous ethnic group that dominates politics and the armed forces. Consequently, apologists for the military argue that in combating separatist movements, the armed forces have been a very important nation-building institution. As one analyst naïvely stated in 1969, 'the military coup is crucial for the continuation and acceleration of nation-building in Asia and Africa' (Chang 1969: 818).

The final factor that contributed to the problems facing the new state of Pakistan was war with India over Kashmir. The new state was initially faced with a crisis as the Hindu ruler of Kashmir, a region dominated by Muslims, decided to transfer his state to Hindu-dominated India. After the first war with India from 1947 to 1948 over the Kashmir issue, the military were seen as the saviours of the state (Siddiqa 2007: 69). Ever since, the threat of India, with its much greater military might and resources, has given the military a crucial role in protecting Pakistan against what is seen as India's goal to divide and destroy the state. In addition, India's failure to fulfil a promise to hold a referendum in Kashmir to decide the future of the region has been resented by all sections of the Pakistani public.[5]

It is difficult to overstate how important the Kashmiri issue is for Pakistan. Indian control of two-thirds of Kashmir and its incorporation into the Indian state are bitterly resented by all sections of Pakistani society. Most Pakistanis believe, with some justification, that Kashmir rightly belongs to Pakistan and that India is illegally occupying Pakistani territory. The dispute between Pakistan and India over Kashmir has been a key factor in tensions between the two countries. It has led to three wars and the very real threat of a nuclear war between the two countries. The future of Kashmir has been the major issue that has poisoned India–Pakistan relations since 1947.

The rise of the armed forces under Ayub Khan

For the first ten years of Pakistan's existence, a series of short-lived, ineffectual governments and the threat of war created a power vacuum which the armed forces were eventually to fill and never entirely relinquish. From 1947 to 1958, for example, Pakistan had seven prime ministers and eight cabinets, which made efficient government and consistent policies virtually impossible (Siddiqa 2007:

69). The political chaos enabled the army Commander-in-Chief, General Mohamed Ayub Khan, to seize power in October 1958.

During Ayub's rule, the army became a key political force in Pakistan. The constitution was abrogated and the general assumed presidential powers with the abolition of the office of the prime minister. For many, both in the West and in Pakistan, the coup was welcomed. Ayub Khan was regarded by many as a strong, professional soldier who would provide Pakistan with the stability and leadership that the state so desperately needed. For others, however, Ayub Khan was an incompetent opportunist. During his rule, his actions and policies weakened civil institutions (Siddiqa 2007: 72–4).

Ayub Khan was viewed very favourably by the United States and its allies because of his very strong, anti-Communist credentials. During his rule, Pakistan was a key state in the Baghdad Pact, a mutual security organization supported by the United States, composed of Turkey, Iran, the United Kingdom, and Pakistan. Support by the West, especially the United States, has since the time of Ayub Khan been an important factor in the continuing dominance of the armed forces in Pakistan.

The other, very important development that occurred during the rule of Ayub Khan was the move of the military into business and the acquisition of large tracts of land, especially state-owned land, particularly by officers. Ayub Khan, his family and other senior military personnel became extremely wealthy landowners.[6] In addition, the armed forces began to develop their own manufacturing and distribution industries, which made them financially largely independent of government. Unfortunately, it also encouraged the armed forces to become involved in politics and to abuse power, partly in order to protect their economic interests.

State terrorism, separatism and the armed forces under Yahya Khan

Anti-government protests against the inefficiency of the rule of Ayub Khan resulted in another coup by General Yahya Khan, who made himself president and imposed martial law. Yahya Khan was regarded as a down-to-earth, professional soldier with contempt for bungling civilians. He attempted a drive against corruption, calling senior public servants 'a bunch of thieves' (Time 1971). Very soon the new regime was faced with a major crisis, which was to tear apart the state, in large part because of the brutal and ultimately counterproductive use of state violence by the military.

Ever since the nation's formation, Bengalis living in the eastern part of Pakistan had resented the dominance of western Pakistan over 1,600 km away. Bengalis were poorly represented in the bureaucracy, the judiciary, and especially the army. Most of the foreign exchange revenue created by the export of eastern Pakistan's rich, agricultural resources went to western Pakistan. There were significant cultural and linguistic differences between eastern and western Pakistan. Western Pakistan Muslims regarded their eastern counterparts as bad Muslims. Many Bengalis had been low-caste Hindus who had converted to Islam, but still shared some of the same religious practices of the Hindus living in their midst. There was also an element of racial prejudice with the taller, fair skinned western Pakistanis contemptuous of the shorter, dark skinned Bengalis.

In elections held in December 1970, the Bengali nationalist party, the Awami League, swept the poll in East Pakistan, winning 167 out of 169 seats and secured an overall majority in the Pakistan national assembly. The result stunned and outraged Yahya Khan and his government. The military and politicians in the west feared that either the politicians of East Bengal would use the results to legislate for a large degree of independence or, even far worse, to assume power. Yahya Khan refused to accept the verdict of the elections and postponed the calling of the national assembly. This led to increased separatist demands by the Bengalis (Guhu 2007: 445–91). In response, the Awami League called for an indefinite strike. In the west, this was regarded as an act of treason by a minority in eastern Pakistan designed to destroy the state of Pakistan.

In March 1971, Pakistan launched a major operation to brutally crush Bengali protests. The army commander in charge of the operation, General Tikka ('Red Hot') Khan, persuaded Yahya Khan to deal harshly with what were regarded as the traitors attempting to destroy Pakistan (Time 1971). The military, dominated almost entirely by recruits from the west, embarked on a particularly brutal form of state terrorism, carried out under the direct orders of the military high command. The ferocity of the army to crush Bengali separatism was tinged with racism. Bengalis were called the *Urdu* word for mosquito: an irritating black pest that needed to be exterminated (Time 1971).

On 25 March, the army attacked Dacca University whose students were among the strongest supporters of the Awami League. Students were rounded up and shot out of hand. Women students were singled out for rape before they were killed. The violence spread from the capital Dacca to the countryside in attempts to crush the armed resistance. Academics, journalists, doctors, and other professionals were prime targets. Hindus, in particular, were singled out for torture and death. As the army attempted to crush the unrest, many soldiers came to regard the fight against the Bengali separatists as a form of *jihad* or holy war against the corrupt Bengali Muslims and their Hindu allies. The massacres, rapes, and other forms of state-sponsored violence failed to crush the separatist movement in Bengal, while the flagrant abuse of human rights outraged public opinion in India and throughout the world (Guhu 2007: 449–51).

India's support for the Bengali rebels led to the third India–Pakistan war and the total defeat of the Pakistani forces. The subsequent breaking away of East Pakistan to form the new independent state of Bangladesh was a crushing, demoralizing blow to the prestige of the army. Not only had Pakistan lost a sizable portion of its territory and its army suffered a humiliating defeat, but its reputation for brutality tarnished the military's reputation both at home and in the outside world. The debacle led to the temporary restoration of civilian power in the now severely truncated state of Pakistan.

The debacle over the failure of the military's use of savage state terrorism to crush Bengali separatism demonstrates the limitations of a simplistic, military solution to complex political problems. It is doubtful whether eastern and western Pakistan would have remained united given the huge problems, particularly the distance between the two parts. But the legitimate grievances of the Bengalis needed to be handled with diplomacy rather than to be crushed by the use of brute force, an expression of extreme state terrorism. The failure of the army leadership to recognize the limitations of the use of force and state terror to resolve complex, political issues was to be repeated in later periods in Pakistani history.

State terrorism and the armed forces under Zia ul-Haq

After a period of civilian rule under Zulfikar Ali Bhutto and his Pakistan People's Party, in July 1977, the chief of army staff General Zia ul-Haq seized power in a bloodless coup. Martial law was imposed and Bhutto was sent to prison. In April 1979, Bhutto was hanged after a trial of dubious legality on what are widely regarded as trumped-up charges of conspiring to murder. The execution went ahead, despite protests inside Pakistan and repeated requests for clemency from foreign governments.[7] The execution was a brutal display of state terrorism, designed in part at least to terrify and silence the civilian opponents of the military regime. Opponents of the regime such as journalists, who criticized the execution and other actions of Zia ul-Haq's government, were imprisoned and flogged.[8] According to one such journalist whom I interviewed in Islamabad: 'The pain was so severe when I was being flogged that I fainted and had to be revived. Then the flogging continued'.[9]

During his rule, Zia ul-Haq, a devout Sunni Muslim, greatly strengthened the alliance between the mullahs and the armed forces. He promoted a particularly narrow form of Sunni Islam to consolidate his power and to legitimate military rule. Military rule, consequently, under Zia ul-Haq accelerated the process of the Islamization of Pakistan. Zia ul-Haq and his military colleagues deliberately developed political alliances with Sunni Islamic parties to support the military regime against its secular opponents. According to Hassan Abbas, who served in very senior capacities in both Benazir Bhutto's and Pervez Musharraf's administrations, Zia was not a religious zealot. Rather, he was a 'tolerant and a tolerable Muslim' (Abbas 2005: 89). If Abbas is correct, then Zia's enthusiastic drive for a more rigid Islamization was more to do with practical politics – winning legitimacy for his rule and political allies among the mullahs – than religious conviction. It is worth noting that this alliance between military and mullah persisted even under the government of the secular-minded General Musharraf.

A major factor in the Islamization of Pakistan was the rapid growth in the number of *madrassas*, religious schools, during the 1980s. In 1971, there were 900 *madrassas* in Pakistan, but by the end of the Zia era in 1988, there were 8,000 registered and 25,000 unregistered *madrassas* (Rashid 2000: 89). The *madrassas* provided education, food, housing, and a very narrow Islamic education for the very poor. Many of these *madrassas* preached a narrow form of Sunni Islam and were, according to Pakistani journalist and author Zahid Hussain, a 'nursery for *jihad*' (2008: chapter four). They were financed to a large extent by the state, by Saudi Arabia and, ironically as it were to turn out, by funds from the United States in support of the guerrilla war against the Soviet Union in Afghanistan. While only a minority of *madrassas* preached violence, nevertheless, a long-term consequence of the growth of the *madrassas* was the development of a narrower form of Sunni Islam, particularly among the poor, and the increase of sectarian violence (Dalrymple 2005).

One of the negative aspects of Zia ul-Haq's Islamization process was the growth of religious tensions between orthodox Sunni Muslims and the minority Shia sects, whose believers comprised about 20 per cent of the population. In 1980, Pakistani Shias strongly objected to Zia's attempts to raise the Zakat tax, the tax to be paid by all Muslims, by the state. The attempt alienated the Shias who protested that it was against their religious traditions to have the state involved. A massive protest mobilized thousands of Shias who stormed the Federal Secretary building in Islamabad. Zia eventually withdrew the demand, but the issue strongly accentuated the differences between Sunnis and Shias (Bansal 2006). Reaction to the Zia legislation led to a mushrooming of extremist groups which targeted Shia mosques, religious processions, professionals, and leaders of the Shia community. In reaction, Shias formed their own anti-Sunni groups and took bloody reprisals. As a result of Zia's attempt to use Sunni Islam to bolster his regime, tensions between Sunnis and Shias have persisted ever since. Sectarian violence, involving shootings, bombings, and political assassinations, have unfortunately remained a feature of Pakistani life (Haleem 2008).

In addition to Muslim sectarian divisions, tensions between Muslims and non-Muslim religions increased under Zia's Islamization process. The introduction of the notorious 1981 blasphemy law was used against Christians in particular. The law made it a serious criminal charge to defile images of Mohammed or to deface the Koran. In some cases, however, it was used unfairly against Christians and secular Muslims. For instance, anti-blasphemy laws could be invoked to harass Christians in personal and land disputes (Samad 2001).

In 1979, Zia ul-Haq's government modified Pakistan's penal code by introducing the *Hudood* ordinance, which discriminated against women in particular. The *Hudood* ordinances addressed crimes under Muslim law such as robbery, the drinking of alcohol, and sexual relations out of marriage. A subcategory of the *Hudood* ordinances was the *Zina* ordinance, which dealt with rape, adultery, fornication and prostitution. The particular *Zina* ordinance which outraged Pakistan feminists, human rights workers, and many Islamic scholars was that a conviction for rape required the testimony of four male, Muslim witnesses or the confession of the suspect. In effect, this requirement meant it was virtually impossible to secure a conviction for rape in Pakistan. To make matters worse, a woman bringing a charge of rape could herself be charged under the *Zina* ordinance for having sex outside of marriage. Numerous innocent women have languished in Pakistani jails before being able to establish their innocence.[10]

The *Zina* ordinance was a threat to every Pakistani woman as relatives, spouses and others could maliciously file charges that could see the woman spending years in jail, even if eventually she was cleared of *Hudood* violations. According to human rights lawyers in Pakistan, of the 7,000 women in jail around the country awaiting trial in 2005, nearly 90 per cent were accused of crimes under *Hudood* and the vast majority had no lawyer. While most are eventually acquitted, they spend an average of five years in jail and have lost their reputations, their livelihoods, and very often, their families, when they are eventually freed (Baldauf 2005). During Zia's rule, protests against the *Hudood* ordinances by female activists were broken up violently, with women being assaulted and imprisoned. Later attempts to reform the *Hudood* ordinances were blocked by religiously conservative supporters and allies of the military. It was not until November 2006 that the Pakistan government passed the Women's Protection Law, which amended the *Hudood* ordinances by taking the crime of rape back to Pakistan's secular penal code (ABC National Radio 2008). The consequences of the *Hudood* ordinances were, according to human rights activists and analysts such as Lisa Sharlach, a form of state-sponsored terrorism potentially directed against all females in Pakistan (Sharlach 2008: 95). President Musharraf himself was highly critical of Zia for his bigotry and total appeasement of the religious lobby (2006: 67).

Military rule under Zia was by no means the only factor in creating Sunni-Shia disputes or discrimination against women, as these also occurred under civilian governments. His rule greatly accelerated these developments, however, as too did the ongoing military alliance with the hard-line religious element. The use of violence to intimidate civilians, such as the innocent women in jail and the Shias who suffered discrimination and violence, were just two aspects of state terrorism that developed directly out of Zia's rule.

State terrorism and the armed forces under Musharraf

In October 1999, the armed forces again seized power when General Musharraf overthrew Prime Minister Nawaz Sharif. Musharraf did not make the mistake of Zia by making Sharif a martyr. Instead, Sharif was sentenced to life imprisonment on hijacking and terrorism charges and was later sent into exile in Saudi Arabia. Musharraf's seizure of power was supported by many in Pakistan who were fed up with the ineffectual, corrupt rule of Sharif.

Musharraf became a key ally of the United States and its allies in the fight against international terrorism, especially after 9/11. He was highly regarded by many Westerners, also because of what was regarded as his moderate and rational policies, 'enlightened moderation' and for his own secularism. He projected the image of a bluff, no-nonsense, former commando officer with little time for religious bigotry; this image was promoted by Western governments and by most of the Western media. He had little time for the lawyers, journalists, academics and human rights workers who criticized the army, stating at a speech on his retirement from the army: 'They are lost people. They don't know that the

army has played an important role in integration and development of Pakistan'
(Shah 2008).

However, Musharraf's rule was characterized by authoritarianism, the subversion of the democratic process, and a reliance on right-wing religious allies
opposed to secular politicians. His government continued to protect vested interests of the armed forces through holding onto political and economic power. His
regime, when threatened, also resorted to state violence. The practice of torture,
kidnapping, and assassinations by agents of the military state against dissidents
and suspected terrorists continued, especially after Pakistan supported the United
States in the global war against terrorism after 9/11 (Haqqani 2005: 320–9).
Thus, state terrorism continued, albeit in a less overt manner, during Musharraf's
rule. Political opponents were intimidated, kidnapped, tortured, and even killed
by agencies of the states, such as the police force, to attempt to quell the growing
unrest against the incompetence of Musharraf's rule and of the arrogant claim of
the military to play the central role in the government. Torture is commonly used
in Pakistani prisons against political opponents, as well as common criminals.
These tortures include: brutal beatings; burning with cigarettes; whipping the
soles of the feet; sexual assault; prolonged isolation; electric shock; denial of
food or sleep; hanging upside down; and public humiliation, in some cases
leading to death. Often magistrates covered up abuses by issuing investigation
reports, stating that the victims died of natural causes (US State Department
2002).

It is highly significant that the same political strategy of allying with religious
conservatives continued under the rule of General Musharraf, who prided
himself on his secularism and tolerance. Ironically, after 9/11, Musharraf was
forced by the United States to use state terrorism against those perceived to be
religious terrorists, including previous supporters of his. Terrorist tactics such as
kidnapping, extra judicial violence, and disappearances were used against supporters of religious and anti-West terrorism, including members of Al Qaeda, as
previously they had been used against the secular opponents of his regime.

One of the central arguments of this chapter is that the Pakistani military has
periodically resorted to state terrorism to protect its economic and political interests. This can well be illustrated through a discussion of what is known as the
Okara Military Farms dispute. The dispute started when Pakistan's Defence
Ministry tried to impose a cash payment contract for tenants occupying more
than 17,000 acres of fertile farmlands in the Punjab, known as the Okara Military Farms. The new cash contract system was intended to replace the usual
share of the harvest. The area was composed of long-term tenants, not the
owners of the land, which is held by the government of the Punjab. The farmers
strongly protested because the unilateral imposition of the new system by the
military would mean they would have to pay their rents in cash, not in crops,
which would, in effect, make them contract workers and thus liable for eviction
(Human Rights Watch 2004a).

When the farmers organized meetings and refused to agree to the new contracts which would severely disadvantage them, a large contingent of the Paki-

stan Rangers was sent to the district (Human Rights Watch 2004a). As a paramilitary internal security force, the Rangers are commanded by seconded Pakistan Army generals and serve as an extension of the Army. The Rangers are notorious for their abuse of human rights. Farmers who refused to hand over their land rights to the army were subjected to various forms of state terrorism, including murder, arbitrary detention, and torture carried out by the paramilitaries and supported by senior military and political officials. On two occasions, the paramilitaries blockaded villages and prevented the movement of people, food and public service officials from entering or leaving the villages. Even children were tortured to coerce their parents into signing the new contracts (Human Rights Watch 2004b).

A typical account of the brutality was given by Bashir Ahmad, who was detained in order to coerce his father-in-law, Mohammad Yaqub, into signing a contract and depositing contract money. He stated:

> We were made to lie on our stomachs and they started whipping us. We were separated from each other one by one after the whipping. I was taken outdoors and made to stand with my hands raised for an hour. Then I was brought to the veranda outside the room. A stick was fixed through my legs and I was ordered to sit down. I was kept in that position for twenty minutes. Then they tried to push the stick up my anus but stopped. Then they started interrogating us again. We were placed together again at midnight.... We were produced before Major Tahir Malik at seven that evening. He threatened us if we told the villagers of the torture then we would be arrested again. I was also threatened with re-arrest if I did not ask my father-in-law to deposit the contract money. Since that day, I have been going to the city for work incognito.
>
> (Human Rights Watch 2004a)

The attitude of the military towards the opposition by the farmers, human rights lawyers and the government in this illegal attempt to gain ownership of state land was summarized by Major-General Shaukat Sultan, the Director General of the public relations wing of the Pakistan Army: 'Nobody has the right to say what the Army can do with 5,000 acres or 17,000 acres. The needs of the Army will be determined by the Army itself' (Human Rights Watch 2004a).

At stake in the dispute were not only the legal rights of the tenant farmers but also the potential threat to the economic and political dominance of the military. According to Brad Adams, the executive director of Human Rights Watch's Asian division: 'For the Pakistani military establishment, control of land is essential for maintaining its position within the country's political structure' (Human Rights Watch 2004c).

As has been argued earlier in this chapter, the Pakistan army is one of the largest, if not the largest, holders of land, both urban and rural, in the country. Valuable urban land is used by the military to dispense patronage to civilians and is distributed as rewards to its own officers. The farmers' revolt then struck at the very foundation of the military's power. Through its extensive landowning, the military had established close links with the traditional, landed elites, as well as peasant farmers. Thus, the revolt threatened the patron–client relationships that the military established with both the traditional landed elites and with peasant farmers (Human Rights Watch 2004a). Control of the land provides the military with huge political patronage among the major political parties (Human Rights Watch 2004a). The fact that all the major political parties in Pakistan are controlled and funded by large landowners means that the military has a huge incentive to maintain tight control over its vast tracts of land.

This fact helps account for the resort to terrorist tactics by the military to suppress the farmers' movements. According to Adams: 'The military is going to great lengths to teach the lesson that anyone who resists its grip on the economy will be severely punished' (Human Rights Watch 2004c). In other words, the violence was not just about coercing the farmers to sign new contracts; rather, it had much wider implications in sending a clear message to farmers and other groups that the military would allow no threat to its control of land. Thus, the military violence quite clearly falls into the category of state terrorism.

One of the major problems inherited by Musharraf was regional unrest in Baluchistan. Baluchistan is rich in natural gas and minerals, which are being heavily exploited by the central government. The province has a long history of resentment and armed insurrection against what is regarded as the exploitative, Punjabi-dominated, central government. The construction of a huge, deep-sea port at Gwardar on the south coast, with Chinese backing, was particularly resented as very few locals were involved in the construction. Land grabs by the army in Baluchistan created a great resentment (Harrison 2006). Insurrections by Baluch nationalists in 1948, 1958–59, 1962–63 and 1973–77 were brutally repressed by the army, which did little to address the fundamental underlying political and economic grievances of the Baluchi that even Musharraf himself admitted were genuine (Hussain 2006). The setting up of army cantonments in Baluchistan was seen to tighten federal control and the presence of large numbers of federal military and paramilitary troops, inevitably resulting in clashes with the locals.

Tensions between the military and the local Baluchis came to a head in 2004 when a Baluchi physician, Dr Shazia Khalid, of the local *Bugti* clan, was raped in her home by a captain in the military (Hussain 2006). Her employers, the government-owned Pakistan Petroleum Ltd, attempted to hush her up while Pakistan defence security guards warned her not to report the rape to the police. She was denied medical treatment and kept under house arrest. The government issued a statement, saying that her house was full of cash and used condoms. Musharraf himself made the extraordinary, insensitive statement on television that the captain accused of the rape was 100 per cent innocent. He compounded his appalling error of judgement by telling the *Washington Post* newspaper that the way to become a millionaire and to get a visa for Canada was to get oneself raped (Sharlach 2008: 97). While it could not be proven that the rape of Dr Khalid was a deliberate act of state terrorism, the reaction to the event most certainly sent a clear message both to the people of Baluchistan and to the women of Pakistan that the military could rape and mistreat women with impunity. As Lisa Sharlach has argued, the function of state rape in Pakistan is to inflict sexual degradation and harm upon women, usually women belonging to a politically restive ethnic or tribal group (2008: 97). The *Bugti* clan saw the rape as an attack on their honour and led to violent unrest, including assaults on government targets while rioters attacked the state-owned gas plant (Hussain 2006; Sharlach 2008: 100).

Instead of attempting to redress the grievances of the Baluchis, the military regime of Musharraf continued to use heavy-handed attempts to quell the regional unrest in Baluchistan. They resorted to scorched-earth tactics, including using US-supplied, F-16 fighter bombers and Cobra gunships to strafe and bomb villages that supported the rebels. Innocent civilians, particularly women and young children, were terrorized and often killed as their villages were strafed and bombed. On 26 August 2006, one of the more important tribal leaders or *sardars*, Akbar Bugti, was killed by military forces in a cave where he was hiding (Harrison 2006). To the military, it was a successful elimination of a terrorist, but to the followers of Bugti, it was state-sanctioned political assassination.

Somewhat to the surprise of political commentators on Pakistan, Musharraf ran afoul of the judiciary. One of the major factors in his eventual loss of power was when his attempt to bully the judiciary backfired. On 9 March 2007, Musharraf summoned the Pakistan Chief Justice Iftikhar Mohammed Chaudhury to Army House, his residence. In the presence of top army and intelligence officers, who were Musharraf loyalists, pressure was put on the chief justice to resign. Attempts to intimidate him included threats, bullying, and physically preventing Chaudhury from leaving. When he refused to resign, he was informed that he was to be suspended and charged with misconduct. When he left Army House, Chaudhury and his wife were roughed up by thugs loyal to Musharraf. Unfortunately for Musharraf and his supporters, the treatment was captured on television and when equipment belonging to an independent station was smashed, all hell broke loose. To the surprise of just about everybody, Pakistan's lawyers rallied in large numbers to the support of the chief justice, risking beatings and arrests. The bizarre sights of well-dressed lawyers demonstrating and being attacked by the police became a regular feature in the Pakistani media (*Tribune* 2007).

One of the main issues that created conflict between Musharraf and Chaudhury was the issue of human rights. According to human rights groups, the Pakistani military, along with civilian authorities, have resorted to extra judicial killings, torture, and house arrest of political opponents and these abuses increased dramatically under Musharraf's rule. Human rights groups have expressed concern at the use of Pakistan's anti-terrorism laws to detain peaceful opponents of the Musharraf government (Human Rights News 2006). Shortly before he was dismissed from office, Chaudhury had angered the military as he began to become increasingly assertive about examining the role of the military intelligence agencies in the disappearance of citizens. These missing citizens included students, businessmen, and civil servants. Many of those who disappeared from Baluchistan were regional separatists. Others were suspected religious terrorists. It was claimed that they were taken by agents of the military to intelligence sites and tortured. Their families unsuccessfully filed petitions to courts, claiming that their relatives were innocent and asking for information about them (Amnesty International 2004). Musharraf attempted to browbeat the media and to arrest opponents and protesters; while Chaudhury and his family were subjected to severe forms of house arrest.

In November 2007, Musharraf declared a state of emergency, suspended the constitution and sacked what he declared were rebellious judges. The crude attempts to silence Pakistan's Chief Justice Iftikhar Mohammed Chaudhury and other members of the legal profession through intimidation and bullying in fact backfired, and helped contribute to the eventual decline of Musharraf's power and that of the military in government. Musharraf was forced to bow to international and domestic pressure to step down as head of the army. He also allowed two exiled former prime ministers, Benazir Bhutto and Nawaz Sharif, to return to lead their parties in the parliamentary elections (OneWorld.net 2008).

Conclusion

It would be incorrect and unfair to suggest that the Pakistani military has been a highly oppressive instrument of state terrorism in Pakistan throughout its existence. Except in the case of the brutal attempt to crush Bangladeshi separatism in 1971, the Pakistan armed forces have not been guilty of acts of state terrorism on a very large-scale. Many Pakistanis, in fact, would argue that the armed forces have at times served Pakistan well. They have provided stability, holding the fragile state together, especially during the early years of the young state. The military has built roads, established communication networks in remote areas, and provided relief during disasters, such as floods and earthquakes. Many Pakistanis take pride in the professionalism and the discipline of their army. In particular, they point with great pride to the bravery of officers and men in the wars against the much stronger forces of India. Despite the persistence of chronic poverty, especially in rural areas, under Musharraf's military-led government the economy has greatly improved, with an 8 per cent growth in 2005 and the emergence of a new consumer middle class (Hussain 2008: 189).

The dominant position of the army and its involvement in politics, have in part, resulted from a number of historical forces. At its formation in 1947, the state was a fragile state, facing the possibility of regional fragmentation. Throughout its history, Pakistan has faced a potentially dangerous neighbour, India, with its vastly superior, economic and military resources. Four times in Pakistani history, the Armed Forces have assumed control as ineffectual, corrupt politicians have mishandled grossly the government and the economy. Many would argue that the military usurpation of power and the use of force against internal and external enemies were justified. Nevertheless, the army's involvement in politics, either directly or indirectly, has at times led to serious abuses of power that constitute state terrorism throughout the history of Pakistan.

This study, therefore, argues that the army's economic and political power and involvement in politics have both weakened the reputation of professionalism of the army and the development of democracy. The very culture of a professional army, like that of Pakistan with its emphasis on authority, obedience and discipline, is not conducive to the uncertainty and the risks inherent in the rule of democracy. Simple, military solutions to complex, political issues often result, as we have seen, in acts of state terrorism. It can be argued that the mistakes of military rulers are in part a consequence of their military training and background. Nevertheless, their actions at times have constituted state terrorism.

The major events discussed above can be categorized as forms of state terrorism when tested against Jackson's four main criteria discussed in the introduction:

- State terrorism is a pre-determined strategy of political violence employed in the pursuit of strategic goals.
- State terrorism is a form of political communication whose primary audience is not the victims of terrorism.
- The central purpose of state terrorism is designed to cause fear and intimidation.
- State terrorism is directed primarily, although not exclusively, against civilians.

The most unambiguous and brutal form of state terrorism by the military was, of course, in the former East Bengal, now Bangladesh. The premeditated mass murder, torture, rape and killings, particularly of natural leaders of Bengali society, politicians, professionals and students in particular by the military was an attempt to ruthlessly crush the demand for regional autonomy. The military also has continued to use brutal tactics in an attempt to repress regional separatist movements in other parts of Pakistan particularly Baluchistan. In both Bangladesh and Baluchistan, the military demonstrated very clearly to all Pakistanis, through the deliberate and brutal targeting of civilians, that attempts to break up the state of Pakistan, and hence challenge the authority and vested interests of the military, were not acceptable.

The execution of the former prime minister of Pakistan, Bhutto, soon after the seizing of power by General Zia ul-Haq was a deliberate message again to all Pakistanis that opposition to his rule and to that of the military would be met by force. Zia's support for a very narrow, exclusivist form of Sunni Islam and the introduction of the *Hudood* ordinances that mandate brutal penalties, such as floggings and execution for the breach of Islamic law, were designed to send a message to all citizens of Pakistan, whether Sunnis, Shias, secular, Christian or Hindu, that Zia and the army were the guardians of a pure form of Islam and as such were the legitimate rulers. While Zia had strong religious convictions, the alliance between the military and religious conservatives was a very deliberate, long-term, political strategy to attempt to browbeat secular opposition that might threaten the political or economic interests of the military. For many women and for human rights activists, the introduction of legislation under the *Hudood* ordinances regarding sexual behaviour constituted state terrorism against women. The appalling treatment of the raped Baluchi physician, Dr Shazia Khalid, is just one instance of how state-approved or at least state-sanctioned terrorism against women by the military has persisted in Pakistan.

Although General Musharraf's rule was welcomed by many in Pakistan because of this commitment to secularization, law and order, and the eventual restoration of democracy, his regime has been tarnished by acts of state terrorism. The use of political assassinations, torture and other forms of intimidation by agents of the state, such as the police, against political opponents has continued under his regime. The military's heavy-handed, violent reaction to legitimate protests in Baluchistan, while a pale shadow of the mass slaughter that took place in East Pakistan, can also be categorized as a form of state terrorism. The crude and violent attempts to suppress the Punjab farmers' movement because it threatened the political as well as economic interests of the military clearly demonstrate why elites often resort to state terrorism.

One may with some justification sympathize with the armed forces' contempt for politicians and the political process. Nevertheless, it seems that if democracy in Pakistan is to take firm root, the armed forces have to return to their barracks and remain under civilian control. Indeed, there are signs that many in the military are concerned about the involvement in politics. The new Chief of Staff, General Ashfaq Pervez Kayani, who has never belonged to Musharraf's inner circle, has made clear that the armed forces must permanently keep out of politics (Hasan 2007). Most Pakistanis would probably agree. Most are convinced that either Musharraf's military-led government was involved in the assassination of Benazir Bhutto or was criminally negligent in failing to protect her (Hussain 2008: XIII). The election held in February 2008 was a sweeping success for Musharraf's opponents: the Pakistan People's Party, headed by Bhutto's husband Asif Zardari, and its rival, the Pakistan Muslim League – Nawaz (PML-N), led by Sharif. The two parties, however, have little in common except to get rid of Musharraf. The future of democracy in Pakistan and of the role of Musharraf in politics is uncertain (OneWorld.net 2008).

There may be a risk in returning to civilian rule but the alternative, as has been shown in Pakistan, is potentially far worse. Unless the military remains under civilian control, its continued involvement in politics, its heavy-handed approach and use of excessive force to resolve complex, political problems and to protect its power and vested economic interests will inevitably continue to lead to further acts of state terrorism.

Notes

1 The Pakistan military has carried on the policy of the former British, colonial rulers by confining recruitment largely to the so-called martial races.
2 Siddiqa (2007) is the best study of the Pakistan armed force's military economy and its detrimental effects on the nation's political and economic development.

3 For a clear discussion of the politics of partition with an emphasis on class interests, see Alavi (1988).
4 Jinnah has been the subject of many monographs and articles. See for example, Ahmed (1997).
5 A concise, balanced discussion of the events surrounding partition is provided by Guhu (2007), especially pp. 74–96.
6 During a research trip to Pakistan in 2005, I was shown the extensive fertile farms in the hills, just outside of Islamabad, still owned by Ayub Khan's family.
7 Constitutional experts in Pakistan gave the judgement that Bhutto's execution was illegal, according to Tanveer (2008).
8 In Pakistan, I interviewed a journalist who was a prisoner of Zia and described the pain and humiliation of being flogged.
9 Ibid.
10 For an excellent discussion of how an understanding of terrorism should be expanded to encompass violence against women, see Sharlach (2008).

References

Abbas, H. (2005) *Pakistan's Drift into Extremism: Allah, the Army, and America's War on Terror*, New York: M.E. Sharpe.

Ahmed, A.S. (1997) *Jinnah, Pakistan and Islamic Identity: The Search for Saladin*, London: Routledge.

Alavi, H. (1988) 'Pakistan and Islam: Ethnicity and Ideology', in Fred Halliday and Hamza Alavi (eds) *State and Ideology in the Middle East and Pakistan*, London and New York: Macmillan Education. Online, available at: www.ourworld.compuserve. com/homepages/sangat/Pakislam.htm (accessed 18 November 2008).

Amnesty International (2004) 'Pakistan: Human Rights Abuses in the Search for Al-Qa'ida and Taleban in the Tribal Areas'. Online, available at: www.asiapacific. amnesty.org/library/Index/ENGASA330112004?open&of=ENG-PAK (accessed 8 July 2008).

Baldauf, S. (2005) 'Pakistan: Pakistani Religious Law Challenged', *Christian Science Monitor.* Online, available at: www.wluml.org/english/newsfulltxt.shtml?cmd%5B157 %5D=x-157–142764 (accessed 8 July 2008).

Bansal, A. (2006) 'Pakistan: New Strands of Sectarianism', *Institute of Peace and Conflict Studies.* Online, available at: www.ipcs.org/whatsNewArticle11.jsp?action=show View&kValue=2027&status=article&mod=b (accessed 8 July 2008).

Chang, D. (1969) 'The Military and Nation-building in Burma, Korea and Pakistan', *Asian Survey*, 9 (11): 818. Online, available at: www.jstor.org/pss/2642226 (accessed 8 July 2008).

Chazan, D. (2002) 'Profile: Pakistan's Military Intelligence Agency', *BBC News.* Online, available at: http://news.bbc.co.uk/1/hi/world/south_asia/1750265.stm (accessed 8 July 2008).

Dalrymple, W. (2005) 'Inside Islam's "Terror Schools"', *New Statesman.* Online, available at: www.newstatesman.com/200503280010 (accessed 8 July 2008).

'Good Soldier Yahya Khan' (1971) *Time.* Online, available at: www.time.com/time/magazine/article/0,9171,878409–1,00.html (accessed 18 November 2008).

Guhu, R. (2007) *India after Gandhi: The History of the World's Largest Democracy*, New York: HarperCollins.

Haleem, I. (2008) 'Creating Frankensteins: The Taliban Movement of Pakistan', *Perspectives on Terrorism*, 11 (5). Online, available at: www.ipcs.org/Terrorism_kashmir

Level2.jsp?action=showView&kValue=2027&subCatID=1022&status=article&mod =g (accessed 8 July 2008).

Haqqani, H. (2005) *Pakistan: Between Mosque and Military*, Washington, DC: Carnegie Endowment for International Peace.

Harrison, S. (2006) 'Pakistan's Baluch Insurgency', *Le Monde Diplomatique* (English edition). Online, available at: www.mondediplo.com/2006/10/05baluchistan (accessed 8 July 2008).

Hasan, S. (2007) 'The Rise of Pakistan's "Quiet Man"', *BBC News*. Online, available at: www.news.bbc.co.uk/2/hi/south_asia/7024719.stm (accessed 18 November 2008).

Human Rights Watch (2004a) 'Soiled Hands: The Pakistan Army's Repression of the Punjab Farmers' Movement'. Online, available at: www.hrw.org/reports/2004/ pakistan0704 (accessed 8 July 2008).

—— (2004b) 'Human Rights Overview: Pakistan'. Online, available at: www.hrw.org/ english/docs/2004/12/14/pakist9852.htm (accessed 8 July 2008).

—— (2004c) 'Pakistan: Military Torturing Farmers in Punjab'. Online, available at: www.hrw.org/english/docs/2004/07/21/pakist9102.htm (accessed 8 July 2008).

Hussain, Z. (2006) 'Musharraf's Other War', *Newsline*. Online, available at: www.news-line.com.pk/NewsJan2006/cover1jan2006.htm (accessed 8 July 2008).

—— (2008) *Frontline Pakistan: The Path to Catastrophe and the Killing of Benazir Bhutto*, London: I.B. Tauris.

Jackson, R. (2008) 'An Argument for Terrorism', *Perspectives on Terrorism*, 2 (2). Online, available at: www.terrorismanalysts.com/pt/index.php?option=com_rokzine& view=article&id=28 (accessed 18 November 2008).

Martin, G. (2008) 'Essentials of Terrorism: Concepts and Controversies', Los Angeles: SAGE publications.

Musharraf, P. (2006) *In the Line of Fire: A Memoir*, London: Simon & Schuster.

'Pakistan: Torture in Counterterrorism Should Top Blair Agenda' (2006) *Human Rights News*. Online, available at: www.hrw.org/en/news/2006/11/16/pakistan-torture-counterterrorism-should-top-blair-agenda (accessed 18 November 2008).

'Politics in Pakistan' (2008) *OneWorld.net*. Online, available at: www.uk.oneworld.net/ guides/pakistan/development?gclid=CNXug5yrm5QCFR8cagodflgEuQ (accessed 18 November 2008).

Rankin-Reid, J. (2008) 'Fighting for the Bottom Line', *ON LINE opinion*. Online, available at: www.onlineopinion.com.au/view.asp?article=6902 (accessed 18 November 2008).

Rashid, A. (2000) *Taliban Militant Islam, Oil and Fundamentalism in Central Asia*, New Haven: Yale University Press.

Samad, Y. (2001) 'Pakistan, "Pro-Taliban Elements" and Sectarian Strife', *MiddleEast-Desk.org*. Online, available at: http://middleeastdesk.org/article.php?id=233 (accessed 8 July 2008).

Siddiqa, A. (2007) *Military Inc. Inside Pakistan's Military Economy*, London: Pluto Press.

'6 Judges Quit' (2007) *Tribune* (Chandigarh). Online, available at: www.tribuneindia. com/2007/20070320/world.htm (accessed 8 July 2008).

Shah, N. (2008) 'Military and Pakistan: An Unending Waltz of Authoritarianism?', *Asiana Press Agency*. Online, available at: www.asiana-press-agency.com/ articles/2008-shah-0202.html (accessed 8 July 2008).

Sharlach, L. (2008) 'Veil and Four Walls: A State of Terror in Pakistan', *Critical Studies on Terrorism*, 1 (1): 95–110.

Tanveer, R. (2008) 'Retired Judges Term Zulfikar Ali Bhutto's Execution', *Daily Times*, Lahore. Online, available at: www.dailytimes.com.pk/default.asp?page=2008%5C04% 5C04%5Cstory_4-4-2008_pg7_25 (accessed 8 July 2008).

'Transcript of Interview with Human Rights Lawyer' (2008) *Law Report, ABC National Radio*. Online, available at: www.abc.net.au/rn/lawreport/stories/2008/2209518.htm (accessed 8 July 2008).

US Department of State (2002) 'Pakistan: Country Reports on Human Rights Practices – 2001'. Online, available at: www.state.gov/g/drl/rls/hrrpt/2001/sa/8237.htm (accessed 18 November 2008).

4 Israel's *other* terrorism challenge

Sandra Nasr

Introduction

In the West, we hear a lot about terrorism in relation to Israel: Palestinian militants in Gaza using rockets to fire at Israeli towns over the 'border'; and Palestinian suicide bombers strapping on explosives and detonating their payloads in Israeli cafes, bars, restaurants and buses. These attacks on civilian targets for the purpose of making a political statement are, indeed, examples of terrorism and Israeli civilians are right to demand that their government act decisively to prevent such acts. Yet Israel often responds to these terrorist tactics by adopting its own. When Israel sanctions and employs tactics which are designed to instil fear, humiliate, injure or otherwise cause harm to a civilian population for a political purpose, the state is guilty of state terrorism. Identifying those policies which constitute state terrorism requires an examination of both the intent and effect of actions (and inaction) by the state. The purpose of this chapter is to evaluate whether various Israeli policies and practices employed in Israel's occupation of the Palestinian Territories constitute 'state terrorism'. This policy analysis, while not exhaustive, is intended to present a broad cross-section of policies in recent and current context. Material has been sourced from reputable, human rights, non-government organizations (NGOs), United Nations (UN) bodies and published eyewitness accounts collated since the commencement of the second *intifada*.

Where the effect of state (in)action is identified as instilling fear, humiliating or injuring a person *and* the broader community, then it *may* constitute state terror. To assess whether the (in)action qualifies as state terror rather than simply state repression, we must look at intent. Ruth Blakeley, in her volume *State Terrorism and Neoliberalism: The North in the South* (2009), identified a key ingredient, 'instrumentality', which set state terror apart. That is, the intended target of the violent act (or threat) is the wider audience, rather than only the immediate victim. As no state is likely to acknowledge that the intended purpose of its policies is to spread terror among a population in order to gain political control advantages, we must deduce intent from the context.

For the purposes of establishing whether the action's purpose is legitimate, the following questions must be asked: Is the action a proportional response?

Does the action adequately and specifically target the individual/s responsible? Can the response be justified under the state's international and domestic legal obligations? Does the response have a *permissible* strategic value?

Proportionality

While the notion of proportionality remains problematic, it is fair to say that it rests on a correlation between the crime and its punishment. Within jurisprudence, of course, a long history of case law has established a basic understanding within society of what (at least in general terms) constitutes a proportionate punishment. Further, the punishment is devised within the realms of the law, i.e. a conviction is obtained, then the appropriate legal statute is consulted for an appropriate punishment.

A disproportionate response does two things: it side-steps the conviction process and it punishes beyond what is reasonable for the crime. In terms of the perpetration of state terror, the state exacts a disproportionate response which terrorizes or physically harms innocents to send a political message to a wider population. The message is intended to project the state's power and quell challenge or resistance.

Specificity

The term 'collateral damage' has been used to describe the supposed, *unintended* injuries sustained by innocent bystanders as a result of a targeted military action. It fails to differentiate between the innocent and guilty and rests on the premise that a certain level of unpredictable, unintended injury – beyond the action's target – is acceptable, as long as the extent of such injuries does not outweigh the expected military advantage. This comes down to what can be reasonably predicted. For example, it should be reasonable to expect that firing from a helicopter gunship into a crowded street or an apartment block, is likely to cause substantial 'collateral damage'. Failure to take all necessary steps to prevent wanton injury during military action – when it is so clearly foreseeable – amounts to, at best, culpable negligence and, at worst, an act of collective punishment, aimed at instilling fear across a broad audience.

Justifiability

The various instruments of human rights, to which Israel is a signatory,[1] were developed in response to the litany of atrocities committed by states against civilian populations throughout history. States' support of these various treaties, which constitute international 'law', is vitally important both to their standing as nations and as an expression of moral integrity to their own citizens. Where a state attempts to circumvent or ignore this fundamental set of human rights in order to pursue its political aims, it is, in effect, instilling fear among people for political advantage. International law is very clear about the rights of civilians to receive protection and no amount of semantic obfuscation or special pleading on the part of states can obviate their responsibilities in this regard.

Strategicality

The strategic value of a military action is its *raison d'etre*. This seems obvious, but often actions are taken which are purely retaliatory, punitive and have very little strategic value. For instance, bombing a civilian population or civil infrastructure does not usually reduce the number of combatants or their offensive capabilities. We can deduce, then, that the aim of the action is to subjugate and intimidate the population to reduce support for a political organization or combatants.

However, it is not enough for an action to have an identifiable strategic value. It must also be *permissible*, by which I mean that it conforms to international laws and the state's own regulations on the use of force by its representatives. Where an (in)action fails, on balance, to have a legitimate purpose, it must be deduced that its intention is to instil fear, humiliate, injure or otherwise cause harm to a civilian population for political purposes and thereby constitutes an act of state terror. First, some background will be provided to the analysis of Israeli state terrorism.

Birth of a state

Even prior to the official birth of the Israeli state, it is clear that groundwork was being done with the aim of depopulating the land of its Arab inhabitants. Early Zionists had decided already that the problem of co-existence would best be cured by driving the Arabs off the land (Morris 2004). This could be assisted by the establishment of an environment of extreme fear among the Arab population. The massacre at Deir Yassin, while not an isolated incident, was pivotal in causing widespread terror among Palestinians in the crucial, pre-state months of 1948.

According to the account of Jacques de Reynier (Khalidi 1971: 761–6), who headed the International Red Cross delegation to Palestine at the time, all but around 50 people out of 400 inhabitants of the village of Deir Yassin were *deliberately* massacred in cold blood by members of the Irgun (an extremist militant Zionist group).[2] As word spread among Arabs of the massacre, their terror was 'astutely fostered by the Jews' (ibid.: 765), leading to many fleeing their homes, including the evacuation of whole towns. Deir Yassin is vivid in the memory of today's Palestinians and remains symbolic of what Palestinians see as a continuing policy aimed at ethnically cleansing the Occupied Palestinian Territories (OPT) of Arabs.

State terror policymaking: Plan D

To understand how the use of terror became Israeli policy, we must go back to the period prior to the establishment of the Israeli state. In March 1948, the head of operations at the soon to be officially established, Israeli armed forces, General Yigael Yadin, launched what became known as 'Plan D' or 'Plan *Dalet*' (*Tochnit Daleth*)[3] (Kimmerling 2003). The official purpose of the plan was to aid the establishment of the state of Israel by providing protection for the new Jewish settlements against 'hostile' forces, specifying certain steps:

> These actions should be executed as following: destruction of villages by fire, explosives and mining – especially of those villages over which we cannot gain [permanent] control. The gaining of control will be accomplished in accordance with the following methods: encircling the village and searching it, and in the event of resistance destroying the resisting forces and expelling the population beyond the boundaries of the State.
>
> (Ibid.: 24)

According to Pappe (2006: 88), the plan was executed according to the directive: 'the principal objective of the operation is the destruction of Arab villages ... [and] the eviction of the villagers so that they would become an economic liability for the general Arab forces'. As Kimmerling (2003) noted, Plan D, instigated following the declaration of a state of emergency, was a spectacular success. Some 20,000 km square of territory were conquered and almost entirely cleansed of Arab inhabitants.[4] In and around Haifa (a northern coastal city of Israel), 15 towns and villages of between 300 to 5,000 people were expelled in quick succession, despite the presence of British soldiers, foreign reporters and UN personnel (ibid.).

State culpability for settler violence

Attacks by settlers on Palestinians in the OPT are daily occurrences, according to human rights organizations. In June 2007, Al-Haq (2007) reported an instance of a 16-year-old boy being attacked and injured by a group of settlers in Hebron. A Red Crescent ambulance was called to assist the boy, but was also attacked by the settlers. Nearby Israeli forces, observing what was happening, made no attempt to intervene. In other accounts, Palestinians were beaten with clubs or rifle butts, verbally abused in foul language and intimidated by large groups of armed settlers, settlement guards and the Israeli Defence Force (IDF). Settlers frequently usurp Palestinian farm land and olive groves, preventing Palestinians from accessing their means of feeding their families.

If the IDF took steps to prevent the settlers' violence – to protect Palestinians from the violence when it occurred and prosecute settlers who perpetrated it – this would simply be a case of criminal behaviour by individuals and groups of settlers. What transforms this issue into one of state terror is the behaviour of the occupying forces. Where IDF soldiers are present during instances of settler violence, they rarely do anything to prevent it and, indeed, often encourage or assist it. The IDF seldom record identifying details of the settlers and almost never arrest a settler (B'Tselem n.d.a). Then the IDF imposes restrictions on the movement of the attacked Palestinians (including curfews), thereby punishing the victims further. Such a policy undermines Israel's obligations under international law to protect civilians on land it occupies. The state's response to settler violence against Palestinians has no legitimate purpose and it must be concluded that the intent is to maintain fear among a population, who know they will not receive protection or recourse under the law (ibid.).

Home demolitions

The IDF use home demolition regularly as a means of collective punishment for the (alleged) terrorist activities of an individual Palestinian or in order to force the individual (or family members) to turn the accused person in to Israeli authorities. B'Tselem statistics on punitive house demolitions for the period October 2001 to January 2005 put the figure at 668 homes (B'Tselem n.d.b). Demolitions of this type, in particular, occur with little warning and without means of redress, as happened in the case of the family of a young man, Ibrahim, who was arrested in 2002. In February 2004, Ibrahim's brother, wife and children (including a newborn child) were forcibly removed from their house in the middle of the night and ten minutes later, their home was demolished (Al-Haq 2004).

Rarely do Palestinians live as single individuals in a single free-standing house. Given the overwhelming crowding within Arab villages and towns, mostly several related and unrelated families are packed into a group of joined apartments within blocks which are attached or built very close to other apartment blocks. A demolition of one 'suspected terrorist's' home equates to the destruction and damage of many other families' homes and often the loss of almost all their personal belongings. Such demolitions are carried out with little regard for the safety and well-being of the families living there (or indeed, of foreign activists trying to prevent the destruction – see the case of Rachel Corrie) (Palestinian Centre for Human Rights Gaza 2003). The demolition policy is disproportionate, unlawful and constitutes collective punishment.

In February 2005, the minister for defense announced a cessation in the policy, following the recommendations of a committee, which found that punitive house demolitions not only failed to deter terrorist activity but in fact, instilled further hate and a desire for vengeance in Palestinians (Margalit 2005). The fact that this policy has been dropped and then resurrected at various times by the IDF suggests that the policy is used as revenge or intimidation, rather than as a strategic military action.

Beatings and abuse

Palestinians may be subjected to verbal or physical abuse by the IDF at any time or place in the West Bank but by far, the greatest risk lies at the many checkpoints dotted throughout the West Bank. Palestinians often queue for hours in all weather conditions with the uncertain hope of finally being able to pass and reach school, work, home or medical centres. Checkpoints are invariably crowded, tense bottlenecks which MachsomWatch (a group of Israeli women who observe and report on checkpoints) described as a 'pressure cooker that's about to explode at any moment' (MachsomWatch 2004). There is a great sense of uncertainty and unpredictability surrounding the checkpoint process, as acknowledged in the statement of an Israeli soldier at Qalandia checkpoint:

> No one knows what is going on; the rules change every minute. Palestinians get shot because no one knows what they're supposed to be doing and everyone is scared. That's why an innocent man died last week. It's all out of control. There's no sense here.
>
> (Al-Haq 2002)

According to MachsomWatch (2004), a soldier was observed attacking a Palestinian in the face with a screwdriver at the Ar Ram checkpoint. When Machsom Watch confronted the officers involved, they were told 'we don't understand why you're so upset, events like this occur ten times a day'. The attacks on unarmed Palestinian civilians by heavily armed IDF soldiers range from verbal abuse (often in Arabic for extra impact) through pushing, slapping, kicking to shooting. One particularly poignant example of the more serious end of the scale is contained in an affidavit by a 23-year-old woman from Zeita, obtained by Al-Haq (2002). The woman was in labour and was being driven by her husband and father-in-law to hospital. Soldiers at a checkpoint ordered the woman to lift her shirt so they could confirm that she really was pregnant and they were motioned to pass through the checkpoint. Yet 600 metres further, the soldiers opened fire on their car, hitting the occupants. The woman was made to undress fully (including her undergarments) and forced to lie on the cold ground. By the time the soldiers allowed a Palestinian ambulance to take them to hospital, the woman's husband was dead, her father-in-law seriously injured and she was left injured.

When challenged concerning incidents of brutality, the IDF mount a limited investigation occasionally but seem unwilling to accept either the scope or prevalence of the problem. The response blames the individual soldier, who may have become 'unhinged' (MachsomWatch 2004)[5] or acted contrary to orders. According to B'Tselem, incidents of IDF brutality towards Palestinians are too common and have increased significantly with the outbreak of the *al-Aqsa intifada*. Many incidents are unreported. To file a report regarding such incidents, Palestinians must follow a convoluted process, which is time-consuming and generally pointless. According to reports by B'Tselem, the Department for the Investigation of Police often close files following incomplete or indifferent investigations due to the 'offender [being] unknown' or there being 'insufficient proof'. At other times, the case has not progressed because the complainant has been unable to obtain the necessary travel permit from the Israeli authorities to attend hearings and provide a testimony. In the few cases where perpetrators are prosecuted, they can expect to receive light sentences (B'Tselem n.d.c).

The message that these responses transmits to soldiers at checkpoints is that abuse of Palestinians is an acceptable means to control a population, whose dignity matters very little. From time to time, senior officers and politicians pay lip service to the idea that such abuse is undesirable or even unacceptable. As B'Tselem (ibid.) noted, however, until the lip service is supported by unequivocal instructions to all security forces operating in the Occupied Territories that abuse of Palestinians is absolutely prohibited and then, complaints are seriously and fairly investigated, the abuse was sure to continue. The message that Israel's inaction in these circumstances conveys to Palestinians is that any Palestinian may be subjected to cruel, degrading treatment at the hands of an all-powerful IDF. There can be no permissible strategic purpose to such humiliation and physical harm; nor can the actions be considered lawful, proportional and specifically targeted. It is reasonable to conclude that until all appropriate steps to prevent IDF abuse against unarmed Palestinian civilians are taken by Israeli authorities, Israel is culpable and guilty of using state terror tactics.

Torture of detainees

The issue of detainee torture has received substantial international media coverage in recent years, primarily as a result of reports of torture at high-profile institutions in Iraq (Abu-Ghraib), Afghanistan, Cuba (Guantánamo Bay) and facilities in various countries under 'rendition' arrangements. The use of torture as a means to extract information, enforce compliance or generally break the will of detainees is nothing new. Humankind's creativity in inventing new forms of torture throughout the ages shows a serious commitment to this form of cruelty. Since the inception of the UN and the various charters, declarations and covenants (particularly the UN Convention Against Torture (UN 1975)),[6] however, torture is no longer popularly acceptable.

A joint investigation of torture of Palestinian detainees was conducted in May 2007 by Hamoked – Center for the Defence of the Individual and B'Tselem (Lein 2007).[7] Their report revealed the nature and scope of torture that Palestinian men, women and children experienced at the hands of IDF captors over a six-month period in 2005–06. The report detailed a policy of torture in the form of 'beating, painful binding, swearing and humiliation and denial of basic needs' which began at the moment of arrest by security forces. This treatment's practical outcome was the 'softening up' of detainees prior to being handed over to the big guns of interrogation, the Israel Security Agency (ISA). The report identified several key elements of the treatment of detainees during interrogation periods which, in the sample, lasted an average of 35 days. Detainees were subjected to isolation (from other prisoners, their families, lawyers and International Red Cross workers) and solitary confinement in poor conditions; they were deprived of sleep, exercise and food. They were cuffed in the 'shabah' position – painfully bound by hands and feet to a chair. Detainees were abused and humiliated (including verbal abuse, swearing, spitting and unnecessary strip searches). Intimidation and threats of torture against the detainees and their family members were common, both to illicit information and to recruit the detainees as informants.

These routine devices are intended to 'break the spirit' or will of detainees and are prohibited under international law. It is the non-routine or 'special' methods involving direct physical violence, however, which are most disturbing. These methods include: sleep deprivation for more than 24 hours; 'dry' beatings; extreme tightening of handcuffs; abrupt forced movements of parts of the body; 'frog' crouching – which involves tip-toeing in a crouched position and extreme arching of detainees' backs while seated (known as the 'banana' position). The use of these non-routine methods are not out-of-the-ordinary, spontaneous responses to exceptional circumstances. The report indicated that the methods were 'pre-authorised and used according to fixed instructions' (ibid.: 8). The report's findings were corroborated by other reports and numerous testimonies, compiled by various human rights organizations and international bodies, including Amnesty International, Human Rights Watch, Al Haq and B'Tselem. Under international law, these methods constitute torture and are prohibited.

Human Rights Watch, in a memorandum to the UN Committee against Torture in May 1998 (Human Rights Watch 1998), noted that Israel had failed to comply with Article 16 of the Convention against Torture. A number of recommendations were made by the UN body and others regarding concrete steps which Israel must take to 'bring its law and practice into compliance'. The Human Rights Watch memo stated: 'Israel has consistently disregarded these recommendations and continues to use torture and cruel, inhuman or degrading treatment during interrogations of Palestinian detainees'. Israel's response to these and other international criticisms of its policy and practice of the torture of detainees was to invoke 'Special Powers of Interrogation of the General Security Services (GSS)' (Israeli Ministry of Foreign Affairs 1999). The document stated, *inter alia*, that:

> The Government intends to introduce to the Knesset a bill that would secure the existing powers of interrogation of the GSS in its struggle against terrorism ... with the proviso that these practices would not involve torture, cruelty or inhumanity.
>
> (Ibid.)

Some eight years and many instances of torture later, Israel still relies on a 'necessity defense' (Public Committee against Torture in Israel 2007); given the environment of defending the state against 'terrorists', the GSS is obligated to use whatever means it deems necessary against anyone it perceives as a threat. This defence is limited, however, in both international and national provisions, such as Article 31 of the ICC Statute and Article 34 of Israel's own Penal Code. Specifically, the interrogation methods used must be 'reasonable', 'necessary' or 'immediately necessary' and 'no alternative means' must be available (Marchesi 2006). Governments who sanction (or fail to prevent) torture during incarceration or interrogation fail in their legal obligations under international law.

Torture as a tactic is clearly designed to instil fear, break the will, humiliate and intimidate its victims and the wider population. It is a disproportionate action because the methods employed are clearly not 'immediately necessary', reasonable and without an alternative. Detainees may be suspected of some kind of involvement in a crime or potential crime, they might be relatives/ friends of a suspect or they might be quite randomly chosen. Given the various reports and entreaties of the many human rights organizations and Israel's inadequate responses, it surely can be deduced that Israel intends to continue the practice.

Use of human shields

The use of civilians as 'human shields', as protection for soldiers conducting house-to-house searches or other similar operations, is prohibited under international law. Article 27 of the Fourth Geneva Convention states that civilians must be treated humanely and protected against acts or threats of violence. Articles 31 and 51 prohibited moral or physical coercion of civilians to make them participate in military tasks. Official commentary of the Convention specifically acknowledged the barbarity and cruelty of the practice of human shields. In the case of children, further protections are afforded and the use of children under the age of 15 to carry out military tasks is considered a war crime under the terms of international criminal law (B'Tselem n.d.c).

The IDF made use of Palestinian civilians as human shields in a number of circumstances. They may be forced to enter buildings before the soldiers to detonate any booby traps or remove occupants that might resist. Where suspicious objects are sighted on roads that the army uses, human shields will be ordered to remove the objects. They may be lined up in front of sites, where the IDF are located, to prevent militants shooting at the IDF. At gunpoint, human shields are forced to walk in front of soldiers to prevent the soldiers from being shot (while the soldier fires over the human shield's shoulder) (B'Tselem n.d.d).

The practice of randomly choosing Palestinian civilians to act as human shields was used extensively by the IDF during the Al Aqsa *intifada* and was particularly prevalent during Operation Defensive Shield, from March to April 2002, which essentially consisted of a series of incursions into Palestinian towns and villages. The testimony of an IDF soldier provides us with an insight:

> Before searching a house, we go to a neighbor, take him out of his house, and tell him to call for the person we want. If it works, great. If not, we blow down the door or hammer it open. The neighbor goes in first. If somebody is planning something, he is the one who gets it. Our instructions are to send him inside and have him go up to all the floors and get everyone out of the house. The neighbor can't refuse; he doesn't have that option. The neighbor shouts, knocks on the door, says that the army is here. If nobody answers, we tell him that we'll kill him if nobody comes out, and that he should shout that out to the people in the house. The basic procedure was

the same no matter who gave the briefing. Maybe the 'we'll kill him' came from the platoon, but the rest came from the brigade level or higher.

(B'Tselem n.d.e)

As a result of this marked increase in the use of human shields, in May 2002, various human rights organizations petitioned the High Court of Justice to obtain a cessation of the practice. The IDF undertook to stop the practice, except for the 'neighbor procedure' (the technique described in the above testimony). Following the death of a Palestinian in August 2002, the Court was petitioned successfully to grant an injunction into this practice. The practice continued anyway. Further petitions resulted in the IDF replacing its 'neighbor procedure' with a 'prior warning procedure', which essentially permitted the use of human shields as long as the individual consented to being so used. In such circumstances of extreme power imbalance and the threat of harm, implicit or explicit in such situations, it is highly unlikely that consent would be withheld very often. As Supreme Court President, Aharon Barak, observed: 'It is very hard to verify willingness, and the fear is that, when a contingent of soldier [*sic*] come at night, out of fear no neighbour will refuse to cooperate with the soldiers' (B'Tselem n.d.f). In October 2005, the High Court of Justice ruled the use of Palestinian civilians during military operations is illegal, regardless of what label is attached (ibid.).

Unfortunately, the Israeli forces still use human shields. In May 2007, a student at A-Najah University, Majd Ghanem, was shot in the back while being used as a human shield. In March 2007, testimonies were received by B'Tselem (B'Tselem 2007) that two children, a 15-year-old boy and an 11-year-old girl, were used by the IDF as human shields in operations. In both cases, the children were forced to enter houses in front of soldiers. Their compliance was unwilling – both feared that they would be killed or arrested if they did not do as they were told.

It is clear from the continuance of human shield use by the IDF, that military orders prohibiting their use have failed to be communicated properly to soldiers in the field nor have violations been investigated thoroughly. The effect of this is a perception by soldiers that the use of human shields is not really a problem. As B'Tselem wrote: 'using a Palestinian as if he were a bulletproof vest turns him into an object whose only purpose is to save soldiers' lives. His needs, his pain and suffering, his very being, are utterly ignored' (B'Tselem n.d.f).

IDF soldiers in the field do not take international law seriously because their military commanders and state leadership do not. It is clearly disproportionate to use an innocent civilian in a way which is likely to cause the person injury or death. Likewise, the human shield is not a 'person of interest' who could be detained reasonably and so, the policy fails the specificity test. The use of human shields violates international law and Israel's domestic laws; while the strategic military advantage is obvious, it is not a *permissible* strategy.

Violent incursions

IDF incursions into Palestinian towns are not unusual – many such operations have been mounted into both the West Bank and Gaza Strip – and there are no signs that incursions will stop anytime soon. They are usually accompanied by the rhetoric of 'security operations' – the need to 'uproot the terrorist infrastructure' – but the IDF is not carrying out a surgical extraction of known terrorists from its bases in these operations. Operation Defensive Shield, launched in March 2002, was easily the most extensive incursion into the West Bank that Palestinians experienced since the expulsions of 1948 (Hamzeh and May 2003).[8] The operation was far from 'defensive'. It was estimated that within less than a month, the damage was USD 465 million and included: the gutting of hospitals and universities; the bombing and bulldozing of homes; and the vandalizing of private and public institutions, business, banks and homes. Up to 270 Palestinians (mostly civilian) were killed and as many as 750 people were injured (ibid.).

During this period, the IDF stepped up its use of all of the terror tactics described previously in this chapter and became even less concerned about the potential for harm to civilians. Eyewitness accounts of the incursion into Jenin refugee camp (Baroud 2003) described civilians being shot at inside their own homes; of having hand grenades thrown in through doors or windows; and tanks driving over everything in their paths, including cars. Those unable to get out of their homes in time were bulldozed along with them and ambulances were prevented from assisting those injured.

At Birzeit University in Ramallah six months after Operation Defensive Shield, I was shown a photo album, full of pictures taken in Jenin immediately following the incursions. I saw mangled, burned, bullet-ridden corpses of men, women and even a few of small children. I counted 30 such photographs before I could bear to look no more. Similar atrocities were reported to have occurred during recent (early 2008) incursions into Gaza. A photojournalist – Mohammed Omer – who resided in Rafah refugee camp, close to the Egyptian border, reported widespread, indiscriminate rocket fire from Israeli warplanes, causing many civilian casualties (Omer 2008).[9]

According to Human Rights Watch (2009a), Israel failed to hold anyone in the IDF to account for violations of international humanitarian laws in the early 2008 Gaza incursion and 2002 West Bank incursions. This failure, according to Human Rights Watch (ibid.) sent the message that serious abuses of civilians would be tolerated in future conflicts. In December 2008, following a spate of rocket attacks by Hamas on Israeli towns, the Israeli Air Force commenced an air offensive against targets in Gaza which escalated in January 2009 with an IDF ground offensive. By 10 January 2009, the UN put the Palestinian death toll at 792 with a further 3,200 injured (United Nations 2009a). Gaza, a small sliver of land between Israel and Egypt, is home to approximately 1.5 million people and one of the most densely populated places in the world. During the course of the fighting, Israel was accused of indiscriminately firing upon civilian targets, including the following national institutions: the education, foreign and justice ministries (Nabulsi 2009); a mosque in Beit Lahiya (Balousha and Syal 2009); Gaza University (Bannoura 2008); and even the shelling of clearly identified UN schools (El-Khodary and Kershner 2009; Human Rights Watch 2009b). Furthermore, attempts by UN agencies to assist civilians and for Red Crescent workers and other medical personnel to access the many dead and wounded were actively hampered by Israeli forces, causing the death of at least one UNRWA driver and injuries to others (Palestine Red Crescent Society 2009; United Nations 2009a; 2009b; 2009c). This was despite the UN facilities being clearly marked, co-ordinates mapped and the agencies receiving specific Israeli approvals (United Nations 2009a; Human Rights Watch 2009b).

Even more disturbing were allegations that Israel unlawfully used a chemical 'obscurant' – white phosphorus – in densely populated areas on a number of occasions during the conflict. White phosphorus is highly incendiary and 'causes horrific burns when it touches the skin' (Human Rights Watch 2009c). Media photographs have shown white phosphorus projectiles bursting in the air above civilian areas with the potential to spread '116 burning wafers over an area between 125 and 250 metres in diameter' (ibid.). Gazans felt extremely vulnerable because: 'in Gaza there is nowhere to evacuate people to safety: they are imprisoned on all sides, with an acute awareness of the impossibility of escape. Land, sea, sky: all will kill you' (Nabulsi 2009).

For Israel to declare these violent incursions to be security operations designed to uproot the terror infrastructure was disingenuous. The sheer scale of the operations and the apparent lack of care taken to avoid civilian loss of life amounted to an unlawful and disproportionate action against the general Palestinian population, with easily foreseeable consequences. The incursions had the effect of parading the overwhelming might of the Israeli forces and to reiterate the inability of the Palestinian authorities to protect the people. Violent incursions (and the ongoing threat of them) are a particularly effective means of causing fear and intimidating large numbers of people.

Extrajudicial assassinations

The practice of 'taking out' a suspect, known as an 'extrajudicial assassination', is widely used by Israel in the OPT. In a ruling in the Israeli High Court of Justice in December 2006 – *The Public Committee against Torture in Israel* v. *Government of Israel* (HCJ 769/02) – the Court found that killing a 'terrorist' was permissible when a person played a 'direct part' in an act (Dugard 2007). The terms were rendered very broad but were tempered by the requirement that such 'extrajudicial assassinations' should not be resorted to when a person could be arrested without undue risk to soldiers, or where the risk of harm to civilians would outweigh any security advantage. It would seem unlikely that Israel would feel restrained by the need to justify its actions, given this ruling. Firing missiles at an apartment block or a moving vehicle – or mounting an armed incursion into a town to kill an individual – always results in some 'collateral damage'.

This disregards civilian safety and results in the perception by Palestinians that their lives are not valued (therefore why should they value Israeli lives?) and that they are being punished collectively for the alleged crimes of particular individuals.

Some commentators, such as Steven David of John Hopkins University (2003), would argue that in this 'post 9–11 world', 'targeted killing is a legitimate and moral response to terrorist attacks'. This is a very dangerous proposition and one with which the UN Special Rapporteur, John Dugard, disagreed (2007). He described the policy as the death penalty via the back door. It is also a means by which a warning is sent to other militants and potential supporters that deadly military force will be used against whomever Israel deems a threat. Extrajudicial assassinations have little strategic value as even Israel acknowledges that for every militant killed in this way, another takes their place. The policy is without merit in terms of proportionality and lawfulness because it does not exact a punishment in line with international humanitarian law standards or Israel's own criminal laws. The action fails to adequately prevent foreseeable injury to innocent bystanders. The context reveals the broader intent of targeted assassinations to be the terrorizing of the population.

IDF training

The IDF, as the official 'face' of Israel to most Palestinians in the territories, wields substantial power and every interaction between the IDF and Palestinians has life-changing potential. Appropriate training, supervision and the enforcement of lawful rules of engagement are vitally important. It is reasonable to expect that the IDF, like any other military force, will attract a few people who really shouldn't be issued with a weapon of any kind. Within the IDF, however, a pattern of systemic brutality has been identified. A Master's research project was conducted by Nufar Yishai-Karim – a clinical psychologist at Hebrew University in Jerusalem and a former soldier in Gaza (Urquhart 2007) – to assess how pervasive was the problem and how it was perpetuated. The report identified a propensity for IDF soldiers to see themselves as above the law:

> The most important thing is that it removes the burden of the law from you. You feel that you are the law ... you are the one who decides ... as though from the moment you leave the place that is called Eretz Yisrael ... and go through the Erez checkpoint into the Gaza Strip, you are the law. You are God.
>
> (Ibid.)

The report proceeded to describe various acts of brutality by soldiers, including the shooting of a 25-year-old man for no reason at all and then, leaving him to die in the street without a second glance. A woman threw a clog at one soldier so he repeatedly kicked her in the groin, rendering her infertile. Another woman spat at a soldier and received a rifle butt in the face.

This is not only a problem of poor discipline among soldiers, it is a problem of example and training. A soldier described the actions of his new commanding officer:

> It's 6 a.m., Rafah is under curfew, there isn't so much as a dog in the streets. Only a little boy of four playing in the sand. He is building a castle in his yard … the officer suddenly starts running and we all run with him … He grabbed the boy … broke his hand here at the wrist, broke his leg here. And started to stomp on his stomach, three times, and left … The next day I go out with him on another patrol and the soldiers are already starting to do the same thing.
>
> (Ibid.)

During the first weeks of basic training, a group of soldiers was escorting arrested Palestinians. The soldiers made the Palestinians, wearing very little clothing, sit on the floor of the bus in sub-zero temperatures. The new recruits spent the journey stamping on and beating the Palestinians, before dousing them in cold water.

If this is the training regime of the IDF and the example set by its officers, then two things must be considered: either the IDF are seriously mismanaging the training of recruits and failing to instil the ethics so proudly displayed on the IDF's website; or the IDF has two ethics policies – the written and unwritten ones – which are at odds with each other. Either way, the state is culpable for the actions of its military. What allows such acts of unrestrained brutality is the notion that Palestinians' lives are worth less than those of the soldiers and that the state, by not enforcing appropriate standards in its military, condones and even encourages such actions. The only possible explanation for this is the terror value gained by maintaining the Palestinians in a perpetual state of fear for themselves, their families and friends. The problem this creates for Israel is simply 'the next generation of terrorists' (B'Tselem 2003).

Israel's *other* terrorism challenge

From the foregoing, it is surely indisputable that Israel is committing acts of state terror of many kinds on a daily basis in the Occupied Territories. In each case considered in this chapter, the action taken shows an unlawful and disproportional response, which fails to target individuals adequately and appropriately for a permissible, strategic purpose. This failure indicates a more generalized policy of employing terror tactics for the purposes of subjugating a population.

Revisionist historians (including Israelis) have acknowledged the truth regarding Israel's violent birth. Early Zionists laid the foundations of state terror and Israel's military has continued on this basis. Despair, hopelessness and rage are engendered by Israeli state policies and practices, which allow Palestinians to be subjected, with little recourse in the law, to beatings, abuse, punitive home demolitions, torture, death as human shields or 'collateral damage' and death by prevention of medical treatment. It is unacceptable and counter-productive to attempt to counter terror with terror. This chapter has sought to expose Israeli state terror for the sake of Israelis as much as for the sake of Palestinians. How can Israel live peacefully as a nation among nations if it fails to uphold the very things it claims to be built upon? How can there be reconciliation with the moderate majority of Arabs in the Middle East when Israel is unwilling to acknowledge the violence of its birth and resolve to adhere to its obligations under international humanitarian law? Israel's future rests on how it rises to this, its *other* terrorism challenge.

Notes

1 Israel is a signatory to many instruments of Human Rights protection, including: The Universal Declaration of Human Rights; The Geneva Convention; The International Covenant on Economic, Social and Cultural Rights; The International Covenant on Civil and Political Rights; The International Convention on the Elimination of All Forms of Racial Discrimination; The Convention against Torture and Other Cruel, Inhuman or Degrading Treatment or Punishment; The Convention on the Rights of the Child; Rome Statute of the International Criminal Court (signed, but not ratified).
2 Full name Irgun Zvai Leumi, headed at the time by Menahem Begin, who was later the sixth prime minister of Israel.
3 Kimmerling, (*Book of Haganah History* published only in Hebrew) sets out the full story of how Plan D provided a blueprint for a policy of ethnically cleansing Palestine of its Arab inhabitants.
4 It is commonly accepted among historians that approximately 750,000 Palestinians became refugees in 1948.
5 MachsomWatch ibid.: 48–9. The case of a brutal beating and shooting of an unarmed student at Beit Iba is one of the few cases where the IDF has proceeded with investigation and prosecution of the IDF perpetrator. It was concluded that the soldier possessed a 'narcissistic personality disorder and the inability to control violent urges'. MachsomWatch had raised concerns with this soldier's commanding officer on previous occasions, but was ignored.
6 Israel has signed and ratified this convention, with the proviso that the nation does not recognize any external right to investigate incidents within its borders. According to the UN Convention against Torture, torture is defined as:

> Any act by which severe pain or suffering, whether physical or mental, is intentionally inflicted on a person for such purposes as obtaining from him or a third person information or a confession ... when such pain or suffering is inflicted by or at the instigation of or with the consent or acquiescence of a public official or other person acting in an official capacity.
>
> (UN Convention against torture and other cruel, inhuman or degrading treatment or punishment, Part 1, Article 1(1))

7 See also: Public Committee against Torture in Israel (2007) *Ticking bombs: testimonies of torture victims in Israel*, Jerusalem. Online, available at: www.stoptorture.org.il (accessed 13 February 2007).
8 For further insights into IDF actions during the operation, see: Pilger, John (2004) *Palestine is still the issue*, Carlton International Media, DVD; Bakri, Mohamed (2002) *Jenin Jenin*, Arab Film Distribution, DVD; Hass, Amira (2003) *Reporting from Ramallah: an Israeli journalist in an occupied land*, Los Angeles, Semiotext(e); and Raheb, Mitri (2004) *Bethlehem besieged: stories of hope in times of trouble*, Minneapolis: Fortress Press.
9 See also reports by Mohamed Omer at www.ipsnews.org.

References

Al-Haq (2002) 'Death traps: Israel's use of force at checkpoints in the West Bank'. Online, available at: www.asp.alhaq.org/zalhaq/site/templates/1stBooks.aspx?keyword Id=26 (accessed 4 March 2005).

—— (2004) 'Four years since the beginning of the intifada: systematic violations of human rights in the occupied Palestinian territories'. Online, available at: www.alhaq. org (accessed 13 January 2005).

—— (2007) 'Field report April–June 2007'. Online, available at: www.alhaq.org (accessed 21 August 2007).

Balousha, H. and Syal, R. (2009) 'Six children among 12 killed in mosque blast', *Guardian*, 4 January. Online, available at: www.guardian.co.uk/world/2009/jan/04/mosque-blast-gaza/print (accessed 11 January 2009).

Bannoura, S. (2008) 'Israeli Air Force shells the Islamic University in Gaza', *International Middle East Media Center*, 28 December. Online, available at: www.imemc.org/article/58198 (accessed 11 January 2009).

Baroud, R. (ed.) (2003) *Searching Jenin: eyewitness accounts of the Israeli invasion*, Seattle: Cune Press.

Blakeley, R. (2009) *State terrorism and neoliberalism: the North in the South*, London: Routledge.

B'Tselem (2003) 'Soldier testimony: "IDF soldiers are creating the next generation of terrorists"'. Online, available at: www.btselem.org/English/Testimonies/20030801_Soldiers_Testimonies_Witness_D_H.asp (accessed 18 March 2005).

—— (2007) 'Human shields – 8 March 07: Israeli soldiers use two Palestinian minors as human shields'. Online, available at: www.btselem.org/english/Human_Shields/20070225_Human_Shields_in_Nablus.asp (accessed 15 February 2008).

—— (n.d.a) 'Settler violence: handling complaints of settler violence by the judicial system'. Online, available at: www.btselem.org/english/Settler_Violence/Judicial_System.asp (accessed 2 January 2008).

—— (n.d.b) 'House demolitions as punishment'. Online, available at: www.btselem.org/english/Punitive_Demolitions/Statistics.asp (accessed 17 January 2008).

—— (n.d.c) 'Beatings and abuse'. Online, available at: www.btselem.org/english/Beating_and_Abuse/Index.asp (accessed 2 January 2008).

—— (n.d.d) 'Human shields: legal background'. Online, available at: www.btselem.org/english/Human_Shields/legal_background.asp (accessed 15 February 2008).

—— (n.d.e) 'Operation Defensive Shield: soldiers' testimonies: Palestinian testimonies'. Online, available at: www.btselem.org (accessed 15 October 2007).

—— (n.d.f) 'Human shields: timeline of events'. Online, available at: www.btselem.org/english/Human_Shields/Timeline_of_Events.asp (accessed 15 February 2008).

David, S.R. (2003) 'Israel's policy of targeted killing', *Ethics and International Affairs*, 17 (1): 111–90.

Dugard, J. (2007) 'Report of the Special Rapporteur on the situation of human rights in the Palestinian territories occupied since 1967', Office of the High Commissioner of Human Rights. Online, available at: www.ohchr.org/english/bodies/hrcouncil/docs/4session/A.HRC.4.17.pdf (accessed 26 February 2007).

Hamzeh, M. and May, T. (eds) (2003) *Operation Defensive Shield: witnesses to Israeli war crimes*, London: Pluto Press.

Human Rights Watch (1998) 'HRW memorandum to UN Committee against torture'.

Online, available at: www.hrw.org/press98/may/isra0515.htm (accessed 13 February 2008).

—— (2009a) 'Israel: Gaza ground offensive raises laws of war concerns'. Online, available at: www.hrw.org/en/news/2009/01/04/israel-gaza-ground-offensive-raises-laws-war-concerns (accessed 11 January 2009).

—— (2009b) 'Gaza: Israeli attack on school needs full UN investigation', 7 January. Online, available at: www.hrw.org/en/news/2009/01/07/gaza-israeli-attack-school-needs-full-un-investigation?print (accessed 11 January 2009).

—— (2009c) 'Israel: stop unlawful use of white phosphorus in Gaza'. Online, available at: www.hrw.org/en/news/2009/01/10/israel-stop-unlawful-use-white-phosphorus-gaza (accessed 11 January 2009).

Israel Ministry of Foreign Affairs (1999) 'Special powers of interrogation of the general security services – GSS Jan 99'. Online, available at: www.israel-mfa.gov.il/MFA/Government/Law/Legal+Issues+and+Rulings/Special+Powers+of+Interrogation+of+the+General+Sec.htm?DisplayMode=print (accessed 13 February 2008).

Khalidi, W. (ed.) (1971) *From haven to conquest*, Washington, DC: Institute for Palestine Studies.

El-Khodary, T. and Kershner, I. (2009) 'Israeli shells kill 40 near a UN school in Gaza', *International Herald Tribune*, 7 January. Online, available at: www.iht.com/bin/print-friendly.php?id+19141745 (accessed 11 January 2009).

Kimmerling, B. (2003) *Politicide*, London: Verso.

Lein, Y. (2007) 'The torture and ill-treatment of Palestinian detainees'. Online, available at: www.btselem.org (accessed 30 October 2007).

MachsomWatch (2004) 'A counterview: checkpoints 2004'. Online, available at: www.machsomwatch.org (accessed 25 May 2005).

Margalit, M. (2005) 'The truth behind formal statistics'. Online, available at: www.icahd.org (accessed 24 January 2008).

Morris, B. (2004) *The birth of the refugee problem revisited*, Cambridge, UK: Cambridge University Press.

Marchesi, A. (2006) 'Getting around the international prohibition of torture: responsibilities of the Israeli Government and the Palestinian National Authority'. Online, available at: www.unitedagainsttorture.org (accessed 11 November 2007).

Nabulsi, K. (2009) 'Land, sea, sky: all will kill you', *Guardian*, 2 January. Online, available at: www.guardian.co.uk/world/2009/jan/03/israel-palestinians-gaza-attacks/print (accessed 11 January 2009).

Omer, M. (2008) 'Reports February, March'. Online, available at: rafah.virtualactivism.net (accessed 21 May 2008).

Palestine Red Crescent Society (2009) 'Gaza situation updates 09/01/2009 till 10/01/2009 (09:00am)'. Online, available at: www.palestinercs.org/news_details.aspx?nid=101 (accessed 11 January 2009).

Palestinian Centre for Human Rights Gaza (2003) 'Israeli Army kills American woman by bulldozer', Press Release 37/2003. Online, available at: www.pchrgaza.org/files/PressR/English/2003/37–2003.htm (accessed 11 March 2008).

Pappe, I. (2006) *The Ethnic Cleansing of Palestine*, Oxford: One World.

Public Committee against Torture in Israel (2007) 'Ticking bombs: testimonies of torture victims in Israel'. Online, available at: www.stoptorture.org.il (accessed 13 February 2007).

United Nations (1949) *The Fourth Geneva Convention.* Online, available at: www.un.org/

children/conflict/keydocuments/english/thefourthgenevac3.html#c190 (accessed 13 February2008).

—— (1975) *UN Convention against torture and other cruel, inhuman or degrading treatment or punishment.* Online, available at: www.hrweb.org/legal/cat.html (accessed 21 February 2008).

—— (2009a) 'Press conference on humanitarian situation in Gaza', 9 January. Online, available at: www.un.org/News/briefings/docs/2009/090109_Gaza.doc.htm (accessed 11 January 2009).

—— (2009b) 'Statement by the Secretary-General (SG/SM/12040/Rev.1)', 8 January. Online, available at: www.un.org/News/Press/docs/2009/sgsm12040.doc.htm (accessed 11 January 2009).

—— (2009c) 'Ambulances face growing difficulty in reaching Gaza wounded, UN warns', 5 January. Online, available at: www.domino.un.org/unispal.nsf/47d4e277b48 d9d3685256ddc00612265/1e4294ca675fb7018525753500613a64!OpenDocument (accessed 11 January 2009).

Urquhart, C. (2007) 'Israel shaken by troops' tales of brutality against Palestinians', *Guardian*, 21 October. Online, available at: www.guardian.co.uk/world/2007/oct/21p/ israel (accessed 20 February 2008).

5 'We have no orders to save you'

State terrorism, politics and communal violence in the Indian state of Gujarat, 2002

Eamon Murphy

Introduction

In 2002, the state of Gujarat in western India was rocked by ferocious communal violence, during which Hindu mobs embarked on a well-planned, coordinated campaign of state terrorism, directed against defenceless, Muslim women, men and children; more than 2,000 were massacred in a particularly brutal fashion. A particularly horrifying feature of the violence was the systematic sexual assault of women and girls, which included rape and mutilation, often culminating in murder. A great deal of the responsibility for the communal violence can be attributed to the state's ruling Hindu nationalist party, the Bharitya Janata Party (BJP) and its Chief Minister, Narendra Modi, who initiated, encouraged and condoned it. State agencies, including the police and government officials, participated in the violence either directly by attacking Muslims, organizing attacks on Muslim settlements and providing lists of victims to the mobs or, indirectly, by making no attempt to curb the violence.

On the surface at least, Gujarat, a medium-sized state in North West India bordering Pakistan, was a most unlikely candidate to have earned the reputation of being one of India's most notorious centres of communal violence. It is in one of India's most prosperous states, embracing modernity and change. In recent years, the state welcomed economic liberalism and globalization, and promoted strong government and business efficiency. Although it has just 5 per cent of India's total population and 6 per cent of the geographical area, Gujarat contributes 16 per cent of India's total investment, 10 per cent of expenditure, 16 per cent of exports and 30 per cent of stock market capitalization (Gujarat Government 2007). Its long coastline has from very early times linked Gujarat economically and culturally to the outside world. Many of the most successful Indians living in the West, particularly in the United States, have come from the state. The state is agriculturally rich, particularly in cotton, dairy farming, textiles, rice, wheat and tobacco. Gujarat's official website, which features the smiling face of the charismatic chief minister, boasts of Gujarat's dynamic administration, its high annual growth rate of between 10 per cent and 12 per cent, and its position as India's leading industrialized state (Gujarat Government 2007).

The 2002 Gujarat communal violence was different from other outbreaks of Hindu–Muslim rioting that had previously taken place in the state: the extent, intensity and savagery were unique. For the very first time, the violence was both a widespread urban and rural phenomena, spreading from urban centres to towns and villages in the countryside that previously had escaped communal violence. In fact, the violence was a direct consequence of state terrorism. The central question of this chapter, then, is why a rapidly modernizing, economically powerful state experienced some of the worst communal violence that has occurred in India in recent times? Such an analysis explores the complexity of the motivations for and the nature of state terrorism, particularly its relationship to modern electoral politics operating at the local level.

The background: the Godhra fire and the communal violence

The trigger for the state terrorism and the subsequent communal violence that followed between 28 February and mid-June 2002 was a train fire. On 27 February 2002, the Sabarmati express pulled in at Godhra station in the town of Godhra in the western Indian state of Gujarat. The train was packed with Hindu pilgrims, known as *karsevaks*, who were returning from a pilgrimage to the holy city of Ayodhya (Nussbaum 2007a: 17). The pilgrims had been shouting aggressive anti-Muslim slogans when the train had stopped at other stations. The town has a relatively high (40 per cent) population of Muslims and a history of strained relations between the Hindus and Muslims, helping to precipitate the spontaneous violence which broke out at the station (Brass 2004: 3).

While the train was stationary, *karsevaks* bought tea and snacks from platform vendors, many of whom were Muslims. An argument broke out between a *karsevak* and one of the Muslim vendors which led to name-calling and minor altercations between the pilgrims and Muslims on the platform, mainly young tea hawkers (Nussbaum 2007a: 18). The violence rapidly escalated and when the train stopped further down the track, it was attacked by a Muslim mob, hurling stones and other missiles. In the confusion, a fire broke out in one coach and spread to the next, burning alive 58 men, women and children. Police arrived soon after and dispersed the Muslim mob (Nussbaum 2007a: 18). The cause of the fire is still vigorously debated. The Nanavati-Mehta Commission, appointed by the Gujarat government, concluded in 2008 that it was a conspiracy by local Muslims, who set the train alight with petrol (Dasgupta 2008). This finding directly contradicted the conclusions of the Justice Bannerjee Committee, appointed by the Indian government's railway minister, which stated in 2005 that the fire that started inside the train was accidental (Rediff News 2005).

Whatever the truth of the events, the next day saw the beginning of systematic violence when Hindu mobs, supported by state agencies and encouraged by the chief minister, embarked on a campaign of revenge against Muslims throughout the state. In the massacres that followed, around 2,000 innocent men, women and children were murdered in many parts of Gujarat state, many in hideously cruel ways. Both the living and the dead were mutilated. Women and young girls were raped in their homes, farms, factories and by the side of the road. Those killed included a former highly-respected Muslim member of parliament who had worked for communal harmony, Ehsan Jafri. Along with other Muslims who had taken shelter in his housing compound, Jafri was burnt alive. For five hours on the morning of 28 February 2002, the mob attempted to storm the housing compound which was surrounded by a high wall. Jafri had frantically but unsuccessfully attempted to contact the police commissioner, the chief minister's office and politicians. Not only did the police do nothing to stop the attack, but the police inspector in charge at the scene told the mob that they had three to four hours to carry out the killings. Finally, they scaled the high walls and forced their way into the compound, where they butchered all the Muslims they could find. According to one of the participants in the murder of Jafri:

> Five or six people held him, then someone struck him with a sword ... chopped off his hand, then his legs ... then everything else ... after cutting him to pieces, they put him on the wood they'd piled and set it on fire ... burnt him alive.
>
> (*Tehelka* 2008)

One unfortunate man witnessed the rape and murder of seven of his family of 11:

> We ran to nearby Gangotri society and took shelter on the terrace. The mob started burning people at around 5 or 6 o'clock in the evening. The mob stripped all the girls of the locality including my 22-year-old daughter and raped them. My daughter was engaged. Seven members of my family were burnt that includes my wife (age 40), my son (18), my son (14), my son (7), my daughter (4), my daughter (2).
>
> (Human Rights Watch 2007)

The fury that was directed against the Muslims is evident in the statements of those who took part in the massacres. According to one of those involved:

> We hacked, we burnt, did a lot of that ... They shouldn't be allowed to breed. Whoever they are, even if they're women or children, there's nothing to be done with them; cut them down. Thrash them, slash them, burn the bastards.
>
> (*Tehelka* 2008)

Particularly chilling were the many accounts of the sexual violence, rape and sexual torture against women deliberately calculated to terrorize, shame and humiliate both the women and their male relatives. One of the common tactics was to gang rape the woman, then torture her and then burn her to death in front5of other family members, who would themselves be butchered. One of the most common forms of torture was to insert large metal objects into the vagina

(Nussbaum 2007a: 17). One of the mob, who was later imprisoned for his role in the killing of Muslims but was released on bail after spending eight months in jail, bragged to an undercover investigating reporter about one of the most infamous incidents during the 2002 violence in Gujarat: the slitting open of the womb of a pregnant Muslim woman and the pulling out of the foetus and then burning both.

> There was this pregnant woman. I slit her open, sisterf**r, showed them what's what, what kind of revenge we can take if our people are killed. I am not a feeble vegetarian. We didn't spare anyone. They shouldn't even be allowed to breed. I say that even today. Whoever they are – women, children, whoever – nothing to be done to them but cut them down, thrash them, slash them, burn the bastards.
>
> (Tejpal 2007)

Another feature of the riots was the destruction of historic, Islamic buildings, particularly mosques and tombs. According to one source, more than 200 Islamic monuments were destroyed. These included the tomb of the famous, Muslim poet respected by both religions, Vali Gujarati, which was smashed by the Hindu gang who built a small, Hindu temple in its place. State authorities completed the destruction by almost immediately tarring over the site of the desecrated tomb (Harding 2002). The systematic destruction of religious buildings, particularly those of historical and symbolic importance, is a common feature of state terrorism directed against a religious or ethnic minority.

State terrorism and communal violence: the role of the Gujarat's chief minister and government

On the day of the train burning, the BJP Chief Minister of Gujarat Narendra Modi irresponsibly claimed that the fire was deliberately caused by local Muslims, in collaboration with Pakistan's notorious Inter-Services Intelligence Agency (Sud 2008: 1272). Although the train fire provided the trigger for the communal violence, Hindu extremists had been planning violence for some time. Members of the Vishwa Hindu Parisad (World Hindu Council), one of the Hindu nationalist organizations, immediately called for a *bandh* or total shutdown of the state as a protest. At 8 p.m. on the same day, the government issued a press note that endorsed the *bandh*. Modi called a meeting of senior police officials and bureaucrats, instructing the police to take no action against the inevitable violence (Sud 2008: 1272). Government approval of the *bandh* was interpreted both by Hindu nationalist groups and by the police as a signal that the government would not intervene when inevitably the violence broke out.

According to numerous media, civil rights and eyewitness accounts, the mob attacks on the Muslims were carefully planned and coordinated. Two cabinet ministers had on 27 February 2002 met with senior members of Hindu nationalist organizations to coordinate the unleashing of violence against Muslims

(Sud 2008: 1272). On the day after the fire, Hindu mobs began coordinated attacks: attackers arrived in trucks, dressed in saffron robes and khaki shorts, the uniform of Hindu nationalist groups. The mobs were armed with swords and other weapons and explosives, gas cylinders which they used to set alight houses and businesses alike. They also had computer printouts obtained from government officials, listing the addresses of the homes of Muslims and their businesses. The attacks were carefully coordinated through the use of mobile phones. In numerous cases, Muslim businesses were looted and burnt down while neighbouring Hindu businesses were left untouched (Narula 2002).

Many attacks were made close to police stations and in view of the police but no attempts were made to stop the violence. Frantic calls by terrified men, women and children were answered by the police: 'We have no orders to save you' (Narula 2002). In some instances, the police fired on Muslims who attempted to defend themselves. Police officers who tried to control the violence were later disciplined. According to one of many witnesses:

> The police were with them and picked out the Muslim homes and set them on fire. The police aimed and fired at the Muslim boys. They then joined with the Hindus to set fire to the homes and to loot the homes. The police were carrying kerosene bottles and shooting and setting the bottles on fire.
>
> (Narula 2002)

In 2007 the Indian magazine *Tehelka* ran a sensational, feature article about those responsible for the massacre. One of the magazine's reporters had infiltrated a right-wing Hindu organization for six months and secretly videotaped interviews with some of the Hindu militants. According to one interviewee, a BJP member of the Gujarat state assembly from Godhra, the state government gave Hindu right-wing activists three days to act with impunity and to take revenge against all Muslims in the state, who were held collectively responsible for the deaths of the Hindu pilgrims in the Godhra fire. He stated:

> He (Modi) had given us three days to do whatever we could. He said he would not give us time after that. He said this openly. After three days, he asked us to stop, and everything came to a halt. It stopped after three days. Even the army was called in. All the forces came, and we had three days and did what we had to do in those three days.
>
> (Tejpal 2007)

Explaining state terrorism: communalism, politics and Hindu nationalism

A key to understanding state terrorism and the communal violence in Gujarat is an analysis of the growth of right-wing Hindu nationalism, both nationally and in the state, in particular, the recruitment strategies and electoral campaigning of the BJP, the electoral arm of Hindu nationalism. Politics in India, both nationally and in states like Gujarat, had been dominated since independence in 1947 by the Congress Party, which in the early years, at least, was committed to a policy of secularism and Hindu–Muslim unity. Both in India nationally and in Gujarat in particular, however, Congress Party domination of Indian politics was challenged by a new political phenomenon that emerged during the 1980s: the rise of Hindu nationalism, known as the *Hindutva* movement, which was made up of a number of different organizations.[1]

The ideological goal of Hindu nationalism is to build a strong, united and proud Indian nation around the concept of *Hindutva* or Hindu-ness, the political ideology that aims to create the Hindu *Rashtra* or Hindu nation. According to this ideology, to be a patriotic Indian is to be a Hindu, or at least to adhere to Hindu values and to the Hindu way of life. *Hindutva* emphasizes that the central, unifying force in India is the common identity created by the cultural heritage of India's rich, Hindu civilization. Inhabitants of India, such as Muslims and Christians, are therefore viewed as potential traitors because of their alleged loyalty to foreign religions. Muslims, in particular, are regarded as dangerous and subversive because they are the largest single minority in India and because of the suspicion that they are all potential fifth columnists for India's greatest enemy, Islamic Pakistan.[2] These claims ignore the fact that the majority of Muslims in India, including those living in Gujarat, have generally lived peacefully alongside Hindus for many centuries. The vast majority of Gujarat Muslims are loyal citizens who provide no support to Muslim extremists operating in other parts of India or in neighbouring Islamic Pakistan.

Hindutva propaganda emphasizes that the weakness of the Hindu nation has been largely due to oppressive rule of various Muslim dynasties that ruled North India before the advent of British rule. Muslim rule in India is portrayed as a disaster for the Hindu motherland. *Hindutva* literature portrayed Muslim rulers as violent, religious bigots, who destroyed numerous Hindu temples and persecuted the Hindus whom they had conquered. According to one *Hindutva* pamphlet 'Awake, Hindu Brothers': 'When there were kings, the Muslim kings forced our Hindus to convert and then committed atrocities against them. And this will continue to happen till Muslims are exterminated' (Ghista 2006: 53). Historically inaccurate, lurid stories of the cruelties of Muslim rulers, such as the rape of Hindu princesses, appeared in *Hindutva* literature. According to the *Hindutva* view of history, the Muslim invasions ended a golden age of peace and prosperity (Nussbaum 2007a: 212). For the very extreme proponents of *Hindutva* ideology, the choices for Muslims living in India are very clear: convert to Hinduism or migrate to Pakistan or die.

Although the *Hindutva* movement had ideological and organizational roots in the 1920s and 1930s, it gained little widespread support or political influence until the 1990s. Over time, however, *Hindutva* forces were able to achieve rapid, widespread support and electoral successes in some parts of North India, particularly in Gujarat. In order to win popular support among Hindus, organizers of the *Hindutva* movement were able to identify a single issue that was to appeal to national pride of many Indian Hindus and to be translated into organizational and electoral successes, both nationally and throughout many North Indian states. That issue was the campaign to build a great temple, dedicated to the Hindu god Ram at his alleged birthplace in the north Indian town of Ayodhya.

It was alleged by Hindu nationalists that the site of Ram's birthplace lay in the ruins of an ancient Hindu temple destroyed by the Muslim Emperor Babur. *Hindutva* followers demanded, therefore, that the mosque, the Babri Masjid, should be pulled down and a brand-new Hindu temple be erected in its place. From 1990 to 1992, Hindu nationalists embarked on a number of campaigns to publicize the Ayodhya issue, including religious processions from various North Indian states, such as Gujarat to Ayodhya. The political agitations culminated in the destruction of the Babri Masjid by Hindu mobs in 1992. The campaign and destruction of Babri Masjid was to inflame communal hatreds and lead to communal rioting throughout much of North India, including Gujarat. Many of those involved in the destruction of the Babri Masjid had come from Gujarat, where riots broke out in 26 places, killing 99 Muslims (Shah 1998: 245). The intense emotions created by the Ayodhya campaign were harnessed and transferred into electoral success for the BJP, both nationally and most spectacularly in Gujarat.

Strong support for the *Hindutva* movement came from the new, vibrant middle class that had emerged with the economic growth and prosperity that globalization and economic liberalism had brought to Gujarat. For many among the newly middle class, the history of India had been a history of shame because for more than1,000 years, Hindu India had been a conquered state under initially foreign Muslim and later British rule. According to nationalist ideology, for far too long Hindus had been humiliated by foreigners, especially Muslims who in the past had destroyed Hindu culture (Shah 1998: 248). Associated with these feelings of shame, impotence and anger was an irrational fear of meat-eating Muslims, who were seen to be physically and sexually more powerful than effete vegetarian Hindus. It was alleged in anti-Muslim speeches, slogans, pamphlets and speeches at public meetings that because of their alleged, uncontrollable lust, all Muslim men were potential rapists of Hindu women, who needed to be protected by a new, strong and self-confident Hindu community (Anand 2005: 208). The BJP and its allies were therefore skilfully able to exploit this sense of insecurity, low self-esteem and an irrational fear of Muslims. Despite the fact that the Muslims only comprise about 12 per cent of India's population, the BJP was able to successfully portray them as a serious threat to India's security and existence.

Indian Muslims were portrayed in *Hindutva* literature as the Other: fanatical, backward, violent and dirty. They were regarded with mixed feelings of 'fear, fantasy, disgust, anger, envy and hatred' (Anand 2005: 207). The Hindu, nationalist agenda was to demonstrate that a Hindu India and a strong Gujarat, governed by the BJP, would be the only force to have the strength, determination and the power to defeat the descendents of foreigners, who had dominated India for so very long. The violence against Muslims that followed the Godhra train fire was, therefore, a 'slap in the face', a humiliating warning to Muslims that if they wished to stay in India and be accepted as citizens, they should demonstrate that they were loyal and patriotic (Ray 2007: 96). The hate literature also stereo-typed Muslim men and women as oversexed and hyper-fertile and who, if allowed to breed indiscriminately, would eventually outnumber the Hindus in their own country. This crude and inaccurate depiction of sexual excesses of Muslims provided the justification for the widespread, sexual violence committed against what were considered to be highly sexed, Muslim women. The pornographic, hate literature claimed that Muslim women enjoyed uncircumcised, Hindu penises yet the rapists also demanded that the women and their children be killed to prevent them from reproducing (Nussbaum 2007b: 114). This potent cocktail of lust, fear and hate in part explains the ferocity of the sexual violence.

Explaining state terrorism: caste, religion and electoral politics

The second key to understanding state terrorism and communal violence in Gujarat is more mundane: an analysis of caste and religion and their role in electoral politics in the state. Understanding the highly complex relationship between castes and religious communities in Gujarat and how this relationship has affected politics is crucial for explaining both the nature of Gujarati state terrorism and the savagery of the communal violence.

The most simple and most clear communal division within Gujarati society is religious. About 90 per cent of the population can be very crudely grouped under the heading of Hindu.[3] As in other parts of India, the caste system in Gujarat is extremely complicated. The so-called Hindu caste groups can be categorized under four broad headings. First, there is a numerically small group of higher and middle castes – about 25 per cent of the population – who traditionally controlled land, the professions, education, dominated the bureaucracy and business and who until recently had traditionally held political power in Gujarat. Second, there is a numerically much larger group – about 43 per cent – of so-called backward or lower castes who are mainly small landowners, sharecroppers, artisans and labourers. The third group are the so-called Untouchables, now more generally known as *Dalits* (the Oppressed) or *Harijans* ('children of God') – about 7 per cent. Traditionally *Dalits* have been the poorest, most disadvantaged within Hindu society. Most work as poor farmers, landless rural workers and urban labourers and often perform ritually polluting tasks, such as disposing of dead animals and cleaning latrines. Finally the term *Adivasis* ('aboriginal inhabitants') refers to the tribal peoples who previously lived in remote areas away from settlements, who are about 14 per cent. Many *Adivasis* have been absorbed into the mainstream society at the very bottom of the caste system, being regarded as *Dalits* and also being discriminated against. Like the *Dalits*, the majority of *Adivasis* live in poverty, either in their own settlements or in slums in urban centres.[4]

To some extent, these broad caste categories parallel class divisions in Gujarati society. In general, the higher castes are economically much better off, better educated and, until recently, dominated politics. The *Dalits* and *Adivasis*, on the other hand, are generally the lowest economically, ritually and socially. This class division is reinforced by the hierarchical and religious basis of the caste system, with its concept of pollution and purity. Although Untouchability is forbidden under the Indian constitution, *Dalits* and *Adivasis*, in particular, are still regarded as highly polluting and often are excluded from using village wells, entering the temples of the high castes or even, in some instances, being allowed to walk through the village. Physical violence, including killing, raping and humiliation, has for generations been used against the lowest castes and *Dalits* by members of higher castes in order to maintain their political, economic and social dominance (Human Rights Watch 2007).

The largest religious minority in Gujarat are Muslims, comprising about 9 per cent of the population. Most of the Muslims in Gujarat are descendents mainly from low caste and untouchable converts, particularly from lower caste groups, *Dalits* and *Adivasis*, who were converted to Islam by Muslim mystics, particularly the Sufis (Muslim mystics). As in other parts of India, most Muslims are extremely poor, often living in urban slums alongside low-caste Hindus or *Dalits*. In most respects, the economic and social positions of most Muslims are very similar to that of the *Dalits* (*Islamic Workplace* 2006). Gujarat had experienced communal rioting in some urban and rural centres but until the 2002 riots, Muslims generally had lived peacefully with their Hindu neighbours, especially in rural areas.

Although the majority of Muslims in Gujarat, as elsewhere in India, are impoverished, there is a small but important class of merchants, businesspeople shopkeepers and moneylenders. Because in many villages and small towns, Muslims own businesses and are moneylenders, they are often resented by poorer peasants, who are forced to pay exorbitantly high interest on their loans for buying seeds, paying their daughters' dowries and meeting everyday expenses. Higher caste and class Hindu nationalist activists and politicians were consequently able to exploit this economic resentment, both in initiating communal violence and later translating this into electoral support (Jaffrelot 2003: 7). Many of the villages involved in the rioting were located in the eastern tribal zone of the state. Similar to the lower castes and *Dalits*, many tribals resented the Muslim economic elite and with the breakdown of law and order, they also took the opportunity to loot Muslim shops and other businesses, as well as killing and raping their hated oppressors and their families (Jaffrelot 2003: 8). Many involved in the looting, raping and killing were unemployed youth or criminals, who also opportunistically took advantage of the breakdown of law and order. A feature of the communal violence in both urban and rural areas is that the state terrorism was planned, organized and instigated by the higher-caste Hindu activists but the worst cases of violence were perpetuated by the lower castes, *Dalits* and *Adivasis*, against their Muslim neighbours.

Although resentment against Muslim businessmen and moneylenders can help explain some of the violence, such an explanation by itself is inadequate to explain why Gujarat became the place where state terrorism led to one of the most horrific cases of communal slaughter in modern Indian history. Gujarat was relatively quiet during the widespread, largely spontaneous communal violence that affected much of northern India during the 1947 partition of the Indian sub-continent into India and Pakistan. It is the home state of the apostle of nonvio-lence in India, Mahatma Gandhi, who strongly preached Hindu–Muslim unity. Many of Gujarat's upper castes have a strong commitment to vegetarianism, non-violence and to the prohibition of alcohol. Although there were outbreaks of communal violence before 2002, these were largely confined to a few large cities and rural centres. In the 1980s and 1990s, however, there had been a build-up of communal violence in Gujarat, initially directed against low castes and *Dalits* and later against Muslims, which was a direct consequence of political develop-ments within the state (Shah 1998: 246).

Caste, community and state terrorism

In order to fully understand why the BJP needed to use state terrorism against Muslims, it is necessary to discuss and analyse how the BJP and its Hindu nationalist allies were able to win over the support of the lower castes, *Dalits* and *Adivasis*, who previously had supported the rival secular Congress party in the state and how this successful mobilization was later translated into spectacu-lar electoral success for the party. Higher-caste dominance of society and pol-itics in Gujarat, as elsewhere in India, had been challenged with the introduction of democratic politics, the principle of adult suffrage introduced with independ-ence in 1947. Voting rights to all Indians had given great electoral power to the numerically larger lower castes, *Dalits, Adivasis* and Muslims. From around 1969, Gujarati politics had been dominated by the Congress Party, at the national level led by Indira Gandhi, which had built a mass-based party in Gujarat, com-mitted to social justice and abolishing poverty. The Congress party success was based on a coalition made up predominantly of the lowest class and caste groups, comprising *Hindu Kshatriyas* (mainly lower castes), *Harijans, Adivasis* and Muslims and called KHAM after the initials of the members of the coalition. Comprising between 70 per cent and 75 per cent of Gujarat's population (Sud 2008: 1262), this vote bloc enabled Congress to dominate electoral politics and thus threaten the political, economic and social dominance of Gujarat's upper castes. In 1980, the KHAM alliance won 141 out of the 182 assembly seats and in 1985, increased its majority, winning 149 seats (Subrahmaniam 2007). As one journalist succinctly put it, 'KHAM brought the depressed, marginalised classes on one platform and delivered stunning results for the Gujarat Congress' (Sub-rahmaniam 2007).

The loss of political power posed a major threat to higher caste dominance of Gujarat. The decision that had particularly alarmed and angered the higher castes was the decision by the Congress-led state government to implement a positive discrimination policy, which legislated that 21 per cent of government jobs, places in education institutions and appointments to government jobs be reserved for *Dalits*. Another 28 per cent were to be set aside for other backward or lower castes (Sud 2008: 1261). Attempts to implement this legislation in Gujarat resulted in violent protests in 1981 and 1985 by upper caste *Brahmins, Banias* and *Patidars*. Hindu nationalists, including members of the BJP, were involved in initiating violence against both *Dalits* and Muslims during the riots. For instance in the 1985 riots, 210 *Dalits* and Muslims were killed by upper-caste protestors, which is ironic given that *Dalits* were among the forefront in the killings of 17 Muslims later in the 2002 riots (Sud 2008: 1262).

By the 1990s, the extensive organizational activities of the Hindu nationalists had begun to pay off, with the BJP winning strong support among upper and middle castes, including government bureaucrats and the police. This organizational campaigning had initially some success in local elections and Gujarat was to emerge as the strongest state in India to support the BJP during the 1980s and 1990s. Eventually the BJP became the major party in the political coalition that ruled Gujarat state in 1995. In 1996, the party controlled the central government. The electoral successes in Gujarat were in large part built upon the fact that the Hindu nationalists were very well organized at a grassroots level. Hindu nationalists, working through the media, local organizations, propaganda and education, were able to take the *Hindutva* message, emphasizing pride in being Hindu and the unity of all Hindus including, for the first time, to large numbers of *Dalits* and *Adivasis*.

Bringing the *Dalits* and *Adivasis* into the Hindu fold was a novel development. The major problem that the Hindu nationalists had faced initially in their attempts to unify all Hindus was that Hinduism does not have a common set of religious beliefs or practices. What is known as Hinduism in the West is higher caste *Brahminical Hinduism* which emphasizes worship of one of the great two Indian gods, *Vishnu* or *Shiva*, holds the ancient religious texts, *Vedas*, as most sacred and encourages worship in large *Brahminical* temples. The lower castes, the *Dalits* and *Adivasis*, have their own gods, beliefs and practices. In fact, many upper castes, and indeed many of the *Dalits* themselves, do not regard *Dalits* as Hindus – and the tribal *Adivasis* even less so. The Hindu nationalists thus embarked on a novel policy of constructing a new Hindu identity that would include the lower castes, *Dalits* and *Adivasis*, who previously had been excluded from higher caste *Brahminical Hinduism*.

Putting it simply, a new inclusive form of Hinduism was constructed that included the elite, highest Hindu castes and the lowest *Adivasis*. For the first time in history, *Dalits* in large numbers were invited to attend Hindu religious programmes, such as chariot processions of Hindu gods. Hindu nationalist activists distributed idols of the two very popular, Indian gods, *Ganesh* and *Ram*, throughout tribal areas (Subrahmaniam 2007). Members of the youth wing of the *Hindutva* movement, the *Bajang Dal*, were asked to dedicate themselves to the abolition of untouchability and to work for the social, economic and educational uplift of their Hindu brothers. Social work, such as the building of schools, was carried out by activists among *Adivasis*, including those living in remote, isolated areas, and the education they provided emphasized the beliefs and values of *Brahminical Hinduism*. For instance *Hindutva* activists distributed food grains, medicine and clothing in tribal areas during times of emergency, such as the 1985–86 drought (Shah 1998: 255). *Hindutva* forces were particular success-ful in winning support in the *Adivasis* areas of central and east Gujarat by por-traying the tribal culture as inferior and offering the *Adivasis* incorporation into what they regarded as a superior, higher religion and culture (Subrahmaniam 2007). *Dalits* and tribals were given leadership positions at the lower levels in *Hindutva* organizations, thus enhancing their self-respect and sense of accept-ance by the upper castes (Shah 1998: 257). The winning over the allegiance of the lower castes, *Dalits* and *Adivasis*, who previously had been such staunch supporters of Congress, was to be the key factor in the electoral successes of BJP in 2002.

Crucial for the construction of a new Hindu identity was the projection of Muslims as a common enemy of all. All Muslims were tarnished with the label of being fundamentalist, anti-national and pro-Pakistan. Hindu nationalists managed to persuade many low castes, *Dalits* and *Adivasis*, that as Hindus and proud citizens of their country, their real enemies were their previous electoral allies: Muslims (Kumar 2002). However, this unity was fragile as many back-ward castes, *Dalits* and *Adivasis*, still resented higher-caste dominance of the top leadership positions in *Hindutva* organizations, as well as what was perceived as the arrogance of the higher castes who, despite the rhetoric of equality, deep down were still contemptuous of those below them in the hierarchy of caste. The Muslims therefore served as a very necessary 'Other' whose existence would unite all Hindus through fear and hate of the common enemy. As backward caste university lecturer and journalist Kancha Ilaiah succinctly put it, the Hindu nationalists successfully created a 'deliberately constructed enemy – Muslims' (Ilaiah 2002). Despite *Dalits*, tribals and Muslims facing similar economic prob-lems, exploitation and marginalization, the BJP had, by making the Muslims the real enemy, destroyed the class alliance that had previously existed among the oppressed communities (Kumar 2002).

State terrorism: the payoff at elections

The *Hindutva* electoral strategy worked brilliantly. In December 2002, Modi and the BJP were returned to power with a landslide victory in Gujarat state assem-bly elections, the best result for any BJP state party (Anand 2005: 21). During the 2002 electoral campaign, the use of anti-Muslim riots and anti-Muslim prop-aganda by the chief minister and his supporters proved to be a highly successful political tactic. The BJP had helped provoke a number of anti-Muslim riots prior to the election, which were to culminate in the 2002 violence, which polarized Gujarati society between Hindus and Muslims (Jaffrelot 2003: 8). In September shortly before the elections, the chief minister made a highly successful tour of the state, symbolically commencing at a very important Hindu temple. During his tour, Modi made many anti-Muslim references, such as the claim that Muslim polygamy and alleged high rates of fertility would, if not stopped, make Hindus a vulnerable minority in their own country (Jaffrelot 2003: 8). Muslims were portrayed as polygamous, disloyal and traitorous supporters of global

Islamic terrorism (Chakravartty and Lankala 2007: 187), a task made easier by the worldwide anti-terrorist hysteria following the events of 11 September 2001. A vote for the BJP, therefore, would demonstrate to Pakistan and its alleged fellow traitorous, subversive Muslims living in Gujarat that terrorism would be resisted at all costs. Huge pictures of the Pakistan President General Musharraf were displayed throughout Gujarat, with the inference that a vote for the rival Congress party would be a vote for Musharraf (Chakravartty and Lankala 2007: 189).

The strategy of playing upon anti-Muslim sentiment was therefore highly successful in the 2002 state elections, with the BJP having an unexpected huge victory, winning 125 out of 182 total seats. The result stunned many commentators, as the BJP had been expected to lose many of the seats it had won during the previous election in 1998 (*socialistworld.net* 2002: 1). The success was even more remarkable as the BJP, both nationally and in other states, had been losing votes, in part because the anti-Muslim message of the BJP had been losing appeal to an electorate concerned with more mundane issues, such as the cost of foodstuffs, corruption and good government. The Gujarat results, therefore, reversed that trend and were hailed as a major victory for the party. The large vote from *Dalits* and *Adivasis* – a combined total of about 22 per cent of the population – made an important contribution to the sweeping victory. In the 2002 elections, for the first time ever, the BJP won massive support among the tribal population, who comprised about 14 per cent of the state's population. There was a particularly high vote for the BJP, where the rioting and violence had been worst (Majumder 2002), with the largest swings to the BJP also in the 2002 elections in areas that were most strongly affected by the rioting (Wilkinson 2005: 154).

Interestingly in the 2007 Gujarat state elections, the BJP electoral campaign was based around Gujarat's spectacular economic development, the effectiveness of the state's administration and on the personal character of Modi rather than on communal issues (Subrahmaniam 2007). While there was an undercurrent threat of further state terrorism, the election instead revolved around the achievements and character of the chief minister, who was portrayed as dynamic, hard-working, shrewd and largely responsible for the state's spectacular economic growth of 11 per cent (Subrahmaniam 2007).

In the 2007 elections, no mention was made either by the BJP or by the Congress Party of the 2002 communal violence. Muslims were not mentioned: they were simply ignored because they were no longer either a threat electorally or a means by which the BJP could win votes through making them scapegoats (Subrahmaniam 2007). The reason for switching tactics appears to some extent to be the revulsion, both in India and overseas, at the 2002 violence, including criticism from more moderate members of the BJP national leadership. Modi had been denied entry to the United States in 2005, apparently because he was held responsible, at least to some extent, for the 2002 communal violence (*Times of India* 2005). The feeling among big business, which strongly supported the BJP in Gujarat, was that communal peace was good for business and for the state.

The key factor, however, was the poor showing of the BJP in the 2004 Indian national elections that had demonstrated that economic issues, such as the cost of foodstuffs, were becoming more important than the question of communal differences and the threat of Islam (Subrahmaniam 2007). In fact, in 2007, Modi paid tribute to successful Muslim businessmen for their contribution to the state's economic growth (*Communalism Watch* 2007). It was also ironic that Modi was criticized by the more extremist members of the *Hindutva* movement for focusing solely on economic development and ignoring the Muslim enemy (Bosmia 2007).

Perhaps the best comment on Modi and his party's use of state terrorism as a political strategy came from a Muslim, small businessman whose business had been burnt down during the 2002 riots. He not only voted for the BJP in the 2007 election but also joined the party. When asked to explain these astonishing decisions, he stated that while Modi had used communalism at election times to win votes, he was a highly efficient administrator and the BJP government was very good for business (Bhatt 2008: 1). Such a comment, of course, would have little comfort for the thousands of Muslim families displaced by the 2002 riots and still living in wretched refugee camps across the state, mourning the loss of loved ones and constantly fearing that they would again be scapegoated.

Conclusion

A description and analysis of the state-sponsored violence in Gujarat is a fascinating, if chilling, exploration of how state terrorism was used to further political goals in a highly complex society. It is extremely difficult for an outsider to fully comprehend the complexity of caste and communal politics in an Indian state such as Gujarat, yet the fundamental motivation for the use of state terrorism and the consequent communal violence was universal and quite simple: the quest for political power. The Gujarat case study of state and religious terrorism, therefore, provides ample empirical evidence to support Richard Jackson's claim that 'most terrorism occurs in the context of wider political struggles' (2007: 248).

The central argument of this chapter, therefore, is that the main motivation for the state terrorism initiated by the Gujarat state government was political: to win the electoral support of the majority of non-Muslims in Gujarat by sending a clear message to Hindu voters that the BJP was the only political party with the determination to combat the alleged threat of Islam, both from within the state and from the neighbouring Islamic state of Pakistan. That such a threat was nonsense was beside the point, so far as the BJP were concerned: the strategy worked brilliantly, bringing unexpected, spectacular electoral success to the party. The state terrorism also sent a very clear warning to Muslims of the consequences of opposing the state, either through the use of their votes or through violence. If they wished to live and work in Gujarat – and some of the more extremist Hindu nationalists claimed that they had forfeited even this right – then they had better conform and demonstrate that they were loyal citizens, who accepted the values of the Hindu majority as was upheld, of course, by the BJP and its allies. The memory of the past violence along with the ever-present, underlying threat of further violence, or even expulsion altogether from the state, ensured Muslim compliance.

When one analyses how the BJP state government used state terrorism so successfully, one can very usefully draw upon the insights of critical terrorism studies commentators who view 'terrorism fundamentally as a strategy or tactic of political violence that can be, and frequently is, employed by both state and nonstate actors and during times of war and peace' (Jackson 2007: 248). This case study of Gujarati state terrorism explains how the Hindu elite, who controlled the BJP party, were able to manipulate religious differences to divide political opponents, previously united by class and social interests. By using state terrorism to demonize Muslims in Gujarat, the BJP was able to create an unlikely, fragile alliance made up of very divergent class, economic and social groups, ranging from the highest, wealthy and powerful castes to the very poorest and lowest of *Dalits* and *Adivasis*, thus ensuring the party's long-term political control of the state. An added bonus was that the terrorization of the Muslim minority ensured that Muslim votes would no longer electorally, even in a minor way, ever again threaten the power of the BJP.

The Gujarat example also strongly supports Marie Breen Smyth's claim that critical terrorism studies 'must be contextualized in an analysis of power relations at a local and global level' (Smyth 2007: 263). Without understanding the competition for power at the local level, an explanation for the state terrorism, communal violence and the successes of the BJP in the 2002 elections would be inadequate. The power relations at the local level were certainly highly complex, involving factional, ideological, class, caste and religious elements, but Gujarat government state terrorism was highly successful in making religious differences become the single, all-powerful major factor, at least for the 2002 elections. As a consequence the BJP, for the very first time, was able to win widespread support from both the highest and lowest Hindu castes. The BJP was successful, therefore, because it won the hearts, minds and souls of the majority of Hindus at the local level, initially in urban centres and later in rural centres including, for the first time, the tribal belt. Simply put, the use of state terrorism was a highly effective strategy by the BJP for winning elections in Gujarat through fomenting communal differences and violence at the local level in order to wrestle control away from other political parties, particularly its major rival, the now-impotent Congress party.

Writing this chapter in the peace and security of my office in Western Australia, I can only imagine the terror, pain and anguish that the innocent victims of state terrorism in Gujarat must have suffered. The importance of such case studies of state terrorism lies not just in a contribution to academic debate on the nature of state terrorism, but in enabling us to understand more fully how politicians in the quest for political power can initiate, encourage and condone horrible abuses of fundamental human rights.

Notes

1 The Sangh Parivar or 'family' of Hindu right-wing organizations include the militant Rashtriya Swayamsevak Sangh (the National Volunteer' Organization), the Vishva Hindu Parishad (World Hindu Council), the youth wing of the Vishva Hindu Parishad, the Bajrang Dal and the Sangh Parivar's electoral and the political party, the Bharatiya Janata Party (the Indian People's Party.)
2 There is a vast literature on the *Hindutva* movement. An excellent concise introduction is Basu (1993). A more detailed study is Jaffrelot (1996). For *Hindutva* ideology, see Jaffrelot (2005).
3 The caste and religious statistics are based on the 1971 census (see Kohli 1991: 241).
4 This, of course, of necessity is a very simplified analysis of a very complex issue. The nature of Hinduism and the caste system is a matter for great debate among academics.

References

Anand, D. (2005) 'The Violence of Security: Hindu Nationalism and the Politics of Representing "the Muslim" as a Danger', *Round Table*, 94 (379): 203–15. Online, available at: www.staff.bath.ac.uk/ecsda/DAnandRTArticle.pdf (accessed 19 November 2008).

'Asghar Ali Engineer on Gujarat elections 2007 and after' (2007) *Communalism Watch*, 30 December. Online, available at: www.communalism.blogspot.com/2007/12/asghar-ali-engineer-on-gujarat.html (accessed 19 November 2008).

Basu, T., Pradip Datta, Sumit Sarkar, Tanika Sarkar and Sambuddha Sen (eds) (1993) *Khaki Shorts, Saffron Flags: A Critique of the Hindu Right*. Delhi: Orient Longman.

Bhatt, S. (2008) 'Why Mohammad Shafi Mansuri will Vote for Modi', *Rediff News*. Online, available at: www.in.rediff.com/news/2007/Dec/15gujpoll.htm (accessed 11 November 2008).

Bosmia, A.J. (2007) 'Why Modi will Score a Landslide Win Again', *Rediff News*. 7 December 2007. Online, available at: www.rediff.com/news/2007/dec/07guest1.htm?zcc=rl (accessed 19 November 2008).

Brass, P. (2004) 'The Gujarat Pogrom of 2002', *Social Science Research Council*, 26 May. Online, available at: www.conconflicts.ssrc.org/archives/gujarat/brass (accessed 11 November 2008).

Chakravartty, P. and Lankala, S. (2007) 'Media, Terror, and Islam: The Shifting Media Landscape and Culture Talk in India', in Amitra Basu and Srirupa Roy (eds) *Violence and Democracy in India*, Calcutta, London and New York: Seagull Books.

'Communalists Profit from Hate' (2002) *socialistworld.net*, 31 December. Online, available at: www.socialistworld.net/eng/2002/12/31gujarat.html (accessed 19 November 2008).

Dasgupta, M. (2008) 'Mob of Muslims Attacked Train, says Nanavati Commission', *Hindu*. Online, available at: www.hindu.com/2008/09/26/stories/2008092657571400.htm (accessed 19 November 2008).

Ghista, G. (2006) *The Gujarat Genocide: A Case Study in Fundamentalist Cleansing*, Bloomington: AuthorHouse.

'Godhra Train Fire Accidental: Report' (2005) *Rediff News*, 17 January. Online, available at: www.rediff.com/news/2005/jan/17godhra.htm (accessed 19 November 2008).

'Gujarat 2002: The Truth – The Truth about Gujarat 2002 in the Words of the Men who Did it' (2008) *Tehelka*, 31 October. Online, available at: www.tehelka.com/story_main35.asp?filename=Ne031107Press_release.asp (accessed 19 November 2008).

Gujarat Government (2007) *Gujarat Official Portal of Gujarat Government: Business*

Investment Opportunities. Online, available at: www.gujaratindia.com/business/business1.htm (accessed 5 January 2009).

Harding, L. (2002) 'Gujarat's Muslim heritage smashed in riots', *Guardian*, 29 June. Online, available at: www.guardian.co.uk/world/2002/jun/29/india.arts (accessed 19 November 2008).

Human Rights Watch (2007) 'Summary List of the Critical Issues Pertaining to India's Periodic Report to the Committee on the Elimination of Racial Discrimination', Human Rights Watch. Online, available at: www.hrw.org/reports/2007/india0207/2.htm#_Toc158704441 (accessed 11 November 2008).

Ilaiah, K. (2002) 'The Rise of Modi', *Hindu*, 26 December. Online, available at: www.hinduonnet.com/2002/12/26/stories/2002122600461000.htm (accessed 19 November 2008).

Jackson, R. (2007) 'The Core Commitments of Critical Terrorism Studies', *European Political Science*, 6: 244–51.

Jaffrelot, C. (1996) *The Hindu Nationalist Movement in India*, New York: Columbia University Press.

—— (2003) ''Communal Riots in Gujarat: The State at Risk?' *Heidelberg Papers in South Asian and Comparative Politics*, 17: 1–20.

—— (ed.) (2005) *The Sangh Parivar: A Reader*, New Delhi: Oxford University Press.

Kohli, A. (1991) *Democracy and Discontent: India's Growing Crisis of Governability*, Cambridge, UK: Cambridge University Press.

Kumar, D. (2002) 'Poisoned Edge: The Sangh Exploits Dalit and Tribal Frustration to Recruit Soldiers for Hindutva's "War"', *Coalition against Communalism*, June 24. Online, available at: www.cac.ektaonline.org/updates/2002_06_23_archive.htm (accessed 19 November 2008).

Majumder, S. (2002) 'Gujarat: BJP's "Testing Ground"', *BBC News Online*, 15 December. Online, available at: www.news.bbc.co.uk/2/hi/south_asia/2578185.stm (accessed 29 December 2008).

'Marginalization of Muslim Minority in India' (2006) *Islamic Workplace.* 29 December. Online, available at: www.makkah.wordpress.com/2006/12/29/marginalization-of-muslim-minority-in-india (accessed 19 November 2008).

Narula, S. (2002) ''"We Have No Orders To Save You": State Participation and Complicity in Communal Violence in Gujarat', *Human Rights Watch*, 14 (3). Online, available at: www.hwr.org/reports/2002/india (accessed 19 November 2008).

'No Entry for Modi into US: Visa Denied' (2005) *Times of India*, 18 March. Online, available at: www.timesofindia.indiatimes.com/articleshow/1055543.cms (accessed 19 November 2008).

Nussbaum M.C. (2007a) *The Clash Within: Democracy, Religious Violence, and India's Future*, Cambridge, MA: Harvard University Press.

—— (2007b) 'Raped and Murdered in Gujarat: Violence against Muslim Women in the Struggle for Hindu Supremacy', in Amitra Basu and Srirupa Roy (eds) *Violence and Democracy in India*, Calcutta, London and New York: Seagull Books.

Ray, R. (2007) 'A Slap from the Hindu Nation', in Amitra Basu and Srirupa Roy (eds) *Violence and Democracy in India*, Calcutta, London and New York: Seagull Books.

Shah, G. (1998) 'The BJP's Riddle in Gujarat: Caste, Factionalism and Hindutva' in Thomas Blom Hansen and Christophe Jaffrelot (eds) *The BJP and the Compulsions of Politics in India*, Delhi: Oxford University Press.

Smyth, M.B. (2007) 'A Critical Research Agenda for the Study of Political Terror', *European Political Science*, 6: 260–7.

Subrahmaniam, V. (2007) 'The Muslim Question in Gujarat', *Hindu*. 9 October. Online, available at: www.hindu.com/2007/10/09/stories/200710095623800.htm (accessed 11 November 2008).

Sud, N. (2008) 'Secularism and the Gujarat State: 1960–2005', *Modern Asian Studies*, 42 (6): 1251–81.

Tejpal, T. (interviewed by Amy Goodman) (2007) 'Explosive Report by Indian Magazine Exposes Those Responsible for 2002 Gujarat Massacre', *Democracy Now!*, 5 December. Online, available at: www.democracynow.org/2007/12/5/explosive_report_by_indian_magazine_exposes (accessed 19 November 2008).

Wilkinson, S.I. (2005) 'Elections in India: Behind the Congress Comeback', *Journal of Democracy*, 16 (1). Online, available at: www.muse.jhu.edu/journals/journal_of_democracy/v016/16.1wilkinson.html (accessed 19 November 2008).

6 The politics of convenient silence in southern Africa

Relocating the terrorism of the state

Joan Wardrop

> This story is not just about the past, but about how the past affects the present.
>
> (Catholic Commission 1999: 8)

> It is possible, of course, to take the position that all wars necessarily involve violence and horror and guerrilla wars more than most, as regimes strike at civilian populations and guerrillas search for 'sell-outs'. But a number of conference participants urged that beyond this inevitable violence there was a need to look at terror – the purposive but illegitimate violence deployed in various ways by both sides in the war. There was a need to look at Rhodesian poisonings, mass graves and public displays of bodies; at guerrilla killings of 'witches' and refusals to allow the dead to be buried. If we did not remember such instances of terror, it was argued, there was a danger that illegitimate violence might survive as one of the legacies of the war.
>
> (Bhebe and Ranger 1995: 21)

In this chapter, I suggest that postcolonial Zimbabwe is frozen in a condition of continuous state terror, a condition nurtured in the terror imposed by the colonial state through the violence of dispossession and the (re)creation of its indigenous inhabitants as illegitimate, and nourished by a postcolonial elite determined on the maintenance of its position and power. I show that the present difficulties in Zimbabwe do not stand isolated from the past, rather they can only be deciphered by repositioning them in a violent history, a collective memory of invasion, betrayal, and suffering in which terror from above is naturalized as both political technique and cultural practice. Collective memory of violence, vulnerability and fear as a way of life for Zimbabweans is accretive, nurtured through the telling and retelling of private stories (Green 1994; Halbwachs 1992), yet silenced and denied public expression. Terror is remembered and internalized generation after generation, incorporated as integral to the sinews of social life (Ricoeur 2004: 123), its quiet narratives an essential condition for the repeated acts of state terror deployed by successive Rhodesian/Zimbabwean regimes. Private memories of past terror make possible the terror of the present. I further suggest that the examples of memories recuperated and reshaped into public narratives through truth (and reconciliation) commissions, such as in South Africa, or through the more

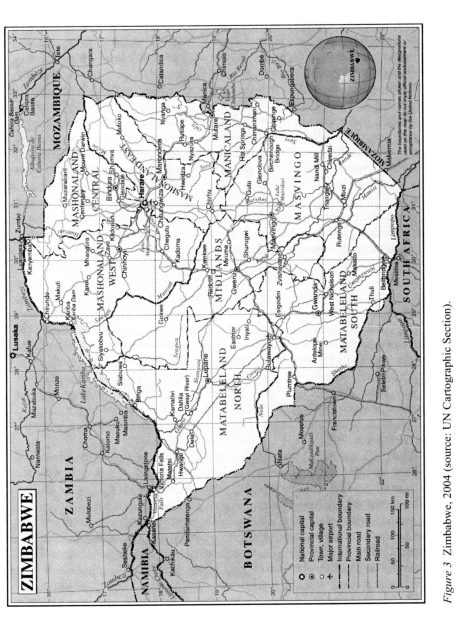

Figure 3 Zimbabwe, 2004 (source: UN Cartographic Section).

localized story-telling of the *gacaca* in Rwandan villages demonstrate the power (if not absolute) of memory and narrative exercised in public spaces in healing the terrorized; a power which, despite the efforts of NGOs and church organizations, has not yet been felt in Zimbabwe. In this, Zimbabweans continue to suffer the effects of rupture with their past (Werbner 1998: 15).

Zimbabweans have lived in a condition of profound social suffering, a shared collective experience of the world (Kleinman *et al.* 1997) in which their voices are unheard, their pain is silenced, the violence against them so horrendous that its meanings become elusive and susceptible to our perception only through an unfathomable distance (Das 1997; Cavell 1997). In Henri Raczymow's evocative phrase, their collective understanding of the past, their collective memory, is 'shot through with holes' (1994), 'but as time elapses, the mind accepts some terrible things and forgets others' (Elizabeth Ndebele in Staunton 1991: 192).

In asking why it is that this state has chosen instrumental and seemingly arbitrary terror as a long-term political strategy, and what its enabling conditions have been, I focus on a series of memory snapshots, exemplary of convenient historical silences, beginning with the Matabeleland massacres of the 1980s (Catholic Commission 1999) as tactical deployment of the power of the state to eliminate potential opponents and create a state of terror in others; as iconic representation of continuities with the culture of violence of the colonial project which preceded them and with the enthusiasm with which the first Independence government adopted those practices of state terror. Different choices would have been possible but these emblematic moments peculiarly demonstrated the continuing power of state terror and its effects, from the colonial period of coercive domination to the current impossibility of political community in Zimbabwe, to the development of what Stephen Chan has called 'unreconciled citizenship' (2005) and of vulnerability and deprivation as practices and conditions of everyday life. In writing back to the past, I draw substantially on the ethnographic and historical research of others, without whose persistence in a difficult and troubling field, my own interrogation of the relationships between memory, silencing and the terror of the state would not be possible.

When, in mid-2008, I originally drafted this interrogation of the cultures of violence that pervade early twenty-first-century Zimbabwe, I thought to begin with the devastation resulting from Operation Murambatsvina ('Restore Order') which Robert Mugabe's government imposed in May 2005. Right at the onset of the southern hemisphere winter, the security forces targeted first street vendors, then informal and formal settlements, destroying stalls, shacks, houses and other property, much of it located in so-called 'opposition' areas. In less than six weeks, by the government's own figures, nearly 600,000 people had been made homeless and nearly 100,000 had lost their livelihoods (cited in United Nations 2005). Its actions were vociferously condemned regionally and internationally by governments which found no means to act to prevent this wholesale devastation of the lives of ordinary people. But events overtook me, and now as I write I do so surrounded by reports of the horrors of a massive cholera epidemic, of dying people being carried across the border with South Africa, of hundreds dying in urban, high-density areas, of unknown numbers of people dying unnoticed and unregistered in rural areas (World Health Organization 2008). The epidemic is a pathological symptom of the decade-long implosion of the Zimbabwean state, its immediate cause the recent collapse of previously efficient water supply and sanitation services, exacerbated by widespread food shortages, malnutrition, hyperinflation, 80 per cent unemployment, ongoing political crisis and increasing levels of public unrest by soldiers and police. More than the carelessness and incompetence of a state spiralling out of control, the current situation enacts the Mugabe government's intention to continue to discipline and control an increasingly unruly population, seeking to impose conditions which force the majority of the population to focus almost entirely on the barest means of survival.

To cling to power, the Zimbabwean state has located itself in a history of low-intensity conflicts punctuated by episodes of massive, systematic, arguably proto-genocidal, violence against the civilian populations of the region. It has systematically deployed the politics of difference, of marginalization and forgetting, silencing wherever possible the memories and dissonant voices of those who recalled different histories, forging and refining structural cultures of violence, 'violence exerted systematically – that is, indirectly' (Farmer 2004: 307), manufacturing 'desocialisation' (ibid.) and the destruction of community (and so diminishing individual agency and capacity for resistance). In choosing to exercise the state's capacity both for the daily uncertainties of structural violence and for pathological, physical violence, the Zimbabwean state draws on its own versions of history to create a culture of terror in which 'solitude, fear and silence' (Taussig 1984: 470) become deliberate agents of state terror. Mired in crisis, it continues to enact these strategies of convenient silence and to deny the recuperation of contested memories which would permit moving beyond the cultures of violence that inscribe it and underpin it.

'Let us understand', the Geneva declaration on terrorism reminds us, 'that the distinguishing feature of terrorism is fear and that this fear is stimulated by threats of indiscriminate and horrifying forms of violence directed against ordinary people everywhere' (United Nations 1987). While state terror is most usually characterized by specific acts of physical violence by a government against a population, detention, torture, suppression of public demonstrations and private resistance (Blakeley this volume) 'as a means of political intimidation and control' (Sluka 2000: 2), here I extend that definition to suggest that the war of the Zimbabwean state against the majority of its own people is now conducted both through acts of physical violence and repression and through the structural violence of systematic neglect of the basic needs of human survival. Ultimately, the consequences are similar: the construction of a shared state of fear and apprehension, the continual and constant expectation of arbitrary and illegal acts by agents of government, the deprivation of means of life, the individual body reduced to an emaciated cipher, the loneliness of unnoticed death, through disease, through the batons, firearms or instruments of torture of the security forces.

Matabeleland

> Telling stories, and being listened to, can allow the healing of these painful memories to begin. While there were some people speaking out at the time atrocities were occurring, these claims were not being 'heard', either in the country or outside the country. Only a few churches and human rights workers and a few journalists from overseas, really listened to these stories. Until the report was released in 1997, the story of the 1980s remained almost entirely unspoken and unheard.
>
> (Catholic Commission 1999: 9)

To silence the stories because we found their representation difficult or disturbing would be a possibility not acceptable to those who struggled to make public spaces for narratives, such as those that began to uncover the silences of the horrific and prolonged Matabeleland massacres (1982–87) in which at least 20,000 people were killed. For them, 'social forgetting is a breeding ground for ideological inscription' (Battaglia 1993: 439) and Alison Brysk's dictum that 'recovery [from state terror] begins with memory' (2003: 238) holds true: a buried unrecuperated traumatic past lurks pathologically in the imagination, continuing to manufacture fear, infecting the future. 'The story of the 1980s remained almost entirely unspoken and unheard' and, we could add, unimaged for, unlike many post Second World War conflicts, few photographic or filmed images were made, so the devastating work of the private memory could flourish, nightmarishly, without the healing of release into a public domain (Werbner, 1998: 97–8; Guérin and Hallas 2007; Moss 2008).

The coordinated purposeful state terror inflicted on the ZAPU heartland of Matabeleland after independence in 1980 exemplified the nature, purposes and potential consequences of state terror in the post-colonial situation. In order to focus government power in his ZANU-PF (mostly Shona-speaking), within three years of independence, in the honeymoon period the international media accorded him, Robert Mugabe took advantage of the intense divisions articulated and emphasized during the fearful years of the war of liberation to devastate his principal opposition, Joshua Nkomo's ZAPU (mostly Ndebele-speaking). As Mugabe declared with foresight in an interview in the late 1970s: 'instead of the enemy wearing a white skin he is soon going to wear a black skin' (1983: 167). Some five years of state and 'dissident' terror brought chaos to the inhabitants of Matabeleland until the remaking of a unity agreement between ZAPU and ZANU-PF in December 1987.

Spearheaded by North Korean-trained shock troops (5 Brigade), the army of the new Zimbabwe entered Matabeleland in pursuit of 'dissidents', many of them former guerrilla fighters, left without employment or retraining, often roaming in armed bands, in an area of the country in which the apartheid regime in South Africa was vigorously fostering and manipulating dissent and unrest as it worked to prevent cadres of the African National Congress using it as a base (Alexander 1991: 586). Many hundreds of civilians had been robbed, injured, raped or killed by the dissidents and many more were to be killed in systematic and massive displays of state power. Curbing the excesses of the dissidents became a cover strategy for a systematic and sustained attack on ZAPU. 'We eradicate them', Mugabe said. 'We don't differentiate when we fight because we can't tell who is a dissident and who is not' (Catholic Commission 1999). Within a very short time of entry into Matabeleland North by the North Korean-trained 5 Brigade (known as Gukurahundi – 'the sweeping away of rubbish') (Alexander *et al.* 2000: 191) which was specifically exempted from usual Army discipline and rules of engagement: 'its troops had murdered more than two thousand civilians, beaten thousands more, and destroyed hundreds of homesteads. Their impact on the communities they passed through was shocking' (Catholic Commission 1999: 14). Gukurahundi troops were trained to utilize their killing for maximum impact on other residents, using public spaces, gang raping women of all ages, humiliating and torturing victims, forcing them to dig their own graves in front of assembled villagers, gathering numbers of people in their huts, setting fire to the thatch and burning them alive. The public nature of their terror sent an overt, unmistakable message to inhabitants of Matabeleland that innocent or not of 'banditry' or of political activity, they could be targeted at any time.

Over the following years, Matabeleland South also was targeted, strategies developed, many thousands of people were forcibly detained, disappeared, tortured, raped, killed, the new state manifesting itself through terror, ridding itself of opponents, destroying community, constructing topographical spaces of terror in order to teach its population how it must be controlled (Sluka 2000: 22). Shallow mass graves grew like strange fruit across the hills and valleys, untold memories haunted and distorted. The lasting lesson for the people of Matabeleland: a naturalized, internalized fear.

> We can still be eliminated at any time ... This wound is huge and deep ... The liberation war was painful, but it had a purpose, it was planned face to face. The war that followed was much worse. It was fearful, unforgettable and unacknowledged.
>
> (Catholic Commission 1999: 15)

In Matabeleland, state terror was deployed as a deliberate strategy of state building through the politicization of ethnicity (Alexander *et al.* 2000: 202), through the creation of widespread, fearful uncertainty, through the construction of a wounded and damaged society whose political community had been torn apart. Hardly a universal strategy of post-colonial states, nonetheless the deliberate use of state terror is not uncommon (e.g. Cambodia, Democratic Republic of Congo). In the new Zimbabwe, Mugabe's willingness to use sustained terror against those he perceived as political opponents (rather than simply as an opposition party) served both to discourage any real opposition and to unify significant sectors of the wider population behind him and ZANU-PF for more than a decade and, effectively, to enable him to build an elite through which he could maintain power long after he had lost electoral control.

In 1997, after the publication of the Catholic Commission's *Breaking the silence* report, Robert Mugabe reacted by acknowledging the power of the historical record yet denying any role for memory in his new Zimbabwe:

> Let us remember that there are those who are bent on mischief-making – persons who see in our unity and the history of the struggle that unites us, a force against their own machinations. If we dig up history, we wreck the nation and we tear our people apart into factions.
>
> (Sokwanele 2005; see also Alexander and McGregor 1999: 256–7)

Memory is required to be absent, the possibilities of countermemory too threatening for a state deeply suspicious of its own legitimacy (Sicher 2001).

The terrible actions of Gukurahundi, the social destruction that ensued, the exemplary demonstration of the power of the state, were to be buried along with the bodies of its victims, to be recalled only efficaciously, as needed to reconfirm the authority and reach of the state. The Matabeleland massacres, made conceivable by a traumatized past, in turn made continued state terror feasible, the anonymity of its victims became a guarantee of continuance.

Colonial memories: states of emergency

> The tradition of the oppressed teaches us that the 'state of emergency' in which we live is not the exception but the rule ... One reason why Fascism has a chance is that, in the name of progress, its opponents treat it as a historical norm. The current amazement that the things we are experiencing are 'still' possible in the twentieth century is not philosophical. This amazement is not the beginning of knowledge – unless it is the knowledge that the view of history which gives rise to it is untenable.
>
> (Benjamin 2003 [1940]: 392)

These types of exercise of state terror served to nurture a pervasive culture of violence which can be traced back into the colonial period of dispossession and the social, economic and cultural disruption of settled societies. The colonial project in Zimbabwe (as elsewhere) was impossible without domination, coercion and the exercise of the violence of the state: physical, coercive, psychological, structural, ultimately instrumental. Cecil Rhodes and his compatriots relied on both force and profound cultural gulfs of understanding to coerce and persuade indigenous leaders to participate in the wholesale transfer of power from indigenous, rural, essentially subsistence-based societies to European colonists who denied indigenous people both individual and collective agency, reading local inhabitants as no more than labour units for large-scale, European-'owned' agricultural enterprises. This is a history of hidden texts (Scott 1990) demanding a further extension of our definition of state terrorism since, as Mazower has argued, 'prioritizing the state's role in the perpetration of large-scale violence had the effect of marginalizing this kind of settler violence, whose victims have tended to be indigenous peoples leaving few historical records behind them' (2002: 1164, and see Mamdani 2001).

Mamdani insists that we remember that from the beginning of the twentieth century, 'it was a European habit to distinguish between civilized wars and colonial wars' (2002: 3): profound moral distinctions were drawn, permitting, encouraging colonial barbarisms to be enacted on subjectified peoples. The maintenance of colonial power depended not only on its capacity to exercise instrumental violence in quelling resistance or on the bewilderment of indigenous people faced with alien practices of governance and bureaucratic machinery, but also on its imposition of coercive cultural technologies. A constantly reinforced and reaffirmed experience of authority, of command, of superiority, of the real power of the conqueror, shaped an expatriate settler culture which came to believe its own myths and yet to deny that the colonial project was, at its heart, a project embedded in and reliant upon continued violence – psychological, cultural, physical. The colonial project of domination, then, in its inherent violence, direct and structural, facilitated the construction of a culture of violence through which the terror of the colonial state could be perpetuated by the post-colonial state.

Late in the nineteenth century, consumed by the potentials and potencies of power, Cecil Rhodes dreamed of a colonial territory and so it came to be, the passionate resistance of Africans denied and overcome by force of arms. Terence Ranger writes of the iconic landscape of the Matopos (where Rhodes chose to buried, looking out over Africa) that for Europeans what was clear was that 'the African inhabitants ... were making no use of the hills. No roads, no parks, no towns, no mines, no castles, no cathedrals, no attempts to exploit the forests – in short, no command over nature' (1999:17). The presumption is of *terra nullius*, a concept both central and essential also to the wider colonial project as it manifested itself in other contemporaneous settler societies, such as Australia. In such 'empty' territory, a new world could be imagined, a new economy built.

Implicit in the colonial project was a rapid reshaping of the indigenous imagination. Thema Khumalo, remembering the colonial past and its imaginative constraints, told Irene Staunton that:

> We were ruled like tame animals. We did not have the opportunity to do things on our own. We did what the white man told us to do. As a result we had no confidence in ourselves and we had no chance to prove ourselves worthy people. We doubted our abilities and could never see ourselves doing something worthwhile. We did not think that black people had rights and could use money as they wished. We thought that money was only supposed to be used profitably and satisfactorily by whites.
>
> (Staunton 1991: 74)

Re-imagined as helpless, as lacking any of the skills or knowledges essential for life in anything but the most basic subsistence economy, black Rhodesians found themselves inhabiting complex, conflicting life-worlds, internally maintaining African cultural understandings and practices while publicly and externally complying with the demands of European colonialism. Public acts of resistance were sporadic but nonetheless intensely felt, as in Bulawayo in July 1960 at a Sunday morning rally of the Youth Front at a city arena, when initial compliance met with unexpected and seemingly arbitrary intransigence, responses escalating, spiralling towards the moment when the violence of police and troops acted to disperse the crowd; it was a binary opposition of African and European reworked and reinscribed (Ranger 1995: 187–8). In mutual misunderstanding of intent and purpose, fear made itself palpable, 'a peaceful rally' turned upside down, its purposes shattered, transformed into 'a riot' which could then be reinterpreted as representing that dangerous Other called African, the stereotypical colonial subject. For those who set out to protest peacefully, the event, as with many other similar events, reinforced a 'sense that one's access to context is lost that constitutes a sense of being violated' (Das 2007: 9). To be misunderstood, wilfully, violently, induced frustration and humiliation, the world turned topsy-turvy, stripped of familiar meaning, purposive acts of instrumental violence deployed by the state to quell resistance and nourish that fear of arbitrary and unpredictable violence that underpins state terror.

Implicit in a state of being-in-the-world as colonial subject were the 'nervous conditions' so powerfully deciphered by the Zimbabwean writer Tsietsi Dangaremba, one of whose protagonists, Nyasha, fails dramatically (and traumatically) in her doomed attempt to be more British than the British, exemplifying that fracture of identity which embodied the psychic violence of colonialism (Fanon 1986 [1952]). Framing his history of nationalism, Terence Ranger's despairing title *Are we not also men?* speaks beyond his immediate subject, the Methodist Samkange family, to evoke masculinities threatened by colonial repositioning, productive of resistance and of demonstrative acts of violence. Yet complicit in the problem was that European identities too were disturbed and frayed by the (literally) outlandish and disconnected nature of Rhodesian colonial society, that the oppressor became the oppressed through the implicit violence of the colonial project itself (Freire 1996). Through imaginative depictions by the novelist and memoirist Doris Lessing, for example, who wrote tellingly of the draining dullness and dislocation of colonial Rhodesia experienced by her autobiographical, central character Martha Quest, we could glimpse an overwhelming sense of non-place (as Marcel Augé would call it). As space became atomized and solitary, colonial settlers lived the desolate loss of that deep-rooted sense of place which anchored individual and collective identities, creating hybrid, confused senses of self which in their dis/placement depended on the demonized Other, imagined both as primitive and violent and, simultaneously, receptive of disciplinary violence (Tuan 1974):

> The white colonial society I grew up in was a bubble ... it was sealed; its inhabitants inhaling and exhaling the same stale, recycled air, unable to breath in any other consciousness for fear of contamination and degradation. Nothing local could be beautiful or important.
>
> (Murray 2008)

Yet paradoxically, many white Rhodesians fleeing to South Africa after independence took with them watercolours of the hills of the Matopos as memory pieces, emblematic of all that they felt they were losing (Ranger 1999: 11), relationships with land and landscapes far different from any that were conceivable or possible in Europe. Landscapes were represented as simultaneously both wild and accessible, magnificent and awe-inspiring yet susceptible to capture in that most delicate of arts, the watercolour. Land too was read through conflicting and contradictory lenses: accessible, yet first it had to be conquered, acquired from residents perceived to have no claims of ownership upon it; fertile, yet demanding of substantial labour inputs, safe and dangerous simultaneously. In this colonial settler society, the conquering of the land metonymically represented the conquering of the people for at the heart of the colonial enterprise lay the appropriation of rural land and consequently the coercion of African labour to work the vast, new agricultural estates, the establishment of settler modes of production.

Most terrible: nothing was as it seemed, the memories and histories of local people were given no space, no privilege, convenient silences reconstructed social and cultural meanings. Being-in-the-world ceased to signify what once, in living memory, it had been able to embody.

Land was instrumental to the colonial project, land was survival for indigenous people. The 90 years of colonial rule, of the systematic allocation of the best land to whites and the forced removal of blacks to the poorest lands (Lan 1985: 173; Iliffe 1990), produced some of the most intense resistance to the colonial state; such as what Ranger called 'the most effective rural protest movements in Zimbabwe – the *Sofasonke* and *Sofasishamba* movements' of the late 1940s (1999:3), and the passionate support of rural, black people for the two nationalist movements (ZANU and ZAPU), which battled first the colonial state and then its successor under the Unilateral Declaration of Independence (UDI, 1965–80) (Palmer 1990: 165) The inequities were manifest: at 'independence, in 1980, population densities were over three times greater in the black than in the white areas, and some 42 per cent of the country was owned by 6,000 white commercial farmers' (Palmer 1990: 165). By 1997, when President Mugabe announced that the government 'would acquire 1,471 farms for redistribution to smallholder famers … over 3.5 million hectares to some 70,000 families' had been transferred (Moyo 2000: 5). But the numbers could be misleading: while peasant production had been badly affected overall during colonial times, it was really the period of UDI which produced the most rapid changes. During the colonial period, most white famers focused on large-scale agribusiness, such as the production of tobacco for export, while peasant farmers produced food (maize and garden crops) for the domestic market. The export sanctions and boycotts that accompanied UDI, however, saw white farmers switch to production for the domestic market 'at the expense of the peasants so that by 1980 the white commercial famers were producing some 90 per cent of the country's marketed food requirements' (Palmer 1990: 167; Ranger 1978: 119–20, cited in Palmer 1990).

This is not the place for a rehearsal of the very complex history of land issues and land redistribution in independent Zimbabwe. What is necessary here is to understand that post-Independence land redistribution to the rural peasantry has been slow and inconsistent (e.g. Ranger 1989; Palmer 1990; Alexander 1991; Coldham 1993; Coldham 2001; Moyo 2000; Mlambo 2005). Further, a profound sense of betrayal by successive British governments has enabled Robert Mugabe and ZANU-PF to capitalize on the pent-up demand for land and on the frustration born of 90 years of settler privilege to cast Britain (and the United States) as fascist colonial/imperialist powers intent on counter-revolution. Constructing independent Zimbabwe as perpetually threatened by external forces both creates internal tension and uncertainty and seemingly legitimizes government violence against its own people.

The sense of betrayal – and the capacity of the Zimbabwean state to brandish the anti-colonial banner – were vastly compounded in 1997 by the actions of the Secretary of State for International Development in the new Blair Labour government, Clare Short, when she wrote to the Zimbabwean Minister of Agriculture and Land, Kumbirai Kanga radically reshaping British undertakings from recognition of an historical colonial responsibility to a simple aid donor–recipient relationship:

> I should make it clear that we do not accept that Britain has a special responsibility to meet the costs of land purchase in Zimbabwe. We are a new government from diverse backgrounds without links to former colonial interests. My own origins are Irish, and as you know, we were colonised, not colonisers.
>
> (Short 2007 [1998])

Apart from the naïve condescension and amateurish attempt to patronize the Zimbabweans, the breathtaking claims of total separation from the past, and the personalization of the issue through the stress on an individual, colonized Irish origin on the part of the secretary of state, however, radically reconstruct contemporary concepts of collective responsibility for past actions. Unlike, for example, the German debates of the 1980s and 1990s (*Historikerstreit)* about the extent of responsibility, actual, moral, financial, on the part of later generations for the actions of Hitler and his National Socialists, in particular for the Holocaust, the reshaping by the British Labour government of existing relational understandings reinforced Zimbabwean sensitivities to their historical experience of patriarchal colonialism, seeming through its lack of acceptance of responsibility, to reiterate, yet again, the psychological violence of 90 years of colonial and post-colonial experience.

Traces from the past

Without memory we become less than ourselves. Memory shapes and structures our practices of everyday life; memory allows us understanding of our pasts and therefore our presents. Silenced memory disrupts and distorts our inscriptions of the past on the present, diverting, suppressing, constructing fantastic spaces for the continued, enervating, practice of illusions and disillusionment. As Miroslav Volf reminds us, 'without memory, you could not be you and I could not be I ... To be human is to be able to remember. It is as simple as that: no memory, no human identity' (2006:147). Yet memories, even those most cruelly silenced, possess form and substance: their dark presence relentlessly capable of disturbing and destroying surface stabilities or equilibria. Therein rests their threat and their power.

Memories swell from the past into the present through stories, evoking embodied experiences, enabling the recall and even the reliving of individual and collective pasts. Veena Das and Arthur Kleinman suggest that 'the choke and sting of experience only becomes real – is heard – when it is narrativized' (2001: 20). But in times of deep, social suffering, past and present are conflated, elided, disturbed. In Zimbabwean narratives of the past and of the present, violence and memory crowd together: television news footage of elderly women, daring to be supporters of an opposition party, bodies beaten and bloodied by police, merges with the voices of the past:

> They really tortured us. Someone had told them that we harboured freedom fighters in our home ... they made us lie down, both me and my husband, and they beat us on our backs. They took a big stick and beat us: me first, then my husband.
>
> (Tetty Magugu describing the Second Chimurenga in Matabeleland in the 1970s, quoted in Staunton 1991: 165)

Through 'discipline', 'punishment' and pain, the individual body is transformed into a site for collective acts of control and dominance: through violent acts against the body, the agency of the individual is cast aside, the disorder of subversion reshaped as order by the collective, the resistant mind attacked through its weakest point, the body which sustains it. 'All these corporeal technologies of violence that open some surface and orifices to signification and close down others effectively reinscribe bodies and selves into new cultural categories', as Vigdis Broch-Due reminded us (2005: 28). For a culture which has lived with systemic structural violence for more than a century, with a history of state terror, of invasion, dispossession, domination and coercion, the narratives of memory represent the only source through which it is possible to record the hidden histories of broken bodies and lives disturbed by the normalization of the inconceivable. No other archive has been possible.

In embedding its ineradicable traces on individuals, I suggest, a violent, wounding, traumatic past is ensured survival (Koshar 2000), its textures made legible through shared social understandings about the omnipresent possibility of arbitrary, unpredictable acts of violence, understandings articulated, if at all, privately and quietly, rarely in public spaces (Young, 1993). When Coronil and Skurski argue that 'violence is wielded and resisted in the idiom of a society's distinctive history' (1991: 290) we can hear the resonances for Zimbabweans: that violence from above, which is characteristic of state terror, is deeply, historically inscribed in their hidden histories, the violence of the present given legitimacy by the violence of the past.

Convenient silences

Some things that happened in the 1970s made what happened after Independence much more likely. In particular, certain laws were passed by the Rhodesian Front, which made it impossible for government officials to be punished for what they did, even if they murdered innocent people. The Rhodesian Front and the Governments before them, passed many laws which severely limited most people's rights to live where they chose, go to school, work, or express any freedom of thought or movement. People in Rhodesia became used to a situation where the Government showed no respect for their civil rights.... The very men who tortured people in the 1970s used the same methods to torture people again in the 1980s. Both times they got away with it and were never punished. Some of these men still hold senior positions in the Zimbabwean Government and armed forces.

(Catholic Commission 1999: 10)

From the early 1960s, the nationalist movement in Zimbabwe was formally divided, both by language and by home territories. Norma Kriger has shown us that even within ZANU or ZAPU, and their respective territories of influence, generational, class and gender differences were enacted, often violently. Kriger quotes Fanon's compelling insight about the French occupation of Algeria, that 'in the colonial context ... the natives fight amongst themselves' (1992: 211) but disagreed with him in his conclusion this aggression would eventually become a united struggle against the colonizers. Rather, her ethnographic interrogation of peasant voices from the second Chimurenga leads her to 'suggest that peasants, even during the anti-colonial war, ranked coming to terms with their internal enemies as more pressing and more worthy of risks than eliminating the white state' (Kriger 1992: 211).

Without coming to such a precise conclusion, Irene Staunton, in listening to women's narratives of the second Chimurenga, had heard similar stories. Agnes Ziyatsha, for example, told of the *mujibas* (scouts/messengers) that:

The Zanlas would address us and tell us that they did not want sell-outs or witches. They killed such people. It was usually the *mujibas* who caused these deaths and what they claimed was frequently not true. A lot of people were killed because of the lies.

(Staunton 1991: 171)

Linda Green, in another context, has written of the emotional power of the cultural ecology of 'living with fear', a condition that became the life world of many rural Rhodesians in the 1970s as the civil war became naturalized across the country. Every party, government and nationalist, deployed unpredictable brutality, seemingly erratically and arbitrarily yet clearly with purpose beyond individual or even collective pathological desire for the pleasures of extreme violence. The terrible spread of unpredictable, extreme violence created a space of terror in which 'everyone was frightened of meeting either the freedom fighters, or the soldiers, on their way to school. It was a really terrible time. Shootings! Ah, people were shot by ... both the soldiers and the freedom fighters' (Staunton 1991: 128). Reflecting each other's understandings of the political ecology, both state and non-state participants rationally and instrumentally deployed atrocity to create cultures of terror as a means of control of populations and territories: 'People were only afraid – not to support one party or another, but being afraid only', as a Gokwe informant told Eric Worby (1998: 568). The depth of the brutality made identification of its perpetrators as state or non-state actors almost irrelevant:

> I can recall when the soldiers came and took people quite unawares and many died. Girls were brutally killed, having had their breasts cut off. One of those girls is still alive but she is crippled: both her legs are paralysed.
>
> (Meggy Zingani to Staunton 1991: 128)

Reading these narratives, we are witnesses to trauma rippling out spatially and temporally, from the bodies on which violence is imposed, seeking out the vulnerable and inscribing itself wherever it can take hold, at once arbitrary and purposeful, deployed with intent to dominate and control; 'enforcement terror', as McCormick calls it (2003: 485), rational choices to utilize tactical violence made by state and non-state players during the Chimurenga in order to control resources, populations and territories (Kriger 1992: 152–7). Mary Gomendo recognized the controlling power of the public performance of atrocity when she described the treatment of suspected informers:

> They tied your legs together and your arms together and they called everyone to collect firewood and make a big fire. They threw the person, alive, on to the fire. They said they wanted everyone to see what would happen to an informer. Everyone had to sit and watch the person die. You were not even allowed to cry. It was terrible.
>
> (Staunton 1991: 143)

Whether such stories were told from firsthand witness, direct testimony, or whether they were circulating in a village or community, they quietly did memory's work in (re)performing atrocity, sheeting home blame to both (all) sides, constructing a culture of violence, a life world of fear, vulnerability and terror.

In their deployment of unpredictable violence to create a condition of terror, the illegitimate state and its insurgent opponents reflected each other mimetically (Warren 2000: 230). Similarly in their spatial strategies to control rural populations and territories, they shared understandings of the tactics of insurgency and counterinsurgency and the need to concentrate and defend localized populations (Cilliers 1985: 79). In the struggle for control of territory, the government followed the examples set in other counterinsurgency actions, in Vietnam in particular, and established 'protected villages' into which it forcibly relocated about 750,000 rural people between 1974 and 1977 (Kesby 1996: 564). The commissioner of police formally had the power 'to confiscate, seize or destroy property in these areas' (Cilliers 1985: 83) in pursuit of systematic surveillance and control of the inhabitants of these new 'protected' spaces (Kesby 1996: 571). Relocation was bitterly resented: 'People's homes were burnt down so that they would not return to them. Everything was burnt – their corn, their fields everything. Many people were tortured' a woman from Chibuwe told Irene Staunton (1991: 142).

Within the protected village, living conditions were difficult, crowded, lacking schools, clean water supplies and sanitation: 'There were no houses. People lived in sheds. There was no sanitation no water: nothing. People were forced to live like animals' (Staunton 1991: 200). In the closer spaces of the protected villages, rural farmers became urban residents, disease and health problems followed, including malnutrition because the villages were so large yet were required to be self-supporting, so people were forced to walk long distances to their crops, gardens and animals (Cilliers 1985: 97). Family and community structures were disrupted, with devastating cross-generational and gendered relational impacts (Kriger 1992: 179–86; Kesby 1996). Even the Rhodesian government recognized publicly that a fundamental failure of the protected villages, which subverted its campaign to win black support for UDI was the 'complete disruption of normal kraal life', which ensued from forcible relocation (quoted in Cilliers 1985: 100). Yet the government failed to fund the protected villages programme at a level that would provide not only the basics of material life but also the protection that the villages were designed to provide. The programme was always undermanned, the planned formation of local militias failed and the government forces were unable to prevent intimidation by nationalist fighters through armed attack, burning huts, torturing and killing residents (Cilliers 1985: 88, 101; Staunton 1991: 202).

Fiona Ross suggests that 'the difficulties involved in listening and attending to stories of pain and loss', are almost impossible to overcome (2001: 250). Yet through these stories of suffering, we can decipher something of the operations of state terror, of that creation of disorder in people's lives which goes against the grain, which disrupts the usual 'flow of everyday life' (and everyday death) through acts of violence, of wounds and deaths (Das 1997: 68). To renarrate the stories offers the possibility of preserving the germ of their meanings and of the experiences of vulnerability and humiliation to which they testify.

The long endgame

By 2000, it was evident that the inflation which had been exacerbated by Mugabe's military adventures in the Democratic Republic of Congo was beginning to bite, bus fares rising too rapidly for wages to keep pace, less food and less variety in the shops and from the informal street traders. Yet only months earlier the publishers of the summary version of the *Breaking the silence: building the peace* report on the Matabeleland massacres of the 1980s wrote, as much in hope as in reality: 'Zimbabwe is currently enjoying a period of stability which did not exist twelve years ago. There are now no emergency powers in force, and people have more freedom of movement and speech than ever before' (Catholic Commission 1999). The government's heavy-handed response to the food riots of 1998, and its lack of a sound economic response to steadily-growing crisis, resonated quietly through urban areas in particular. Lingering resentments and social suffering were carving deeper marks on wider swathes of the population.

Agricultural land, which had become symbolic of continued European control of the Zimbabwean economy, shifted into a new focus, at least for the international community as farm invasions by so-called 'war veterans'. Land has been focus of much international media and diplomatic attention yet even now, the silences are perpetuated as reporting has centred on evictions (often very violent) of white farmers, failing to address either the desperation for arable land felt by many Zimbabweans or the systematic state violence against any forms of opposition to the government. But other narratives are formed by the actions of the security forces in both urban and rural areas, of actions against members or supporters of opposition parties, in Operation Murambatsvina, an unprecedented emptying of the cities, reminiscent in its vast scope of the emptying of the cities of Cambodia in Pol Pot's Year Zero.

The hopefulness expressed in *Breaking the silence* has long dissipated in electoral manipulation, state violence, hyperinflation, malnutrition and disease. The government of Robert Mugabe retains power, relying on the only, remaining capability of a collapsed state, its residual capacity to inflict state terror on its people.

Through repositioning narratives of the current state terror in Zimbabwe, I have demonstrated its historical roots and shown that it should be understood as having been enabled and facilitated by the violence, direct and structural alike, of the colonial project and by nationalist responses to invasion and appropriation. In understanding the contexts and continuities of state terror in Rhodesia/Zimbabwe, I have drawn out the complex relationships between state terror, memory and narrative, suggesting that the work of private memory (so useful in creating and sustaining a state of fear and uncertainty) has been counterpointed by the convenience of public silence, forbidding the healing of recuperated memory and public narrative.

Epilogue

In 1984, Edinburgh University conferred an honorary doctorate to Robert Mugabe for his services to education in Africa. It seems that one lone voice from among the university's academic staff protested this, on the grounds of the atrocities already known to be occurring in Matabeleland. The degree was finally revoked only in July 2008 (McAlister 2007).

References

Alexander, J. (1991) 'The unsettled land: the politics of land distribution in Matabeleland, 1980–1990', *Journal of Southern African Studies*, 17 (4): 581–610.

Alexander, J., JoAnn McGregor and Terence Ranger (2000) *Violence and memory: one hundred years in the 'dark forests' of Matabeleland*, Oxford: James Currey.

Alexander, J. and McGregor, J. (1999) 'Representing violence in Matabeleland, Zimbabwe: press and internet debates', in T. Allen and J. Seaton (eds) *The media of conflict: war reporting and representations of ethnic violence*, London: Zed.

Augé, M. (1995) *Non-places: introduction to an anthropology of supermodernity*, trans. J. Howe, New York: Verso.

Battaglia, D. (1993) 'At play in the fields (and borders) of the imaginary: Melanesian transformations of forgetting', *Cultural Anthropology*, 8 (4): 430–42.

Benjamin, W. (2003 [1940]) *Selected writings volume 4 1938–1940*, in H. Eiland and M.W. Jennings (eds) Cambridge, MA: Belknap Press.

Bhebe, N. and Ranger, T. (eds) (1995) *Soldiers in Zimbabwe's liberation war*, London: James Currey.

Blakeley, R. (2009) 'State terrorism in the social sciences: theories, methods and concepts', in *Contemporary state terrorism: theory and practice*, Routledge: London.

Broch-Due, V. (2005) 'Violence and belonging: analytical reflections', in V. Broch-Due (ed.) *Violence and belonging: the quest for identity in post-colonial Africa*, Abingdon: Routledge: 1–40.

Brysk, A. (2003) 'Recovering from state terror: the morning after in Latin America', *Latin American Research Review*, 38 (1): 238–47.

Catholic Commission for Justice and Peace and Legal Resources Foundation (1999 [1997]) *Breaking the silence: building true peace: a report on the disturbances in Matabeleland and the Midlands, 1980–1988: summary report*, Harare: CCJP; LRF.

Cavell, S. (1997) 'Comments on Veena Das's essay "language and body: transactions in the construction of pain"', in A. Kleinman, Veena Das and Margaret Lock (eds) *Social suffering*, Berkeley: University of California Press.

Chan, S. (2005) 'The memory of violence; trauma in the writings of Alexander Kanengoni and Yvonne Vera and the idea of unreconciled citizenship in Zimbabwe', *Third World Quarterly* 26 (2): 369–82.

Cilliers, J.J. 1985) *Counter-insurgency in Rhodesia*, London: Croom Helm.

Coldham, S. (1993) 'The Land Acquisition Act, 1992 of Zimbabwe', *Journal of African Law* 37 (1): 82–8.

—— (2001) 'Land Acquisition Amendment Act, 2000 (Zimbabwe)', *Journal of African Law*, 45 (2): 227–9.

Coronil, F. and Skurski, J. (1991) 'Dismembering and remembering the nation: the semantics of political violence in Venezuela', *Comparative Studies in Society and History*, 33 (2): 288–337.

Dangaremba, T. (1988) *Nervous conditions*, London: The Women's Press.

Das, V. (1997) 'Language and body: transactions in the construction of pain', in A. Kleinman, Veena Das and Margaret Lock (eds) *Social suffering*, Berkeley: University of California Press.

—— (2007) *Life and words: violence and the descent into the ordinary*, Berkeley: University of California Press.

Das, V. and Kleinman, A. (2001) 'Introduction', in V. Das, Arthur Kleinman, Margaret Lock, and Mamphela Rampele (eds) *Remaking a world: violence, social suffering and recovery*, Berkeley: University of California Press: 1–30.

Das, V., Arthur Kleinman, Margaret Lock, and Mamphela Rampele (eds) (2000) *Violence and subjectivity*, Berkeley: University of California Press.

—— (eds) (2001) *Remaking a world: violence, social suffering, and recovery*, Berkeley: University of California Press.

Fanon, F. (1986 [1952]) *Black skin: white masks*, trans. C.L. Markmann, Paris and New York: Groves.

Farmer, P. (2004) 'An anthropology of structural violence', *Current Anthropology*, 45 (3): 305–25.

Freire, P. (1996) *Pedagogy of the oppressed*, revised edition, London: Penguin.

Green, L. (1994) 'Fear as a way of life', *Cultural Anthropology*, 9 (2): 227–56.

Guérin, F. and Hallas, R. (eds) (2007) *The image and the witness: trauma, memory and visual culture*, London: Wallflower.

Halbwachs, M. (1992) *On collective memory*, trans. L.A. Coser, Chicago: University of Chicago Press.

Iliffe, J. (1990) *Famine in Zimbabwe 1890–1960*, Gweru: Mambo Press.

Kesby, M. (1996) 'Arenas for control, terrains of gender contestation: guerrilla struggle and counter-insurgency warfare in Zimbabwe 1972–1980', *Journal of Southern African Studies*, 22 (4): 561–84.

Kleinman, A., Veena Das and Margaret Lock (eds) (1997) *Social suffering*, Berkeley: University of California Press.

Koshar, R. (2000) *From monuments to memory: artifacts of German memory, 1870–1990*, Berkeley: University of California Press.

Kriger, N.J. (1992) *Zimbabwe's guerrilla war: peasant voices*, Cambridge, UK: Cambridge University Press.

Lan, D. (1985) *Guns and rain: guerrillas and spirit mediums in Zimbabwe*, London: James Currey.

Lessing, D. (1952) *Martha quest*, London: M. Joseph.

McAlister, J. (2007) 'Revoked: the story of Robert Mugabe and his honorary degree from Edinburgh University'. Online, available at: www.eusa.ed.ac.uk/news/229 (accessed 2 February 2009).

McCormick, G.H. (2003) 'Terrorist decision making', *Annual Review of Political Science*, 6: 473–507.

Mamdani, M. (2001) *When victims become killers: colonialism, nativism, and the genocide in Rwanda*, Princeton, NJ: Princeton University Press.

—— (2002) 'Making sense of political violence in postcolonial Africa', *Identity, culture and politics*, 3 (2): 1–24.

Mazower, M. (2002) 'Violence and the state in the twentieth century', *American Historical Review*, 107 (4): 1158–78.

Mlambo, A.S. (2005) '"Land grab" or "taking back stolen land": the fast track land reform process in Zimbabwe in historical perspective', *History Compass*, 3: 1–21.

Moss, M. (2008) *Toward the visualization of history: the past as image*, Lanham, MD: Lexington.

Moyo, S. (2000) 'The political economy of land acquisition and redistribution in Zimbabwe, 1990–1999', *Journal of Southern African Studies*, 26 (1): 5–28.

Mugabe, R.G. (1983) *Our war of liberation: speeches, articles, interviews 1976–1979*, Gweru: Mambo Press.

Murray, B. (2008) '*Two tone: an essay*'. Online, available at: www.chimurengalibrary.co.za/essay.php?id=24&cid=24_1 (accessed 9 November 2008).

Palmer, R. (1990) 'Land reform in Zimbabwe, 1980–1990', *African Affairs*, 89 (355): 163–81.

Raczymow, H. (1994) 'Memory shot through with holes', *Yale French Studies*, 85: 98–105.

Ranger, T. (1978) 'Growing from the roots: reflections on peasant research in central and southern Africa', *Journal of Southern African Studies*, 5 (2): 99–133.

—— (1989) 'Matabeleland since the amnesty', *African Affairs*, 88 (351): 161–73.

—— (1995) *Are we not also men? The Samkange family and African politics in Zimbabwe 1920–64*, Harare: Baobab.

—— (1999) *Voices from the rocks: nature, culture and history in the Matopos Hills of Zimbabwe*, Harare and Oxford: Baobab and James Currey.

Ricoeur, P. (2004) *Memory, history, forgetting*, trans. K. Blamey and D. Pellauer, Chicago: University of Chicago Press.

Ross, F.C. (2001) 'Speech and silence: women's testimony in the first five weeks of public hearings of the South African Truth and Reconciliation Commission', in Das, V., Arthur Kleinman, Margaret Lock, and Mamphela Rampele (eds) *Remaking a world: violence, social suffering, and recovery*, Berkeley: University of California Press.

Scott, J.C. (1990) *Domination and the arts of resistance: hidden transcripts*, New Haven, CT: Yale University Press.

Short, C. (2007 [1998]) 'One bad letter with long-lasting consequences', *New African* (May). Online, available at: www.findarticles.com/p/articles/mi_qa5391/is_200705/ai_n21288044 (accessed 2 February 2009).

Sicher, E. (2001) 'The future of the past: countermemory and postmemory in contemporary American post-Holocaust narratives', *History and Memory*, 12 (2): 56–91.

Sluka, J.A. (2000) 'Introduction: state terror and anthropology', in J.A. Sluka (ed.) *Death squad: the anthropology of state terror*, Philadelphia: University of Pennsylvania Press: 1–45.

Sokwanele (2005 [1997]), 'A chronicle of post-independence massacre', (6 April 2005, from *Africa News* 16 July 1997). Online, available at: www.sokwanele.com/articles/supporting/achronicleofpostindependencemassacre_16july1997.html (accessed 2 February 2009).

Staunton, I. (comp. and ed.) (1991) *Mothers of the revolution: the war experiences of thirty Zimbabwean women*, Bloomington: Indiana University Press.

Taussig, M. (1984) 'Culture of terror – space of death. Roger Casement's Putamayo Report and the explanation of torture', *Comparative Studies in Society and History*, 26 (3): 467–97.

Tuan, Y.-F. (1974) *Topophilia: a study of environmental perception, attitudes and values*, Englewood Cliffs, New Jersey: Prentice-Hall.

UNICEF (2008) *Zimbabwe statistics*, Online, available at: www.unicef.org/infobycountry/zimbabwe_statistics.html (accessed 2 February 2009).

United Nations General Assembly (1987) *The Geneva declaration on terrorism*, document A/42/307, annex. Online, available at: www.i-p-o.org/Gdt.htm (accessed 2 February 2009).

—— (2005) *Report of the fact-finding mission to Zimbabwe to assess the scope and impact of Operation Murambatsvina by the UN special envoy on human settlements issues in Zimbabwe, Mrs. Anna Kajumulo Tibaijuka.* Online, available at: www.un.org/News/dh/infocus/zimbabwe/zimbabwe_rpt.pdf (accessed 2 February 2009).

Volf, M. (2006) *The end of memory: remembering rightly in a violent world*, Grand Rapids, MI: W.B. Eerdmans.

Warren, K.B. (2000) 'Death squads and wider complicities: dilemmas for the anthropology of violence', in J.A. Sluka (ed.) *Death squad: the anthropology of state terror*, Philadelphia: University of Pennsylvania Press: 226–47.

Werbner, R. (1998) 'Smoke from the barrel of a gun: postwars of the dead, memory and reinscription in Zimbabwe', in R. Werbner (ed.) *Memory and the postcolony: African anthropology and the critique of power*, London: Zed: 71–102.

Worby, E. (1998) 'Tyranny, parody and ethnic polarity: ritual engagements with the state in northwestern Zimbabwe', *Journal of Southern African Studies*, 24 (3): 561–78.

World Health Organization (2008) 'Cholera in Zimbabwe'. Online, available at: www.who.int/csr/don/2008_12_02/en/index.html (accessed 2 February 2009).

Young, J.E. (1993) *The texture of memory: Holocaust memorials and meanings*, New Haven, CT: Yale University Press.

7 Revenge and terror

The destruction of the Palestinian community in Kuwait

Victoria Mason

Introduction

The 1990–91 Gulf conflict claimed a victim largely forgotten by the world: the community of approximately 400,000 Palestinians who lived in the emirate of Kuwait. The vast majority of Palestinians within Kuwait opposed the Iraqi occupation; however, their image was badly damaged by the perceived support of the invasion by the Palestinians outside of Kuwait. Consequently, Palestinians in general were tarred as Iraqi 'collaborators'. As a result, frenzied revenge attacks took place after the liberation of Kuwait, with Palestinians in the emirate being beaten, tortured and in some instances, brutally killed. While these attacks were initially carried out by Kuwaiti vigilantes, once sovereign rule returned to Kuwait, they became part of a more systematic state campaign of terror aimed at 'cleansing' the emirate of Palestinians. As a result, the Palestinian community in Kuwait was reduced from 400,000 to around 30,000 people. While this campaign was driven to a certain extent by scapegoating and revenge, it was also part of a more systematic process of state terrorism. Due to the size and influence of the Palestinian community in Kuwait, by the 1980s, they were increasingly seen as a potential demographic threat. Thus, the actions taken against Palestinians following liberation also had more sinister motives – to terrorize the entire Palestinian civilian population to force them to leave the emirate. Although Kuwaiti actions received harsh criticism from human rights groups and NGOs, the plight of Palestinians from Kuwait was soon forgotten by the international community. This chapter explores this largely untold story: the acts of state terror perpetrated by the Kuwaiti government against its Palestinian population following the 1990–91 Gulf conflict.

Palestinians in Kuwait

The 1948 establishment of the state of Israel and resultant dispossession of around 700,000 Palestinians – known by Palestinians as *al nakbah* (the catastrophe) – coincided with the massive development of Kuwait following the discovery of oil. The intersection of these two events resulted in large-scale migration of Palestinian refugees to Kuwait and united the Palestinians and

Kuwaitis in a relationship which would prove, at least initially, to be mutually beneficial (Longva 1997: 25; Lesch 2005: 163). Palestinians played a central role in the development of post-oil Kuwait, and soon became the most numerous expatriate worker group and a semi-permanent community within the emirate. By 1965, Palestinians comprised 41 per cent and 48 per cent of employees in Kuwait's private and public sectors respectively (Ghabra 1987: 41–9, 77; Longva 1997: 26–34). In return, the Kuwaitis provided very good conditions for expatriate workers, including no income tax, inexpensive or free medical care, free telephone services and subsidized water, electricity, petrol and essential foodstuffs (Longva 1997: 52–64). As a result, Kuwait became a 'haven in exile' for Palestinians.

Yet despite this initially mutually beneficial relationship, Kuwait did not follow a policy of integration when it came to its expatriate workers (Mason 2001: 13–20; Longva 1997: 44; Lesch 2005: 164–7). Furthermore, as the expatriate worker community expanded, Kuwaitis found they had become a minority in their emirate and came to see the large number of expatriate workers as a potential threat (Lesch 2005: 167–8; Brand 1988: 112–13). While Kuwaiti fears stemmed from the overall numbers of expatriates, Palestinians constituted one of the single largest non-Kuwaiti populations in Kuwait – in 1975, they comprised nearly 40 percent of Kuwait's expatriate population – and so came under particular scrutiny (Mason 2001: 13–20; Shah 1986: 815). Kuwaiti fears then resulted in the emergence of a siege mentality and a 'discourse of exclusion' becoming a central part of Kuwait's government policy from the 1960s. This discourse of exclusion was manifested in a number of ways, including moves to nationalize all sectors of the Kuwaiti economy and the blatant differentiation in the position and wages of Kuwaitis over non-Kuwaitis (Longva 1997: 43–112; Lesch 2005:164–8). Expatriates were banned from buying property and owning and operating businesses. The latter meant that setting up a business required a Kuwaiti business partner to hold at least a 51 percent share, with only the Kuwaiti partner able to undertake legal contracts, creating rife exploitation of non-Kuwaitis (Longva 1997: 77–108; Brand 1988: 114). Non-Kuwaitis were denied the right of franchise and election to government bodies, and were barred from setting up companies in areas, such as oil ventures and financial services (Al Moosa and McLachlan 1985: 105; Brand 1988: 114). Residency within Kuwait was furthermore dependent upon the *kafala* sponsorship system, which required workers to be employed (and thus sponsored) by a Kuwaiti institution or individual. Under the *kafala* system, workers' passports were kept by employers as security and employer's permission was necessary to change jobs (Longva 1997: 77–108).

All of the above meant that Kuwaiti employers had great power over expatriates. When an employment contract ended, moreover, expatriates were required to leave the country within two weeks, regardless of how long they had been in Kuwait (Brand 1988:113–14; Longva 1997: 84). While these policies affected all expatriate workers, their impact on Palestinians was particularly pronounced because many Palestinians were stateless and had nowhere else to go (Mason

2008; Brand 1988: 115). The only other way to remain in Kuwait was through naturalization, which occurred in only the most select of circumstances. Reflecting this trend, the 1975 Kuwaiti census counted only 374 people of Palestinian/ Jordanian origin as naturalized Kuwaitis, out of the 204,000 Palestinians residing there at that time (Al Moosa and McLachlan 1985: 109).

This matrix of exclusionary policies within Kuwait only became more entrenched during the 1970s and 1980s. The economic malaise during these decades resulted in further 'Kuwaitization' of the workforce. There was a drop in the number of positions held by Palestinians and increasing limitations placed on their career opportunities (Lesch 2005: 165–6). While Kuwait did not allow a military presence among its Palestinians, the Kuwaitis were nonetheless disconcerted by the conflicts that emerged between Palestinians and their hosts in Jordan and Lebanon in the 1970s and 1980s (Ryan and Stork 1977: 14). More generally, distrust of non-Kuwaitis in the emirate was exacerbated by a series of events in the 1980s, including a number of explosions at foreign embassies and the airport in 1983 and an assassination attempt on the emir in 1986. While Palestinians were not involved in any of these actions, these events intensified the feeling that expatriates represented a threat (Brand 1988: 112, 124: Stanton Russell 1989: 38). By the end of the 1980s, therefore, a number of measures had been instituted with the aim of decreasing the overall numbers of expatriates – particularly Palestinians – in Kuwait (Van Hear 1998: 86; Graham-Brown 1992: 4; Peretz 1993: 56–7). As Gil Feiler tells us, the measures included forbidding:

> Migrant workers from changing jobs without first leaving the country. It was not unusual for Palestinian tourists visiting gulf states [*sic*] to be detained and prohibited entry. Kuwait sometimes refused Palestinian researchers permission to participate in academic projects there. The Kuwaiti government even obtained a computer programme ... that compares the passport details of persons entering the country with a list of Palestinian names and determines if the place and date of birth have been altered. The Kuwaitis used it as part of their policy of restricting the number of Palestinians entering the country irrespective of their citizenship.
>
> (Feiler 1993: 639)

By the eve of the Iraqi occupation of Kuwait, the 400,000 Palestinians in Kuwait were largely viewed by the 600,000 Kuwaiti citizens as 'a potentially explosive demographic' (Lesch 1991c: 42). As Ann Lesch argues:

> Palestinians were the one group that could outweigh Kuwaitis. Palestinians had large and growing families, a multigenerational presence, and a vibrant society. Their cohesion and influence – along with their deepening perception of Kuwait as their home, in which they were entitled to certain benefits – threatened Kuwaitis.
>
> (Lesch 2005: 168)

As anti-Palestinian sentiment became increasingly entrenched, Kuwait's news-papers called for Palestinians and Jordanians (with many Palestinians classed as Jordanians because they held Jordanian citizenship) to be deported, and the motto of 'Kuwait is for Kuwaitis' became widespread (Swaiden and Nica 2002: 5). Yet while the position of Palestinians grew ever more tenuous, few Palestinians could have foreseen that the August 1990 Iraqi invasion of Kuwait would provide the catalyst for, and justification of, the destruction of their com-munity by the Kuwaiti government.

The Iraqi occupation

The vast majority of Palestinians in Kuwait saw the Iraqi occupation as an unmitigated disaster – not least for the threat it presented to the prosperous lives they had created in Kuwait (Mason 2008). The harsh Iraqi occupation also pre-sented a very dangerous situation for everyone living in Kuwait. Consequently, many of those Palestinians who had Jordanian passports (and were therefore able to leave Kuwait) sought refuge in the Hashemite Kingdom. Others decided to stay and either resist, or at least wait out, the Iraqi occupation. Some – such as those Palestinians with Egyptian Travel Documents (ETDs) – faced a much more difficult situation. ETDs were granted to Palestinians in the Gaza Strip by Egypt during their control of the area between 1948 and 1967. These documents are notoriously problematic for Palestinians, making it difficult to even enter Egypt and effectively rendering their holders stateless. As a result, those Pales-tinians within Kuwait that had ETDs had little choice but to remain in the emirate after occupation (Mason 2008; Shiblak 1996: 40).

Most of the Palestinians who remained within Kuwait, including the local PLO leadership, opposed the occupation. Many Palestinians, furthermore, actively assisted Kuwaitis. This aid included food and medical assistance, pro-tecting Kuwaitis and their property from Iraqi soldiers and being active members of the armed anti-Iraqi Resistance (Mason 2008; Lesch 1991c: 45–7, 2005: 169; Ghabra 1991: 122–4; MNSRC 1992: 12). In comparison, very few Palestinians assisted the Iraqis (Mason 2008; Ghabra 1991: 122–4; Lesch 1991c: 45–7).

The ranks of the small number of Palestinians in Kuwait who were sympa-thetic to the Iraqis, however, were buoyed by the creation of an armed group known as the 'Iraqi Popular Army' (IPA). This 'army' was initially created from 200 to 400 members of the Iraqi-sponsored Palestinian organization of the *al-Tahrir al-Arabiya*, or the Ba'athist Arab Liberation Front (ALF), who arrived in Kuwait during the occupation. These Palestinians were then reinforced with 400 members of the pro-Iraq Palestine Liberation Front (PLF), led by Muhammad Zaidan, and 400 members of the Iraqi-controlled Palestine Liberation Army (PLA). Consequently, the IPA – which was regarded as a Palestinian army – was predominantly made up of Palestinians from Iraq and included very few Pales-tinians from Kuwait (Lesch 1991c: 45–6; 2005: 169; Ghabra 1991: 122–3; Mattar 1994: 41–2; Mason 2008). According to Lesch, the IPA joined *al-jaish al-sh'abi* (the neighbourhood Iraqi guard forces), manned roadblocks and assisted Iraqis in torture chambers. Such actions, although not carried out by Palestinians from Kuwait, increased the perception that Palestinians were acting as a 'fifth column' (Lesch 2005: 169).

Compounding this perception of 'active' support of the Iraqis by the IPA was the contentious issue of those Palestinians who continued to work following the Iraqi occupation. While it has been estimated that more than 70 per cent of Palestinians did not work under the Iraqis, the remaining 30 per cent were strongly resented by Kuwaitis. This was despite the fact that the vast majority of those Palestinians who returned to work did so under pressure from Iraqi soldiers or because their dire financial situations left them with no other option (Mason 2008; Lesch 1991c: 46–7; Ghabra 1991: 123). Perhaps the biggest factor in the tarring of Palestinians en bloc as collaborators, however, was the position taken by PLO leader Yassir Arafat and Palestinians in the Occupied Palestinian Territories (OPT). Soon after the Iraqi invasion, a photograph of Arafat embracing Saddam Hussein made world headlines. This was interpreted internationally as Palestinian support for Iraq's invasion (Lesch 2005: 169). The PLO then attempted to walk the precarious tightrope of not alienating Hussein, who was linking the Palestinian question to his invasion, while at the same time not being seen to support him overtly. As a result, the PLO was largely ambiguous in its formal position on the invasion, particularly in relation to Arab League statements (Lesch 1991a; Khalidi 1991: 14–17; Mattar 1994: 31–4). To many, particularly to Kuwaitis, this sense of ambiguity surrounding the PLO translated to de facto support for Hussein's invasion (Lesch 2005: 169). This perception was then exacerbated by widespread support of Hussein by Palestinians in the OPT (Lesch 1991b: 46–50). This support, however, was not so much about support of Iraq's invasion of Kuwait as it was of Hussein's stance on Israel, which was seen as a long-overdue response to the Israeli-inflicted suffering of the Palestinians (Lesch 1991a: 46–50; Muslih 1992: 22–3).

Revenge and terror

Following the liberation of Kuwait by coalition forces in February 1991, Kuwaitis started to come to terms with the widespread destruction that had occurred during the Iraqi occupation (Al-Hammadi 1995; Tetreault 1992). Enraged Kuwaitis, unable to retaliate directly against the Iraqis, instead started to re-direct their anger at those they saw as 'collaborators'. They regarded 'collaborators' as the foreign workers from countries that had either openly supported, or failed to condemn Iraq's invasion. Sudanese and Yemenis were grouped under the former category, while Jordanians, Palestinians and Iranians were in the latter. Palestinians, however, made up the largest and most conspicuous group. As a result, Palestinians became the primary target of Kuwaiti fury.

As early as January 1991, the Kuwaiti government in exile in Jeddah: 'harp[ed] on the theme that Kuwaiti society had been infiltrated by agents provocateurs [*sic*], and that the loyalties of Palestinians resident in Kuwait were suspect and needed to be determined' (Tetreault 1992: 8). Martial law was declared on 26 February 1991 and lasted until 26 June, providing the Kuwaiti police with the right to arrest and detain individuals without charge. In addition, martial law courts were set up to deal with those charged with collaboration (MEED 1991: 17; MNSRC 1992: 15). Palestinians became the main targets of retribution. At first, these revenge attacks were at the hands of vigilantes (allegedly including members of the Kuwaiti royal family) and the Kuwaiti resistance. Once sovereign rule returned to Kuwait, however, violent and hostile acts against Palestinians became part of a more systematic, state campaign of terror, aimed at 'cleansing' the emirate of Palestinians (Mason 2008; Lesch 1991c, 2005: 170–1; HRW 1992a). While an element of this campaign was unarguably undertaken in 'revenge' for what Kuwaitis regarded (unfairly, as we have seen) as Palestinian collaboration with Iraqis, it also provided an opportunity for Kuwait to act on its pre-existing desire to decrease radically the Palestinian population in the emirate. At the time, Human Rights Watch (HRW) characterized the actions of the Kuwaitis as being driven partly by revenge, but also aiming to 'restructure Kuwaiti society to make it more *reliable politically*' [my italics] (1992a: 1.) As Lesch outlined more pointedly, the labelling of Palestinians as collaborators enabled the mass expulsion of Palestinians, which then '"solved" the demographic problem and eliminated the perceived threat to Kuwaiti identity that they posed ... Expulsion was only feasible in the context of an upheaval that transformed the political and social order' (2005: 173). As I argue in this chapter, the range of measures undertaken by the Kuwaiti government to 'solve' this 'demographic problem' constituted state terrorism.

As demonstrated in the emergent field of critical terrorism studies, and by Blakeley in the first chapter of this volume, acts of terrorism perpetrated by states have been largely absent from the traditional literature examining 'terrorism' (Jackson 2008b, 2007; Blakeley 2007; Stohl 2006, 2008). As shown by scholars in this area, acts of terrorism need to be defined according to the rationale and objectives of particular acts of terror, rather than on the identity of the perpetrator. In line with this, the generally accepted definition of acts of terror is that they are deliberate, coercive actions designed to terrorize civilians to achieve particular political objectives (Jackson 2008a, 2007; Blakeley 2007; Burke 2008; Zulaika and Douglass 1996, 2008; Stohl 2006, 2008). On the basis of this definition, it is clear that states are among the actors utilizing terror tactics (Blakeley this volume; Rummel 1997; Sluka 1999; Hayner 2002; Pilger 2004). Indeed, as Stohl summed up, the 'most persistent and successful use of terror ... has been demonstrated by governments' (2006). The failure to recognize the reality of state terrorism has resulted in atrocities being allowed to be committed and legitimized in the name of 'national security'.

With this definition in mind, Kuwaiti actions against its Palestinian community discussed below – including violent attacks, 'disappearances', killings, detentions, torture, mass deportations and a raft of associated measures to consolidate feelings of intense fear – constitute a clear case of state terrorism. It is important here to explain why such actions constitute state terrorism, rather than more general acts of state repression. While such acts taken individually might constitute repression rather than terrorism, they need to be evaluated within the wider context, particularly in terms of the motives and instrumentality of the totality of such measures. In terms of motive, the range of actions taken against Palestinians were not isolated acts of repression, but a comprehensive campaign aimed at terrorizing the Palestinian community to achieve a particular political objective. In terms of instrumentality, the raft of actions were designed to reach beyond individual victims – sending a message to the broader Palestinian community that the terrorizing would be all-encompassing and relentless until they left Kuwait. Seen within this context, these acts, which created pervasive fear amongst Palestinians, were clearly part of a campaign of state terror.

Acts of terror

The worst of the attacks on Palestinians, as part of this far-reaching campaign, came between March and May 1991, when many Palestinians were beaten, tortured and executed. During this first wave of extrajudicial attacks and killings by vigilantes and members of the Kuwaiti resistance, an estimated 400 to 600 Palestinians – mostly males – were detained. While it was unknown exactly how many of these people were executed, the number was thought to be in the hundreds. In March 1991, one Kuwaiti Resistance member claimed to know of at least 80 'collaborators' who had already been killed by the Resistance. Former Kuwaiti Minister of State for Cabinet Affairs, Abdul Rahman al-Awdi, who was advising the prime minister in 1991, believed the figure was around 1,000 (Lesch 1991c: 47–9; Kramer 1991: 33; HRW 1992a: 4). As Kuwaiti rule was consolidated, attacks on perceived collaborators started to be undertaken by Kuwait's army and police (HRW 1992a: 1, 3; Graham-Brown 1992; Lesch 1991c: 47–50; AI 1991b). Kuwaiti checkpoints became notorious locations for security forces to identify and target foreign nationals they believed to be traitors – particularly Palestinians (Lesch 1991c: 49; Graham-Brown 1992; AI 1991b; Mason 2008).

Few Palestinians escaped harassment or attacks by either vigilantes or the security services. According to the chronicles compiled by Amnesty International (AI), victims were:

> Gunned down in public, or taken away, tortured and killed in secret. Hundreds of victims were plucked from their homes, taken from the streets, or arrested at check-points, many to be tortured in police stations, schools, and other make-shift detention centres.
>
> (AI 1991b: 1)

Lesch, who spent the period from 25 May until 3 June 1991 in Kuwait on behalf of Middle East Watch, documented a number of largely arbitrary and vigilante attacks on Palestinians. Many Palestinians I interviewed also attested to the intense persecution and violence that occurred during this period.[1] One man told me that his father had been tortured and had a stroke as a result. The interviewee himself was then tortured:

My landlord came to my house with relatives of his carrying guns. He said 'I want these people tortured – they haven't paid their rent'. They took five of us away and tortured us … one of my friends that was taken never returned. I don't know what happened to him.

(Mason 2008)

Another man told me: 'My wife's brother was taken by Kuwaitis … We ended up getting reports from the Red Cross that people had seen him tortured and killed by being burnt to death in a rubbish bin two weeks after liberation'. A third interviewee told an equally chilling story:

I was afraid of the Kuwaitis. They arrested and tortured so many. They raped women … Kuwaitis came to take my neighbour to jail and when I looked out of the window they threatened to shoot me. They accused my neighbour of being a collaborator. They [the neighbour] were found dumped in a bag – killed and chopped into pieces.

(Ibid.)

Within the security forces, some of the worst offences were carried out by members of the *Mabaheth Amn al-Dawla* or State Security Investigative Police (SSIP). The security forces were reported to have recruited hundreds of Kuwaiti youths and given them discretionary powers to arrest, beat and detain individuals (HRW 1992a: 2). Seized at roadblocks, on the street and in their homes, Palestinians suffered everything from humiliation to violent attacks and killings. One account, reported by Lesch, included the case of four young men (three of whom were Palestinians) who were arrested at a roadblock in May 1991. They were taken to Sabah Salem police station, where they were hit with clubs, heated and electrified rods, twisted cable wires, as well as burnt with cigarettes and made to drink something that they said smelt like urine or sewerage. The young men were subjected to sexual abuse and two had bones broken (Lesch 1991a, 1991c: 49).

Two of the most commonly targeted groups of Palestinians were the most visible groups to have continued work during the occupation – health workers and teachers (Lesch 1991c: 48; HRW 1992a: 8). One such story was that of Khalil Bakhour, a headmaster of a secondary school. He was arrested and did not return home. When his wife finally found his body at a hospital nine days later, she found horrifying evidence of torture including: his nose and ears having being cut off, his head being smashed and having a hole drilled in it, his neck apparently broken (his head was moving freely), his legs and hands broken and burns to his body. The Kuwaiti death certificate gave the reason for death as a 'heart attack and kidney failure' (Lesch 1991a).

Attacks were also indiscriminate in terms of age and gender, with women, children and the elderly being targeted. In one case, the body of a 16-year-old Palestinian boy was found in a garbage dump. Autopsy reports showed he had been tortured and raped (Marzoued 1994: 206). Similarly, the body of 13-year-old Iyad

Aqrabawi – who went missing with his cousins after they went to buy petrol – was found with a bullet in his forehead and other signs of torture (Lesch 1991c: 48). Palestinian youths and children were arrested and tortured in attempts to get them to say that other family members had been collaborators (Marzoued 1994: 206). At the other end of the age scale, there were many reports of attacks on elderly Palestinian men. One eyewitness reported that a 65-year-old man in the military prison had two soldiers take him in the early hours of the morning. They reportedly poured hot tea on his head and put out cigarettes on him (Lesch 1991a).

Human rights organizations found it almost impossible to gauge how many non-Kuwaiti nationals were extra-judicially killed after liberation, as neither they nor the families of those arrested were given information on detainees' whereabouts (AI 1991a). As much of the abuse was undertaken by members of the Kuwaiti security forces, it was not surprising that minimal official efforts were made to investigate reports of missing non-nationals, particularly Palestinians (HRW 1992a: 4). Some verification of the extent of violations, however, was able to be ascertained from cemetery records. In one example, entries in the logbook at Riqqa cemetery listed the cause of death for 54 unidentified bodies buried in March and April 1991 as 'killed' or 'executed' (HRW 1992a: 3; Lesch 1991c: 48).

Alongside violent attacks and extra-judicial executions were the large-scale detention and torture of Palestinians. In June 1991, Palestinian, Red Cross and embassy sources within Kuwait estimated that 6,000 Palestinians had been detained since Kuwait's liberation, with 2,000 still incarcerated in August (Lesch 1991c: 48–9; Dumper 1991:121; HRW 1992a: 7). While most detainees were held in four main prisons, people were also held in police stations and schools, where they were often beaten or tortured overnight, with some detained for indeterminate periods prior to going to trial. In the earliest days following liberation, there were accounts of people being imprisoned in private Kuwaiti houses (HRW 1992a: 6; Lesch 1991c: 49). Those who were taken into custody before the end of March were largely held incommunicado (HRW 1992a: 5).

Conditions for detainees varied according to the particular location; however, some of the worst brutality was catalogued by AI:

> Savage beatings with sticks, hose-pipes, and rifle butts, and whippings with electric cables appeared to be the norm for many detainees … [as is] the use of electric shocks, burning with cigarettes, candles and acid, cutting with knives, biting and threats of execution, and sexual assault. Teams of torturers often appeared to work in relays, maintaining the torture for hours. Daily torture of captives appeared to have been common.
>
> (AI 1991a: 2)

AI also discovered a number of instances where detainees were not given necessary medical treatment, with Kuwaiti army and security personnel refusing to follow doctors' recommendations (1991a: 2). Systematic torture remained common until September 1991, when the Kuwaiti authorities began to clamp down on it, in response to Kuwaiti doctors and the Red Crescent Society demanding more humane practices (HRW 1992a: 1,6). While the use of torture decreased after this time it was, however, not totally eradicated. Those who were tortured and released, moreover, were generally intimidated into keeping quiet on the details of their experiences, including menacing phone calls and further threats to themselves and their families (Mason 2008; Lesch 1991a). Those who were not released generally faced a 'collaborator' trial and/or deportation, as discussed below.

Following international concern, largely by human rights organizations, at reports of attacks on Palestinians and other perceived 'collaborators', in April and May 1991, the Kuwaiti government announced efforts to try to stamp out violent attacks. At the same time, however, the Kuwaiti leadership was not only turning a blind eye to the majority of abuses, but was making inflammatory comments that intensified anti-Palestinian feeling (Lesch 1991c: 50; HRW 1992a). These comments included the Emir's statement on 8 April that Hussein still had supporters within Kuwait seeking to 'shake our security and stability' and that Kuwait had not yet been 'cleansed' of that 'fifth column' (cited in Lesch 1991c: 49–50). In his first address to the Kuwait National Council on 9 July 1991, Crown Prince (and prime minister) Shaikh Sa'ad al-Abdulla al-Sabah declared that the emirate was continuing its attempt to 'purify the country of the evil elements that constitute a danger to its security' (in HRW 1992a: 7–8). In November, Minister of Defence Shaikh Ali al-Sabah made statements about Kuwait harbouring 'fifth columnists' (in HRW 1992a: 7–8). As HRW noted at the time, such statements 'amounted to invitations to abuse' (1992a: 1). Reflecting the impact of these comments, while there appeared to be a stronger effort to rein in police and prison officers from early June 1991, and the level of brutal killings abated, as Lesch outlined, 'political and extra-judicial torture, killings and disappearances continued into the mid-1990s, and ID-checking roadblocks remained pervasive' (2005: 172).

Consolidating the campaign of terror

The widespread and arbitrary attacks, detentions and torture of Palestinians were then compounded by a range of other measures, such as 'collaborator' trials, deportations and systematic discrimination, designed to make life unbearable for the Palestinian community. Again, it is important to reiterate here that while such measures on their own might not necessarily be acts of terror per se, they need to be evaluated within the wider campaign being conducted against Palestinians. All of these measures served to consolidate the environment of violence and intimidation that created pervasive terror amongst the Palestinian community.

In May and June 1991, so-called 'collaborator' trials were held by Kuwait's martial law courts. Human rights groups and international observers argued that little regard for due process was demonstrated in the trials. Criticisms of the trials included: interrogations being conducted without counsel; the use of torture in achieving confessions; many lawyers not being able to speak to their clients until after their trials had commenced; and the judge not having to read the charges against individuals unless the defendant's lawyer specifically requested it (HRW 1992a: 2–10; Lesch 1991a; Mason 2008). Of particular concern was a significant number of trials taking place with the defendants in absentia, with it feared that many such defendants were kept out of the courts to conceal evidence of torture. According to HRW, a 'substantial majority' of defendants relayed stories of extreme beatings to force confessions. Many appeared before the courts with injuries ranging from broken bones, cigarette burns and burns from handcuffs through which electric current had been passed (HRW 1992a: 6–8).

The court's ruling during these 'collaborator trials' was final and subject to review only by the emir himself.[2] Many Kuwaiti lawyers who acted for individuals charged with 'collaboration' were also themselves harassed. This meant that many lawyers were then reluctant to take on the role (HRW 1992a: 10). Kuwait traditionally imposed heavy sentences, so it was not surprising that the majority of the sentences were harsh, including 29 death sentences. Following severe international criticism, however, the death sentences were commuted by the emir to life imprisonment (HRW 1992a: 8; AI 1991a). Under Kuwaiti law, simply being charged with an offence was sufficient grounds for deportation, so many of the non-Kuwaitis who had been tried were deported, regardless of whether they were acquitted or convicted (HRW 1992a: 11–12, 31; Neier 1991: 327). Following the liberation of Kuwait, at least 2,500 expatriate workers and their 5,000 dependents (at least one-third of which were Palestinians) were formally deported from Kuwait (Graham-Brown 1992: 5; HRW 1992a: 11). While the deportation of suspected collaborators had begun soon after liberation, once martial law ended in June 1991 and suspects could no longer be tried in military courts, deportation was used as a more general punishment. Deportation could be ordered by either a court ruling or by an 'administrative deportation'. Deportation by the former applied to people who had been detained but cleared of charges, and some who were acquitted in the military courts. Administrative deportation orders were authorized by an order of the ministry of interior and could be issued by police officers. Administrative deportation was used widely against those without valid identity cards or residence permits (HRW 1992a: 12; Graham-Brown 1992: 5). Deportation orders had no appeals process and an order for one family member – such as a father – usually resulted in the departure of the entire family (Lesch 2005: 164–5).

The deportations played a central role in the terrorizing of Palestinians. As well as achieving the objective of decreasing the number of Palestinians in Kuwait, it sent waves of fear and panic throughout the community, many of whom were stateless. This sense of terror was particularly so in light of the widespread stories of people being 'dumped' just outside the border of Kuwait. The fate of deportees was often arbitrary: some were flown to Jordan, while others were simply ejected from Kuwait at its border with Iraq (Lesch 1991c: 51). For example, one group of 115 people (including 20 children) was left stranded just outside the Kuwaiti border and had to navigate a one-mile, mine-infested walk to the closest Iraqi checkpoint (HRW 1992a: 11).

Human rights organizations were also concerned about the conditions people were subjected to in the various deportation centres. For example, the main deportation prison in al-Shuwaikh was generally filled beyond capacity (with around 1,000 people held there at any time) and according to HRW, it exhibited some of the worst conditions in the country. Detainees were denied access to their families and lawyers, with the International Committee of the Red Cross (ICRC) only able to gain access to the prison in early June 1991. Even then, the ICRC was not allowed to interview detainees (HRW 1992a: 12).

For those Palestinians who were not officially forced to leave, systematic pressure was employed to 'encourage' their departure through 'economic penury, social discrimination and police checks on permits' (Graham-Brown 1992: 3). This harassment included people receiving visits from state security officials, telling them they had 'no future' in Kuwait and having their papers stamped with exit permits at checkpoints, which then made it difficult for the person to stay in the country for more than a month or so (Graham-Brown 1992: 5; Mason 2008).

One of the most effective methods of forcing Palestinians to leave Kuwait, however, was to deny them employment. Many government agencies were ordered to reduce the number of expatriate workers to 35 per cent of the pre-war level – overall numbers being slashed from 142,000 to 38,000 (Peretz 1993: 60; Kramer 1991: 33; Graham-Brown 1992: 4). To this end, Kuwait either sacked, or refused to renew the work contracts, of most Palestinians (Lesch 1991c: 50; Dumper 1991: 121). To further discourage the employment of Palestinians, ordinances forbidding even the entry of Palestinians into particular buildings – such as the government ministries, utility sites and army camps – were introduced soon after liberation (Dumper 1991: 121; Lesch 2005: 171).

The Kuwaiti government introduced new residence permits that had a validity of only one year and required applicants to 'prove' that they had not collaborated with the Iraqis. Palestinians were excluded from receiving most of the subsequent visas granted to non-Kuwaitis (Peretz 1993: 60; Graham-Brown 1992). As the campaign against Palestinians intensified, Palestinian children were banned from attending government schools, and Kuwait University's non-national quota was reserved solely for students from the Gulf States (Graham-Brown 1992: 4; Lesch 1991c: 51). Free medical care for Palestinians was rescinded. The extent to which Kuwait was prepared to take this was illustrated in the example of 42 Palestinian patients on kidney dialysis being told they were no longer eligible to continue their treatment, despite fundraising within the Palestinian community to pay for the medication. This situation continued for the dialysis patients until intervention by the German ambassador in Kuwait (Dumper 1991: 122). In mid-August 1991, the Kuwaiti government demanded utility payments accrued during the Iraqi occupation (from which Kuwaitis were exempted) (Lesch 2005: 171) and many landlords started asking for back-dated rent and threatening to confiscate belongings left in apartments if the rent was not paid. The landlords' actions were legalized on 17 July 1991, when the Kuwaiti cabinet approved the confiscation of absentee property (Kramer 1991:

32–3; HRW 1992a: 15). Other, more insidious 'punishments' designed to make life difficult for remaining Palestinians included garbage not being collected from Palestinian areas, such as Hawalli (Lesch 1991c: 51).

The international response

Given the lack of recognition of state terror discussed earlier, it was not surprising that Kuwait justified the measures taken against Palestinians after liberation in terms of national security and received little censure within the international state system. Indeed, outside of human rights organizations, NGOs, and concerned journalists and academics, the international community did little to stop the attacks on Palestinians. In fact, the United States, which had a troop presence in Kuwait following liberation, was seen to support tacitly Kuwaiti actions and deflect any effort to censure them. As HRW's damning report on the matter concluded:

> The thousands of U.S. troops in the country played an active role in rebuilding Kuwait's ruined infrastructure – even preparing a palace for the emir's return – but adopted a hands-off attitude when it came to preventing vengeful Kuwaiti forces from executing scores of perceived Iraqi sympathizers and torturing hundreds more ... the Administration acted as the foremost apologist for the emirate, rebutting human rights criticisms and actively seeking to deflect attention from Kuwaiti abuses. There were no public calls to punish those responsible for murder and torture, to release or retry those convicted of 'collaboration' after farcical trials, or to stop the summary deportation of refugees and stateless residents of Kuwait.
>
> (HRW 1992b: 10–11)

The hands-off attitude of the United States was reflected in one notorious incident, when journalist Robert Fisk witnessed US special forces troops looking on as Kuwaiti soldiers attacked Palestinians and Iraqis. Fisk and a colleague intervened to stop three of the Kuwaiti soldiers, who were beating up a Palestinian boy, but were laughed at when they asked the Special Forces to help. One of the officers told Fisk: 'We don't want your sort around here with your rumours. This is martial law, boy. You have a big mouth. Fuck off' (interview with author 2006; Fisk 2005: 799).

US President George H.W. Bush attracted considerable criticism for his response to reports of Kuwaiti atrocities. At a press conference on 1 July 1991, President Bush commented that:

> The war was not fought about democracy in Kuwait ... I think we're expecting a little much if we're asking the people of Kuwait to take kindly to those that had spied on their countrymen that were left there, that had brutalized their families there and things of that nature.
>
> (HRW 1992a: 25)

This statement was interpreted by many in Kuwait as tacit approval of their actions. Kuwait's daily newspaper, for example, published Bush's comments under the headline: 'Bush declares his understanding of Kuwaitis' attitude towards collaborators' (Neier 1991: 327). In its 1992 report, HRW castigated the Bush administration for what it saw as inaction over Kuwaiti human rights abuses:

> The crucible of the Bush Administration's human rights policy in 1991 was the Middle East. President Bush cited Iraqi abuses of human rights in rallying support for a military solution to the invasion of Kuwait. Yet as soon as the war was over, the cry for human rights was lost.
>
> (HRW 1992b: 10–11)

The US reaction to the acts of terror being perpetrated by the Kuwaiti state against its Palestinians is important. For in the United States being seen as giving tacit approval to Kuwaiti actions, and then being their strongest apologist when such actions were criticized in the international arena, the Kuwaiti government clearly felt they could terrorize Palestinians with impunity. This reaction by the United States, and the more general apathetic international reaction, is emblematic of the appalling consequences of the failure to recognize, and designate, acts of terror by states.

Conclusion

By May 1992, as a result of this comprehensive campaign of violence, intimidation and discrimination against Palestinians, only 30,000 of the original community remained in Kuwait (Graham-Brown 1992; Peretz 1993: 60). Kuwaiti government officials made it clear that their aim was to decrease this number further – to 10,000 or 15,000 – as soon as possible. The campaign of state terror against Palestinians had completed its main aim: the once-thriving Palestinian community in Kuwait had been destroyed (Mason 2008). By allowing the Kuwaiti government to couch their actions in the name of national security, the complicity of the United States and the inaction by the world community, Kuwait was able, with impunity, to brutalize and destroy an entire community.

Notes

1 Between 2000 and 2003, I conducted interviews with 103 Palestinians who lived in Kuwait at the time of the Iraqi invasion. This research was part of a wider study on the experiences of Palestinians in Kuwait as a consequence of the 1990–91 Gulf conflict (Mason 2008).
2 In August 1991, after international pressure, Kuwait amended its laws, giving a limited right of appeal (HRW 1992a: 11).

References

Al-Hammadi, A. (1995) *Torturing a Nation: A Documented Study of the Iraqi Aggression Towards the Kuwaiti People*, Kuwait: A1 Wazzan International Press.

Al Moosa, A. and McLachlan, K. (1985) *Immigrant Labour in Kuwait*, Kent: Croom Helm.

Amnesty International. (AI) (1991a) 'Kuwait: Three Years of Unfair Trials', 24 February 1994. Online, available at: www.web.amnesty.org/library/Index/ENGMDE170011994?open&of=ENG-KWT (accessed 16 January 2007).

—— (1991b) 'Amnesty International Calls on Emir to Intervene over Continuing Torture and Killings', April. Online, available at: www.amnestyusa.org/document/php?lang=e&id=D45F2AF72CFB7A7E802569A600600E2C (accessed?)

Blakeley, R. (2007) 'Bringing the State Back into Terrorism Studies', *European Political Science*, September, 6 (3): 228–35.

Brand, L. (1988) *Palestinians in the Arab World: Institution Building and the Search for State*, New York: Columbia University Press.

Burke, A. (2008) 'The End of Terrorism Studies', *Critical Studies on Terrorism*, April, 1 (1): 37–49.

Dumper, M. (1991) 'Letter from Kuwait City: End of an Era', *Journal of Palestine Studies*, Autumn, 21 (1): 120–3.

Feiler, G. (1993) 'Palestinian Employment Prospects', *Middle East Journal*, Autumn, 47 (4): 633–51.

Fisk, R. (2005) *The Great War for Civilisation: The Conquest of the Middle East*, London: Fourth Estate: 799.

—— (2006) Interview with Author, 20 March, Wellington, New Zealand.

Ghabra, S. (1987) *Palestinians in Kuwait: The Family and Politics of Survival*, Boulder: Westview Press.

—— (1991) 'The Iraqi Occupation of Kuwait: An Eyewitness Account', *Journal of Palestine Studies*, Winter, 20 (2): 112–25.

Graham-Brown, S. (1992) 'Palestinians in Kuwait: Report on a visit to Kuwait, May 1992, Gulf Information Project', London: British Refugee Council.

Hayner, P. (2002) *Unspeakable Truths: Confronting State Terror and Atrocity*, New York: Routledge.

Human Rights Watch (HRW) (1992a) 'Kuwait: Human Rights Developments since Liberation', Kuwait: Human Rights Watch, Country Reports. Online, available at: www.hrw.org/reports/1992/WR92/MEW2.htm#P8_0 (accessed 23 December 2008).

—— (1992b) 'Human Rights Watch World Report 1992: Kuwait', Online, available at www.hrw.org/legacy/reports/1992/WR92/INTRO.htm (accessed 23 December 2008).

Jackson, R. (2007) 'The Case for Critical Terrorism Studies: A Symposium', *European Political Science*, 6 (3).

—— (2008a) 'The Ghosts of State Terror: Knowledge, Politics and Terrorism Studies', Paper Presented at the Annual Meeting of the ISA's 49th Annual Convention, Bridging Multiple Divides, San Francisco.

—— (2008b) 'An Argument for Terrorism', *Perspectives on Terrorism*, 2 (2): 25–32.

Khalidi, W. (1991) 'The Gulf Crisis: Origins and Consequences', *Journal of Palestine Studies*, winter, 20 (2): 5–28.

Kramer, M. (1991) 'Kuwait: Back to the Past: Liberation has Brought Little Change to Kuwait's Way of Life or Its Politics', *Time*, 5 August, 138 (5): 32–40.

Lesch, A.M. (1991a) Fieldwork notes (unpublished), Kuwait, 25 May–3 June 1991. Cited with permission.

—— (1991b) 'Contrasting Reactions to the Persian Gulf Crisis: Egypt, Syria, Jordan, and the Palestinians', *Middle East Journal*, winter, 45 (1): 30–50.

—— (1991c) 'Palestinians in Kuwait', *Journal of Palestine Studies*, summer, 20 (4): 42–54.

—— (2005) 'No Refuge for Refugees: The Insecure Exile of Palestinians in Kuwait', in Ann M. Lesch and Ian J. Lustick (eds) *Exile and Return: Predicaments of Palestinians and Jews*, Philadelphia: University of Pennsylvania Press: 162–3.

Longva, A.N. (1997) *Walls Built on Sand: Migration, Exclusion, and Society in Kuwait*, Boulder: Westview Press.

Mason, V. (2001) 'Needed but not Accepted: The Ambiguous Role of Palestinian Migrant Workers in Kuwait Following the Discovery of Oil', in Cathy Cupitt and Gemma Edeson (eds) *On the Edge: Refereed Proceedings*, Perth: Black Swan Press: 13–28.

—— (2008) *Occupation, War and Exile: The Consequences of the Gulf Conflict (1990–91) for Palestinians in Kuwait*, unpublished PhD thesis, Social Sciences, Department of Humanities, Curtin University, Western Australia.

Mattar, P. (1994) 'The PLO and the Gulf Crisis', *Middle East Journal*, winter, 48 (1): 31–46.

Marzoued, M. (1994) 'Palestinian Youth in Kuwait', in Saul Bloom, John Miller, Phillippa Winkler and James Warner (eds) *Hidden Casualties: Environmental, Health and Political Consequences of the Persian Gulf War*, London: Earthscan Publications: 206.

Middle East Economic Digest (MEED) (1991) 'Government Quells Political Fears (Kuwait)', *Middle East Economic Digest*, 15 March, 35 (10): 17.

Migration and Naturalization Service Resource Center (MNSRC) (1992) 'Draft: Alert Series: Kuwait: Human Rights after February 28, 1991', March, Washington. Online, available at: www.uscis.gov/graphics/services/asylum/ric/documentation/alkwt92–001. pdf (accessed 23 December 2008).

Muslih, M. (1992) 'The Shift in Palestinian Thinking', *Current History*, January, 91: 22–8.

Neier, A. (1991) 'Watching Rights: Human Rights Violations in Kuwait', *Nation*, 23 September, 253 (9):327–8.

Peretz, D. (1993) *Palestinians, Refugees, and the Middle East Peace Process*, Washington, DC: United States Institute of Peace.

Pilger, J. (2004) *Tell me no Lies: Investigative Journalism and Its Triumphs*, London: Jonathan Cape.

Rummel, R. (1997) *Death by Government*, New Jersey: Transaction Publishers.

Ryan, S and Stork, J. (1977) 'Palestinians and the Political Situation in Kuwait', Interviews, *MERIP Reports*, February, 54: 14.

Shah, N.M. (1986) 'Foreign Workers in Kuwait: Implications for the Kuwaiti Labor Force', winter, *International Migration Review*, 20 (4): 815–32.

Shiblak, A. (1996) 'Residency Status and Civil Rights of Palestinian Refugees in Arab Countries', *Journal of Palestine Studies*, spring, 25, 3: 38–42.

Sluka, J. (ed.) (1999) *Death Squad: The Anthropology of State Terror*, Philadelphia: University of Pennsylvania Press.

Stanton Russell, S. (1989) 'Politics and Ideology in Migration Policy Formulation: The Case of Kuwait', *International Migration Review*, spring, 23 (1): 24–47.

Stohl, M. (2006) 'The State as Terrorist: Insights and Implications', *Democracy and Security*, 2: 1–25.

—— (2008) 'Old Myths, New Fantasies and the Enduring Realities of Terrorism', *Critical Studies on Terrorism*, April, 1 (1): 5–16.

Swaidan, Z. and Nica, M. (2002) 'The 1991 Gulf War and Jordan's Economy', *Middle East Review of International Affairs*, June, 6 (2). Online, available at: www.meria.idc. ac.il/journal/2002/issue2/jv6n2a7.html (accessed 23 December 2008).

Tetreault, M. (1992) 'Kuwait: The Morning After', *Current History*, January, 91 (561): 6–10.

Van Hear, N. (1998) *New Diasporas: The mass exodus, dispersal and regrouping of migrant communities*, London: UCL Press.

Zulaika, J. and Douglass, W.A. (1996) *Terror and Taboo: The Follies, Fables and Faces of Terrorism*, New York: Routledge.

—— (2008) 'The Terrorist Subject: Terrorism Studies and the Absent Subjectivity', *Critical Studies on Terrorism*, April, 1 (1): 27–36.

8 Winning hearts and mines

The Bougainville crisis, 1988–90

Kristian Lasslett

Introduction

In the early hours of the morning on 26 November 1988, the managing director of Bougainville Copper Limited (BCL) received a phone call. Militant landowners, he was told, had begun a campaign of industrial sabotage directed towards shutting BCL's lucrative copper and gold mine in the Panguna region of central Bougainville, an island province over 500 km off the Papua New Guinea (PNG) mainland. Over the coming months, the mine would become the focus of a complex struggle in which the PNG state would undertake the first major counterinsurgency campaign in the nation's history, sponsored and encouraged by BCL and the regional hegemon Australia.

PNG security force tactics included the burning of villages, extra-judicial killings, the harassment and torture of villagers, journalists and politicians, as well as the progressive installation of a blockade around Bougainville that was 'tighter than that placed around Saddam Hussein's Iraq' (Spriggs 1992: 13). When this war formally ceased in 1998, between 5,000 and 20,000 people had died, the majority of whom were civilians.

Since the military tactics employed in this counterinsurgency campaign fit within the rubric of state terrorism – that is they involved the state directing extreme violence at particular categories of civilians, in order to communicate a general message to the civilian population as a whole – this chapter will focus on identifying and defining the basic social conditions in which state terrorism became a cogent political practice for state actors in PNG. To begin this task, I will provide a brief overview of PNG's historical development before shifting to a more condensed narrative that plots the key moments of the counterinsurgency campaign during 1988–90.

Uneven and combined development in PNG and Bougainville

In order to approximate the forces which fostered state terrorism's employment in the Bougainville crisis, we must familiarize ourselves with the basic social structures that frame life in PNG and the peculiar social tensions they excite. Given PNG's 'late development', this process must begin by considering the

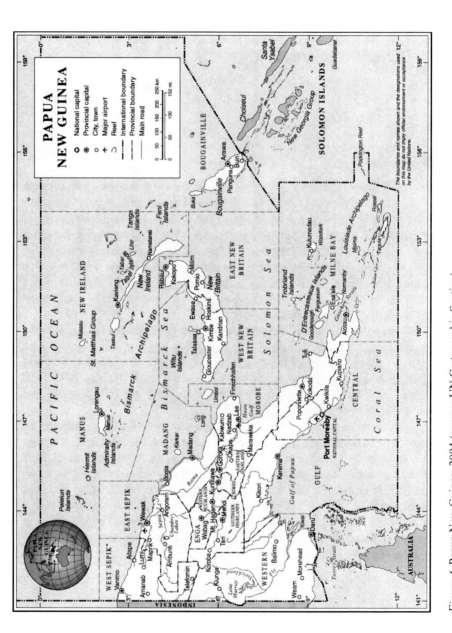

Figure 4 Papua New Guinea, 2004 (source: UN Cartographic Section).

primary social units of pre-colonial PNG and their evolution in PNG's colonial and post-colonial history.

The population of pre-colonial PNG lived generally in scattered hamlets or villages organized around kinship-based clans. The clan lineage, based on bonds of blood, acted as a corporate body which held ultimate ownership over land. Households acquired managerial rights to land on the basis of lineage membership. The household reproduced itself through the cultivation of root crops, supplemented by hunting and gathering. Surplus labour was devoted to raising pigs for ceremonial exchange and warfare. Generally, a small number of closely connected hamlets formed a political unit, the clan community, under the leadership of a big man (the Melanesian form of chieftaincy). Thus, by the nineteenth century, PNG consisted of thousands of hamlets, populated by an agricultural community whose connection with the objective conditions of production was mediated through the social form of the clan. As a consequence, wealth, culture, custom and politics were devoted to preserving this higher unity on which the household's life and identity hinged.

The first, formal stage of colonial expansion into PNG began in 1884 with Britain's annexation of the south-eastern half of New Guinea and Germany's more or less simultaneous annexation of the island's north-eastern half. By the end of the First World War, the New Guinea mainland and a number of islands to the east, including Bougainville, had passed to Australian control. Australia's predominant concern was to secure an inert island shield that would protect its northern flank from imperial aggressors. The poorly funded Australian administration focused on pacification of the indigenous population, as well as the development of rudimentary forms of colonial regulation and governance. Irregular patrols by colonial field officers meant that the administration relied on the cooperation of indigenous leaders.

Penetration of plantation, mining and merchant capital was weak. While the colonial administration was active in encouraging indentured labour, it nevertheless fundamentally sought to preserve the clan community by protecting it from excessive forms of exploitation and land alienation. After all, for a colonizer starved of funds and personnel, the clan structure was central to the regulation of PNG's dispersed communities.

Following the Second World War, Australia devoted more resources towards developing a stable, capitalist political economy in PNG. A conservative development policy aimed to expand smallholder production through the social framework of the village, while at the same time mapping PNG's natural resources, in the hope of attracting injections of foreign capital that could develop a solid revenue base for a national government.

Initially, the provision of expanded agricultural extension services was monopolized by big men. In Bougainville, however, it was observed that the intense social obligations placed on these actors, limited their ability to integrate into the structures of global capitalism. Consequently, it was often young men who had standing in their clan community but were not so tightly bound by traditional obligations that were able to utilize their superior education and training to manipulate customary land tenure and cultural obligations, in pursuit of economic aims based increasingly on the logic of capital (Connell 1978: 230, 249–50; Ogan 1972: 180). Thus, we begin to see an important, incremental and uneven *process* of qualitative change in the social structures of villages, both in Bougainville and PNG generally; 'progressive' subjects, more intensely involved in the circuits of global capitalism, begin to act as agents of change, subordinating clan, custom and culture to private, accumulation strategies based on commodity production.

In 1963–64, indigenous smallholder production of cocoa totalled 174 tonnes. By 1969–70, this cocoa production had 'risen to 1,461; by 1979–80 to 10,151; and by 1988–89 to 13,841 tonnes' (Oliver 1991: 163). By 1980, only 19 per cent of Bougainville's population was engaged wholly in subsistence agriculture (Oliver 1991: 162). Thus, village households, whose access to land was mediated through the clan community, were involved increasingly in production for exchange; they were employing revenues to pay for goods and services essential both for the reproduction of the household (e.g. education, tinned fish, rice), and customary obligations (luxury items). In addition, these village households needed to purchase steel tools and labour power (in the case of expanding smallholdings). Consequently, clan, custom and culture became more widely subordinated to the accumulating strategies of private households.

With the expansion of commodity production in Bougainville, and the subordination of customary structures to the private, accumulation strategies of households, there began a process of social fracturing; households differentiated into new, social strata with distinct, accumulation strategies. Those able to expand production and diversify surplus into business/investment, accompanied on occasion by salaried labour, formed a rural bourgeoisie and rich peasantry. While households lacking access to essential resources, such as land, labour and finance, resorted to temporary participation in unskilled/semi-skilled wage labour. These disadvantaged villagers tended to form a new rural poor. As a result of the growing divisions in Bougainville, Tanis (2005: 457–8) claimed: 'the people started seeing each other not as brothers and sisters and clan mates with common ownership of wealth, but more as business competitors, with only the fittest to survive'.

Accompanying these social changes in PNG's predominantly rural population was a rapid process of political development, instigated by the Australian administration. When PNG was granted independence in 1975, there existed an elected parliament (which by 1977 contained 109 seats), a bureaucracy with more than 50,000 employees (40 per cent of formal sector employment), a judiciary, a defence force and a police constabulary. In addition, there was a provincial and local level of government (see Connell 1997; Dinnen 2001; Mapusia 1986; Turner 1990).

This structure placed enormous pecuniary pressures on the independent PNG state, whose size outweighed its revenue base; this demanded that the government pursue domestic policies focused on expanding the most promising national forms of commodity production, balanced with a pressing need to also attract foreign capital and foreign aid. The minerals industry, in particular, became integral to the funding of the expanded state apparatus, a fact which manifested itself in a minerals tax regime that prioritized capturing rents (Wesley-Smith 1990: 6–7).

The national government's capacity to regulate the essential operating conditions for expanded commodity production, particularly in the mineral extraction industry, was however limited by the peculiar character of PNG's political system. The most fundamental social unit underpinning PNG's national polity was and remains the evolving clan community, which regulates most forms of everyday social metabolism in rural areas. As a political whole, the clan community tends to take the form of a unified bloc, composed increasingly of antagonistic, social groups, forming an alliance under the leadership of the social fraction, which successfully forges a popular definition of the community's general interest (usually based on notions of economic development, social progress and respect for tradition). Thus, the private practices of households in PNG are mediated through the structures of clan communities, whose character is itself the site of political struggle between fractured social groups.

This political foundation has two important consequences for the character of PNG's nation-state. First, with the state lacking a monopoly over the regulation of everyday social interaction, it relies on the structures and the lead social fractions of clan communities to produce the essential, operating conditions for expanded, commodity production (Jackson 1992: 81–2). In addition, as the state's relationship with its citizens is mediated through the clan structure, the state derives its legitimacy on the basis of its ability to promote the interests of the clan community, as defined by the hegemonic social fraction (Connell 1997: 303). National MPs, therefore, generally obtain their support base through circuits of patronage with clan networks, giving rise to a national polity where atomized, political representatives compete for positions in government to access the necessary resources to repay their local supporters.

In situations where the state must actively penetrate local communities to facilitate essential public infrastructure, or to promote economic developments of national significance (such as mining), the leadership of local communities have tended to exploit this moment; employing their integral position in the regulation of social reproduction to obtain patronage outside of the electoral relation by impeding these developments. As the interruption of essential, national projects increased in the 1980s, a tension has developed between the need for political stability and PNG's particular form of indirect informal political rule. In lieu of either a developed, civil society through which consent may be forged at a local level, or of formal mechanisms to integrate effectively local clan structures into the state apparatus, agents of the state have turned to 'special policing operations (often with the Defence Force) ... with ... [a] para-military orientation' (Dinnen 1994: 107). In this instance, state violence becomes a mechanism for enforcing the stability necessary for particular national projects, while at the same time presenting the state generally as a credible force to PNG's clan communities. Bougainville was, and remains, the most extreme manifestation of this important, political dynamic.

The Bougainville copper mine and the struggle for its closure

The Bougainville copper and gold mine developed on this changing social and political terrain. Beginning production in 1972 during its life (until 1989), the mine accounted for 17 per cent of the nation's internal revenue, 12 per cent of its gross domestic product (GDP) and 45 per cent of its export income (CRA 1990: 2–3). Being a large, open-cut mine, surrounding villages suffered from land appropriation, environmental damage, village relocation and social inconvenience. BCL attempted to ameliorate villagers' grievances through the payment of occupation fees and compensation to primary right holders, who were expected to distribute these cash sums to subsidiary right holders. While absolutely small, these payments were relatively significant, being 'the initial impetus to business development' as households sought to take advantage of opportunities opened by the mine (Applied Geology Associates 1989: 4.16). Consequently, compensation payments, mediated through custom, became another site of struggle for socially fractured households.

In 1980, certain landowners in the mine lease area created a formal organization to unite scattered landowners into a larger social bloc, initially led by the middle and rich peasantry, along with the rural bourgeoisie. Known as the Panguna Landowners Association (PLA), this organization impressed more intensely on BCL the landowners' social ability to mediate their access to the minerals. This effort won an improved compensation agreement, which included a provision for the setting up of the Road Mine Tailings Lease Trust Fund (RMTLTF). This fund would administer certain compensation payments, diversifying them into investments that would survive the mine's life. By 1983, the trust was chaired by prominent Bougainvillean businessman Severinus Ampaoi, who directed that the trust's investments be determined by rate of return, not local needs. This strategy intensified a wider perception among the poor peasantry, wage-labourers and the still largely 'traditional' clan communities in the mine lease area that the region's wealth was being monopolized by self-interested individuals and organizations, motivated by rates of profit rather than the needs of local households. Other organizations that would become subject to this charge included the Bougainville Development Corporation (BDC), as well as BCL and its associated benevolent organization, Bougainville Copper Foundation (BCF).

Consequently, as households in the mine lease area became more intensively affected by the process of social differentiation during the 1980s, those denied access to key economic resources (land, compensation, skilled jobs, business contracts, finance, agricultural extension services), found common ground in chastising the PLA, RMTLTF, BCL, BCF and BDC. This was particularly the case for a rapidly growing, youth population – lacking in land, education and finance – who were forced often into underemployment and unemployment. These groups, squeezed by the development process, found representation in a number of radical, young leaders, the most prominent of whom were Francis Ona, a truck driver at the mine, and his cousin, Perpetua Serero. These leaders set about a forward-looking project, albeit dressed in traditionalist garb, of inverting the existing social balance by subordinating the production of profit to the needs of the clan community, viewed through the lens of egalitarianism.

These new, radical leaders became hegemonic within the PLA, with Ona and Serero elected to the organization's executive on 21 August 1987. Under their leadership, the PLA acquired a markedly different social character. No longer would the landowners' customary title be principally employed to extract increased compensation and benefits from BCL. Rather, the landowners' title would be directed towards the subordination of capital to the egalitarian clan community. On 12 April 1988, BCL was to learn of the PLA's new social character when the PLA executive delivered a letter to demand formally PGK 10 billion compensation (about USD 12 billion) from the company and 50 per cent of BCL's future profits. Also, the PLA called for the total transfer of company ownership to the landowners after five years (Panguna Landowners Association 1988a). Failure to meet these demands, it was warned, would lead to the mine's closure.

For the remainder of 1988, BCL attempted to encourage the new PLA to soften its demands, offering a public works programme valued at PGK 3 million (about USD 3.6 million). In addition, the national government ordered an official inquiry into the social and environmental effects of the mine. Yet Ona informed the company and national government that 'we are not worried about money. Money is something nothing'.[1] 'We are', Ona claimed, 'determined to close the mine' (Bougainville Copper Limited 1988a). The company found its interests and those of the new PLA in intense opposition. The social mechanisms that could placate the old PLA executive had little effect.

On 22 November 1988, Ona began to fulfil his promise to shut down the mine. The PLA entered what was described as 'stage 2' of its political project (Panguna Landowners Association 1988b). This new phase began with armed men forcing their way into BCL's explosives magazine to steal a considerable quantity of dynamite. In response, BCL organized crisis meetings with senior national government officials in Port Moresby, the nation's capital.

Late in the night, after the first day of crisis talks (25 November), a campaign of industrial sabotage began that was directed against mine property, causing damage estimated at PGK 620,000 (about USD 750,000). BCL's managing director phoned senior ministers immediately to arrange a meeting the following morning to discuss their joint response. During the meeting, BCL's policy was made clear: this was an act of 'highly organised terrorism'. Consequently, the militant landowners must be arrested, the legitimacy of the PLA executive re-examined and, most importantly, the terrorists must not be 'given indication that increases their expectations and therefore vindicates their actions' (Bougainville Copper Limited 1988b).

BCL wanted the national government to employ the security apparatus to remove the radicals and restore the leadership of moderates from the old executive. The company requested that the Royal PNG Constabulary's (RPNGC) mobile squads be employed, arguing it 'was necessary to have at least two riot groups and flight arrangements to get them to Bougainville' (Bougainville Copper Limited 1988b). Further reinforcements were requested by BCL's Managing Director on 2 December (Cornelius 1988).

A senior official from the RPNGC[2] explained to me, the mobile squads 'are semi-military, they are aggressive ... they go in there and they beat a few heads in ... burn a few houses down, shoot a few pigs ... the mobile squads operated with a modus operandi of frightening people' (Personal Communication, 10 July 2006). BCL was well aware of the mobile squads' character. A senior manager from BCL explained:

> We knew the riot squads were heavy handed, that was well known in PNG ... If you threw a rock at them you would get ten rocks thrown back ... We knew that the heavy handed approach wouldn't work if they were there long term. It was a case, somebody has to come ... and put a lid on things before it gets out of hand.
>
> (BCL Manager, Personal Communication, 26 October 2006)

Despite BCL's policy position, the National Executive Committee (NEC) – PNG's cabinet – restrained temporarily the mobile squads, preferring to negotiate a political solution. BCL's reaction was recorded in an internal memorandum of its chairman: 'The PM's priority was to "appease" the landowners. I expressed the view that CRA [BCL's parent company] would want to review its assessment of PNG as a place to invest' (Carruthers 1988). BCL had been presumptuous in assuming an identity of interests between mining capital and the national government. While both share a common interest in maintaining the operating conditions of mining production, perspectives on how this is to be achieved can differ as a result of BCL's preeminent concern with the security of tenure and profit rates, and the state's priority to balance fiscal liquidity, international reputation and domestic legitimacy. The chairman's reaction did little to ingratiate the company in Port Moresby.

A ministerial envoy arrived in Bougainville on 4 December 1988 and four days later, it was agreed that Ona would assist the police to find the remaining explosives. In return, the government promised to restrain the mobile squads and review the conditions of the company's mining agreement. BCL 'expressed amazement at [the] outcome of the Minister party's actions over the past week' (Bougainville Copper Limited 1988c) and so did the hard-talking Police Commissioner Paul Tohian. Like the company, Tohian believed it was a strategic failure on the government's part to 'appease' landowners, a decision that could reverberate elsewhere in the country. As a result, early on 9 December, the police commissioner 'pulled the rug from underneath' the national government (NEC Official, Personal Communication, 5 July 2006), ordering a raid on four landowner villages. Landowners were arrested, women harassed, villages burnt; however, Ona and other radicals escaped (BCL Manager, Personal Communication, 7 June 2006).

Heightened tensions necessitated that the mobile squads remained and this placed a considerable burden upon BCL. A senior BCL manager informed me:

There were absolutely no arrangements for accommodation, no arrangements for messing, or transportation, so it was expected that the company was going to feed, and house, and transport these guys ... [The mobile squads said:] 'If you want us to drive around give us some f*** vehicles [asterisks added]. We are not going to be very effective if we are dying from hunger, we need to be fed'. So what do you do?

(Personal Communication, 26 October 2006)

Consequently BCL became the de facto logistical network for PNG's security apparatus, who at the time were one of the few government organs openly sympathetic with the company's aims.

In January 1989, the rebels – who named themselves formally the Bougainville Revolutionary Army (BRA) – began attacking the property of local businessmen and murdered Matthew Kove, a prominent member of the old PLA and a relative of Ona. In late March, the murder of a Bougainvillean nursing sister by a Highlands labourer increased tensions.[3] In revenge, two Highlanders were killed and riots broke out in Toniva on the east coast of Bougainville. Government infrastructure was damaged and three militants were killed near Buin in south Bougainville in armed skirmishes with the mobile squads (Hiambohn 1989a).

The government characterized these events as a serious law and order breakdown, provoked by the rebels. In a joint statement, the police minister and police commissioner warned: 'Any person who steps out of line will ... bear the brunt of the law ... Give us a month and we will get everything in order' (quoted in Hiambohn, 1989b). This time, it would appear, the government was prepared to defer to PNG's security apparatus, hoping they could 'put a lid' on the situation via their trademark 'reactive', 'paramilitary' style of policing. These punitive methods had been employed with varying success in other law and order operations during the 1980s (Dinnen 2001; Mapusia 1986). To assist operations, the existing contingent of 250 mobile squad officers was supported by approximately 100 defence force soldiers. On 10 April 1989, 'a full-scale military operation against militant landowners' was launched (Rea 1989: 1). The prime minister argued: 'No responsible government can allow this to continue. Our nation depends upon the unity of all its people ... unity is strength' (quoted in Avei 1989: 2).

The operation employed a number of well-established tactics. First, 'villages were burnt as a form of punishment and in retaliation for ambushes or simply on suspicion of harbouring rebels. Soldiers believed that all Bougainvilleans should be made to suffer for the actions of those few militants' (Rogers 2002: 252). A BCL official, who surveyed the damage, reported that 'forty, fifty villages, and the crops [were destroyed]. Villages were varying from five or six houses to twenty or thirty houses' (BCL Manager, Personal Communication, 31 May 2006). Those left homeless were placed into government 'care centres'. A witness from this period recalled: 'we were not allowed any contact [with people in the "care centres"] ... even priests going in trying to minister to the people were beaten up' (Havini 1997: 31).

The security forces also engaged in the harassment, torture and execution of suspected BRA supporters. The predominant victims of these attacks were young Bougainvillean men, provincial politicians, young women, as well as national and international journalists, perceived to be either supporting the BRA or undermining the national government by reporting atrocities (Amnesty International 1990; Layton 1992). Indeed, on 21 March 1989, journalists and diplomats were banned officially from entering the island.

Commentators often characterized these atrocities as examples of undisciplined behaviour. Poor discipline may have exacerbated the brutality of these operations; however, the general tactics were by then institutionalized and had been employed systematically in reactive law and order operations throughout the 1980s. State violence had become an 'ongoing ... instrument of state rule' (Gurr 1986: 50) for a government that lacked a monopoly over social regulation on the ground. In the specific case of Bougainville, the destruction of villages served to demoralize and reduce the BRA's support network while its arbitrary character, often based quite simply on village proximity to militant operations, sent a message to the surrounding communities: 'control your young men, or we will destroy you'. Additionally, the detention, torture and execution of individuals from specific social groups made clear to all those of a similar social identity that they were under suspicion. Facing an elusive enemy, violence against civilians became one of the few mechanisms available to the underprepared and poorly equipped security forces to pressure the militants.

As stories and rumours surrounding the state's terrorist campaign began to disperse around and beyond central Bougainville, it had the ontological effect of creating a social vacuum. That is, villagers' immediate fear of personal destruction transcended temporally their socially generated interests; so that households and communities were guided for a period by a natural desire to secure their existence as organic beings. Under these conditions, the space was opened for the state to assert its hegemony through forging a definition of the community's social interests which also promised to secure villagers' personal safety.

In this instance, however, the social vacuum created by the climate of fear was harnessed initially by the BRA, who emphasized ethnic solidarity and secessionism as the means through which to protect Bougainville from the 'marauding' security forces. Ethnicity and secessionism are phenomena that have a complex lineage in Bougainville. In the immediate term, ethnicity and secessionism allowed the BRA to forge a definition of the community's general interests in areas beyond their immediate zone of influence in central Bougainville, creating alliances with leaders who, under normal conditions, would be opposed to the BRA's anti-capitalist ideology.

This ability of the BRA to exploit the social vacuum created by the state's terror campaign was a new phenomenon in PNG. Ordinarily, these types of security operations were directed at tribal fighting in the Highlands and rascal gangs situated in urban centres. Unlike the latter two scenarios, the Bougainville crisis featured the BRA, who was organized around an ideology that mixed forms of proto-socialism and Melanesian communalism. These basic elements of

BRA's ideology – when mediated through the lens of Bougainvillean nationalism and a respect for tradition – had popular appeal, allowing the BRA to turn the ontological effect of state terrorism in its favour.

Nevertheless, the BRA was still manoeuvring within difficult social terrain. Given that Bougainville was an island made up of hundreds of tightly bound clan communities, which collaborated in regional and provincial organizations of a more tenuous nature, it was difficult for any one social fraction to create a new national unity under their leadership. While the BRA could obtain support temporarily through ethnic solidarity, its anti-capitalist stance and radical practice were inconsistent with the general interests of most scattered clan communities, defined as they tended to be by the middle and upper peasantry. This tension could be exploited by the national government through encouraging community leaders to break any alliance with the rebels. If this could be achieved, then the disenfranchised young men who had joined the hardcore element of the BRA could be persuaded to desist by clan-mates.

Accordingly in late April 1989, the national government attempted to exploit this fractured, political fabric by offering a substantial peace package, which provided landowners with increased royalties, compensation, employment, business contracts, public works, business advisory assistance and investment opportunities. When the package was presented to moderate members of the old and new PLA on 25 April, the minister for minerals and energy made clear his desire that this would enable a new, unified PLA to be formed, under the leadership of moderates. It was anticipated that these moderates could employ the patronage from the peace package to reclaim community support, thus creating the conditions under which local pressure could be brought to bear on the disenfranchised, young men who had fled with Ona into the dense, mountain regions of central Bougainville (PNG 1989). It was hoped this loss of local support would persuade the BRA to engage in dialogue with the national government.

Instead, the BRA responded to this initiative by refocusing its attacks on the mine. On 15 May, the mine unions decided to withdraw their labour while several days later, BCL management resolved that until operating conditions were safe, the mine would remain closed. The company informed the national government that 'protection for such a diverse operations as ours is virtually impossible against a determined militant effort' (Cornelius 1989). BCL hoped that the increased, pecuniary pressure from the mine's closure – in conjunction with the negative impact it was having on PNG's international reputation (which BCL was keen to highlight publicly) – would encourage the national government to adopt the only strategy that could restore stability: to neutralize the militants.

Initially, the national government persisted with its political project of isolating the BRA. However, by the beginning of June, a NEC reshuffle had placed a number of capable and highly influential 'hawks' into key ministerial positions. The company's request for more decisive action was now being supported actively in the cabinet room. The hawks' position was strengthened as the mine's closure began to undermine political stability. BCL's contribution to PNG's internal revenue, according to its parent company CRA, fell from 17 per cent in 1988 to 6 per cent in 1989 (CRA 1990: 2). In response, the government initially made a number of smaller adjustments to the national budget, including a PGK 25 million reduction in government expenditure. By January 1990, this amount was increased to PGK 100 million (about USD 120 million), supplemented by a number of other serious austerity measures (Weisman 1990: 49).

Consequently on 8 June 1989, BCL was told by the newly appointed Minister of State, Ted Diro, that the government was prepared to 'neutralize' the BRA, employing 'brutal firepower' (Bougainville Copper Limited 1989a). Diro noted more ominously, 'it will take time, democracy'. The reasoning behind this shift in strategy was articulated in parliament soon after the government declared a state of emergency on 26 June. The newly appointed Defence Minister, Benias Sabumei, claimed:

> For the first time in the history of PNG, we are witnessing a well organised group of landowners, supporters, and other Papua New Guineans using arms and opting for violence as a primary bargaining power to achieve their objectives. Objectives they all know will destroy the economic and political unity in our country.
>
> (Hansard 11 July 1989)

The Foreign Minister, Michael Somare, elaborated on this point:

> We are faced with huge compensation claims today. You cannot build a teachers' college, you cannot build a hospital or improve the highway from Watabung to Chuave because the people are calling for compensation. We must think seriously when dealing with the Bougainville situation because similar problems will arise when other mines go into operations in the future.
>
> (Hansard 11 July 1989)

Consequently, in order to restore the operating conditions of mining capital and deter radical forms of landowner practice, it was announced that the BRA would be isolated from its civilian support base and militarily harassed, showing Ona the 'hopelessness of the situation that he is facing' (Hansard 11 July 1989). The minister for police warned that 'people who obstruct, hinder, assist rebels and who disobey lawful orders are bound to be assaulted and harassed' (Hansard 12 July 1989). BCL was broadly supportive of this new offensive strategy. One senior manager informed me:

> We did everything they [the security forces] asked of us to make their life more comfortable, and better able to manage through, with transport, communications, provisions, whatever, fuel ... as far as we saw it we were hoping that they were going to solve the situation, so we could start operating again.
>
> (BCL Manager, Personal Communication, 26 October 2006)

As the conflict escalated in seriousness, another party became active in making its presence felt: the Australian state.[4]

Publicly the Australian government was reserved, with the foreign minister stating the Bougainville crisis was an 'internal matter' for PNG, which he hoped would be resolved through a 'peaceful solution' (see for example, Hansard 8 November 1990). This official position was a predictable one for a regional hegemon aware that its 'otherness' demanded that particularly sensitive diplomatic issues be handled on an 'informal' and 'discrete' basis (Evans 1989: 43). Nevertheless, given that Australia's highest foreign policy concern was the security of its immediate region (Evans 1989:1), Bougainville in fact became a 'fairly big part' of the Australian government's life (Department of Defence Official, Personal Communication, 31 August 2006).

It was generally felt within the Australian government that the escalating crisis on Bougainville could 'rip the fabric of PNG in ways where the repercussions would simply be unpredictable' (Department of Defence Official, Personal Communication, 28 August 2006). Would secessionism spread to other parts of PNG? Would this legitimize landowner violence in other provinces? Would the security forces crack under the pressure? Would the state collapse? All of these contingencies were discussed, with a general conclusion drawn that any of these outcomes would be potentially deleterious for Australia's regional security, mining companies and its credibility as an international actor.

Consequently, Australia's *actual* position during 1989–90 was that it supported an expanded counterinsurgency campaign and would do everything it could to assist the PNG security forces, short of sending its own infantry. Thus, as a senior official from Australia's High Commission informed me:

> We were, early on, supporting a stronger PNGDF role than they actually played ... we were ... pushing them to get more troops over there ... Ben Sabumei was the Minister, and I use to see him all the time saying get your people over there.
>
> (Personal Communication, 25 August 2006)

To facilitate this policy directive, Australia played an enhanced, logistical role in supporting the counterinsurgency, both through its defence cooperation programme and High Commission presence. A senior defence staff official stationed in the High Commission at the time informed me that during the 1989–90 period:

> Without our support they couldn't have done what they did ... we'd be training them at training camps, we'd be supplying them with weapons, we'd be supplying them with uniforms, everything. And then we'd say these companies are now fit to be used, let's send them now to Bougainville. We'd even fly them to Bougainville for God's sake.
>
> (Personal Communication, 1 September 2006)

This intensive support of the PNG security apparatus presented Australia with a particular moral dilemma. The aforementioned Australian defence staff official explained:

> We had good knowledge about what was going on ... they [the PNG security forces] were involved in some pretty awkward situations where there was large losses of life ... [Yet] to step back completely and let them just sink was not really a palatable option.
>
> (Personal Communication, 1 September 2006)

As Australia's support for PNG in this instance served to consciously reinforce the state's capacity to continue and intensify its campaign of terrorism, it may be characterized as an instance of 'surrogate' state terrorism.[5]

With BCL and Australia providing logistical and moral support for an expanded counter-insurgency operation, and the NEC now increasingly influenced by the 'hawk' faction, the PNG security apparatus would proceed to engage in three major military offensives during 1989 and 1990. The first offensive began in July 1989. Employing 500 soldiers and 200 mobile squad officers (Oliver 1991: 219), the offensive aimed to clear the strategically important port mine access road, as well as the mine operations area (Rogers 2002: 224–9). In doing so, it was hoped the security forces would create the stability necessary for the mine to reopen; at the same time, they would neutralize key BRA members, as well as demoralize and remove their civilian support base.

The clearing of these key strategic zones was facilitated by the threat of force by the deputy controller Colonel Dotaona. Havini observed:

> They [villagers] were actually invited to come down but the invitation is 'if you don't come down, you cop what you get'. We are going in there on a military operation. If you are not down there in care centres you are fair game.
>
> (Havini 1997: 31)

Those who remained were indeed subject to the sort of violent destruction witnessed during the April operations. For example, Irenaeus Ivomei of Puempe village reported that on 18 July 1989, soldiers had been observing his village, which consisted of 18 adults and 40 children. At around 1 p.m. these soldiers opened fire abruptly 'with automatic weapons, destroying our houses'. Then, according to Ivomei: 'A helicopter appeared which also rained automatic fire down onto the village ... all food gardens [were] destroyed, and the air was foul with the smell of dead pigs, dogs, cats and chickens' (Quoted in Havini 1990: 35–7). Furthermore, as with the April operations, young men in the area were tortured and murdered by the security forces. One example cited by Amnesty International is particularly gruesome:

> The body of Ambrose Leo of Guava village arrived at Arawa General Hospital on 18 July 1989 with a note attached to it which read: 'this is the first

billion of your ten billion' ... Ambrose Leo had been beaten, kicked and
stabbed in the ear before being shot at close range.

(Amnesty International 1990: 23)

Symbolic forms of violence such as the above example linked the extra-judicial
killings to the landowners' radical demands in the minds of villagers. Indeed, the
fact that 'body after body' was reported to have been dumped at the Arawa
General Hospital (*Four Corners* 1991), rather than being disposed of quietly,
indicated there was a definite, instrumental dimension to the security forces' brutality; that is, to terrorize the general civilian population of Bougainville into
abandoning their support of the BRA and its radical demands.

While the operations were not successful in neutralizing key BRA personnel,
BCL felt the security environment in the mine area was safe enough to begin
repair work in August 1989. In this same period, the national government withdrew the security forces from offensive operations. The conciliators in cabinet
hoped that because the BRA was faced with a unified PLA, dwindling civilian
support and military demoralization, the organization may be prepared to join
the peace process.

During late August and early September, it was announced publicly that the
mine would reopen on 5 September while the peace package would be signed on
11 September, with or without BRA support. In response, the BRA shut down
the mine successfully only a day after reopening, while on the morning of 11
September, the peace package signing was derailed after the BRA assassinated
John Bika, a provincial minister who was involved in its negotiation. The conciliators in PNG's cabinet were disillusioned, strengthening the standing of the
'hawks', whose preferred solution was the annihilation of the BRA's core
element. This new complexion in cabinet manifested itself in October with the
replacement of the operation's deputy controller, Colonel Dotaona, with Colonel
Nuia. It was believed that Dotaona was not aggressive enough in pursuing the
BRA, whereas Nuia had a reputation for being a 'hard man', with a 'punitive'
approach to military operations (RPNGC Official, Personal Communication, 10
July 2006).

While building his offensive capacity, Nuia attempted to isolate the BRA
strategically by placing a goods and services embargo on areas known to be
under BRA influence. It was hoped that 'when people start to feel the hardships
in education and health they might start to turn against the militants', particularly
in those areas where the alliance with the BRA was most tenuous (Bougainville
Copper Limited 1989b). To assist this process of subversion, the security forces
and provincial government opened a dialogue with community leaders, encouraging them to turn over the young men in their area suspected of supporting the
BRA. By late December, the provincial administrative secretary Peter Tsiamalili
reported that in Boku 'the leaders ... are identifying the hardcore and turning
them into the authorities. A similar thing is happening down in Buin' (Bougainville Copper Limited 1989c). Thus, the perception grew that by placing pressure
on clan communities through a goods and services blockade while establishing

communications with local leaders, moderates in regions of weak BRA penetration could be encouraged to break their alliance with the BRA and reassert their leadership. It was hoped this government policy would allow the security forces to concentrate their limited offensive capacity on the most hardcore BRA region, Kongara, in central Bougainville.

Nuia's much-awaited military offensive began on 11 January 1989. It involved 500 soldiers, supported by 300 police officers and 100 correctional services staff (Hansard 14 March 1990). Rogers (2002: 241–2) observed that, 'the operation had two phases; phase 1 would force the rebels onto the run while phase 2 would see the rebels rounded up'. Phase 1 was enacted by a surprise aerial bombardment of villages in the Kongara region, employing Iroquois helicopters, grenades and mortars supplied by the Australian government (including white phosphorous mortar rounds). Rogers (2002: 228–9) noted that 'mortar rounds often fell indiscriminately, wounding civilians and terrorising the local population'. Indeed, Amnesty International (1990: 35) received reports that at least 27 villagers, 'including elderly people and children, were killed between mid-January and mid-February as a result of heavy mortar fire and aerial bombing into areas of suspected rebel activity'. As with previous operations, the security forces implemented 'destructions' while arresting, torturing and, in some cases, killing young Bougainvillean men, often simply on the justification they had 'dreadlocks, a hairstyle worn by some BRA members' (Amnesty International 1990: 26).

The BRA counterattacked successfully and an increasingly frustrated security force responded by summarily executing six civilians, throwing five of the corpses into the sea from an Iroquois helicopter. Knowledge of these desperate acts of state terrorism filtered throughout the island and the BRA earned pan-Bougainville influence (see Spriggs 1990). As early as 6 February 1990, the chairman of BCL warned the PNG prime minister:

> I am alarmed at the rate at which the situation in Bougainville has deteriorated in the last month. To the best of my knowledge the militants now appear to be in control of virtually the entire Province with the principal exception of the area around Arawa, Panguna, Kieta and Aropa.
>
> (Carruthers 1990)

The national government, realizing they 'could not control it [the island] anymore', negotiated a cease fire with the BRA (NEC Official, Personal Communication, 8 July 2006). It was agreed that the security forces would leave the island, to be replaced by an international, peace-monitoring group. By the end of March, the island was completely abandoned by the PNG state and by BCL. In May 1990, the BRA declared independence and formed an interim government.

Neither PNG, nor Australia nor BCL were prepared to see the island abandoned. Indeed, PNG and BCL still shared the sincere hope that the mine would re-open. The NEC was also particularly wary of the strategic implications an independent Bougainville would have for an already fragile national polity. Similarly, Australia saw no particular advantage in having yet another non-viable micro-state in the region, which they speculated would only further undermine an increasingly hazardous regional security environment. Thus, while initiatives aimed at opening dialogue with the BRA were pursued, the Defence Intelligence Branch (DIB) of PNG's Department of Defence, in conjunction with Australian Defence Force officers stationed both in the Papua New Guinea Defence Force and the Australian High Commission, began to develop a strategy to retake the island, known as Operation *Bung Wantaim.*

The first pillar of the operation was a full military blockade of the island (including Buka just off its northern tip). Officially beginning on 6 May 1990, it aimed to prevent all goods and services, including humanitarian assistance, from reaching Bougainville's general population. The DIB (1990: 10) observed 'the people have been waiting for S. Kauona [a BRA leader] to bring in the assistance of four foreign nations to provide goods and services', the denial of which will be 'detrimental for the NSP [North Solomons Province] population's well being and good for the government'. The DIB (1990: 11) claimed that these hardships would create the conditions for carefully 'planned and executed psychological warfare', aimed at turning areas of weak BRA influence against the militants. This tactic – as we know from similar, smaller-scale blockades in late 1989 – aimed to strengthen the influence of moderate community leaders, who could utilize customary relations to encourage support for the security forces, with promises of restored services and increased forms of patronage.

The effect of the blockade on the civilian population was enormous. An observer from the Australian Council for Overseas Aid, who visited the island in March 1991, claimed the blockade had created 'an emergency situation', with medical experts on the island suggesting 'over 3,000 people have died as a direct consequence of the blockade' (Evans 1992: 45–6). This general finding was supported by Médecins Sans Frontières, who observed in 1993 'elevated death rates in the population, and most especially among the most vulnerable groups such as children and pregnant women' (Médecins Sans Frontières 1993). Despite reports of the suffering being made public on numerous occasions in 1990, BCL in December lent its moral support to maintaining the blockade, telling the government to 'starve the bastards out' (Somare 2001). While the Australian government 'did everything it could' to support the embargo in terms of logistics (High Commission Official, Personal Communication, 25 August 2006).

The second and third pillars of Operation *Bung Wantaim* were enacted in September 1990 when the security forces re-entered the island, with the support of a Bougainvillean paramilitary force, known as the Buka Liberation Front (BLF). The BLF was led by prominent politicians and businessmen from north Bougainville and equipped by the national government. This had been pre-planned by the DIB (1990: 14), who hoped that the 'hardships' caused by the blockade would create an environment where Bougainvillean leaders, loyal to the national government, could turn BRA members in the north and south of

Bougainville through the provision of patronage and cash bribes (DIB 1990: 14; PNG Department of Foreign Affairs Official, Personal Communication, 11 July 2006). If successful, the DIB (1990: 13) claimed, the BRA's expanded opposition could be militarized, creating a 'civil war' situation where central Bougainville would be pitted against north and south Bougainville. Under these general conditions, the security forces could retake the island and surround the militants in central Bougainville. This latter aspect of the operation was given particular attention by Australian Defence Force officers in the PNGDF and the Australian High Commission, who:

> Started to devise an operation to win back Bougainville. Which was to start by getting back Buka, getting Buka, and then working into expanding your basis and thereby winning it back in a military sense, when it was in total darkness, the case was totally hopeless.
> (High Commission Official, Personal Communication, 1 September 2006)

By the end of 1990, the security forces had successfully recaptured Buka. BRA suspects were reportedly executed at escalated rates, while those villages in Buka that were accused of supporting the BRA were subject to brutal reprisals by the BLF (Spriggs 1992: 11–13). Thus, by 1991, the security forces had been successful in militarizing the social tensions on Bougainville, cultivating a 'civil war' which eased its military reengagement. This military reengagement proceeded in 1991, in close liaison with community leaders. Furthermore, additional anti-BRA forces were militarized. By 1992, government control had been established over north and south-west Bougainville, setting the conditions for a long and complex civil war that would not formally cease until 1998.

Conclusion

In this case study, we have seen that the traditional clan communities of PNG were exposed to the structures of global capitalism under the guidance of a conservative, colonial administration. Consequently, a unique trajectory of historical development was created, wherein households, bound together by clan relations, became increasingly differentiated as a result of their uneven access to essential social resources such as land, credit, labour and compensation. It was on this social base that radicalized youth, squeezed by the development process into underemployment and unemployment, squared off against capital in an intensive form, corresponding to the intensive penetration of capital in central Bougainville. This struggle absorbed the PNG state, whose carrot-and-stick approach symbolized the tension between political legitimacy and political stability in PNG.

In these circumstances, state terrorism first became a tool utilized by the national government to restore the hegemony of moderates in the PLA, an organization which mediated capital's access to the conditions of production. Once the BRA attempted to unify Bougainville in a class alliance under its own leadership, state terrorism became a tool which could exploit the fragmented social fabric of the island, encouraging local leaders to reassert their authority and regulate the activities of the hardcore youth. In both instances, state terrorism's cogency arose from the elusiveness of the militants, which made the targeting of civilians a practical way in which the state could induce the BRA to abandon its hard-line position and join the peace process.

Australia, as the regional hegemon, brought its weight to bear on the crisis at a subtle level, employing discrete political connections at cabinet, High Commission and defence force levels to encourage a more militarized approach to the conflict. With enhanced defence cooperation assistance, Australia proved to be a surrogate agency of state terrorism.

BCL lacked the continuity, depth and form of connection that Australia possessed with PNG's political rulers. Therefore, BCL found its support for offensive operations was less persuasive in Port Moresby than hoped. Nevertheless, BCL's decisive position in the economic fabric of PNG – and direct support of the military apparatus – entailed that in the absence of an ability to forge a genuine, strategic consensus with the PNG state, it could at least manoeuvre in a way that added moral weight to existing national political forces that were sympathetic to its position. BCL was assisted in this aim by Australia's strategic position, illustrating how the geopolitical interests to arise out of a world economy, organized around a system of nation states, can create international, political forces which attempt to assist capital's secure movement across spatial barriers.

Notes

1 Ona's idiosyncratic mode of expression captures how money, as the higher object of the private household's accumulation strategy, has corroded increasingly the kinship structures through which this drive has been mediated, and placed definite limits on the ability of poorer households to realize the new commodified use values that have become available through integration into the world economy. Hence money is certainly 'something', but for the radicalized subjectivities of the PLA, it is also 'nothing'; in other words, it is symbolic of new, destructive relationships that inhibit households from evenly realising the universal, historically generated, social forces of humanity (e.g. use-values of all varieties, forms of knowledge, cultural media, health services etc.), that were becoming available through integration into a global society.
2 The identities of the informants cannot be disclosed for confidentiality reasons.
3 The Highlands are a densely populated mountainous inland region of mainland PNG. Significant historical tensions exist between Bougainvilleans and migrant Highlands labourers.
4 PNG's stability was a major strategic concern for the Australian government, given its geographical proximity to Australia's northern coastline and sea-lanes. Australian capital also had significant investments in PNG (AUD 1.8 billion in 1989 or the equivalent of USD 1.4 billion), with a large, expatriate population living throughout the country. Accordingly, after granting PNG independence, Australia continued to provide untied budget support for the PNG state (15 per cent of PNG's revenue in 1989). Australia assisted PNG's security forces through a significant, defence aid programme. This programme accounted for 51.1 per cent of Australia's total defence aid of AUD 72.2 million (about USD 56 million) in 1989–90.

5   When a government sells, grants, and in other procedures provides favorable
         terms by which a coalition partner, ally, friend, or client state ... obtain equipment
         that a 'reasonable person' should perceive would likely be used to *continue* prac-
         tices of repression and terrorism ... [or] when governments train the personnel
         that conduct the terror operations, consult with and advise (for 'reasons of state')
         the security services of a 'friendly' state in its use of terrorism ... [these are forms]
         of surrogate terrorism.

                                                                           (Stohl 1984: 53–4)

References

Amnesty International (1990) *Papua New Guinea: Human Rights Violations on Bougain-
    ville 1989–1990*, London: Amnesty International Secretariat.
Applied Geology Associates (1989) *Environmental, Socio-economic and Public Health
    Review of Bougainville Copper Mine Panguna*, New Zealand: Applied Geology Asso-
    ciates Limited.
Australia, Senate (1990) Hansard, Canberra: AGPS. Online, available at: http://parlinfo.
    aph.gov.au/parlInfo/search/display/display.w3p;query=Id%3A%22chamber%2Fhansar
    ds%2F1990-11-08%2F0180%22 (accessed 19 June 2009).
Avei, P. (1989) 'PM Seeks Islanders' Support for Sake of Nation', *Post-Courier*, 10
    April: 2.
'Blood on the Bougainvillea' (1991) *Four Corners*, ABC Television, Sydney, 24 June.
Bougainville Copper Limited (1988a) Minutes from 31 July 1988, Panguna.
—— (1988b) Minutes from 26 November 1988, Port Moresby.
—— (1988c) Minutes from 8 December 1988, Siromba Hotel, Papua New Guinea.
—— (1989a) Minutes from 8 June 1989, North Solomons Government Office.
—— (1989b) Minutes from 22 December 1989, Location unknown.
Carruthers, Donald S. (1988) Memorandum to Directors, CRA Limited, Melbourne, Vic-
    toria, 6 December.
—— (1990) Letter to Hon. Rabbie L. Namaliu, Morauta Haus, Waigani, Port Moresby, 6
    February.
Connell, J. (1978) *Taim Bilong Mani: The Evolution of Agriculture in a Solomon Island
    Society*, Development Studies Centre Monograph, no. 12, Canberra: Australian
    National University.
—— (1997) *Papua New Guinea: The Struggle for Development*, London: Routledge.
Conzinc Riotinto of Australia (CRA) (1990) 'Bougainville Update: The Economic Impact
    of Bougainville Copper', supplement to *CRA Gazette*, 25 (6).
Cornelius, Robert J. (1988) Letter to Hon. Rabbie L. Namaliu, Office of the Prime Minis-
    ter, Waigani, Port Moresby, 2 December.
—— (1989) Letter to Hon. Rabbie L. Namaliu, Office of the Prime Minister, Waigani,
    Port Moresby, 18 May.
Defence Intelligence Branch (1990) *An Intelligence Resume for Contingency Planning
    for North Solomons Province*, Port Moresby: Department of Defence.
Dinnen, S. (1994) 'Public Order in Papua New Guinea: Problems and Prospects', in A.
    Thompson (ed.) *Papua New Guinea: Issues for Australian Security Planners*, Can-
    berra: Australian Defence Studies Centre.
—— (2001) *Law and Order in a Weak State: Crime and Politics in Papua New Guinea*,
    Honolulu: University of Hawai'i Press.

Evans, G. (1989) *Australia's Regional Security: Ministerial Statement*, Canberra: Department of Foreign Affairs and Trade.

Evans, L. (1992) 'The Health and Social Situation on Bougainville', in M. Spriggs and D. Denoon (eds) *The Bougainville Crisis: 1991 Update*, Bathurst: Crawford House Press.

Gurr, T.R. (1986) 'The Political Origins of State Violence and Terror: A Theoretical Analysis', in M. Stohl and G.A. Lopez (eds) *Government Violence and Repression*, London: Greenwood Press.

Havini, Moses (1990) 'Human Rights Violations and Community Disruptions', in R.J. May and M. Spriggs (eds) *The Bougainville Crisis*, Bathurst: Crawford House Press.

Havani, Marilyn (1997) 'Questions and Answers', in *Women Speak out on Bougainville: National Forum*, Neutral Bay: Women for Bougainville.

Hiambohn, W. (1989a) 'Three More Deaths in Buin Shoot-out', *Post-Courier*, 23 March: 2.

—— (1989b) 'Soldiers under Specific Orders to Flush Out Ona', *Post-Courier*, 28 March: 2.

Jackson, R. (1992) 'Undermining or Determining the Nature of the State', in S. Henningham and R.J. May (eds) *Resources, Development and Politics in the Pacific Islands*, Bathurst: Crawford House Press.

Layton, S. (1992) 'Fuzzy-wuzzy Devils: Mass Media and the Bougainville Crisis', *Contemporary Pacific*, 4 (2): 299–323.

Mapusia, M. (1986) 'Police Policy towards Tribal Fighting in the Highlands', in L. Morauta (ed.) *Law and Order in a Changing Society*, Canberra: Australian National University.

Médecins Sans Frontières (1993) Letter to Hon. Michael Ogio, Waigani, Port Moresby, 11 November.

Ogan, E. (1972) *Business and Cargo: Socioeconomic Change Among the Nasioi of Bougainville*, New Guinea Research Bulletin, no. 44, Canberra: Australian National University.

Oliver, D. (1991) *Black Islanders: A Personal Perspective of Bougainville 1937–1991*, Melbourne: Hyland House.

Panguna Landowners Association (1988a) Letter to the Managing Director, Bougainville Copper Limited, Panguna, North Solomons Province, 5 April.

—— (1988b) Letter to the Managing Director, Bougainville Copper Limited, Panguna, North Solomons Province, 18 November.

Papua New Guinea National Government (1989) Minutes from 25 April 1989, Port Moresby.

Papua New Guinea National Parliament (1989) Draft Hansard, Port Moresby: National Parliament.

—— (1990) Draft Hansard, Port Moresby: National Parliament.

Rea, S. (1989) 'Soldiers to Step up Action', *Post-Courier*, 11 April: 1.

Rogers, T.A. (2002) 'The Papua New Guinea Defence Force: Vanuatu (1980) to Bougainville (1990)', unpublished thesis, Australian National University.

Somare, M. (2001) 'Draft declaration', *Alexis Holyweek Sarei, et al.* v. *Rio Tinto PLC, et al.*, United States District Court (Central District of California), Case No. 00-11695 MMM AIJx.

Spriggs, M. (1990) 'Bougainville, December 1989 – January 1990: A personal history', in R.J. May and M. Spriggs (eds) *The Bougainville Crisis*, Bathurst: Crawford House Press.

—— (1992) 'Bougainville update: August 1990 to May 1991', in D. Denoon and M. Spriggs (eds) *The Bougainville Crisis: 1991 Update*, Bathurst: Crawford House Press.

Stohl, M. (1984) 'International dimensions of state terrorism', in M. Stohl and G.A. Lopez (eds) *The State as Terrorist: The Dynamics of Governmental Violence and Repression*, London: Greenwood Press.

Turner, M. (1990) *Papua New Guinea: The Challenge of Independence*, Middlesex: Penguin Books.

Wesley-Smith, T. (1990) 'The politics of access: Mining companies, the state, and land-owners in Papua New Guinea', *Political Science*, 42 (2): 1–19.

9 Paramilitarism and state terror in Colombia

Sam Raphael[1]

Introduction

The strategically important Republic of Colombia, located in the north west region of continental South America, has been rocked by sustained civil violence for several decades. With substantial natural resources (including significant oil reserves), vast cocoa-producing regions, and Pacific and Caribbean coastlines, the country has been the site for ongoing political struggle to an extent not seen elsewhere in the region. For decades, ruling elites have governed through two political parties (Conservative and Liberal), and successive administrations have worked to open the Colombian economy to foreign capital, and to ensure a healthy investment climate. Through this, elites have both garnered extensive support from the United States, which has provided billions of dollars in economic and military aid to the government, and have entrenched their domestic rule.[2] Colombian society remains deeply inequitable, with vast wealth differentials between the landowning oligarchy and the wider population sustained by the continuing consolidation of capitalist social relations.

Despite relative consensus across the ruling elite regarding the desired structure of the economy, there exists a set of significant political forces in Colombia who remain deeply opposed to the prevailing socioeconomic order. A wide range of people from within Colombian civil society have adopted a position of confrontation against the state, either through taking up armed struggle or through peaceful political organization. Such opposition manifests itself in a varied and complex way, with a myriad of groups who seek to modify or even overturn existing distributions of power and wealth. In response, the Colombian elite, acting through both the state and allied institutions of social, economic and military control, have led a concerted effort to disrupt, dismantle and destroy all viable opposition. As a central strategy within this effort, these elites have undertaken a coordinated campaign of violence against Colombian civilians, specifically in order to instil fear and dissuade political organization from below. As a discrete element within the wider civil conflict, ongoing since the 1960s, tens of thousands of civilians have been victims of violence from a complex network of rightwing paramilitary groups tied to core elements of the state security forces, and to the ruling class. Through the use of unrestrained violence delivered against the civilian population, the Colombian state aims to silence those who would otherwise work openly for better working and living conditions, and for a more equitable redistribution of land, wealth and power. As Adam Jones noted:

> It is ... the defense of the political and economic status quo that is most important [for (para)militarism in Colombia]; one does not need to be a presumed auxiliary of a formal rebel organisation, merely to adopt – or belong to a collectivity deemed to hold – a rebellious stance towards existing socio-economic arrangements.
>
> (Jones 2004: 129)

The prevalence of pro-state violence in Colombia, conducted primarily by paramilitary groups but often alongside military 'counter-insurgency' forces, forms one of the most brutal campaigns of (state) terror in the world. This is so despite the fact that it is carried out largely unremarked upon by commentators, academics and politicians in the West. It is also so despite oft-repeated claims which suggest that the paramilitary groups act independently from the state, and that the civilian government and security forces are focused on *combating* right-wing violence against the population. As will become clear throughout this chapter, state terrorism has had – and continues to have – profound ramifications for the people and society of Colombia, is intimately wrapped up with paramilitary violence and is a key tool for governance by the country's ruling elites.

State terrorism and paramilitarism

Despite clichéd and regular references within the field of 'terrorism studies' to the ongoing difficulty in defining terrorism, there is in fact a clear consensus among scholars regarding the core elements which mark out this form of violence. Terrorism is understood by most experts in the field as:

1   violence (or the threat thereof); which is
2   instrumental, as opposed to aimless; and conducted for
3   political (i.e., non-personal) ends; in order to
4   influence an audience wider than the immediate target(s), generally through the creation of fear; achieved through
5   the deliberate and systematic violation of the established norms surrounding the use of force.

(Raphael 2009: 58)

Despite the fact that most terrorism scholars subsequently refuse (explicitly or otherwise) to discuss the phenomenon of state terrorism, this core definition is explicitly designed to be act-centred (rather than actor-centred), and can clearly be applied to those acts conducted by state forces. Certainly, there exists no *substantive* (non-arbitrary) reason why violent acts conducted by the state which conform to the above definition should not be considered to be terrorist. In this light, and with reference to her chapter in this volume, these core elements can be recast to fit within Ruth Blakeley's more focused definition of state terrorism. Consequently, state terrorism can be understood as a deliberate act of violence against individuals that the state has a duty to protect, or a threat of such an act if a climate of fear has already been established through preceding acts of state violence; which is perpetrated by actors on behalf of, or in conjunction with, the state (including paramilitaries and private security agents); which is intended to induce extreme fear in some target observers who identify with the victim(s); and which is designed to force such observers to adapt their behaviour in some fashion. It is this carefully constructed definition which will be used here to frame the discussion of state terror in Colombia. The ongoing civil conflict in the country has, over the past 50 years, resulted in the violent deaths of hundreds of thousands of people from a variety of forms of violence. For the purposes of this chapter, however, it is important to identify that strategy of violence which is conducted by, or on behalf of, the state against protected civilians in order to induce fear and change behaviour. It is this that forms the campaign of state terror in Colombia and, as we shall see, comprises what is perhaps the central problem of security for Colombian society.

Given the extensive use of paramilitary groups by the Colombian state to terrorize key sections of the population, it is first worth exploring the reasons for employing such clandestine groups. States use paramilitary groups for two main reasons. First and most obviously, it allows for the maintenance of a veneer of innocence. 'Plausible deniability' is often sought by governments engaged in terrorism, given the opprobrium with which it is met by domestic and international opinion. This is perhaps particularly the case where a state receives substantial financial, political or military support from a liberal democracy, given the restrictions often imposed upon such aid by legislators. As a recipient of vast amounts of security and economic assistance from the United States, much of which is subject to key human rights conditionalities, the desire to maintain plausible deniability is clear in the case of Colombia. In particular, the provisions of the so-called 'Leahy Law', which extends to all security assistance provided through the US State and Defense Departments, ensure that funds, training and equipment cannot be provided to 'any unit of the security forces of a foreign country if the Secretary of State has credible evidence that such unit has committed gross violations of human rights' (Center for International Policy *et al.* 2007: 11–12). Although such provisions have been shown to be easily and repeatedly circumvented by US policymakers eager to keep the funding taps open (Stokes 2005; Barry 2002), there is little doubt that such restrictions influence the way in which violence against civilians is 'contracted out'. Commanders in the field in Colombia have a clear rationale for ensuring that evidence concerning gross violations of human rights is difficult to compile. 'Independent' paramilitary forces allow for the application of terrorist force without endangering the primary funding and training source used to conduct the campaign. This logic has long been understood, with a key Colombian investigator into the military–paramilitary nexus during the 1980s, Carlos Jiménez

Gómez, describing military commanders implicated in paramilitary violence against civilians as:

> Officials who go overboard when faced with the temptation to multiply their ability to act and take advantage of private agents ... whom they end up using as a hidden weapon so that, with this plan of hired killers, they can do officiously what they cannot do officially.
>
> (Human Rights Watch 1996)

This was also the conclusion drawn by a detailed report from the Inter-American Commission on Human Rights, which found that the Colombian military:

> Recognised that they could avoid the political costs of engaging in war without limits by leaving to the paramilitary groups the tasks which violated human rights and international humanitarian law and which would attract the attention of the public and the international community.
>
> (IACHR 1999)

Second and of equal importance, paramilitaries are employed by the state to increase the terror experienced by the target audience. Indeed, it is the very 'independence' of the groups used, and associated perception of a lack of control by any higher power, that can instil such fear. This logic has been acknowledged by Michael Stohl: fear is maximized through the use of 'notoriously viscous vigilante groups who are widely recognized in society to act as agents of the state but who are not "legally" constrained in ways that official organs might be felt to be'. Specifically:

> Such extensive use of groups who appear to be virtually 'uncontrolled' and who are notoriously unrestrained in their use of viscous methods is *not* a strategy designed primarily to effectuate the physical elimination of the adversary; that can be accomplished easily by efficient, technologically-sophisticated police organs. Rather, it is a strategy designed primarily to induce extreme fear in a target population. It is a strategy of terrorism and is understood as such by the populations of targeted societies.
>
> (Duvall and Stohl 1988: 245–6; Stohl 2006: 10)

This logic is clearly at play in Colombia, where the viciousness with which paramilitary groups conduct their campaign against civilians, the impunity with which they operate, and the inability of the population to receive protection from the state, heightens the terror experienced. As we shall see in the next section, paramilitary groups in Colombia routinely target not only those they specifically wish to remove; in addition, their strategy is designed to spread fear within the wider population. It is, as Stohl acknowledges, a strategy of terrorism.

Colombian paramilitaries and the use of terror

In their war against insurgents, the Colombian security forces and their paramilitary allies have engaged in a wide variety of military operations against the major armed groups which are positioned against the state: specifically, the *Fuerzas Armadas Revolucionarias de Colombia* (Revolutionary Armed Forces of Colombia, FARC), and the smaller *Ejército de Liberación Nacional* (National Liberation Army, ELN). Alongside covert operations and targeted airstrikes, the Colombian military – backed by massive US support – has engaged these insurgent forces in large-scale battle at numerous points since the 1960s.[3] However, in parallel to this, military–paramilitary violence is consistently deployed against *civilians* in violation of international humanitarian law.

This violence has resulted in the vast majority of overall violations in the country, with the military–paramilitary war waged primarily against a wide array of unarmed progressive forces throughout Colombian civil society. In a war which has routinely claimed a staggering 3,500 to 4,500 political and extrajudicial killings each year, statistics compiled from a variety of sources paint a clear picture as to which groups are primarily responsible for targeting civilians. This has long been the case, with Human Rights Watch reporting by the end of the 1980s that the 'main actors in the political violence are the so-called "paramilitary groups" that operate against left-wing politicians, union leaders, grass-roots organizers and human rights monitors'. Indeed, violence by these groups 'continued to be the country's most serious human rights problem', and was 'responsible for the largest number of both targeted and multiple killings' (Human Rights Watch 1989, 1990). By the mid-1990s, 'multiple, credible reports' suggested that paramilitary activity had increased significantly. At this stage, paramilitaries were known to be committing no less than 70 to 80 per cent of all politically motivated extrajudicial killings; many hundreds, if not thousands, each year (Human Rights Watch 1994, 1997). The proportion of overall violence attributed to the paramilitaries was maintained throughout the late 1990s, with hundreds of people killed illegally each year, many times the number attributed to insurgent forces (US Department of State 1998, 2002a; Chomsky 2000: 65). During the current paramilitary 'ceasefire', negotiated by the Uribe administration, groups continued to be active throughout the countryside and, joined by military units in ever-increasing numbers, are still responsible for around 70 per cent of all illegal killings (Amnesty International 2008a).

In this light, security forces and their paramilitary allies have long posed the greatest threat to the security of Colombians. Crucially this campaign against civilian targets has been deliberately designed to instil extreme fear in a *wider target audience*. This has been acknowledged by the US Government, with the Department of State (1999, 2002a) repeatedly stating that paramilitary groups in Colombia have 'killed, tortured, and threatened civilians suspected of sympathising with guerrillas *in an orchestrated campaign to terrorise them* into fleeing their homes, thereby depriving guerrillas of civilian support' (emphasis added). Indeed, the use of terror has been confirmed by key figures within paramilitary groups, with former AUC leader Carlos Castaño stating that: 'The methods the "self-defence" forces used to recover Urabá were no less violent or disgusting that those used by [guerrillas] ... This should be absolutely clear! We copied the guerrillas' methods and confronted them with the same tactics' (Human Rights Watch 2002). The deliberate intent by the paramilitaries to instil fear among a wider group than their direct targets was clearly identified by the IACHR's (1999) detailed study. According to the final report:

> Many of the acts of paramilitaries are designed to spread terror among the civilian population. In fact, although all of the violent actors in Colombia issue threats and engage in other acts intended to intimidate the civilian population, actions of this type committed by the paramilitary groups are undoubtedly the most extreme and frequent.

As we have seen, it is this characteristic which marks out the violence as terroristic. As terrorism expert Bruce Hoffman (1998: 43–4) makes clear, terrorism is 'specifically designed to have far-reaching psychological effects beyond the immediate victim(s) or object of the terrorist attack. It is meant to instil fear within, and thereby intimidate, a wider "target audience"'. Indeed, this characteristic – the 'terror' within terrorism – is nothing less than the 'hallmark' of this mode of violence (Jenkins 1985: 4).

Working alongside state security forces, paramilitary groups employ several strategies to instil terror. First, specific groups often warn potential targets of the presence of paramilitaries and the likelihood of being attacked if some identified behaviour does not change. This occurs when paramilitaries move into an area for the first time, with general threats issued to stoke fear. For example, when the AUC established a presence in the Arauca Department in May 1998, it released a set of communiqués declaring that 'our armed presence is already a reality in this Department', and that it was embarking upon the first phase of a 'General Plan which has been designed for the department and consists of the location and identification of targets' (Amnesty International 2004a: 32). Combined with knowledge of previous paramilitary campaigns against identified targets, such declarations cause immense fear among a wide section of the population. Similarly groups have frequently targeted their threats at specific actors deemed troublesome, whether trade unionists, human rights campaigners, or community activists. For example in May 2008, several employees of a community radio station in the north-eastern department of Arauca received an identical text message from the local branch of the AUC, after reporting on a local human rights case: 'For the wellbeing of you and your loved ones, do not meddle in subjects that do not concern the radio station'. This message was followed a fortnight later by the letters AUC being painted on the front door of the station's building, ensuring that those working in the building were clear as to the group's intent (Amnesty International 2008b).

Second, when violence is delivered upon its targets, its context is often designed specifically to send a wider message. In particular, massacres of large numbers of

civilians – whereby a local paramilitary unit enters a village, rounds up its population, pulls out those 'guerrilla sympathizers' on a pre-published list, and executes
them in public or 'disappears' them – is a method of violence which ensures that
entire communities live in fear. Paramilitaries have often conducted literally hundreds of massacres in a year, so examples of this practice abound. In one of the
more notorious instances, more than 400 paramilitaries entered the district of Alto
Naya in April 2001, set up extensive roadblocks trapping thousands of villagers
and proceeded to execute more than 120 'guerrilla sympathizers' over a period of
three days (Craig-Best and Shingler 2001). Most were pulled out onto the street
and shot in full view of others. More than 3,000 people were displaced through
fear in a pattern repeated throughout Colombia over the past three decades.

Third, the ways in which actual acts of violence are carried out is clearly
designed to have a profound psychological impact upon witnesses and those who
hear reports. Paramilitary groups specialize in gruesome acts of torture during
terrorist attacks and deploy this systematically. Indeed, according to a 2007
report by a Chatham House working group on the conflict:

> The order of magnitude of paramilitary human rights violations sets them
> apart from abuses carried out by other violent actors ... Despite numerous
> past violations by a range of actors, paramilitary abuses are in a league
> apart, involving not only massacres but systematic rape and dismemberment
> of living victims.
>
> (Chatham House 2007)

The record in this regard is shocking, with paramilitaries employing 'horrifying
techniques of torture, including the use of chainsaws and other techniques to dis-
member their victims' (IACHR 1999). This use of terror has been documented
in vivid detail. In one of numerous cases, for example:

> On February 21, 1996, in the community of Las Cañas, in the municipality
> of Turbo, Department of Antioquia, members of the ACCU paramilitary
> group tortured and then killed Edilma Ocampo and her daughter Stella Gil.
> The paramilitaries, some of whom wore hoods, arrived at the home of the
> victims at 10:30 a.m. Stella's three children were present at the time. The
> paramilitary members tied the hands of the victims and told them that they
> would receive a special treatment, since they were guerrillas. The two
> women were taken out of the house approximately 100 meters and were
> beaten and decapitated in front of the three children. The victimizers then
> opened the stomachs of the victims, from the waist to the neck. They then
> placed Stella's dead body on top of Edilma's body and threatened the other
> residents of the community to leave the area or suffer the consequences.
>
> (IACHR 1999)

In this sense, then, paramilitary groups tied to state security forces clearly
form the premier terrorist threat in Colombia: they target individuals who are

protected by international humanitarian law to an extent far greater than other groups in the country, and specifically in order to instil extreme terror in the wider civilian population. None of this is random; rather it is the product of a concerted attempt by the state and sections of the economic and landholding elite to defend the political and economic status quo from significant challenge, whether that be armed or otherwise. As we shall see in the next section, this is achieved primarily through identifying a wide range of elements within Colombia civil society as *subversive*, as closely connected to the armed insurgency and therefore as legitimate targets for (para)military operations.

The function of state terror in Colombia

States which undertake campaigns of terrorism against elements of their own populations tend to be concerned primarily with combating 'subversion', where this is understood in an extremely loose sense to refer to 'any activity or idea that challenges the status quo', whether that be through the organization of peasants, workers or worshippers, the reporting or campaigning against specific human rights violations, or the promotion of a political or economic agenda in opposition to that of the ruling elite (Sluka 2000: 5). In many states across the world, the list of those who engage in such activities rapidly becomes extensive, with governments identifying a wide range of civil society as a threat to their continued rule (Chomsky and Herman 1979). This has clearly been the case in Colombia, where those subjected to pro-state terrorist violence are often civilians who are in some way organized against the severe political and economic inequalities throughout Colombian society, or who have otherwise spoken up against repression by the state and the paramilitaries.

Given their record of investigating pro-state terrorist crimes, human rights activists and organizations are often targeted ruthlessly. As the IACHR reported, many such workers:

> Receive constant threats against their lives in reprisal for their work. These threats sometimes come in the form of anonymous phone calls and notes. In other cases, unknown individuals approach human rights workers and inform them that they must discontinue their work or suffer the consequences.
>
> (IACHR 1999)

Such threats are made all the more real given the frequency with which they are carried out, with many workers physically attacked, executed by unidentified gunmen or simply 'disappeared'. In particular such workers are identified as 'insurgent-supporting' by paramilitary groups, and therefore as legitimate targets. For example, in one publicly released death threat, published in Barrancabermeja in 2000, the AUC was clear that it:

> Identifies the human rights workers and especially members of CREDHOS as guerrilla sympathisers, and for this reason from this moment forward we

consider them military targets of our organisation. It is important to say that all of this crap that they are doing is the policy of the FARC and ELN guerrillas, since we know who you report to at the end of the day. The AUC is an antisubversive organisation and we are going to carry out a social cleansing in Barrancabermeja and all of Colombia ... We carry out this cleansing for the future of Colombia because if we eliminate them we will be constructing the country we desire. We have in our power a cleansing list and we are going to give some statistics to these S.O.B.S., if they don't clear out, we will kill them.

(reprinted in Amnesty International 2001: 46)

This generalized threat was followed up by specific threats made to individuals working in Barrancabermeja. In one case Audrey Robayo – an employee of the nongovernmental organization Women Family and the Community Organisation – received a phone call from a neighbour who identified himself as a member of the AUC: 'If you want to save your skin, retire from all this shit, close [the Corporation] there, work for yourself, for your personal benefit and that of your family, don't work for others and not at all for the left' (Human Rights Watch 2001: 63). It is the fact that such workers speak out for change on behalf of others and challenge the interests of those in power which makes them such frequent targets.

In a similar vein, paramilitary groups have systematically targeted trade unionists in large numbers since the 1980s, with more than 2,500 killed in the 20 years between 1986 and 2006 (more than two each week) and the majority of these at the hands of the paramilitaries. Such assassinations are not an unintended by-product of the wider conflict; most instances have occurred at the point at which union branches have been involved in organizing drives or collective negotiations for better wages and working conditions. Indeed paramilitaries have been clear on this point, with Carlos Castaño responding to claims that his group 'blindly attacked' civilians with the following reply: 'Blind attacks? Us? Never! There's always a reason. The trade unionists, for example. They keep people from working! That's why we kill them' (Sanchez-Moreno 2007).

Those from the left who attempt to organize themselves politically, and to run for office through the Colombian electoral system, have also been systematically targeted by the military–paramilitary nexus. Nowhere is this clearer than the terrorist campaign conducted throughout the 1980s and 1990s against members of the newly formed political party *Unión Patriótica* (Patriotic Union, UP). The UP had been established by FARC in 1985 to represent guerrillas and those otherwise marginalized from the political process and was combined with a countrywide ceasefire. In response, and in a clear attempt to prevent the successful incorporation of the guerrillas into the political process, the military–paramilitary nexus decimated the party's membership. More than 4,000 UP activists were assassinated in the first decade of its existence (more than one per day on average), and all candidates were declared to be legitimate military targets. As a result, many of the party's members 'retreated into exile, others into a terrified anonymity that mutes their political activism' (Schemo 1997).

Overall, then, pro-state terrorism is routinely deployed throughout Colombia and is specifically directed at those social and political forces pushing for accountability for past crimes, or for significant change within state-society relations. Through the creation of extreme fear, paramilitaries work to silence observers to the violence inflicted upon their victims and thus to remove challenges to the existing elite. To the extent that the Colombian and US authorities have acknowledged the problem of paramilitary violence for the security of the Colombian people, however, they have tended to represent such groups as operating independently from the state (see Romero 2007). This has been matched by several high-profile studies, which underplay the extent of the relationship between the Colombian state and such groups, locating the cause of any documented state-based violations in an infrequent and unfortunate breakdown of the chain of command under the stress of armed conflict (Rabasa and Chalk 2001: 63). Crucially, however, the record of military–paramilitary collusion in the terrorist violence delivered against Colombian civilians clearly demonstrates that it is not the result of occasional 'bad apples'; on the contrary, the connection between paramilitary groups and the Colombian ruling elite is longstanding, multifarious and significant. As former AUC leader Carlos Castaño made clear: 'We started out as a reaction to the guerrillas, but we have evolved and now represent the social interests of big sectors of this country' (Wilson 2001b). Such collusion will be discussed in the next section.

Paramilitaries and the state

The Colombian government has long had a close hand in the formation of paramilitary terrorist groups designed to combat armed and unarmed challenges to elite rule. The formalization of the military–paramilitary nexus and the explicit turn to a terrorist strategy has many of its roots in the resolution of the decade-long civil war – known as *La Violencia* – which rocked Colombia during the 1950s, and the establishment of a 'consensus' National Front government between the Liberal and Conservative parties. The newfound harmony within a relatively narrow political elite was matched by an acceleration of a counter-insurgency campaign designed to destroy those from the left who refused to relinquish their political autonomy. This turn was fully supported by Washington, and Colombia became a recipient of vast quantities of counter-insurgency training and equipment (Stokes 2005). This training, as Doug Stokes has discussed in detail, was designed to enhance the covert and anti-subversive capabilities of the Colombian security forces, primarily through the creation and arming of pro-government *civilian* units to conduct 'search, control and destructive operations' (Stokes 2005). As well as targeting guerrilla forces, these units employed terrorism extensively, targeting a wide variety of government critics, trade union officials, human rights activists and opposition politicians, with many forms of nonviolent protest for social justice recast by the military as 'the unarmed branch of subversion' (Human Rights Watch 1996).

The war against 'subversion' in Colombia resulted in thousands of civilian deaths during the 1960s and 1970s, although little progress was made against the strength and popularity of the insurgent groups. With frustration mounting, the military became increasingly involved in the formation of terrorist groups to target progressive sections of Colombian society. In 1978, the Battalion of Intelligence and Counterintelligence (BINCI) – one of the key Colombian military units responsible for 'anti-subversive' operations – established a covert paramilitary organization with the specific goal of instilling fear in communist supporters. According to then-US Ambassador Diego Asencio, BINCI planned to 'create the impression that the American Anti-Communist Alliance (AAA) has established itself in Colombia and is preparing to take violent action against Colombian communists'. This plan was approved by then Commander of the Army, General Jorege Robledo Pulido, and resulted in the covert bombing of the headquarters of the Colombian Communist Party in December 1978, the bombing of Communist Party newspaper *Voz Proletaria*, and the assassination of a wide variety of leftist political targets (US Embassy Colombia 1979; Gurza 1980).

Ultimately more significant, however, was the formation of a new paramilitary organization in the early 1980s: *Muerte a Secuestradores* (Death to Kidnappers, MAS). Modelled on a group created by key drug traffickers to retaliate against high-profile kidnapping by the guerrilla group M-19, MAS was designed to mobilize civilians against 'anti-subversive' elements throughout the region. According to Human Rights Watch (1996), the formation of MAS was driven by the Colombian military: 'in essence, the army authorized and actively encouraged civilians to pursue and kill suspected guerrillas'. Its goals quickly expanded from defence against insurgent groups, and MAS began actively targeting anyone who opposed its actions, including politicians, activists and doctors. Throughout the 1980s, MAS and other paramilitary groups conducted a widespread campaign of massacres, assassinations and death threats, spreading fear throughout the regions in which it operated. During a government investigation in 1982–83, no less than 59 of the 163 people found to have links with MAS were active-duty police or military officers. Later evidence demonstrated that military intelligence was closely directing the so-called 'self-defence groups' and arming them with forms of heavy weaponry prohibited from civilian use (Pearce 1990: 177).

Increasing violence by the paramilitaries during the 1980s eventually led to the outlawing of the 'self-defence' groups by the Colombian state. As we have seen, however, this did little to change the facts on the ground and paramilitary terrorist violence continued to ravage Colombian society throughout the 1990s. Moreover links between the Colombian military and the paramilitaries, which were unified in 1997 under the umbrella of the AUC, continued to be extensive. Indeed by the turn of decade, Amnesty International (2001: 13) had been able to document this pervasive collusion to such an extent that it could declare that in 'areas of long-standing paramilitary activity, reliable and abundant information shows that the security forces continued to allow paramilitary operations with little or no evidence of actions taken to curtail such activity'. Likewise Human Rights Watch (2001: 1) had compiled substantial primary data, which pointed to a clear conclusion: there existed 'abundant, detailed and compelling evidence that certain Colombian army brigades and police detachments continue to promote, work with, support, profit from, and tolerate paramilitary groups, treating them as a force allied to and compatible with their own'.

With the election of President Alvaro Uribe in 2002, a high-profile demobilization programme was launched, ostensibly to disarm paramilitaries and reintegrate fighters into Colombian society. However, despite official proclamations of success in this regard, evidence abounds that the programme has in fact been designed to facilitate the incorporation of the paramilitary networks within the Colombian *security forces*.[4] For example, Amnesty International (2001) was clear that one Colombian military unit set up specifically to deal with paramilitarism was no more than a 'paper tiger', with the official Colombian government office that allegedly monitored paramilitary massacres 'a public relations mouthpiece for the government'. In reality the demobilization process has simply meant the recycling of illegal, paramilitary networks into more formal (and overt) Colombian military units, coupled with large-scale impunity and the closing down of investigations of collusion. Indeed, the entire process is largely a 'contradictory concept given the long-standing and close links between the security forces and paramilitaries, and the fact that the raison d'être of paramilitarism is the defence of the Colombian state and the status quo against real or perceived threats'. (Amnesty International 2005). Uribe has also provided a blanket amnesty for paramilitary leaders which amounts to 'check-book impunity' (Human Rights Watch 2003), while the Bogotá field office of the United Nations High Commissioner for Human Rights has condemned the legislation, arguing that it 'opens the door to impunity' because it 'voids prison sentences by allowing responsible parties to avoid spending a single day in jail' (UNHCHR 2003).

The extent of the collusion between Colombia's death squads and the Colombian state has continued to emerge, with the capture of a laptop computer in 2006 belonging to one of Colombia's leading paramilitary commanders, Rodrigo Tovar (also known as 'Jorge 40'). This laptop computer contained evidence that unemployed peasants were paid to pretend that they were in fact paramilitary fighters and to participate in the demobilization process. Meanwhile, the real paramilitaries continued to carry out human rights abuses and civilian massacres. According to information on the laptop, the abuses included the killing of 558 individuals in one region of northern Colombia during the ceasefire that the paramilitaries were required to implement in order to participate in the demobilization talks (Bronstein 2006). This confirmed the UNHCHR's analysis of the paramilitary demobilization process, which concluded that throughout this period 'the paramilitary groups, despite their declared cessation of hostilities ... continued their expansion and consolidation, including social and institutional control at the local and regional levels' (UNHCHR 2005). Continued violence has been a clear feature of the 'peace process'. Amnesty International spelt out the situation in stark terms in its 2004 report: 'Despite the declared ceasefire, paramilitaries were still responsible for massacres, targeted killings, "disappearances", torture, kidnappings and threats', and continued to be responsible for more than 70 per cent of all attributable killings of noncombatants. Consistent with a long-standing strategy, much of this violence was conducted through large-scale massacres of active community members (as well as family and friends) in communities designated as 'guerrilla-supporting' by the military–paramilitary network, with lists of 'sympathizers' often circulating in the days before villages were attacked (Amnesty International 2004b).

On the ground, this collusion has long manifested itself in several, overlapping ways. Often local security forces simply fail to react in a timely fashion when provided with information that a paramilitary attack is underway, or planned for the future. In the face of attacks on neighbouring communities, combined with explicit warnings by paramilitaries of an impending attack – a deliberate strategy to increase fear levels – villagers often make direct pleas to local army units to defend them. In response, however, there have been countless cases of such pleas going unanswered and massacres taking place regardless. Indeed, as the US Central Intelligence Agency (CIA) noted in a 1999 intelligence brief:

> Armed paramilitary groups dominate many regions because rural landowners and businessmen see them as the best defence against kidnapping, extortion, and murder at the hands of the insurgents. Police and military garrisons are often passive, preoccupied with their own security, and not responsive to calls to protect the citizenry ... Local military commanders do not challenge paramilitary groups operating in their areas because they see the insurgents as a common foe.
>
> (CIA 1999)

This report confirmed the findings of the Defense Intelligence Agency (DIA 1999), which stated in the same year that the 'Colombian armed forces have not actively persecuted paramilitary group members because they see them as allies in the fight against the guerrillas, their common enemy'. This reluctance to act against paramilitaries has facilitated massacres across the country. For example, the US Department of State had information that Colombian security forces 'did not intervene during 19 separate attacks in which 143 were killed over four days in January' (US Department of State 1999). Likewise, the free hand provided to paramilitaries by the Colombian military was mirrored during the summer of 1999, when paramilitaries from the AUC moved into the region surrounding the towns of La Gabarra Tibú, killing around 150 people over the following three months. According to Colonel Victor Hugo Matamoros, commander of the Fifth Mechanised Brigade, when interviewed by a US embassy officer, the explanation for inaction was clear:

> If you have so many tasks to do with so few resources, and you're faced
> with two illegal armed groups, one of which (guerrillas) is shooting at you
> and the other (paramilitaries) is shooting at them, you obviously fight the
> guerrillas first, then worry about the paramilitaries.
>
> (US Embassy Colombia 1999b)

Collusion is often more than tacit, however. Indeed, in the case of the massacres
around La Gabarra and Tibú, the US Ambassador to Colombia made clear in a
classified cable to Washington that 'an area police detachment commander [was
sacked] for apparent complicity in the 29–30 May massacre, and the Vice President's office privately reported that army soldiers had donned AUC armbands
and participated in the same massacre' (US Embassy Colombia 1999a). Other
intelligence held by the US Department of State confirms the reality of such in-
depth collusion with, for example, Major Alirio Antonio Urena firmly linked to
a paramilitary group involved in the infamous Trujillo massacres during 1988 to
1994, where Urena 'personally directed the torture of 11 detainees and their subsequent execution. The killings were carried out by cutting off the limbs and
heads of the still living victims with a chainsaw' (US Embassy Colombia 1990).
Even when not directly participating in attacks, particular military units often
provide airborne surveillance of villages for paramilitary groups preceding and
following a massacre, and conduct mock battles with nonexistent insurgent
forces so as to seal off the area and disguise the terrorist attack. This support was
provided to an AUC unit which attacked the village of Chengue in January 2001,
where paramilitaries pulled 24 men from their houses, assembled them in two
groups, and publicly killed them by crushing their heads with stones and sledge-
hammers (Wilson 2001a). Overall 'evidence pointing to continued coordination
is compelling' (Amnesty International 2004a: 30), with countless instances
where military units have provided logistical support (such as transport and communications), shared intelligence on 'guerrillas', 'guerrilla-sympathizers' and
other 'subversives', and transferred personnel for roadblocks and the conduct of
terrorist operations.

Moreover, links between the military and paramilitary stretch far wider than
those documented at the tactical and operational levels. Contrary to the official
narrative claiming that collaboration has been limited to a few, low-level 'rogue
elements' in the Colombian military, it has in fact reached into the highest levels
of command. For example, General Mario Montoya – who was the chief of the
army in Colombia until his resignation in November 2008 as the result of accusations regarding military ties to civilian deaths (BBC 2008) – has had a long
record of close association with paramilitaries. Assigned to BINCI in 1979,
Montoya was part of the unit which established and staffed the paramilitary
AAA, responsible for numerous terrorist attacks (Evans 2007). Links with pro-
state terrorist groups continued as Montoya worked his way up the chain of
command. As commander of the US-funded Joint Task Force South, he oversaw
the extensive collusion between the Twenty-fourth Brigade and paramilitaries,
which resulted in the massacre of hundreds of civilians. Indeed during a visit to

the region in 2001, Human Rights Watch obtained 'extensive, detailed and consistent evidence showing that the Twenty-fourth Brigade maintained a close alliance with the paramilitaries, resulting in extrajudicial executions, forced disappearances and death threats' (Human Rights Watch 2001: 17). Violations and collusion existed to such an extent that the US Department of State was forced to suspend all assistance to the brigade in 1999, although US-trained units from other formations continued to cooperate closely with the brigade (US Embassy Colombia 2000). Collusion between the Twenty-fourth Brigade and paramilitaries existed at the highest levels, up to and including Montoya. A CIA report leaked in 2007 noted concrete evidence of Montoya's involvement with paramilitaries, with evidence that they 'jointly planned and conducted a military operation in 2002 to eliminate Marxist guerrillas from poor areas around Medellin'. Operation Orion resulted in at least 14 deaths, with allegations of dozens more disappearances. Information obtained by the CIA, confirming prior intelligence from 'a proven source', was clear that 'jointly conducting the operation, the army, police and paramilitaries had signed documents spelling out their plans'. Signatories included Montoya, as well as paramilitary leader Fabio Jaramillo (Miller and Richter 2007).

High-level links with paramilitaries are not restricted to the Colombian military. The capture in 2006 of Tovar's laptop revealed the extent to which paramilitary groups had links with Colombia's political elite and sparked what has become known as the 'para-political scandal' (Lakshmanan 2007). Detailing individual meetings with a wide range of figures from within the Uribe administration, the laptop identified dozens of mayors, governors, members of congress and judges and included the foreign minister (Ceaser 2006). The subsequent investigation by the Supreme Court had, by April 2008, conclusively linked more than 60 current and former politicians to the paramilitaries, including President Uribe's cousin, the Senator Mario Uribe. Specifically such links have been used by members at the very top of the Colombian government to silence civil society through the use of state terror. In February 2007, for instance, the former intelligence chief, Jorge Noguera, was arrested and charged with supplying the names of trade unionists and human rights workers to paramilitary groups (BBC 2007). Investigations widened still further in 2008, with accusations from a former member of a paramilitary group that the president himself had helped plan a 1997 massacre in which 15 had died (AFP 2008). Whether solid evidence will be unveiled to substantiate such claims is currently unclear; however, what is known is that Uribe has long publicly identified human rights workers and other elements of civil society as a subversive threat to the state and as closely linked to insurgent forces, thereby reinforcing the rhetoric which legitimates the campaign of state terror (Leech 2004).

Conclusion

Colombia's ongoing conflict has had tragic consequences for many millions of people, whether through the murder, torture or displacement of themselves or family members. Within this, however, a clear strategy of state terror – conducted primarily by paramilitary organizations which are ostensibly independent, but in fact intimately linked to the state – has had a profound impact upon the people and society of Colombia. Designed to destroy any significant challenge to the political and economic status quo, this 'war' has been carefully targeted at those who would organize themselves in opposition to those in power, with a clear intention of sending a message to all Colombians regarding the desirability of speaking out for what they see as a better future. If nothing else, pro-state violence in Colombia targeted against noncombatants is designed as a form of communication to those watching, and therefore can be understood as a clear form of state terror.

Notes

1 My thanks go to Doug Stokes and Andy Higginbottom, both of whom read and commented on an earlier draft.
2 For an in-depth examination of the longstanding support provided by the United States for ongoing state terror in Colombia (a record which is not examined in any detail here), see Stokes (2005); Stokes and Raphael (forthcoming).
3 On Colombian military strategy and posture vis-à-vis the insurgents and parallel US support, see Rabasa and Chalk (2001).
4 My thanks here to Doug Stokes for discussions over the primary underlying objective of the 'demobilization' process, and for pointing me in the direction of key sources cited in this paragraph.

References

AFP (2008) 'Colombia's Uribe under probe over 1997 massacre', *AFP*, 23 April.
Amnesty International (2001) *Colombia: human rights and USA military aid to Colombia II*, AMR 23/004/2001, London: Amnesty International.
—— (2004a) *A laboratory of war: repression and violence in Arauca*, AMR 23/004/2004, London: Amnesty International.
—— (2004b) *World report: Colombia*, London: Amnesty International.
—— (2005) *The paramilitaries in Medellín: demobilisation or legalisation?*, 1 September, AMR 23/019/2005, London: Amnesty International.
—— (2008a) *World report: Colombia*, London: Amnesty International.
—— (2008b) *Colombia: fear for safety/death threats*, 13 June, AMR 23/017/2008, London: Amnesty International.
Barry, J. (2002) 'From drug war to dirty war: Plan Colombia and the US role in human rights violations in Colombia', *Transnational Law and Contemporary Problems*, 12 (1), Spring: 139–61.
BBC (2007) 'Colombia's ex-spy chief charged', *BBC News*, 23 February.
—— (2008) 'Colombian army commander resigns', *BBC News*, 4 November.
Bronstein, H. (2006) 'Colombian warlord incriminated by his own laptop', *Reuters*, 13 October.
Ceaser, M. (2006) 'Key Colombian leaders linked to death squads', *San Francisco Chronicle*, 16 December.
Center for International Policy, Latin America Working Group Education Fund and

Washington Office on Latin America (2007) *Below the radar: US military programs with Latin America, 1997–2007*, March, Washington, DC: LAWGEF, CIP and WOLA.

Chatham House (2007) *Paramilitarism and politics*, report of Colombia Study Group Meeting, 29 May, London: Chatham House.

Chomsky, N. (2000) *Rogue states: the rule of force in world affairs*, London: Pluto Press.

Chomsky, N. and Herman, E. (1979) *The Washington connection and third world fascism: the political economy of human rights, volume I*, London: South End Press.

CIA (1999) *Senior executive intelligence brief*, 16 September, Top Secret.

Craig-Best, L. and Shingler, R. (2001) 'The Alto Naya massacre: another paramilitary outrage', *Colombia Journal*, 21 May.

Defense Intelligence Agency (DIA) (1999) 'FARC guerrilla commanders and paramilitary group members comment on their organisations and activities', *Intelligence Information Report*, 23 February, Secret.

Duvall, R.D. and Stohl, M. (1988) 'Governance by terror', in M. Stohl, (ed.) *The Politics of Terrorism*, 3rd edition, New York: Marcel Dekker: 231–71.

Evans, M. (2007) *The truth about triple-a: US document implicates current, former Colombian army commanders in terror operation*, National Security Archive Electronic Briefing Book no. 223, Washington, DC: National Security Archive.

Gurza, T. (1980) 'Militares colombianos presos denuncian crímenes de colegas', *El Día*, 29 November.

Hoffman, B. (1998) *Inside terrorism*, New York: Columbia University Press.

Human Rights Watch (1989) *Human Rights Watch world report 1989*, New York: Human Rights Watch.

—— (1990) *Human Rights Watch world report 1990*, New York: Human Rights Watch.

—— (1994) *Human Rights Watch world report 1994*, New York: Human Rights Watch.

—— (1996) *Colombia's killer networks: the military-paramilitary partnership and the United States*, New York: Human Rights Watch.

—— (1997) *Human Rights Watch world report 1997*, New York: Human Rights Watch.

—— (2001) *The 'sixth division': military-paramilitary ties and US policy in Colombia*, New York: Human Rights Watch.

—— (2002) *Colombia: terror from all sides*, 23 April, New York: Human Rights Watch.

—— (2003) *Colombia's checkbook impunity*, 22 September, New York: Human Rights Watch.

Inter-American Commission on Human Rights (1999) *Third report on the human rights situation in Colombia*, 26 February, OEA/Ser.L/V/II.102, document 9, revision 1.

Jenkins, B.M. (1985) *International terrorism: the other world war*, Santa Monica, CA: RAND.

Jones, A. (2004) 'Parainstitutional violence in Latin America', *Latin American Politics and Society*, 46 (4): 127–48.

Lakshmanan, I. (2007) 'Colombia political scandal imperilling US ties: Congressional support for ally eroding', *Boston Globe*, 25 February.

Leech, G. (2004) 'Newsworthy and non-newsworthy massacres', *Colombia Journal*, 22 June.

McClintock, M. (1992) *Instruments of statecraft: US guerrilla warfare, counterinsurgency and counter-terrorism, 1940–1990*, New York: Pantheon Books.

Miller, G. and Richter, P. (2007), 'Colombia army chief linked to outlaw militias', *Los Angeles Times*, 25 March.

Pearce, J. (1990) *Colombia: inside the labyrinth*, London: Latin American Bureau.

Rabasa, A. and Chalk, P. (2001) *Colombian labyrinth: the synergy of drugs and insurgency and its implications for regional stability*, Santa Monica, CA: RAND.

Raphael, S. (2007) 'Putting the state back in: the orthodox definition and the critical need to address state terrorism', paper given at the British International Studies Association Annual Conference, Cambridge, UK.

—— (2009) 'In the service of power: terrorism studies and US intervention in the global South', in R. Jackson, M.B. Smyth and J. Gunning (eds) *Critical terrorism studies: a new research agenda*, London: Routledge.

Romero, S. (2007) 'Colombia rejects paramilitary report', *New York Times*, 26 March.

Sanchez-Moreno, M. (2007) *Violence against trade unionists and human rights in Colombia*, testimony before the US House of Representatives, 27 June.

Schemo, D.J. (1997) 'Colombia's death-strewn democracy', *New York Times*, 24 July.

Sluka, J., (ed.) (2000), *Death squad: the anthropology of state terror*, Philadelphia: University of Pennsylvania Press.

Stohl, M. (2006) 'The state as terrorist: insights and implications', *Democracy and Security*, 2 (1): 1–25.

Stokes, D. (2005) *America's other war: terrorising Colombia*, London: Zed Books.

Stokes, D. and Raphael, S. (forthcoming) *Imperial logics: US energy security and the long war*, Baltimore: Johns Hopkins University Press.

United Nations High Commissioner for Human Rights (UNHCHR) (2003) *Observaciones al Proyecto de Ley Estatutaria que trata sobre la reincorporacion de miembros de grupos armadas*, Bogotá Field Office, Bogotá: UNHCHR.

—— (2005) *Report of the High Commissioner for Human Rights on the situation of human rights in Colombia*, 28 February, E/CN.4/2005/10, Bogotá: UNHCHR.

US Department of State (1998) *Country reports on human rights practices 1997*, Washington, DC: US Department of State.

—— (1999) *Official informal for Ambassador Kamman from WHA/AND Director Chicola and DRL DAS Gerson*, cable to US Ambassador Curtis Kamman, 25 January, Confidential.

—— (2002a) *Country reports on human rights practices 2001*, Washington, DC: US Department of State.

—— (2002b) *Patterns of global terrorism 2001*, Washington, DC: US Department of State.

US Embassy Colombia (1979) *Human rights: estimate of the present situation in Colombia*, cable to US Secretary of State, February, Secret.

—— (1990) *Human rights in Colombia: widespread allegations of abuses by the army*, cable to US Secretary of State, 27 July, classification excised.

—— (1999a) *Paramilitaries massacre as many as 50 in Norte de Santander*, cable to US Secretary of State, 29 July, classification excised.

—— (1999b) *Visit to Cucuta, on Colombian–Venezuelan Border*, cable to US Secretary of State, 15 November, confidential.

—— (2000) *Part of the 1st CN battalion deployed to Southern Putumayo: logistical support from 24 Brigade*, cable to US Secretary of State, 26 June, confidential.

Wilson, S. (2001a) 'Chronicle of a massacre foretold: Colombian villagers implicate army in paramilitary strike', *Washington Post*, 28 January.

—— (2001b) 'Colombia's other army: growing paramilitary force wields power with brutality', *Washington Post*, 12 March.

10 'We are all in Guantánamo'

State terror and the case of Mamdouh Habib

Scott Poynting

Introduction

Mamdouh Habib was one of two Australians detained at the US prison camp in its naval facility at Guantánamo Bay, Cuba.[1] Habib was kidnapped[2] in October 2001 from a bus bound for Karachi, after intervening, as what might be described as a solicitous bystander, in the hauling off the bus in Pakistan of two young German national Muslim men whom he had befriended (Habib 2008: 84–7; *Dateline* 2005). He was taken, shackled and hooded, to Islamabad. He was tortured by the Pakistani security forces and interrogated by American agents, in communication with (and Habib claims in the presence of) Australian officials (Habib 2008: 100–8; Wilkinson 2005).[3] He was then handed over to US forces and unlawfully 'rendered' by the US military in a 'ghost flight' to Egypt, where he was tortured while imprisoned and interrogated over six months, before transfer to Guantánamo in May 2002, via Bagram air base in Afghanistan. He was demonstrably tortured in US custody. In early 2005, details of his kidnapping, rendition and torture reached US courts – and thus the media – during a habeas corpus case,[4] and the presumptively innocent Habib was repatriated to Australia in January 2005 without charge or trial. Australia's security forces and government were evidently complicit in the unlawful mistreatment of Habib. He was certainly not 'the worst of the worst', nor had much, if any, security-sensitive intelligence. What rationale was there for his long-term detention and interrogation? What purpose underlay his abuse and humiliation (including sexual assault) in custody? This chapter argues that these forms of terrifying and well publicized crimes by the states involved serve to terrify and repress the wider communities from which the victims come, making an example of the victim-detainee for political purposes.

Habib was 46-years-old at the time he was abducted in Pakistan. He was married (to Maha, who became a stalwart of the campaign for his release), and lived with their four children in Birrong, in suburban south-west Sydney. He said that he was in Pakistan pursuing the possibilities of a new life there with his family, including a potential livelihood in contract cleaning, and schools for their children. He and Maha had run several small cleaning businesses prior to running a coffee shop in Lakemba, a very multi-ethnic area with a large Muslim population and Australia's largest mosque.

Mamdouh was born in Egypt and in 1982 had immigrated to Australia, where he had first worked in factories and as a railway fettler. By many accounts, including his own, Habib was a fractious person. A staunch Muslim, he relates that he stood up against the notorious corruption in the New South Wales railways, and was victimized for it (Habib 2008: 20–4). He received workers' compensation after a life-threatening accident which he regards with suspicion. He recounts how in the 1990s his firm's major cleaning contract with the Defence Housing Authority was revoked after anti-Muslim racism and harassment. By the end of the 1990s, the family was surviving on social security payments and Habib was on medication for depression (Habib 2008: 36–40). He was involved in disputes in the local Muslim community (Habib 2008: 41–5). He was an eccentric, local figure, described (by antagonists in the community) as rather erratic or unstable and was seen around the suburb in karate gear, in army pants, and wearing a t-shirt celebrating Osama Bin Laden. He was an unlikely terrorist operative.

Definitions

Before we discuss the state terrorism in which Mamdouh Habib became a victim, it is useful to lay some definitional groundwork. The difficulties of defining state terrorism are legion, as Ruth Blakeley has pointed out in her chapter of this book (see also Blakeley 2009). This current chapter therefore takes a very simple approach. It accepts, for the purposes of its argument, the definitions of 'international terrorism' and of 'terrorism' legislated by the United States and Australian federal law in, respectively, the US Code Section 2331 and the Criminal Code Amendment (Terrorism) Act 2003. Following Blakeley's (2009) argument that the key criteria apply to the *acts* of terrorism rather than the *actors*, where such acts are perpetrated directly or by proxy, or are abetted, by nation-states, these will be taken to constitute state terrorism.

Section 2331 of the US Code defined 'international terrorism' as activities that:

a   involve violent acts or acts dangerous to human life that are a violation of the criminal laws of the United States or of any State, or that would be a criminal violation if committed within the jurisdiction of the United States or of any State;

b   appear to be intended –

    i   to intimidate or coerce a civilian population;

    ii   to influence the policy of a government by intimidation or coercion; or

    iii   to affect the conduct of a government by mass destruction, assassination, or kidnapping; and

c   occur primarily outside the territorial jurisdiction of the United States, or transcend national boundaries in terms of the means by which they are accomplished, the persons they appear intended to intimidate or coerce, or the locale in which their perpetrators operate or seek asylum.

The relevant circumstances in the Habib case are A, B (i) and (since the definition here applies to *international* terrorism), C.[5]

The Australian Criminal Code Amendment (Terrorism) Act 2003 defined 'terrorist act' (not surprisingly) in very similar terms:

1   *Terrorist act* means an action or threat of action where:

    a   the action falls within subsection (2) and does not fall within subsection (3); and

    b   the action is done or the threat is made with the intention of advancing a political, religious or ideological cause; and

    c   the action is done or the threat is made with the intention of:

        i   coercing, or influencing by intimidation, the government of the Commonwealth or a State, Territory or foreign country, or of part of a State, Territory or foreign country; or

        ii   intimidating the public or a section of the public.

2   Action falls within this subsection if it:

    a   causes serious harm that is physical harm to a person; or

    b   causes serious damage to property; or

    c   causes a person's death; or

    d   endangers a person's life, other than the life of the person taking the action; or

    e   creates a serious risk to the health or safety of the public or a section of the public; or

    f   seriously interferes with, seriously disrupts, or destroys, an electronic system.

The relevant criteria in Habib's case are clearly: (a), (b) and (c) (ii) along with 2 (a).

Illegality, violence, dangerousness and serious harm

Let us consider, to begin with, the questions of illegality (US) and violence, dangerousness and serious harm. Then incoming US Attorney General, Alberto Gonzales, admitted in a congressional hearing that the kind of 'rendering' to which Habib was subjected is illegal (Eggen and Babbington 2005; Wilkinson 2005b). The unlawfulness of torture should not need to be demonstrated, but suffice it here to note that it was Gonzales himself, who as White House legal adviser, devised the new, looser and now almost universally discredited, definition of torture (Effron 2005). Despite these semantic ploys, the official of the George W. Bush administration overseeing the Guantánamo military tribunals, former judge Susan J. Crawford, admitted publicly in January 2009 that prisoners had been tortured there and that this unlawful treatment had tainted evidence and meant that some suspects could not be brought to trial (Woodward 2009).

Some of the seriously physically harmful treatment meted out to Mamdouh Habib was detailed in a document submitted in a US court just before they decided to release him. Habib was, while under questioning in Egypt, hung from hooks on the wall, with his feet on a drum which was electrified. When thus electrocuted, 'The action of Mr Habib "dancing" on the drum forced it to rotate, leaving him suspended by only the hooks in the wall' until he passed out in agony (Wilkinson 2005a: 9). He was also blindfolded and locked in rooms flooded with water and charged with electricity (Habib 2008: 119). He was burnt with cigarettes[6] and given electric shocks, including in the testicles. There was psychological, as well as physical torture. In Guantánamo, during interrogation, Habib was told his family had been killed, and he was shown 'doctored' family photographs of them (presumably obtained by agents in Australia). His lawyer related testimony of sexual humiliation of Habib both in Egypt and at Guantánamo. In Egypt, he was sexually assaulted with a rod (Habib 2008: 119). He was stripped naked and threatened with being raped by guard dogs that his captors said were trained to do so (McLean 2005; Habib 2008: 120). In Guantánamo, Habib says, he was threatened with rape by a naked marine wearing a condom with 'Allah Akbar [God is great]' written on it (Snow 2008). Prostitutes were used to humiliate him sexually. 'One of the prostitutes stood over him naked while he was strapped to the floor and menstruated on him', he said. (McLean 2005). This evidence is very consistent with the accounts of other former Guantánamo inmates. The account of British former Guantánamo detainee, Jamal al-Harith, accords with Habib's in this respect, and also (inter alia) with regard to beatings, short-shackling and other painful physical contortion, forced drugging and withholding of medical treatment (Prince and Jones 2004). Such aspects of torture at Guantánamo are further corroborated by other Britons detained there and since released (Rasul *et al.* n.d.; Shiel 2004), who also bear witness to the torture of Habib. Many more have attested to the regime there of sleep deprivation, extreme temperatures, noise torture, menacing with dogs, in addition to bashings and draggings occasioning broken bones, organ damage, bruising, scarring. A released Briton who was imprisoned there, Tarek Derghoul, reports that he saw Habib beaten and dragged around in chains. He confirms that Habib was told his family were dead and that he believed this (*Dateline* 2004). Habib has physical as well as mental scars from his three years in Guantánamo. His medical records there regularly indicated blood in the urine, consistent with blows in the kidney region; marks on the skin of this area examined by medical experts in Australia corroborate this (Brissenden 2005).

Intimidating sections of the public

There is a contradiction involved with state-terroristic kidnappings which is well discussed by Green and Ward (2005: 116–17): they must be seen and not seen. They must be secret, not openly talked about, in order to protect the state's claim that it does not engage in such practices; but they must be known about and privately spoken of, in order to spread the requisite fear for political purposes among sections of the public. This is equally so for abduction and temporary 'disappearances' through extraordinary rendition, such as in Mamdouh Habib's case. The same logic applies to the state crime of torture (Stanley 2008), in instances where there is a political objective. Near the concentration camps of Argentina under the Junta, whose existence was implacably denied by the state but repeatedly announced by screaming, gunfire and helicopters removing corpses, neighbours reported that they 'lived under constant stress, as if we ourselves were also prisoners' (witness quoted by Feitlowitz, cited in Green and Ward 2005: 116–17).

Thus, in a deft two-step by the state 'Egyptian intelligence officers informed their Australian counterparts that Mamdouh Habib was being held', while the Egyptian government could formally deny all knowledge of such to the Australian government (Skehan *et al.* 2002), who would repeatedly say so publicly (*Dateline* 2005; *Four Corners* 2007; Standing Committee on Legal and Constitutional Affairs 2007). A similar logic to that of the Australian government's knowledge of Habib's whereabouts (in a torture cell in Cairo) applies to the US government's knowledge that torture takes place there. The architect of the rendition programme, the Chief/Special Advisor of the Central Intelligence Agency (CIA) Bin Laden Unit from 1996 to 2004, Michael Scheuer, proudly described it as 'the most successful counter-terrorism programme in the history of the country'. He 'didn't care' whether people rendered to Egypt would be tortured and he scorned the suggestion that he would believe Egyptian assurances they would not be: 'Why would I believe that?' (*Four Corners* 2007). Meanwhile US Secretary of State Condoleezza Rice could publicly aver: 'The United States has not transported anyone, and will not transport anyone, to a country when we believe he will be tortured. Where appropriate, the United States seeks assurances that transferred persons will not be tortured' (*Four Corners* 2007). Bob Baer, former CIA officer and author of *See No Evil*, was even more blunt than Scheuer in his certainty: there was 'no doubt at all' that prisoners rendered to Egypt (or Syria for that matter)[7] would be tortured (*Four Corners* 2007).

What makes rendition to other countries for certain, but deniable, torture such a 'successful counter-terrorism programme'? Certainly not conviction on the evidence obtained, since such evidence is inadmissible. Neither can it be the quality of the intelligence so gained, since it is widely recognized that such information is unreliable, as the tortured are moved to tell their interrogators lies, what they want to hear, anything to make the pain stop (Marton, cited in Green and Ward 2005: 131).[8] With any criminal state practising disappearance and torture, the effectiveness of these measures is through the reappearance of mutilated bodies of some of the disappeared, bespeaking torture, or – as in this case – the stories of those released into their communities, often for the purpose. The terror is spread among the communities concerned, and is expected to act as a deterrent, or at least to disrupt subversive organization.

One of the two young Germans who was imprisoned with Habib in Pakistan, Ibrahim Diab, telephoned Maha Habib, on his release, as Mamdouh had asked him to do (Habib 2008: 102). (Both young men were released after questioning in the German Embassy.) So she learned of his kidnapping and doubtless some of the conditions of his imprisonment. The Department of Foreign Affairs and Trade (DFAT) phoned Maha on 18 October 2001, to say that her husband was being detained without charge by the Pakistanis (Habib 2008: 99). One way or another, word gets out. The disappearances are known about. DFAT may (or may not) have been concerned about the well-being of Habib and his family, but they effectively communicated to the Muslim communities of south-west Sydney what could happen to any of their fellows with radical sympathies or big mouths.

A similar message had already been sent by Australian security services and police. In late September 2001, the Australian Security Intelligence Organisation (ASIO), along with Australian Federal Police and NSW police, raided 30-odd households and workplaces in south-western Sydney. All those raided were Muslim. The raids were clearly meant to be a public gesture: the media were taken in tow. They were also clearly intended to intimidate. In one case, five specially armed officers burst into a house, forced a man at gunpoint to lie on the floor and conducted a body search. His wife was escorted downstairs by federal police officers, without time to cover her body adequately. The house was thoroughly searched. The man was threatened that his small children might not see him for years. He was warned the security forces would be back and searching again. The family was traumatized. One woman in another household, a mother of two young children, complained (as did others raided) that a gun was put to her head and she was made to lie on the floor. She said police ransacked the house and interrogated her in front of her family. There were dozens such raids around the country (Poynting *et al.* 2004). In one such, according to Habib's then lawyer, Stephen Hopper, a gun was put to the head of a woman who was breast-feeding her baby (Rhiannon 2005). One of the houses raided was that of Mamdouh and Maha Habib.

Information, such as mobile phone contacts, gleaned in the raid on the Habibs' house was used in interrogating Mamdouh Habib under torture in Egypt. Attorney-General Philip Ruddock was quite approving of such intelligence sharing, though not conceding official knowledge of Habib being in Egypt and not – spare the thought! – condoning torture (*Dateline* 2005).

The raids had the effect of instilling fear. As one middle-aged, Lebanese-background tradesman explained of menacing visits from the ASIO:

> It was increasing, the scare and frightening when they accused me. I felt it was accusation. Maybe not officially, but the way they talked to me, three, two from Federal Police and one from ASIO, to come and talk to me like this ... At home I'm scared that one day they'd come in the same way they did to some people in Sydney and other places, we heard, break things and scare children, scared women.
>
> ('Aladdin', quoted in Poynting and Noble 2004)

I am not claiming that the Australian state committed torture in these instances, though it was complicit with it through feeding to torturing interrogators information gathered in its own raids, and in receiving the results. Further, in the regime of state terror by proxy, and 'subcontracting out' of torture, it matters little whether it was the state apparatuses of Pakistan, Egypt or the United States actually perpetrating the crime or indeed (as was the case) all three. Australia, as a client state of the United States,[9] acquiesced in the Guantánamo regime, including the violently abusive, unlawful treatment there (and in Pakistan, and in Afghanistan, and aboard a US naval vessel) of its own citizens. The Australian state did not effectively request their repatriation (as not chargeable with offences) as did Germany in the case of Habib's companions, Ibrahim Diab and Bekim Ademi, or as (eventually) did the United Kingdom in the cases of Moazzam Begg; the 'Tipton Three' – Shafiq Rasul, Asif Iqbal and Rhuhel Ahmed; Tarek Derghoul and others. More than that, there is evidence that the Australian government, for political reasons, actually discouraged the United States from repatriating its two citizens incarcerated at Guantánamo Bay, knowing they could not be charged with any offence in Australia. All of these nation-states – Pakistan, the United States, Egypt and Australia – acted with common purpose in this collective commission of state terror in the case of Mamdouh Habib; it makes no sense to say that it was the sole work of a particular state, acting alone. Australian officials were present at all three places where Habib was unlawfully held and tortured, where it was plain that the torture was taking place and allegedly in front of their eyes.

Political purpose

A common feature of terrorism is its apparent randomness, in that its victims are often selected arbitrarily. To spread the apprehension that 'it could happen to any one of us' is a key objective of terrorism. It is, in this respect, almost beside the point to insist that the majority of the victims of the prison camps at Guantánamo and other – many more secret[10] – places are innocent, or the damaged collateral of 'mistakes'. It is functional that they be so.

Nor should all the rhetoric about protecting 'America' (or the 'West', or 'democracy') against the forces of irrationality and unfreedom that hate its values and seek to destroy its way of life obscure the politics of purblind revenge and collective punishment. 'Gitmo', Camp X-ray, Camp Delta (and Bagram, Abu Ghraib and the rest of these places) did not function primarily to isolate dangerous enemies,[11] nor to extract accurate intelligence and useable evidence. They made a public and humiliated example of – not the 'worst of the worst' – but many who were not even a little bit bad. The important thing is that they belonged to the category of the enemy 'other' against whom both vengeance was to be extracted and might to be overwhelmingly demonstrated.

In January 2002, the Pentagon distributed photos of prisoners at Guantánamo Bay, blindfolded and forced to kneel. This contravenes Article 13 of the Third Geneva Convention, which provides that: 'Prisoners of war must at all times be humanely treated.... [P]risoners of war must at all times be protected, particularly against acts of violence or intimidation and against insults and public curiosity'. At this stage, however, President Bush and key members of his administration, notably and most vehemently Defense Secretary Donald Rumsfeld, were already suggesting that the Geneva Convention did not apply to the Guantánamo – and other – prisoners captured in the 'War on Terror', since they were not prisoners of war, but 'unlawful combatants'.

'These are killers ... We are not going to call them prisoners of war.... These are terrorists' said Bush (Campbell 2002). Rumsfeld revealed why:

> He has said that both al-Qaida and Taliban prisoners were 'unlawful combatants' and therefore did not qualify as prisoners of war. If they were accepted as prisoners of war, the men would only have to give their name, rank and number and could not be interrogated.
>
> (Campbell 2002)

There was not a lot of public asking until the atrocities of Abu Ghraib became infamous, but it did not take much imagination to reflect on what sort of thing would happen in this convenient limbo away from US jurisdiction and international scrutiny, to those who refused to give more than their name, rank and serial number and be subjected to interrogation. That message came along with the photo of the men paraded in orange jumpsuits. As Douglas Kellner writes:

> Images of the prisoners ... taken from Afghanistan and landing in Cuba in fluorescent orange jumpsuits, blacked-out plastic goggles, turquoise face masks around their mouths and noses, knit hats pulled over their heads, ear cups to block out sound, mittens encompassing their hands and shackles on their legs created intense controversy, leading to claims that the prisoners were being submitted to excessive sensory deprivation.
>
> (Kellner 2003:178)

It is reasonable to surmise that these very deliberately released pictures created widespread fear along with the controversy – but only among certain sectors of the population. Kellner continues:

> Likewise reports that the prisoners were shaven of their beards and hair, which were part of their religious identity, and were housed in concentration camps, exposed to the weather, lit at night with beaming fluorescent lamps, forced to sleep on concrete slabs, and made to live in a glare of publicity, created controversy about the conditions under which the prisoners were housed.
>
> (Kellner 2003: 178)

We know now that these were only part of the cruel and inhumane treatment to which the Guantánamo inmates were subjected. In an environment in which the access of the media was stringently limited and controlled, we must conclude that the relevant arms of the US state wanted these particular conditions widely known.

In fact, that same month of January 2002, Defense Secretary Rumsfeld authorized the use of aggressive interrogation methods at Guantánamo Bay, including stress positions and the use of dogs to intimidate prisoners (Stephens 2005). After all, it was 'not a country club', and these were 'the hardest of the hard core'. In November 2001, a Justice Department memorandum had conveniently provided the CIA with a spurious interpretation of the international anti-terror convention that permitted 'stress and duress' techniques The extremes of these conditions are by now well documented; the point here is that Rumsfeld made little secret, for anyone who would listen, that the conditions would be extreme.

There is little doubt that 'tough', exceptional measures were politically populist ones in the prevailing climate in the United States. A senior republican, Bob Stump, visiting 'Camp X-ray' on a delegation from Congress, made plain his impatience over complaints of human rights violations, which he viewed as 'anti-American': 'I take a dim view of ... the bleeding heart people always looking for a cause' (Borger 2002). Porter Goss, Chairman of the House intelligence committee, contributed, 'This has nothing to do whatsoever with treatment of prisoners ... I'm not interested in any of that' (Borger 2002). Internationally, the images circulated of the humiliated inmates of Camp X-ray showed the might of the empire in its retribution – that it retained the power to punish shockingly and awfully and would use it unsparingly.

The regime at Guantánamo, in summary, was violent, dangerous, unlawful, and intended to intimidate those sections of the civilian population who may be suspected of supporting *jihad* against the United States or its interests – a situation in which almost any Muslim may randomly become caught up, if they happen to be in the wrong place at the wrong time. The political cause is the 'War on Terror': that the American (and Australian) states can represent themselves domestically as 'tough on terror', and internationally that the empire can reassert its potency after the challenges posed by the tumbling of the twin towers.

There is another reason that Habib was targeted by the Australian security services, and hence, to an extent, the Pakistani, US and Egyptian ones. On a number of occasions, including well before 9/11 and shortly before that date, he had rejected ASIO's attempts to recruit him as an informant. When he and Maha had been in New York in 1990 visiting his sister, after visiting his family in Egypt, Habib had encountered friends in the Arab community and had learned of the hubbub surrounding the trial of El Sayyid Nosair, who was in court at the time over the murder of 'Rabbi Meir Kahane, a Zionist who hated Arabs' (Habib 2008: 27). Though he did not know Nosair, Habib – not one to shy away from a controversy – attended the trial with Maha and friends in solidarity. Nosair was acquitted on the murder charge, but convicted of assault and a firearms offence and sentenced to seven years' jail. When, in 1993, 'the 'blind sheik', Omar Abdel-Rahman was arrested in a case arising from the investigation into the bombing of the World Trade Centre in February, Abdel-Rahman was convicted of 'seditious conspiracy'; Nosair was named as one of the co-conspirators, and eventually convicted along with eight other of Abdel-Rahman's followers. Some time later, back in Australia, ASIO approached Habib in his coffee shop and offered to pay him to return to New York and inform on the people he had met there during Nosair's trial in 1990. He flatly refused (Habib 2008: 29).

After Abdel-Rahman's 1995 conviction, Habib believed he had been wrongly convicted. Following his life sentence in 1996, and upon learning in the Arabic press of his denial of treatment for diabetes, and other mistreatment, Habib ran off pamphlets and organized a demonstration among Sydney Muslims in his support. Police and ASIO visited mosques and warned people off participating, and no-one turned up, relates Habib (2008: 29). ASIO then visited Habib and accused him of communications with New York over the World Trade Centre bombing; Habib says that this was 'rubbish' and mere intimidation, and that the faxes had all been about Nosair's trial. Subsequently, Habib was again in 1996 harassed by ASIO in connection with his support for refugees and asylum seekers in Sydney (Habib 2008: 30–1). He was badgered further in 1998 and rumours began to circulate that he was working for ASIO, generating considerable antipathy in the Muslim communities (Habib 2008: 37–45). It was at this stage that he began to consider emigrating.

In Dubai in July 2001, while pursuing a cleaning contract there which would give them a new start, Habib was again visited by ASIO, once more seeking his 'help'. They asked him to inform on various members of Muslim communities in Australia.

> They kept telling me I had to work for them, and report to them immediately if I came across any of these people [that they had named]. I told them over and over again that I would never work for them as a spy. Then, in a flash, their moods turned, and they started threatening me.
>
> (Habib 2008: 49)

One of them began brandishing Habib's old Egyptian passport, which he had not used since 1982 and not been able to find since the early 1980s. How ASIO came into its possession is a disturbing question; certainly their use of it in mid-2001 for intimidation is ominous, given the subsequent events (Habib 2008: 50).

There is other evidence that ASIO behaves vindictively and at times improperly towards those who spurn its advances to engage them as informers. In the case of the young Sydney medical student, Izhar Ul Haque, ASIO had attempted to recruit him as an informant in its anti-terrorism case against Faheem Lodhi. When he refused, the Australian federal police proceeded with terrorism charges against Ul Haque himself, in relation to his having attended a Lashkar-e-Taiba training camp in Pakistan in 2003, when they had, more than six months earlier, decided that he was no risk and that he would not be charged. Not only were these charges thrown out of court, but Justice Adams found that the activities of the ASIO officers concerned had constituted the criminal offences of kidnapping and false imprisonment (Allard 2007; Brown 2008: 313).

Habib's homecoming

When Habib was eventually repatriated to Australia in 2005, he remained under security surveillance, as required of Australia by the United States and the attorney-general announced that he 'would not have an option in terms of leaving Australia' (Banham *et al.* 2005). The Habibs' house was burgled many times: 'usually only tapes, files, photos ... were stolen' (Habib 2008: 249). Habib continued to be outspoken, in the media and at public meetings, about his own case and those of others. ASIO warned him off speaking to the media after two young Australians were arrested in Yemen on accusations of terrorism (they were later released without charge) (Habib 2008: 248). He also received an anonymous telephone call with the menacing message, 'Do you think the Egyptians are going to let you go?' (Habib 2008: 249).

In August 2005, mysteriously, since Habib was under constant ASIO surveillance and the attack must have happened under their watch, Mamdouh and Maha Habib were followed by a car and then accosted by three men in the street one night near their home. Mamdouh was struck on the head from behind, then stabbed shallowly in the stomach. According to Maha Habib, as the assailants fled, the man with the knife shouted 'something like "this should keep you quiet"' (Wilkinson 2005c). When they returned home for private medical treatment (fearing to leave the children to go to the hospital), there was a brief and unexplained power cut to the house (Wilkinson 2005c, Habib 2008: 243).

Police harassment of Habib continues (Bassi 2008), some of it violent and frightening. In March 2006, Habib and his son Mustafa witnessed a street shooting, while driving home at night. Despite their being bystanders and their actually phoning the police, a uniformed police inspector ordered officers to 'take this terrorist'. Mamdouh and Mustafa were apprehended, roughed up, sprayed with pepper spray, and told to 'shut the fuck up', as police used batons and dogs to keep back the crowd (Tayler 2006). They had valuables and money confiscated, Habib complains, and most of the money (USD 756 out of USD 800) was not returned. Police obliged Habib to take a blood test, despite his protests that it was under duress. Police threatened Mustafa that they would charge him with assaulting police if he did not sign a form saying he accompanied them to the police station voluntarily. Of course, neither was charged in relation to the shooting. Subsequent to being 'threatened and terrified by the police', Mustafa has suffered insomnia, depression and become withdrawn, needing to see a psychologist (Habib 2008: 247). This ongoing and cumulative sort of terrifying by state forces, clearly politically motivated, is a form of state terrorism when it applies, as it does, across entire sections of the civilian population.

Conclusion

In August 2005, Mamdouh Habib was addressing students at the University of Western Sydney, about draconian new anti-terrorism laws which would have far-reaching consequences for civil liberties. The Federal Minister for Education,

Brendan Nelson, the following day underlined Habib's point, by demanding a 'please explain' from the Vice Chancellor about why Habib was allowed to speak. In his determined and dignified broken English, the unbroken but damaged Habib related to the students some of his experiences of detention without trial and incommunicado incarceration under abusive conditions. 'We are all in Guantánamo', he said.

Notes

1 The other was David Hicks. See Sales (2007).
2 As the wrongfully detained British prisoner in Bagram and Guantánamo, Moazzam Begg, emphasized of his own kidnapping in Islamabad, to use the term 'arrest' 'implies some legal system was involved, but it was pure abduction, which in itself is terrifying' (Murray 2006).
3 This is corroborated by Ibrahim Diab, who was arrested at the same time as Habib, and shared a cell with him in Pakistan (*Dateline* 2005). An anonymous ASIO official testified in court that he met Habib under detention in Islamabad. The presence of Australian officials at 'interviews' of detainees at Camp Cropper, near Baghdad Airport, was eventually admitted by the Australian government, after much prevarication, when his own interrogation of orange-suited detainees at gunpoint was attested to by 'skilled intelligence analyst', former weapons inspector Rod Barton (Brissenden 2005), so there was little reason to disbelieve Habib's story that such events took place in Pakistan.
4 *Mamdouh Ibrahim Ahmed Habib* v. *George Bush* (Civil Action no. 02-CV-1130).
5 An almost identical definition of 'domestic' terrorism, with C replaced accordingly, can be found in the USA Patriot Act (2001).
6 The scars from this, and skin discolouration indicative of beatings were examined by two professors of medicine after Habib's return to Australia (Brissenden 2005).
7 The infamous case of Maher Arar, an innocent Canadian citizen (of Syrian origin and dual citizenship), rendered by the United States to Syria and tortured there, attests to the accuracy of Baer's assessment.
8 Elizabeth Stanley (2008) notes that the unreliability of evidence obtained under torture has been remarked on since ancient Roman times.
9 Australia loyally sent troops to the wars of the British Empire in the Sudan (New South Wales Regiment, 1885) and the Boer War. Australia was automatically at war in 1914 because Britain was. Only in 1942 did the Australian parliament adopt the 1931 British statute which gave it independence over its international relations. In December 1941, with Japanese troops on the Malayan peninsula and key British naval defences sunk, Australian Prime Minister John Curtin announced, 'Without any inhibitions of any kind, I make it clear that Australia looks to America, free of any pangs as to our traditional links or kinship with the United Kingdom' (Curtin 1941). Since then, Australian foreign policy has seen various degrees of obsequiousness to its successor 'great and powerful friend' the United States of America, somewhat (but not hugely) more under conservative Coalition governments than labour ones. The 'ANZUS' Security Treaty between Australia, New Zealand and the United States of America was effected in 1952 under the longest such (the Menzies) government, during the Korean War to which Australia also sent forces, as it later did to Vietnam. The Howard Liberal-National Coalition government (1997–2008) was no exception to this pattern. November 2001 saw it re-elected in the 'Khaki election' (Hogg 2002) with the government enthusiastically joining the War on Terror. It sent troops to Afghanistan and Iraq; in fact Australia is 'the only country that has joined forces with

the US in every major war of the 20th century and the 21st century, no matter how noble, no matter how misguided' (Hartcher 2008).

10 Afghanistan, Qatar, Thailand, the island of Diego Garcia in the Indian Ocean, Poland and Romania have been instanced (Cornwell 2006). They do not *remain* entirely secret, as I have argued.

11 Be they a child of 15 (Carrell 2006), or an ancient of 110 (Habib 2008: 141, 143).

References

Allard, Tom (2007) 'ASIO conduct was grossly improper: judge', *Age*, 13 November. Online, available at: www.theage.com.au/news/national/asio-conduct-grossly-improper-judge/2007/11/12/1194766590209.html?s_cid=rss_news (accessed 30 January 2009).

Banham, Cynthia, Wilkinson, Marian and Noonan, Gerard (2005) 'Habib comes home to surveillance and a hostile PM', *Sydney Morning Herald*, 13 January. Online, available at: www.smh.com.au/articles/2005/01/12/1105423562693.html accessed 30 January 2009.

Bassi, Raul (2008) 'When is the harassment of Mamdouh Habib going to stop?', press release, Sydney Indymedia, 27 July. Online, available at: www.sydney.indymedia.org. au/story/when-harassment-mamdouh-habib-going-stop (accessed 30 January 2009).

Blakeley, Ruth (2009) *State terrorism and neoliberalism: the North in the South* London: Routledge.

Borger, Julian (2002) 'Congress delegates scorn x-ray fears', *Guardian*, 26 January. Online, available at: www.guardian.co.uk/world/2002/jan/26/usa.afghanistan (accessed 30 January 2009).

Brissenden, Michael (2005) 'Habib was tortured, psychiatrist says', *7:30 Report*, 16 February. Online, available at: www.abc.net.au/7.30/content/2005/s1304488.htm (accessed 26 January 2009).

Brown, David (2008) speech delivered at the launch of Governing through Globalised Crime, Futures for International Criminal Justice, Sydney, 13 May 2008, *Current Issues in Criminal Justice* 20, 2, November: 313–16.

Campbell, Duncan (2002) 'Bush hints at more legal rights for Camp X-ray prisoners', *Guardian*, 29 January. Online, available at: www.guardian.co.uk/world/2002/jan/29/afghanistan.guantanamo (accessed 30 January 2009).

Carrell, Severinn (2006) 'The children of Guantanamo Bay', *Independent*, 28 May. Online, available at: www.independent.co.uk/news/world/americas/the-children-of-guantanamo-bay-480059.html (accessed 28 January 2009).

Cornwell, Rupert (2006) 'Investigation: the CIA's secret prisons', *Independent*, 10 September. Online, available at: www.independent.co.uk/news/world/americas/investigation-the-cias-secret-prisons-415337.html (accessed 28 January 2009).

Curtin, John (1941) 'The task ahead', *Herald* (Melbourne), 27 December.

Dateline (2004) 'The trials of Mamdouh Habib', 7 July, reporter Bronwyn Adcock. Online, available at: www.news.sbs.com.au/dateline/the_trials_of_mamdouh_habib_130421 (accessed 26 January 2009).

—— (2005) The extraordinary rendition of Mamdouh Habib', reporter Bronwyn Adcock, 9 March. Online, available at: www.news.sbs.com.au/dateline/the_extraordinary_rendition_of_mamdouh_habib_130489 (accessed 26 January 2009).

Effron, Sonni (2005) 'Torture becomes a matter of definition', *Los Angeles Times*, 23 January: 1. Online, available at: www.articles.latimes.com/2005/jan/23/nation/na-torture23 (accessed 24 January 2009).

Eggen, Dan and Babbington, Charles (2005) 'Torture by US personnel illegal, Gonzales tells senate', *Washington Post*, 19 January: 4. Online, available at: www.washington-post.com/wp-dyn/articles/A19264-2005Jan18.html (accessed 24 January 2009).

Four Corners (2007) 'Ghost prisoners', Australian Broadcasting Corporation, reporter Sally Neighbour. Online, available at: www.abc.net.au/4corners/content/2007/s1945119.htm (accessed 27 January 2009).

Green, Penny and Ward, Tony (2005) *State crime: governments, violence and corruption*, London: Pluto.

Habib, Mamdouh with Julia Collingwood (2008) *My story: the tale of a terrorist who wasn't*, Melbourne: Scribe.

Hartcher, Peter (2008) 'Curtin call an excellent debut', *Sydney Morning Herald*, 27 June.

Hogg, Russell (2002) 'The khaki election', in Phil Scraton (ed.) *Beyond September 11: an anthology of dissent*, London, UK and Sterling, VA: Pluto Press: 135–43.

Kellner, Douglas (2003) *From 9/11 to terror war: the dangers of the Bush legacy*, Lanham, MD: Rowman & Littlefield.

McLean, Tamara (2005) 'Prostitute used in Habib torture: lawyer', *Sydney Morning Herald*, 27 January: 3.

Murray, Craig (2006) 'Enemy Combatant: Moazzam Begg publishes book on his experiences in Guantanamo', review from the *Herald*, 9 March. Online, available at: www.craigmurray.org.uk/archives/2006/03/enemy_combatant.html (accessed 24 January 2009).

Poynting, Scott and Noble, Greg (2004) *Living with racism: the experience and reporting by Arab and Muslim Australians of discrimination, abuse and violence since 11 September 2001*, report to the Human Rights and Equal Opportunity Commission. Online, available at: www.hreoc.gov.au/racial_discrimination/isma/research/index.html (accessed 28 January 2009).

Poynting, Scott, Noble, Greg, Tabar, Paul and Collins, Jock (2004) *Bin Laden in the suburbs: criminalising the Arab other*, Sydney: Institute of Criminology.

Prince, Rosa and Jones, Gary (2004) 'My hell in Camp X-ray', *Mirror*, 12 March.

Rasul, Shafiq, Iqbal, Asif and Ahmed, Rhuhel (n.d.) *Composite statement: detention in Afghanistan and Guantanamo Bay*. Online, available at: www.freebabarahmad.com/downloads/detentioninguantanamo.pdf (accessed 24 January 2009).

Rhiannon, Lee (2005) Debate on Terrorism Legislation Amendment (Warrants) Bill, Legislative Council, Parliament of New South Wales, Hansard, 22 June: 17153. Online, available at: www.parliament.nsw.gov.au/prod/parlment/HansArt.nsf/V3Key/LC20050622012 (accessed 28 January 2009).

Sales, Leigh (2007) *Detainee 002: the case of David Hicks*, Melbourne: Melbourne University Press.

Shiel, Fergus, (2004) 'Ex-detainees allege Habib and Hicks abused', *Age*, 5 August. Online, available at: www.theage.com.au/articles/2004/08/04/1091557920149.html (accessed 24 January 2009).

Skehan, Craig, Kremmer, Christopher and Fray, Peter (2002) 'Suspect's US detention not a surprise', *Sydney Morning Herald*, 21–22 April: 10.

Snow, Deborah (2008) 'ASIO watched torture: Habib', *Sydney Morning Herald*, 2 October: 1.

Standing Committee on Legal and Constitutional Affairs (2007) letter to Mr Robert Cornall, Secretary, Attorney-General's Department. Australian Senate, 25 July. Online, available at: www.aph.gov.au/SENATE/COMMITTEE/legcon_ctte/estimates/habib/ag_habib1.pdf (accessed 27 January 2009).

Stanley, Elizabeth (2008) 'Torture and terror', in Thalia Anthony and Chris Cunneen (eds) *The critical criminology companion*, Sydney: Hawkins Press.

Stephens, Tom (2005) 'A chronology of US War crimes and torture, 1975–2005: the crimes of Empire', *Counterpunch*, 13 May. Online, available at: www.counterpunch. org/stephens05132005.html (accessed 30 January 2009).

Tayler, Simon (2006) 'State harassment of Mamdouh Habib continues', *Green Left Weekly*, 26 April. Online, available at: www.greenleft.org.au/2006/665/6828 (accessed 30 January 2009).

Wilkinson, Marion (2005a) 'Australian official saw torture, Habib alleges', *Sydney Morning Herald*, 7 January: 9.

—— (2005b) 'Kidnapping Habib illegal: Gonzales', *Sydney Morning Herald*, 8–9 January: 11.

—— (2005c) 'Men trailed and knifed me – Habib', *Sydney Morning Herald*, 24 August. Online, available at: www.smh.com.au/news/national/men-trailed-and-knifed-me– habib/2005/08/23/1124562863772.html (accessed 30 January 2009).

Woodward, Bob (2009) 'Detainee tortured, says US official', *Washington Post*, 19 January: 1. Online, available at: www.washingtonpost.com/wp-dyn/content/article/ 2009/01/13/AR2009011303372_pf.html (accessed 24 January 2009).

11 From garrison state to garrison planet

State terror, the War on Terror and the rise of a global carceral complex

Jude McCulloch

Introduction

Through the military and the police, states have enormous capacity to coerce citizens and inflict violence. It is not surprising then that state terrorism, looked at in terms of numbers killed and harmed, is far more prevalent and significant than that of non-state actors (Green and Ward 2004). And yet, 'terror', 'terrorism' and 'terrorist' are concepts that are considered almost exclusively in terms of the individual and sub-state groups. As a consequence of this myopia, 'counter-terrorism' has frequently become the justification for state terror and violence that far outweigh the harm and violence they are purporting to counter (Jackson 2008). When state terror and terrorism are considered, it tends to be in the context of 'failed states' rather than the democracies of the West (Blum 2000). This chapter focuses on the violence and harm inflicted on prisoners and detainees in US prisons in the War on Terror and links this to the regular, routine and normalized state terror practised daily on millions of prisoners held within US domestic prisons. This state terror, experienced vastly disproportionately among criminalized and racialized communities, amounts to state terrorism as it sends a warning to whole communities about their place in the social and economic hierarchy and the price of transgression.

Revelations of torture and abuse of prisoners in the US-led War on Terror have led to a growing body of critical research on the relationship between US domestic prisons and War on Terror prisons. The responses from the mainstream within the United States have included outright denial alongside declarations that the horrendous cruelty inflicted on prisoners is unrepresentative of the values for which America stands (Rajiva 2005). Critical scholars, on the other hand, pointed to parallels and connections between torture and abuse in US offshore prisons and the routine and normalized state terror inflicted upon prisoners and detainees within the United States (Davis 2005; Greene 2004: 2–4; Gordon 2006: 42–59). There is also an emerging body of critical commentary, research and scholarship that focuses on the role of private corporations, profit and corruption in the War on Terror (Whyte 2007a: 177–95; Whyte 2007b: 153–68; Scahill 2007; Singer 2003; Klein 2007). This chapter extends these critiques by elaborating on the significance of the role of the United States as a self-appointed jailer to the world and by building an understanding of the drivers behind this development, including the role of private corporations and private profit. It argues that the War on Terror reflects, extends and reinforces the penal punitiveness and state terror that have taken root at the heart of the criminal justice system in the United States and many other Western countries. More specifically, it argues that the US role as global jailer and the way it executes this role need to be understood as logical extensions of the mass incarceration in which the United States is global leader and exemplar. Understanding mass incarceration and its global spread under the banner of the War on Terror warrants a consideration of private prisons along with the processes, dynamics and consequences of neoliberal globalization. While critiques of the War on Terror often set out to document its many and manifest failures, the purpose here is to consider and analyse who and what benefits, particularly the ways that the War on Terror and the state terror which accompanies it *succeed* in opening new markets for private capital and profit, thereby maintaining a fertile climate for the advance of neoliberal globalization more generally.

The United States as global jailer

In November 2001, shortly after the September 2001 attacks on the United States (hereafter known as 9/11), President George W. Bush issued a Presidential Military Order for the 'Detention, Treatment, and Trial of Certain Non-Citizens in the War Against Terrorism'. The order allows for the arrest, detention and possible military trial of non-US citizens, regardless of their location, by the US Defense Department. The category of non-citizens subject to this order is extraordinarily broad, including those believed to 'have caused, threaten to cause, or have as their aim to cause injury to or adverse effects on the United States, its citizens, national security, foreign policy, or economy', or simply anybody who the United States believes it is in their interest to detain (Bush 2001). Prior to the issue of the order, the United States was at the forefront internationally of punitive, long-term imprisonment (Christie 2003: 91–109; Garland 2001: 1–3; Parenti 1999: 163–9). The United States was also well-established as the world's laboratory for penal technologies of coercion and control and a trailblazer of prison privatization (Christie 2003; Shichor 1995; Coyle *et al.* 2003: 9–15). The Presidential Order, by overcoming the territorial limits of sovereignty, transformed the United States from global trendsetter to self-appointed world jailer.

The number of people being held in US offshore prisons and detention centres is difficult to accurately calculate. It has been estimated, however, that since 2001, there have been approximately 60,000 people incarcerated by the United States, outside of the United States, in places such as Guantánamo Bay in Cuba, Iraq and Afghanistan. Between them, the US military and the Central Intelligence Agency (CIA) run approximately 25 prisons in Afghanistan and 17 in Iraq (Johnson 2006: 36). The volume of prisoners in offshore US prisons is significant and increasing. The number of prisoners in Iraq, for example, is continually expanding. After the closure of Abu Ghraib following the 2004 release of photographs and videos revealing torture and abuse of prisoners there, the first permanent US prison – a USD 60 million supermaximum security prison – was opened at Camp Cropper, near Baghdad airport. Additionally, despite the release of many prisoners, a new USD 38 million facility is being built at Guantánamo Bay (Gordon 2009).

Prisoner Torture R US

The 2004 publication of photographs depicting torture, abuse, degradation and humiliation of prisoners at Abu Ghraib prison in Iraq focused world attention on the issue of terror inflicted upon prisoners in the US-led War on Terror. Mainstream opinion and official commentary in the United States were quick to dismiss the revelations as unrepresentative of US practices in the War on Terror and more profoundly unrepresentative of the values at the heart of the nation. The president dismissed the practices as not 'American' while others, wedded to the idea of the United States as an international paragon of virtue and a model of democracy, framed the revelations in the context of the idea of the nation as longstanding global moral exemplar (Davis 2005; Rajiva 2005). For these commentators, the damage done to the prisoners was secondary and insignificant compared to that done to the nation's reputation. Typical was the lament by one US senator that:

> Worst of all, our nation, a nation that, to a degree unprecedented in human history, has sacrificed its blood and treasure to secure liberty and human rights around the world now must try to convince the world that the horrific images on their TV screens and front pages are not the real America, that what they see is not who we are.
>
> (MacMaster 2004: 1–22)

US patriots were anxious to present the abuse as atypical: not representative either of the treatment of prisoners in the War on Terror or of the values of liberty, democracy and human rights that they believed the United States held dear. Despite these protestations, it is abundantly clear that the documented abuse, humiliation, sexual degradation, brutality, and torture by US personnel in Iraq and at other locations is not aberrant but systematic and institutionalized in the US-led War on Terror (Hersh 2004; Johnson 2006: 33–45). Beyond this, the torture and gross mistreatment practised in US offshore prisons mirror the experiences of millions of US prisoners incarcerated in domestic prisons and immigration detention centres. These practices amount to and are experienced as forms of state-perpetrated terror. Furthermore, because such practices are experienced so disproportionately by particular groups – Arabs and Muslims in the War on Terror and African Americans in domestic prisons – they send a message to these communities beyond the prison walls about their collective vulnerability to state violence, thus traumatizing and terrorizing entire communities. While the Abu Ghraib photographs and other revelations and documentation of torture and abuse in US offshore prisons are rightly the focus of moral outrage there is no basis for being surprised or shocked (Gordon 2006: 44).

Millions of US citizens have first-hand experience of similar treatment and conditions in domestic prisons and thousands of non-citizens have been subject to such in immigration detention facilities inside the United States. In 2000, Joy James wrote of the 'institutionalization of torture, abuse and repression in the US penal system' (2000: 483–93). In short, US prisons constitute an apparatus of state terror. The tens of thousands of US citizens who work in prisons have authorized, supervised, witnessed or directly participated in this state terror. Judith Greene stated 'experienced observers ... are quick to recognize that the Abu Ghraib photos reek of the cruel but usual methods of control used by many US prison personnel' (2004: 4). The dehumanization exposed by the photo-graphs 'is the modus operandi of the lawful, modern, state-of-the-art prison' (Gordon 2006: 49). Angela Davis argued that the permissive, 'barbaric' prac-tices revealed in US detention in the War on Terror were a reflection and exten-sion of the 'normalization of torture within domestic prisons' (2005: 114). She maintained that the torture of prisoners in offshore prisons had foundations laid deep in the 'routine, quotidian violence that is justified as the everyday means of controlling prison populations in the US' (2005: 115).

One aspect of the photographs and videos from Abu Ghraib that aroused par-ticular outrage and disgust was the depiction of the sexual coercion and humilia-tion inflicted on prisoners. The Physicians for Human Rights report into the 'systematic use of psychological torture by US forces' in the War on Terror stated 'the use of humiliation as a means of breaking down the resistance of detainees, including forced nudity ... began when the "war on terror" began' (2005: 5). This statement, and the outraged surprise accompanying the public revelations of sexual abuse and humiliation, belies the reality that sexual coer-cion, most particularly in the form of routine strip searches, is a longstanding and normalized aspect of state terror within US domestic prisons, as well as in prisons in other advanced liberal democracies (McCulloch and George 2009). There are 'deep connections between sexual violence and the gendered processes of discipline and power embedded in systems of imprisonment' (Davis 2005: 115).

There are also similarities in the design of the newly built War on Terror prisons and domestic prisons. The maximum security prison at Guantánamo Bay, for example, which imposes cruel, dehumanizing sensory deprivation con-ditions that break down and destroy human beings, physically and psychologi-cally, is based on the design of a Miami prison (Rosenberg 2004). Additionally, Guantánamo Bay mirrors and extends the trend within the United States to ware-house prisoners in supermaximum security facilities (Rhodes 2004). Another indication of the connection and continuity between US global prisons and domestic prisons is the overlap in personnel. Many of those revealed to be tor-turers at Abu Ghraib gained their initial experience in prisons inside the United States. One, who took on a leadership role at Abu Ghraib, infamously remarked in a comment that reflected a perverted take on job satisfaction: 'The Christian in me says it's wrong, but the corrections officer in me says "I love to make a grown man piss himself"' (Greene 2004: 2). As US prison activist Judith Greene put it, the 'vengeful penal philosophy and harsh prison culture have led to a dreadful level of brutality and human rights abuses in our own prisons, and now this maliciously punitive mentality has been exported to Iraq by US prison personnel' (2004: 4). Since 2003, more than 5,000 civilian prison guards were called up to military service (Gordon 2009: 169).

Conditions, trends, technology and other innovations circulate between the various spaces of incarceration so that the borders between the US criminal justice system and the expanding US global carceral complex are intertwined and increasingly indistinct. The connections between the institutionalized state terror in the War on Terror and state terror in US domestic prisons are demonstrated on a number of levels, including the exchange of personnel between domestic prisons and War on Terror prisons, and the routine state terror inflicted upon prisoners and detainees in both the global and domestic prisons. In addition, the routine denial of the systematic and institutionalized nature of state terror is a feature of both domestic and War on Terror prisons. Increasingly, the state's coercive capacities are paralleled or mirrored inside and outside national borders (Hardt 2002). The evidence of state terror against prisoners in the War on Terror is both foretold and prescient in relation to state terror in domestic prisons.

Circulating state terror: from criminal injustice to military injustice

The borders between foreign and domestic policies, and between military action and criminal justice, were incrementally but extensively eroded over the past three decades. Since the end of the Cold War, the traditional boundaries between an internally-oriented domestic police sphere and an externally-oriented military sphere became increasingly blurred (Andreas and Price 2001: 31–52). This process accelerated markedly in the post-9/11 era. The War on Terror extended the trend established with the continuing US-led wars on drugs, organized crime and early iterations of the War on Terror, which was first declared using similar rhetoric during the presidency of George Bush senior in the 1980s (Chomsky 2002: 2). The blurring of traditional boundaries was manifested in hybrid military and criminal justice configurations and operations at both the national and global levels (McCulloch 2004: 309–26; Andreas and Price 2001: 31–52; Alliez and Negri 2003: 109–18). National defence, internal security and law enforcement increasingly merged (White 2005: 265–78; Kraska and Kappeler 1997: 1–18; Hardt and Negri 2000: 189). President George W. Bush, setting out the US national security strategy in 2002, observed, 'today, the distinction between domestic and foreign affairs is diminishing' (2002). The War on Terror consolidated and extended the blending of crime and war so that 'securitization' at home paralleled closely war abroad (Kaplan 2003; McCulloch 2004: 309–26).

The War on Terror and the accompanying state of emergency became infinite because it was not temporarily or geographically bounded, being, as President George W. Bush termed it, a global enterprise of uncertain duration (2002: i). In these circumstances, the state of emergency and the exceptional measures that followed became the permanent norm (Agamben 2005: 3). The opening of a global militarized polity subjected to continuous 'peacekeeping' by an army of 'globocops', that emerged and intensified post-9/11, combined the coercive powers of war with the punitiveness of the criminal justice system to create a framework seeking to deny the basic human rights of individuals, caught within the net of what became known as counter-terrorist military interventions. It denied them the protection of international laws embodied in instruments such as the Geneva Convention and the protections traditionally afforded criminal suspects (Butler 2004: chapter 3; McCulloch and Carlton 2006: 397–412). The conflation of the rules of war and criminal justice has precedent in the colonial past (Saada 2003: 10–17).

Prior to 9/11, the United States had already taken some initial steps along the road to becoming jailer to the world. In 1989, it invaded Panama in line with its 'war on drugs', purportedly in pursuit of 'narco-terrorists'. In the wake of the invasion, 5,000 Panamanians were held in detention inside Panama without charge for many years by the United States (James 1996: 63–83). The US behaviour towards and within Panama provided an early example of the extension of the long arm of US criminal justice into extraterritorial contexts. The 2001 Presidential Order (referred to above) represented a formalization and extension of US domestic policing and punishment into global spaces. To understand the nature and significance of the growth of a US global carceral complex, as well as the impetus that underpins this system, it is necessary to first appreciate the nature, extent and function of mass incarceration within the United States.

Mass incarceration and state terror in the United States

Prior to 9/11, prison populations in most Western countries expanded rapidly. The forerunner of this trend was the United States, with an unprecedented increase in prisoners since the 1980s (Sparks 2003: 30). In the two decades between 1980 and the turn of the millennium, the US prison population rose by 319 per cent (Austin *et al.* 2003: 433). The 1990s were 'the golden age of prison expansion in America', with a near doubling of the number of incarcerated men and women, from 1.1 million in 1990 to nearly 2 million in 2000, while spending on incarceration approached USD 40 billion (Pranis 2003: 156). The extent of mass incarceration in the United States was unprecedented in the history of liberal democracy and had no parallel in the Western world (Sparks 2003: 30). The phenomenon was not confined simply to numbers and rates of imprisonment. Another significant dimension concerned the 'social concentration of imprisonment's effects' (Garland 2001: 1). In 2001, 66 per cent of inmates in private prisons were racial minorities, with African Americans constituting the single largest group (43.9 per cent) (Hallett 2006: 4). In 2003, for every 100,000 black males in the United States aged between 20 and 44, there were 36,932 men in prisons. The number for white males was 4,954 (Hallett 2006: 7–8). The upward spiral of incarceration, combined with the over-representation of particular communities and groups of people as prisoners and detainees, meant that incarceration is too frequently a defining experience for these groups and communities. Beyond reflecting broader social inequalities and structural violence, imprisonment also played a defining role in amplifying these phenomena. Imprisonment is racialized and gendered, mirroring and extending the painful, burdensome legacies of slavery and colonization, along with the myriad and intersecting oppressions of patriarchy (Davis 2003; Davis 2005). Prison was also used to punish political dissidents throughout US history (Churchill and Wall 1992). The prison and detention centre provided key experiences for the increasing number of people who worked inside these institutions, particularly as other employment opportunities and the ability to escape such employment contracted markedly (Gilmore-Wilson 2007).

Private prisons

The term, prison-industrial complex, was coined by activists and scholars 'to contest prevailing beliefs that increased levels of crime were the root cause of mounting prison population' and to underline the connections between corporate interests and incarceration (Davis 2003: 84). The concept of a prison-industrial complex drew upon and built from the term, military-industrial complex, first used in the early 1960s by US President Dwight D. Eisenhower to warn about the dangers of the conjunction of an immense military establishment and a large arms industry (Johnson 2004: 39). Eisenhower's early warning proved prescient. In 2003, Robert Higgs summarized the military-industrial complex as:

> A vast cesspool of mismanagement, waste, and transgression not only bordering on but often entering into criminal conduct … The great arms firms have managed to slough off much of the normal risks of doing business in a genuine market, passing on many of their excessive costs to the taxpayers while still realizing extraordinary rates of return on investment.
>
> (Johnson 2004: 309)

The boom in prison populations and rates of imprisonment within the United States coincided with the establishment of private prison corporations during the 1980s. The ability of private corporations to profit through punishment and imprisonment was a significant driver of punitive penal policy and associated increases in imprisonment within the United States. As governor of Texas, prior to being elected president, George W. Bush was instrumental in positioning that state as 'the world capital of the private-prison industry' (Greene 2001). During his time as governor, the number of private prisons in Texas grew from 26 to 42 (Klein 2007: 294).

The unprecedented nature of mass incarceration in the United States provoked speculation on the limits to which it could be taken (Garland 2001: 3). In 1995, a senior executive of Correction Corporation of America argued that 'the USA market would expand "almost indefinitely"' (Harding 1997: 4). Prior to the advent of the 2001 War on Terror, commentators assumed, however, that national borders provided at least a territorial limit on mass incarceration facilitated through US penal policy. James Austin and his co-authors published a chapter in 2003, but clearly written prior to 2001, observing that:

> America has had to construct its locations of banishment within its border. This has been done at feverish pace. As was done in eighteenth-century England, we even tried using barges in New York City. Although we lack an Australia where we can set up prison colonies, we are increasingly building huge megaprison settlements in isolated rural communities where land is cheap.
>
> (Austin *et al.* 2003: 441)

The November 2001 Presidential Order, however, substantially demolished the limits of territory. The 1989 invasion of Panama (see above) provided one early example of the extraterritorial imposition of imprisonment by the United States. The involvement of transnational corporations in prisons and immigration detention centres provided another means by which the limits of territory on mass incarceration were breached prior to the Presidential Order.

Shortly after they emerged in the 1980s in the United States, private prison companies actively pursued expanding markets and profits beyond their home base (Nathan 2003: 190). US private prison corporations are running prisons in or have run prisons in countries including Australia, Canada, New Zealand, the United Kingdom and South Africa (Coyle *et al.* 2003: 1). Despite these successes in market expansion, transnational private prisons corporations encountered some significant barriers in entering the international market. Governments in countries ideologically well-disposed to neoliberal principles were willing to embrace private prisons as part of the trend away from public ownership and state control towards privatization. Nevertheless, it often took companies several years of lobbying to persuade governments outside of the United States, particularly in the face of labour union opposition, that privatization was a good option for prisons (Nathan 2003: 164). Even in countries like Australia, where state governments enthusiastically embraced prison privatization (Moyle 2000: 1), private prisons ran into sustained and sometimes passionate public opposition. A long-running campaign by prison activists in Victoria (a state in Australia), for example, forced the government to use its emergency powers to step in and take over the management of a women's prison from the US private corporation that had been running it for four years. The campaign succeeded in documenting and publicizing escalating violence, mismanagement, cover up, and multiple and serious breaches of contract which endangered both prison staff and prisoners. The campaign, linked to similar activist groups within the United States, was critical not only of the particular circumstances of the specific prison and the private prison company that ran it, but of the whole concept of prisons for profit (George 2003).

Private prisons also had some success in penetrating markets in the global South. The World Bank and the International Monetary Fund, global crusaders for neoliberalism, attempted to impose private prisons on developing countries as part of structural adjustment programmes, but such efforts met resistance (Nathan 2003: 198–201). Even in the United States, where the companies wielded considerable political influence, the behaviour of the companies, combined with philosophical objections to punishment for profit, resulted in community campaigns that succeeded in revealing them 'as cheats, liars and liabilities'. These revelations led to a decline in profits and a slowdown in private prison growth. The massive expansion of private prisons within the United States in the 1980s and 1990s did not continue into the new millennium (Parenti 2003: 30–8).

The deceleration in the expansion of private prisons within the United States coincided with an expanding international market for profit from prisons. Invasion and occupation overcome the limitations of national territory and provide spaces and human beings that can be captured and imprisoned, thus expanding the US project of mass incarceration. Despite the massively disproportionate incarceration of people of colour within the United States and the racism manifest at every level of the criminal justice system, long-term incarceration there still requires the application of some formal process and determination of guilt, although since 9/11 domestic legislation has substantially eroded due process protections. The declaration of the War on Terror, the Presidential Order, and invasions of and subsequent occupations of Afghanistan and Iraq, however, disposed with even the pretext of due process. People in Afghanistan, Iraq and indeed anywhere in the world could be captured, abducted and incarcerated indefinitely by the United States. This capture and detention was not based on what people did, or even on what they were suspected to have done or were planning to do, but on what they *might* do at some unspecified time in the future to harm the interests – however these might be defined – of the United States (McCulloch and Carlton 2006: 397–412). There are tens of thousands of people in offshore US prisons, held without charge or evidence, sometimes for years. These people, many of whom have had nothing to do with insurgency or violent opposition at all, including children, women and the elderly, make up the next wave of US mass incarceration.

Disaster capitalism: state terror, the War on Terror and private profit

There is little empirical evidence available detailing the profits made by private prison corporations in the War on Terror. What we do know, however, is that private corporations are making huge profits in the War on Terror and that prisons are an important and significant aspect of the War on Terror. Peter McLaren and Gregory Martin, commenting on the profits flowing to major US companies from the invasions of Afghanistan and Iraq, observed that 'the best business in the global marketplace these days appears to be the business of bombing the infrastructure of a country to the Stone Age and then receiving millions of dollars to rebuild it' (McLaren and Martin 2004: 281–303). Post-invasion reconstruction and the provision of 'services' during occupation created huge opportunities for private firms. The enthusiastic exploitation of these opportunities was dubbed disaster capitalism and hailed, as 'the rise of the disaster capitalism complex' (Klein 2005; Klein 2007: 281). During the first 14 months of the occupation of Iraq, the US-led regime spent around USD 20 billion in Iraqi oil revenue, most of which was distributed to US corporations (Whyte 2007a). The private contractors and mercenary armies are making huge profits in Iraq (Klein 2007: 13–14; Scahill 2007; Singer 2003). Since the first year of occupation 'reconstruction funds' have been redirected to pay for the military and security costs of the occupation (Whyte 2007b: 159). While money for reconstruction in Iraq has slowed down, money for building prisons continues to flow. The US State Department's *only* request for rebuilding funds from Congress in 2006 was USD 100 million for prisons (*Age* 2006). At the time of writing, there were calls out to private firms for up to USD 5 million of services for the newly-constructed Camp Cropper prison in Iraq (*FBO Daily* 2007). By mid-2004, multinational Halliburton's income from Guantánamo Bay was approximately USD 155 million (Rose 2004: 54).

I am not aware of any specific research on the role of private prison corporations in the War on Terror. Yet joining the dots between the behaviour of these corporations within the United States and other markets they have penetrated previously, such as Australia, and the behaviour of private corporations within Iraq generally, where systematic and institutionalized corruption has been documented, one can speculate that the distinction between private profit and public interest is non-existent and that profit is seen as an end in itself, regardless of human costs.

In a book published in 1995, David Shichor, considering the arguments for and against private prisons, claimed that:

> Nobody seriously recommends that the military be privatized, that wars be fought by soldiers and sailors employed by IBM, or say, Fighting Forces of America, Inc. If death and disaster on a considerable scale are inevitable products the rule seems to be that the responsibility is the business of government. The government is at least responsive to the will of the electorate, and it presumably will not declare or wage war with profit as its major goal.
> (Shichor 1995: vii)

More than ten years after these words were written, with the widespread use of contractors, even combat forces, in every aspect of the War on Terror, the idea of a privatized military, including private military prisons and war-driven by the pursuit of profit became less absurd, though no less morally repugnant or confronting to notions of accountable government (Klein 2007: 13–14). When considering profit, however, particularly profits from prisons, as one of the drivers of the War on Terror, it is important not to get too caught up in focusing on the role of specific corporations, though work has barely begun even in relation to that aspect. It is of a higher level of importance to examine the capitalist system as a whole and the broader politics that drive global mass incarceration, along with the state terror and terrorism that accompany it (Parenti 2003: 30). Criminologist Dave Whyte concluded, based on field research in Iraq, that 'virulent and institutionalized corruption in Iraq has extended the neocolonial reach of the US sustaining a much broader strategy of domination' (Whyte 2007b: 164).

Prisons for the free world

Violence and incarceration, including torture, abuse, sexual violence and super-maximum security conditions, domestically and in the wake of military aggression, amount to state terror because they are inevitably experienced as a form of terror by incarcerated people. Beyond this, violence and incarceration, both domestically and in the War on Terror, are a form of state terrorism. The impacts of violence and incarceration are concentrated in racialized and criminalized groups. Violence and incarceration are part of a political strategy designed to send a message about the social, political and economic system as a whole and strike fear into those communities that are disproportionately the victims of violence and incarceration.

Beyond the purely economic rationale of the prison, mass incarceration in the United States serves an important ideological function: 'the prison industrial complex is not only a set of interest groups and institutions. It is also a state of mind' (Hallett 2006: 80). Neoliberalism and repressive social control are a 'package deal' through which the 'rhetoric of criminalization and punishment legitimizes states that have reneged on their commitment to the social wage' (Mariani 2001: 2–4). As Angela Davis argued, the prison:

> Functions ideologically as an abstract site into which undesirables are deposited, relieving us of thinking about real issues afflicting those communities from which prisoners are drawn in such disproportionate numbers ... It relieves us of the responsibility of seriously engaging with the problems of our society, especially those produced by racism, and increasingly global capitalism ... The prison has become a black hole into which the detritus of contemporary capitalism is deposited.
>
> (2003: 16)

Within the United States, criminalization of African and Indigenous Americans resonates with the slavery and genocides of former times and assists in maintaining African Americans and Indigenous people as marginalized and vilified minorities, thus working to obscure the continuing history of state terror and terrorism. Mass incarceration of the poor, a category which substantially overlaps with 'race', blames the victims for the myriad and intensifying failures of capitalism under conditions of neoliberal globalization. Those that actively oppose and resist neoliberalism are also exiled and isolated, if not silenced, through incarceration. Mass incarceration is driven as much by the political profit as the material profit that goes hand in hand with the promotion of fear and the punishment of criminalized and racialized groups. States no longer willing or able to respond to demands for social justice under the tenets of neoliberalism are quick to respond to, exacerbate and create the fears that underlie the demands for security in its most repressive and coercive forms. As Giroux observed: 'What has emerged is not an impotent state, but a garrison state that increasingly protects corporate interests while stepping up the level of repression and militarization on the domestic front' (2002: 143) – a shift from welfare to warfare state. The United States as the exemplar of neoliberalism is also the exemplar of this process. The fear and anxiety maintained and even manufactured around crime, and more recently and intensely around national security, serve to detract attention from problematic domestic politics. Law, order and security politics mask a range of insecurities that arise from government policies by associating notions of security exclusively with the state or nation rather than with individuals or communities.

In the same way that domestic mass incarceration and state terror reflect and amplify social and 'racial' hierarchies within the United States, the emerging global practice of incarceration assists to maintain hierarchies between different states, primarily the United States and the rest, but also the West and the rest, and between peoples within states. The labelling of a broad range of social movements, armed struggles and protagonists in conflicts hostile to the 'interests' of the United States as terrorists works to obscure the reality of the United States' pursuit of self-interest through state terror in the form of military aggression and incarceration.

In the same way that neoliberalism and punitive penal policy have marched hand-in-hand domestically the spread of neoliberal globalization has extended and intensified this process throughout the world. As Naomi Klein noted, there is a direct connection between military 'shock and awe', the economic shock treatment of coerced neoliberal restructuring and the physical and psychological shock delivered through mass incarceration and endemic torture in the War on Terror (2007: 7).

Internationally, the United States suffers from a 'superiority complex' which provides it with the justification for conquest, invasion and colonial rule, and serves to reduce qualms over the moral rightness of domination (Johnson 2004: 29). Even thoughtful critiques of punitive, penal regimes assume that such practices do not impact on the fundamental nature of Western societies as the home of civilized people. James Austin and others, for example, reflecting on mass incarceration in the United States, commented that: 'as a civilized people we must not tolerate this' (2003: 463). The idea that mass incarceration may be uncivil but nevertheless undertaken by civilized people suggests that such practices, when carried out in putative liberal democracies, may be problematic but not defining.

The failure to consider uncivil practices of state terror through mass incarceration to be defining is related to the long-held and firmly established notion of

Western democracy as the original and natural home of ideas of freedom, equality and justice. The development of postcolonial studies and critical race scholarship has revealed liberal democracies' historical tendency towards violence against and incarceration of identifiable groups, who are socially, politically and culturally constructed as uncivilized. Democratic states have routinely denied access to rights and citizenship on the grounds of 'race', both at home and in 'their' colonies. Exclusion from rights via renewed notions of dangerousness, related particularly to class and 'race', was established at the inception of modern penal systems (Hudson 2003: 35–6).

Imperialist narratives have also incorporated the idea of Western liberal markets as fair, open and transparent as opposed to the corruption and backwardness associated with 'primitive' less developed states (Whyte 2007b: 153–63). As William Pfaff argued, the claim to virtue underlay notions of Manifest Destiny as a claim to power (2007: 54–8). In previous eras, the idea of Manifest Destiny involved spreading white civilization, whereas today such claims are likely to be made in terms of democracy, human rights and free markets (Perera 2007: 119–46). Ironically, the claims to moral virtue translated into Manifest Destiny laid the foundations for the violation of the rights and processes underpinning those claims, coupled with endemic corruption in the form of the active promotion of war, pain and wholesale disaster for profit. The myth of moral virtue works to hide, silence, minimize and deny the continuing brutal history of mass incarceration and the systemic corruption of private profit linked to punishment and prisons within Western countries, the United States in particular. The myth of moral virtue, exemplified by the hypocritical response to the revelations of torture and abuse in US global prisons, fuels the moral basis for the pursuit of the War on Terror and the expansion of mass incarceration internationally. The invasion of Iraq was, among other things, touted as a way of ending the corruption of the Saddam Hussein regime. Such statements are now viewed, in light of revelations of post invasion corruption, as 'breathtakingly hypocritical' (Whyte 2007b: 160).

Conclusion

The War on Terror, and specifically the expansion of US mass incarceration to encompass the entire planet, provide an emblematic example of states' strategic deployment of 'counter-terrorism' to engage in the widespread use of terror against people and communities stereotyped as terrorists. Despite protestations to the contrary the documented state terror and torture of prisoners and detainees in the War on Terror are not outside the moral framework of the United States but instead reveal the values put into practice daily upon the bodies of millions of prisoners by thousands of American citizens, both in the country itself and increasingly in its global prisons offshore. Increasingly, the boundaries between 'homeland' and global security, domestic and offshore prisons, are rendered porous as state terror and terrorism circulate between spaces of violence and incarceration. The internal drivers of mass incarceration in the United States –

inequality, racism, prisons for profit and neoliberalism – more generally are embracing new frontiers and capturing new markets. The people of the world represent the bodies upon which US state terror, in the form of mass incarceration and torture, will be practised. The War on Terror, including the Presidential Order that allows for the capture and detention of non-citizens of the United States anywhere in the world, the invasions of Iraq and Afghanistan, and the establishment of a global carceral complex, have extended and transformed mass incarceration from a US-based phenomenon to a process that encompasses the entire globe: a move from garrison state to garrison planet.

References

Agamben, G. (2005) *State of Exception*, Chicago: University of Chicago Press.

Age (2006) 2 March, Melbourne.

Alliez, É. and Negri A. (2003) 'Peace and War Theory', *Culture and Society*, 20, 2: 109–18.

Andreas, P. and Price, R. (2001) 'From War Fighting to Crime Fighting: Transforming the American National Security State' *International Studies Review*, 3, 3: 31–52.

Austin, J., Irwin, J. and Kurbin, C. (2003) 'It's About Time: America's Imprisonment Binge' in T. Blomberg and S. Cohen (eds) *Punishment and Social Control*, New York: Aldine De Gruyter.

Blum, W. (2000) *Rogue State: A Guide to the World's Only Superpower*, London: Zed Books.

Bush, G.W. (2001) 'Military Order of November 13, 2001', *Federal Register*, November, 16, 66: 222.

—— (2002) *The National Security Strategy of the United States of America*, Washington, DC: The White House.

Butler, J. (2004) *Precarious Life: The Powers of Mourning and Violence*, London: Verso Books: chapter 3.

Chomsky, N. (2002) *Pirates and Emperors, Old and New: International Terrorism in the Real World* London: Pluto Press.

Christie, N. (2003) *Crime Control as Industry: Towards Gulags, Western Style*, London and New York: Routledge.

Churchill, W. and Wall, V. (eds) (1992) *Cages of Steel: The Politics of Imprisonment in the United States*, Washington, DC: Maisonneuve Press.

Coyle, A., Campbell, A. and Neufeld, R. (2003) 'Introduction' in A. Coyle, A. Campbell and R. Neufeld (eds) *Capitalist Punishment: Prison Privatization and Human Rights*, Atlanta and London: Clarity Press and Zed Books.

Davis, A. (2003) *Are Prisons Obsolete*, New York: Seven Stories Press.

—— (2005) *Abolition Democracy: Beyond Empire, Prisons and Torture*, New York: Free Press.

Garland, D. (2001) 'The Meaning of Mass Imprisonment', in D. Garland (ed.) *Mass Imprisonment: Social Causes and Consequences*, London: Sage.

George, A. (2003) 'Women Prisoners as Customers: Counting the Costs of the Privately Managed Metropolitan Women's Correctional Centre: Australia' in A. Coyle, A. Campbell and R. Neufeld (eds) *Capitalist Punishment: Prison Privatization and Human Rights*, Atlanta and London: Clarity Press and Zed Books.

Gilmore-Wilson, R. (2007) *Golden Gulag: Prisons, Surplus, Crisis, and Opposition in Globalizing*, Berkeley: University of California Press.

Giroux, H. (2002) 'Global Capitalism and the Return of the Garrison State', *Arena Journal*, 19: 141–60.

Gordon, A. (2006) 'Abu Ghraib: Imprisonment and the War on Terror', *Race and Class* 48, 1: 42–59.

—— (2009) 'The US Military Prison: The Normalcy of Exceptional Brutality' in P. Scraton and J. McCulloch (eds) *The Violence of Incarceration*, London: Routledge.

Green, P. and Ward T. (2004) *State Crime: Governments, Violence and Corruption*, London: Pluto Press.

Greene, J. (2001) 'Bailing Out Private Jails' *American Prospect*, 10 September. Online, available at: www.justicestrategies.net/Judy/AmericanProspect.pdf (accessed 21 November 2008).

—— (2004) 'From Abu Ghraib to America: Examining Our Harsh Prison Culture', *Ideas for an Open Society: Occasional Papers from OSI-US Programs*, 4: 2–4.

Hallett, M. (2006) *Private Prisons in America: A Critical Race Perspective*, Chicago, IL: University of Illinois Press.

Harding, R. (1997) *Private Prisons and Public Accountability*, Buckingham: Open University Press.

Hardt, M. (2002) 'Sovereignty', *Theory and Event*. Online, available at: www.muse.jhu.edu/journals/theory_and_event/v005/5.4hardt.html (accessed 21 November 2008).

Hardt, M. and Negri, A. (2000) *Empire*, Cambridge: Harvard University Press.

Hersh, S. (2004) 'The Other War', *New Yorker*, April 12. Online, available at: www.newyorker.com/archive/2004/04/12/040412fa_fact (accessed 21 November 2008).

Hudson, B. (2003) *Justice in the Risk Society: challenging and re-affirming justice in late modernity*, London: Sage.

Jackson, R. (2008) 'The Ghosts of State Terror: Knowledge, Politics and Terrorism Studies', Paper Prepared for the *International Studies Association (ISA) Annual Conference*, San Francisco.

James, J. (1996) 'Hunting Prey: The US Invasion of Panama' in J. James (ed.) *Resisting State Violence: Radicalism, Gender, and Race in the US Culture*, Minneapolis and London: University of Minnesota Press: 63–83.

—— (2000) 'The Dysfunctional and Disappearing: Democracy, Race and Imprisonment', *Social Identities* 6, 4: 483–93.

Johnson, C. (2004) *The Sorrows of Empire: Militarism, Secrecy and the End of Empire*, London: Verso.

—— (2006) *Nemesis: The Last Days of the American Republic*, New York: Metropolitan Books.

Kaplan, A. (2003) 'Homeland Insecurities: Transformations of Language and Space' in M. Dudziak (ed.) *September 11 in History: A Watershed Moment?*, Durnham, London: Duke University Press.

Klein, N. (2005) 'The Rise of Disaster Capitalism', *Nation*, 2 May 2005. Online, available at: www.thenation.com/doc/20050502/klein> (accessed 19 June 2009).

—— (2007) *The Shock Doctrine: The Rise of Disaster Capitalism*, Camberwell, Victoria: Allen Lane.

Kraska, P. and Kappeler V. (1997) 'Militarizing American Police: The Rise and Normalization of Paramilitary Units', *Social Problems*, 44, 1: 1–18.

McCulloch, J. (2004) 'Blue Armies, Khaki Police and the Cavalry on the New American Frontier: Critical Criminology for the 21st Century', *Critical Criminology*, 12, 3: 309–26.

McCulloch, J. and Carlton, B. (2006) 'Preempting Justice: The Suppression of Financing of Terrorism and the "War on Terror"', *Current Issues in Criminal Justice*, 17: 397–412.

McCulloch, J. and George, A. (2009) 'Naked Power: Strip-Searching in Women's Prisons' in P. Scraton and J. McCulloch (eds) *The Violence of Incarceration*, New York: Routledge.

McLaren, P. and Martin, G. (2004) 'The Legend of the Bush Gang: Imperialism, War and Propaganda' *Cultural Studies: Critical Methodologies*, 4, 3: 281–303.

MacMaster, N. (2004) 'Torture from Algiers to Abu Ghraib', *Race and Class*, 46, 2: 1–22.

Mariani, P. (2001) 'Overview: Law, Order, and Neoliberalism', *Social Justice*, 28, 3.

Moyle, P. (2000) *Profiting from Punishment: Private Prisons in Australia: Reform or Regression?* Annandale: Pluto Press.

Nathan, S. (2003) 'Prison Privatization in the United Kingdom' in A. Coyle, A. Campbell and R. Neufeld (eds) *Capitalist Punishment: Prison Privatization and Human Rights*, Atlanta and London: Clarity Press and Zed Books.

Parenti, C. (1999) *Lockdown America*, London, New York: Verso.

Perera, S. (2007) 'Our Patch: Domains of Whiteness, Geographies of Lack and Australia's Racial Horizon in the "War on Terror"' in S. Perera (ed.) *Our Patch: Enacting Australian Sovereignty Post 2001*, Perth, Western Australia: Network Books: 119–46.

Pfaff, W. (2007) 'Manifest Destiny: A New Direction for America', *New York Review of Books*, 54, 2: 54–8. Online, available at: www.nybooks.com/articles/19879 (accessed 21 November 2008).

Physicians for Human Rights (2005) 'Break Them Down: Systematic Use of Psychological Torture by US Forces', Washington, DC: Physicians for Human Rights: 5.

Pranis, K. (2003) 'Campus Activism Defeats Multinational's Prison Profiteering' in T. Herviel and P. Wright (eds) *Prison Nation – The Warehousing of America's Poor*, New York, London: Routledge.

Presidential Documents (2001) 'Detention, Treatment, and Trial of Certain Non-Citizens in the War against Terrorism', 57831–6. Online, available at: www.fas.org/irp/offdocs/eo/mo-111301.htm (accessed 21 November 2008).

Rajiva, L. (2005) *The Language of Empire: Abu Ghraib and the American Media*, New York: Monthly Review Press.

Rhodes, L. (2004) *Total Confinement: Madness and Reason in the Maximum-Security Prison*, Berkeley: University of California Press.

Rose, D. (2004) *Guantánamo: The War on Human Rights*, New York: The New Press.

Rosenberg, C. (2004) 'Permanent Jail Set for Guantánamo', *Miami Herald*, December 9. Online, available at: www.commondreams.org/headlines04/1209–09.htm (accessed 26 February 2008).

Saada, E. (2003) 'The History Lessons: Power and Rule in Imperial Formations', *Items and Issues*, Social Science Research Council, 4, 4, fall/winter: 10–17.

Scahill, J. (2007) *Blackwater: The Rise of the World's Most Powerful Mercenary Army*, London: Serpent's Tail.

Shichor, D. (1995) *Punishment for Profit – Private Prisons/Public Concerns*, London, New Delhi: Sage.

Singer, P. (2003) *Corporate Warriors: The Rise of the Privatized Military Industry*, Ithaca: Cornell University Press.

Sparks, R. (2003) 'State Punishment in Advanced Capitalist Countries' in T. Blomberg and S. Cohen (eds) *Punishment and Social Control*, New York: Aldine Transaction.

White, J. (2005) 'Terrorism in Transition', in P. Reichel (ed.) *Handbook of Transnational Crime and Justice*, Thousand Oakes: Sage Publications: 265–78.

Whyte, D. (2007a) 'The Crimes of Neo-Liberal Rule in Occupied Iraq' *British Journal of Criminology*, 47, 2: 177–95.

——— (2007b) 'Hire an American! Economic Tyranny and Corruption in Iraq', *Social Justice*, 34, 2: 153–68.

'Y – Multiple Award Task Order Contract (MATOC) for Construction projects at Camp Cropper within Camp Victory installation, Baghdad, Iraq' (2007) *FBO Daily*. 5 April. Online, available at: www.fbodaily.com/archive/2007/04-April/05-Apr-2007/FBO-01265724.htm (accessed 20 November 2008).

12 The deterrence logic of state warfare

Israel and the Second Lebanon War, 2006

Karine Hamilton

Introduction

In 2006, a high school textbook used in Australia sparked controversy for informing students that 'throughout history, most terrorist acts have been carried out by nation states'. The textbook referred to various cases of state terrorism, including the United States in Nicaragua during the 1980s, as well as 'other examples of state-run terrorist campaigns ... in Russia (in Chechnya most recently), Turkey (in Kurdistan), Israel (in Palestine), Indonesia (in Aceh, West Papua and East Timor most recently)' (Heinrichs 2006). The national education minister demanded the withdrawal of the book from school curriculums, declaring 'it is inconceivable that information is being taught in schools which claims Australia is "reaping the harvest" of our foreign policies and our "Western imperialism"' (Heinrichs 2006).

The minister's response to the textbook encapsulated a closely guarded tenet of Australian public discourse that 'the West is always the innocent victim of terrorist attacks, never its perpetrator' (Burchill 2006). Any notion to the contrary – that the counter-terrorism measures of democratic governments worldwide need to be open to the same criticisms and analytical groundwork as the terrorist actions of non-state groups – is indeed rejected routinely by Western governments.

Yet, in a period of international relations dominated by a War on Terror, the artificial distinction drawn between terrorism and democratic governance offers the reassurance of moral certainty but ultimately reinforces and masks the global imbalances which clearly underpin contemporary conflicts. As Thomas Kapitan argues, the term terrorism 'is *the* expression of choice for illegitimate violence, exempting states from being agents of terrorism yields an unfair rhetorical advantage to established governments, especially since states usually inflict greater harm upon civilians than do non-state agents' (emphasis added) (2004: 178). In this chapter, I take my cue from Kapitan's above observation and I examine the use of terror tactics by the state of Israel in its response to a cross-border attack by Hezbollah in 2006.

On 12 July 2006, the Lebanese group Hezbollah or 'Party of God' launched a series of rockets against northern Israeli towns and simultaneously attacked two

Israeli army vehicles, patrolling the Lebanese border. Three Israeli soldiers were killed, two were wounded and another two were abducted in the assault. The Israeli response was immediate and forceful, but hardly proportional. Using naval and aerial bombardments, as well as a ground offensive, the Israel Defence Forces (IDF) targeted the communal centres of Hezbollah's support in the mostly Shia localities of the Beqaa Valley, southern Lebanon and Beirut. The IDF also targeted Lebanon's civilian infrastructure including main roads, bridges, water and sewage plants, petrol stations and airports. In turn, Hezbollah carried out guerrilla-style campaigns against Israeli soldiers and launched thousands of rockets against northern Israeli communities, including the major port city of Haifa. The July War or the Second Lebanon War, as Lebanese and Israelis refer to the conflict respectively, lasted 34 days and resulted in the deaths of more than 1,000 civilians, mostly Lebanese people.[1]

The intensity of the Israeli response to Hezbollah followed a distinct logic of deterrence. By displaying their military might and the will to use it, Israeli leaders purportedly aimed to pressure Hezbollah into releasing the Israeli hostages but, in the long term, they sought to deter the group from engaging in future operations against Israel. As Nadav Morag, a political scientist and former Israeli foreign policy advisor, maintained, 'the Israeli wars with Hezbullah [*sic*] in Lebanon and with the Palestinians in Gaza must be seen in the context of the pressing Israeli need to re-establish some semblance of a deterrent capacity' (Morag 2006). Such deterrence clearly uses terror to achieve its objectives: a point best illustrated in the Israeli case by the deliberate bombing of civilian targets in order to dissuade the Lebanese population from supporting Hezbollah. In spite of its terrorist qualities, the strategy of deterrence is a popular military measure employed by governments around the world. Its popularity, I argue below, relates to the ways in which deterrence draws on notions of a strong national identity and images of an undifferentiated enemy, who is conceived of as unable to dialogue outside a relationship of violent domination.

Israel's deterrence strategy and the conflict in Lebanon 2006

When Hezbollah abducted the two Israeli soldiers in 2006, the Israeli military and government held a long-established policy of deterrence as one of the key objectives of their response. Since the establishment of Israel in 1948, deterrence, along with warning and defeat, has been one of the three pillars of Israeli military doctrine. Deterrence is understood as a cost-benefit calculation which supposes that overcoming an opponent involves demonstrating the capacity to inflict a degree of pain and destruction against your enemies and their supporters which goes beyond their 'cost-tolerance level' (Shultz 1979). Israeli leaders adopted a policy of deterrence primarily with the aim of persuading surrounding states that Israel is impervious to military attacks and that a Jewish state is an unchallengeable presence in the Middle East (Inbar and Sandler 1993). Over the course of its history, Israel used deterrence in two main forms: denial and punishment. In the former, Israel uses pre-emptive military strikes to deny opportunities for Arab governments to gain military success against Israel, such as the air strikes against Iraq's nuclear facilities in 1981. In the latter, Israel reacts to Arab confrontations punitively, also known as a 'reprisal policy'.

The Israeli response to Hezbollah's cross-border raid in 2006 exemplified deterrence in its retaliatory form. Immediately following the incursion, the Israeli Cabinet authorized a 'severe' reaction to the raid, predominantly involving the use of aerial strikes against Hezbollah rocket sites along Israel's northern border, as well as a range of targets across Lebanon (Harel *et al.* 2006). The Defense Minister Amir Peretz explained that 'the goal is for this incident to end with Hezbollah so badly beaten that not a man in it does not regret having launched this incident' (Harel *et al.* 2006). In greater depth, the IDF Chief of Staff Dan Halutz summarized the military objectives of an Israeli campaign which, as well as aiming to compel Hezbollah to return the hostages, included 'deepening Israeli deterrence in the expanse and shaping relations with Lebanon. Cessation of the terror from ... Lebanon ... while pushing the Lebanese administration and the international establishment to realize Lebanon's national responsibility, including security control in southern areas' (Schiff 2006). The inclusion of Lebanon in Israel's strategic objectives and the far-reaching military campaign that ensued were justified by the Israeli cabinet's unique definition of the Hezbollah attack as the act of a sovereign state, rather than as a terrorist act. The Israeli prime minister declared 'the events this morning are not terror attacks but actions of a sovereign state ... Lebanon is responsible and it will bear responsibility' (Sofer 2006). Furthermore, an IDF major general stated 'this affair is between Israel and the state of Lebanon ... Where to attack? Once it is inside Lebanon, everything is legitimate – not just southern Lebanon, not just the line of Hezbollah posts' (Labott 2006). Similarly, the defense minister surmised: 'the Lebanese government, which allows Hezbollah to operate freely against Israel from within its sovereign territory, will bear full responsibility for the consequences. The State of Israel considers itself free to act in any way it sees fit' (Sofer 2006). By attributing blame to the Lebanese government, then, Israeli leaders broadened their strategic intentions beyond using force as a corrective measure against Hezbollah and opened the whole of Lebanon to declaredly legitimate attack by the IDF.

The strategic rationale to punish and deter Hezbollah *and* Lebanon translated into the bombing of multiple and diverse Lebanese locations. In more than four weeks of combat, the Israeli Air Force performed 7,000 air strikes on an equal number of targets in Lebanon at the same time as the Israeli Navy carried out a further 2,500 bombardments. In a population of fewer than four million people, close to 1,200 Lebanese were killed (around a third of whom were under 18 years of age), more than 4,000 people were wounded and nearly one million people were displaced by the IDF campaign. In addition to these human losses, the IDF inflicted extensive damage to Lebanon's civilian infrastructure, including the destruction or damage of an estimated 31 crucial facilities such as airports, water, electrical and sewage factories, as well as five hospitals, 25 petrol stations, 80 bridges, 94 road ways, 900 businesses and more than 30,000 residential homes and shops (Amnesty International 2006). The enormity of the damage conformed to one of the cornerstones of Israel's deterrence policy, the need to make victories commanding and indisputable against Arab enemies: Israel's ability to deter hostile Arab forces was regarded as dependent on its ability to demonstrate *overwhelming* force and conquest (Inbar and Sandler 1993). Particularly given that Hezbollah's initial attack represented a failure of Israeli deterrence then, in line with traditional Israeli military thinking, only a 'decisive victory' *(hachra'a)* or 'extracting a painful price from the Arab side' could re-establish deterrent power. The vast destruction of crucial public facilities, homes, lives and businesses was not an inadvertent outcome of Israeli actions; but rather it was the calculated component of a military strategy based on achieving deterrence through inflicting 'decisive' and 'painful' penalties against Lebanon.

Indeed, it is the aim to demonstrate crushing force and to inflict painful enemy losses against a wider Israeli goal of compelling the entire Middle East to accept its occupation of Palestinian territories, which most affords the strategy of deterrence its terrorist qualities. Israeli state officials rationalized the damage to Lebanese lives and infrastructure by emphasizing that 'Israel only aimed at targets which directly served the terrorist organizations' and that 'Hizbullah's [*sic*] deliberate placing of missile launchers and stockpiles of weapons in the heart of civilian centers, frequently inside and beneath populated apartment blocks, meant that this risk [of collateral damage] was tragically high' (Israel Ministry of Foreign Affairs 2007). A United Nations (UN) commission of inquiry, headed by three international law experts, however, concluded the IDF *intentionally* targeted civilians. The commissioners found 'that, cumulatively, the deliberate and lethal attacks by the IDF on civilians and civilian objects amounted to collective punishment' (Soares *et al.* 2006). Even the stated intentions of Israeli leaders blatantly contradicted the proposition that the civilian casualties of IDF bombings were the unfortunate by-products of the targeting of Hezbollah or the fault of Hezbollah itself for deliberately hiding among civilians. The head of the IDF, for example, asserted that 'nothing is safe (in Lebanon), as simple as that' (Farrell 2006) and that 'if the soldiers are not returned, we will turn Lebanon's clock back 20 years' (Labott 2006). Such comments by Israel's military chief belied the official rationalization of Lebanese casualties by reflecting a policy of collective punishment, which equated to an intentional lack of discrimination between civilians and combatants by the IDF in Lebanon.

The precision bombing of two Lebanese Red Cross ambulances on 23 July 2006 illustrated the purposefulness of the Israeli offensive against civilians and further exemplified the terrorist attributes of Israeli tactics in Lebanon. When an artillery shell exploded outside the home of the Fawaz family in the village of Tibnine, five family members in the household were injured by shrapnel and shattered glass. After seeking treatment at their local hospital, the Fawaz family was advised that their most seriously injured – 41-year-old Ahmad, 13-year-old Ahmad and 80-year-old Jamila – should go to the better-equipped medical facility in Tyre. A local ambulance carried the three Fawaz members to Qana and transferred them to a second ambulance, which intended to transport them the rest of the journey to Tyre. At the ambulances' meeting point, while both had maintained their headlights, flashing blue lights and an illuminated Red Cross sign, Israeli missiles hit the vehicles. The elder Ahmad recalled that after regaining consciousness, 'I extended my hand to my leg, and realized I had lost my leg. It was my right leg. I did not feel anything. I also received shrapnel to my left leg, and it was broken' (Human Rights Watch 2006). His son Ahmad and mother Jamila received further shrapnel wounds, while the ambulance workers ear drums were damaged and they received minor shrapnel wounds (they were wearing flak jackets and helmets). An Israeli military spokesperson later rationalized that the missile attacks 'occurred in an area used to fire hundreds of rockets into Israel ... The army warned the population in the area to stay clear of rocket launching sites because we intended to operate there against activity by Hezbollah terrorists' (Smiles 2006). However the argument that the ambulance casualties were complicit in their fate due to the proximity of Hezbollah munitions or due to their failure to heed Israeli warnings lacked credibility, given the stated intentions of Israeli leaders quoted above. Moreover the bombing of the two ambulances in Qana represented a common pattern of attack in which civilian convoys, often heeding Israeli warnings and attempting to flee for safety, were the target of Israeli bombs (Cambanis 2006).

More tellingly, Israeli actions collectively punished the Lebanese and adopted terrorist methods in the ways that they represented a form of political communication whose main audience was not the immediate casualties of Israel's military violence. One of the core features of terrorism is 'the deliberate use of violence, or threat of its use, against innocent people, with the aim of intimidating some other people into a course of action they otherwise would not take' (Primoratz 2004). The Israeli bombings were designed to communicate a political message to the Lebanese collectively: allowing Hezbollah to exist would come at the expense of your personal and national wellbeing. In the words of one former Israeli army colonel:

> Israel is attempting to create a rift between the Lebanese population and Hezbollah supporters by exacting a heavy price from the elite in Beirut. The message is: If you want your air conditioning to work and if you want to be able to fly to Paris for shopping, you must pull your head out of the sand and take action toward shutting down Hezbollah-land.
>
> (Wright and Ricks 2006)

The head of the Israeli army reiterated the communicative function underlying the bombings which aimed to send 'a clear message to both greater Beirut and Lebanon that they've swallowed a cancer and have to vomit it up, because if they don't their country will pay a very high price' (Erlanger 2006). In effect, the Israeli bombings were intended to coerce and intimidate not only Hezbollah members, but all Lebanese citizens. As Robert Fisk described: 'Lebanon's infrastructure is being steadily torn to pieces, its villages razed, its people more and more terrorised – and terror is the word they used – by Israel's American-made fighter bombers' (Fisk 2006). The Israeli message – to remove Hezbollah or collectively face military punishment – was reiterated during the 2006 conflict and again after the prisoner exchange between Hezbollah and Israel in 2008, when Israel sent automated phone messages to Lebanese residents in Beirut and southern Lebanon. The message warned them not to let Hezbollah form 'a state within a state' and threatened 'harsh retaliation' for any future Hezbollah assault signing the message from 'the state of Israel' (Mahdawi 2008). The Israeli campaign then represented a form of collective punishment, which used fear and intimidation with the purpose of sending a political message to Lebanese civilians that they should dispose of Hezbollah from their territory or be held collectively responsible for the group's actions.

This collective punishment and terrorization of the Lebanese population continued well after the formal end of hostilities between Israel and Hezbollah in the form of the unexploded cluster munitions, deliberately scattered by the IDF throughout southern Lebanon. During the last three days of the conflict, a period in which the UN was brokering a ceasefire, Israeli forces engaged in saturation cluster bombing. Among the four million cluster bombs dropped on Lebanon throughout the IDF campaign, 90 per cent of them fell during this final window of combat (Human Rights Watch 2008). Cluster bombs were released from the air or ground and contained dozens to hundreds of smaller bombs or submunitions, many of which were designed to act as 'duds' – to fail to detonate on initial impact and to create lasting minefields in the process. In a 1,400 km square area of southern Lebanon, populated by 650,000 residents, the IDF used more than double the number of submunitions used by the coalition forces in Iraq in 2003 and more than 15 times the number employed by the United States in Afghanistan between 2001 and 2002. As a result, the post-war presence of submunition explosives was worse in Lebanon than in other high-profile war zones in Iraq, Afghanistan and also Kosovo. With an approximate 25 per cent dud rate, the number of unexploded munitions left in Lebanon was estimated to have been between 500,000 to one million. In the two years since the conflict ended in Lebanon, 20 Lebanese were killed and 194 others were maimed due to unexploded submunitions left by the IDF. As well as these human casualties, the submunition duds damaged the economic security of southern Lebanese communities by transforming agricultural grounds into unusable minefields and interfering with local tobacco, citrus, banana and olive crops.

The use of saturation cluster bombing during a period in which the end of hostilities between Israel and Lebanon was a known outcome represented a terrorist tactic, given the known and therefore intended impact of the notoriously imprecise cluster bomb on civilians. One commander of an IDF rocket unit explained that in order to overcome the cluster bomb's known imprecision, he was ordered to 'flood' areas of Lebanon with the submunitions and he concluded that 'what we did was insane and monstrous; we covered entire towns in cluster bombs' (Rapoport 2006b). Just as Hezbollah's firing of thousands of rockets into Israeli cities was defined as terrorism for its obvious lack of discrimination between combatants and civilians, so too the IDF's flooding of Lebanese towns with cluster munitions was to be viewed as a terrorist act because of its non-discrimination. This symmetry of tactics between the IDF and Hezbollah was considered by a morally troubled reservist in an IDF artillery battalion, who had participated in combat in Lebanon. The reservist said: 'I told myself that the people left in that village [southern Lebanon] must be the weaker ones, like in Haifa ... I felt that we were acting like Hezbollah. Taking houses and turning them into targets. That's terror' (Rapoport 2006a). The use of imprecise weapons by the IDF created long-term economic and safety impacts on Lebanese communities and constituted a terrorist tactic in its deliberate employment within civilian areas.

Deterrence strategies and national identities

States resort to far-reaching military offensives as a way of not only deterring enemy forces, but also of strengthening national pride. As Bruno Frey observes, governments worldwide readily opt for deterrent approaches because their citizens demand actions which are decisive, prompt and which, essentially, maintain 'a "macho" image' (Frey 2004).[2] The use of force and deterrent strategies to deal with terrorism is popular because affected populations consider alternative non-violent responses as somehow soft or 'cowardly'. As a result, coercive counter-terrorism practices dominated government responses to terrorism internationally in places such as the United States, Britain and Israel. These states use deterrence strategies because by adopting a hard line against designated terrorist groups, they can hold up an image of national unity and invulnerability.

This connection between deterrence and national identity is particularly noticeable in military campaigns, which follow the perceived humiliations of previous armed conflicts. This was the case in America's armed foray into Iraq in the first Gulf War in 1991, which as Allen Feldman writes, represented a 'post-Vietnam political fantasy of American re-empowerment' (Feldman 2004: 209). Similarly in Israel 'there is always an old trauma in the inventory, which must be erased in order "to rehabilitate our deterrence"' (Benn 2002). In 1982 then Israeli Prime Minister Menachem Begin declared the first Lebanon War would help to heal the trauma of the war in 1973 when Egypt and Syria surprised Israel with a coordinated military attack (Mairovich 2007). Likewise in 2006, the Second Lebanon War was regarded as a remedy to the perceived damage affected by the withdrawal of IDF forces from Lebanon in 2000.

The contentious withdrawal of Israeli troops from southern Lebanon in May 2000 was widely seen as a shameful surrender: a lesson in failed deterrence. In the popular Israeli judgement, the renewal of violent confrontations between Palestinians and Israelis, which ensued in the second *intifadah*, was 'a direct consequence of Israel's ignominious departure from Lebanon, which convinced Israel's enemies that Israel would no longer allow casualties – that they had gone soft' (Rosenthal 2003: 50–1). In greater depth, the Israeli political scientist Yoram Peri writes:

Withdrawal from southern Lebanon was interpreted by the IDF as weakening Israel's ability to deter attack. The Hizbullah [*sic*] portrayed it as a heroic victory for its warriors, and it was clear that this claim would strengthen the Palestinians' belief that they could drive Israelis out of the West Bank if they adopted the methods of a war of attrition like the one in southern Lebanon. The need to restore Israel's deterrent power in the eyes of its enemies and equally to restore the honor of the military in the eyes of the Israeli public and in its own estimation would henceforth be factors that would have considerable impact on Israeli military policy against the Intifada.

(Peri 2002)

This impact was observable in the attempt to reverse the seeming weakness of military withdrawal and political compromise by then Israeli Prime Minister Ariel Sharon, who aimed to 'clarify the balance of power' and to 'make sure Palestinians understand that Israel is not getting chased out by Hamas and Islamic Jihad. The most obvious way to make this point is to eliminate the leaders of these groups before pulling up stakes' (Chafets 2004). More generally, the IDF responded to the second *intifadah* by aiming to 'nip it in the bud by inflicting heavy losses on the Palestinians while keeping its own casualties to a minimum' (Peri 2002). As with the bombings in Lebanon discussed above, the employment of assassinations and deliberately high fatalities in the Palestinian territories exemplified the use of terror to demoralize and persuade a civilian collective into accepting a particular political reality. Hence, the withdrawal of Israeli troops from Lebanon in 2000 was seen as an embarrassing retreat, which could only be rectified through a demonstration of military force borne out by high casualty numbers and controversial policies, such as targeted assassinations.

In a context of perceived national weakness then, deterrence clearly denotes more than just a military strategy; it represents a source of collective strength and pride. In this way governments use deterrent strategies to shape national identities and in so doing, employ massive force to send a message not just to their enemies but also to their citizens: 'we are strong, we do not compromise, we will protect you and we will defend your honour'. As Peri's above statement explains, consequent to the withdrawal of Israeli forces from Lebanon, the renewed focus on Israeli deterrence and tough military action aimed to repair the reputation of the armed forces *in the eyes of the Israeli public*. Hence, military campaigns based on deterrent tactics are not only aimed at transmitting a message of costly consequences to one's enemies, but convey a message of internal strength to a domestic audience.

When deterrent strategies inform national pride, however, an image of strength becomes dependent on continually reiterating uncompromising political positions and severe military actions. On the one hand, a deterrence strategy does not necessarily equal armed force 'but the difference between deterrence and brute force tends to vanish, because deterrence is only credible and therefore effective if it is regularly used' (Frey 2004: 28). The regular use of massive force becomes even more compelling in the event that deterrence appears lost or weakened. Such is the case in the Second Lebanon War, in which criticisms levelled against the Olmert administration's handling of the conflict suggested that it failed to beat Hezbollah and thus marked an end to Israel's regional deterrence capacity. In the words of a *Jerusalem Post* reporter: 'with every day's evidence of underwhelming military success, the chorus swells in Israel that this is a no-brainer. The army is being humiliated, the argument runs; Israel's critical deterrent capability is being shattered' (Horovitz 2006). This perceived Israeli defeat was already laying the basis for the rationale of the next campaign: 'the third Lebanon War will be declared as a correction of the Second Lebanon War' (Mairovich 2007). As one Israeli queries, does the Israeli prime minister 'think about how to prevent the next war or how to rehabilitate his lost pride ("the deterrence") and that of the IDF? ... perhaps he indeed is planning the "campaign for bringing back pride"' (Shohat 2007). Within the military establishment, the seeming defeat of Israel in Lebanon prompted speculation that the IDF should reoccupy Gaza 'in order to bleach the stain of defeat in Lebanon' (Peled 2008: 284). The need to maintain a credible threat, coupled with the strong association of military force with national pride, reinforces a recurring pattern of violence in which state leaders habitually select massive force as a way of (re)appearing strong.

While deterrence taps into Israeli notions of national identity, it simultaneously draws on images of an undifferentiated enemy, who is unable to communicate outside a relationship of violent domination. As Israel's deterrence strategy sent a message to the whole of Lebanon, in effect it represented a form of collective punishment that positioned every Lebanese person as deserving of, and receptive to, massive force. The Israeli journalist Gideon Levy cautioned against the extreme military measures that collective forms of punishment encourage, such as when:

> Haim Ramon 'doesn't understand' why there is still electricity in Baalbek; Eli Yishai proposes turning south Lebanon into a 'sandbox'; Yoav Limor, a Channel 1 military correspondent, proposes an exhibition of Hezbollah corpses and the next day to conduct a parade of prisoners in their underwear, 'to strengthen the home front's morale'.
>
> (Levy 2006)

Deterrence strategies are commonly underpinned by the sorts of cultural simplifications which lump entire populations together with stereotypical notions that 'the only thing they understand is force' (Morgan 1983). Since deterrence essentially uses threat and violence to manipulate behaviour, it is a seemingly uncivilized way of acting and in turn, people are more at ease using deterrence when they believe that it is being applied to unreasonable and 'primitive-like' people.

In Israel the notion that 'the *Arabs* only understand force' has been a bedrock of national narratives of the Israeli–Arab conflict and underpins Israeli support for deterrent strategies. The Israeli historian Benny Morris encapsulates this view:

> In the 1950s, there was a dispute between Ben-Gurion and Moshe Sharett. Ben-Gurion argued that the Arabs understand only force and that ultimate force is the one thing that will persuade them to accept our presence here. He was right. That's not to say that we don't need diplomacy. Both toward the West and for our own conscience, it's important that we strive for a political solution. But in the end, what will decide their readiness to accept us will be force alone. Only the recognition that they are not capable of defeating us.
>
> (Shavit 2004)

Morris' above statement conveys a belief about Arab peoples which I heard continuously during mid-2004 throughout fieldwork I conducted in Israel. During everyday encounters, from family members to taxi drivers, I regularly heard justifications of Israeli military actions in the Middle East which, it was argued, were misunderstood by naïve Western critics, unfamiliar with the true nature of Arab culture: 'you have to understand, they don't think like we do'.[3] In a related manner Israelis popularly expressed the belief that 'the Middle East is a jungle, where only might speaks' (Laor 2008). This is particularly the case in terms of Israeli perceptions of Lebanon which, since the first Lebanon War in 1982, involve a sense that Lebanon, a Wild West-like nation, drags Israel unwillingly into military combat despite the overt unilateralism of IDF actions (Hamilton 2007). This stereotyping of Arabs as a constellation of people uniformly receptive to violence, as opposed to other forms of political communication, lends itself to harsh forms of *collective* punishment, such as those which characterized the IDF's deterrence strategies in the Second Lebanon War.

Moreover this pigeonholing of Arabs as seemingly stuck in a violent pre-modern mindset draws on and recreates a much more widely held sense of Western superiority vis-à-vis the Islamic Middle East. Israel, like other states which connected their national conflicts to a global War on Terror, uses stereotypes such as 'they only understand force' in part of a broader positioning of itself as a Western nation, defending freedom and civilized values. The counter-terrorism actions of Western governments, following the al-Qaeda attacks against the United States on 11 September 2001 in particular, employed a language in which 'terrorists are endlessly vilified as being evil, barbaric and inhuman, while America and its coalition partners are described as heroic, decent and peaceful – the defenders of freedom' (Jackson 2005). This definition of Western nations specifically in opposition to terrorism transformed Edward Said's notion of 'orientalism from a European-based vision of modernity that could be used to "domesticate" non-Europeans, into a program that established a frontier between "Civilization" and "the new Barbarism"' (Crooke 2006). The cultural stereotypes of enemy groups, which accompany the deterrence measures of Israel and other states fighting self-proclaimed wars against terrorism, offer the building blocks of a national identity based on crudely-formed divisions between a righteous 'us' and a barbaric 'them'.

Conclusion

The Israeli response to Hezbollah's cross-border attack in July 2006 was a military punishment intended to deter Hezbollah from future attacks by inflicting a degree of pain and suffering outside acceptable thresholds. In practice the employment of this deterrence strategy relied on terrorist tactics, which was illustrated by the thousands of overwhelmingly *civilian* deaths, injuries and permanent displacements, as well as the destruction or impairment of basic public amenities across Lebanon. While Israeli state officials rhetorically justified this demolition as the unintended consequences of the IDF's targeting of legitimate military objectives, these human and material casualties were rather the planned outcome of a strategy specifically designed to target and terrorize civilians. The Israeli state targeted Lebanese civilians to convey to Lebanese citizens that they should oppose Hezbollah and to communicate more widely to the Middle East that attacks against Israel are futile. The demonstration of overwhelming force which underpinned the deterrence logic of these messages clearly translated into the use of terror and intimidation by Israeli forces.

The massive force used by states such as Israel is domestically popular because they appear to reflect national strength and resilience. As the Israeli campaign demonstrates, deterrence tactics are tools of national identity enabling state leaders to project collective strength and to react to frightened or angered public sentiments with immediate and resolute action. The propensity to use military muscle as the dominant criterion by which national strength and pride are perceived, however, propels states into bolstering collective identities through new exhibitions of force.

The collective nature of the punishment meted out to Lebanon likewise pointed to the central role of the politics of 'othering' in the deterrence logic used by Israel where the notion that the *Arabs* only understood force had long been pivotal to military strategy. In the global climate of a War on Terror, these sorts of cultural stereotypes about Arab or Islamic people were powerful instruments of identity in Israel and in other states using military force to combat terrorism. Indeed states use deterrence tactics and the cultural divisions which rationalize them because they uphold basic notions of political legitimacy, in which the nation-state, the guardian of civilized values, continually reiterates its authority through its self-appointed battle against the barbaric non-state actor. This is particularly true of Israel, which views and presents itself as 'the only democracy in the Middle East' and as an embattled state struggling against Islamic terrorism.

Ultimately though, the exclusion of the state from the term 'terrorism' shields state leaders from the questions of legitimacy, which acts of politically-motivated violence against civilians (i.e. terrorism) provoke in contemporary political discourses. In so doing, this uneven 'rhetoric of "terror"' is itself a mechanism of state-terrorism' in which governments validate and mask their use of terror tactics by defining their actions as defensive or rationally strategic, while yet employing the illegitimate label 'terrorist' to opponents (Kapitan 2004). The deep resistance shown by state leaders to acknowledging their use of terrorism precisely lies in the political utility of upholding images of righteous combat while maintaining certain groups outside accepted political norms and narratives.

Notes

1 In total there were 1,109 fatalities (overwhelmingly civilian), 4,399 injured and around one million people displaced in Lebanon. In Israel, there were 43 civilian fatalities and 12 soldiers killed with hundreds more civilians injured (Human Rights Watch 2007: 4).
2 In Israel, for example, the public approval rates for the IDF campaign against Hezbollah in 2006 were very high. Following the first two weeks of the campaign, 82 per cent of the Israeli public approved of the war and 71 per cent believed that *added* force should be employed against Lebanon (see Gavriely-Nuri 2008: 7).
3 The notion that 'the Arabs only understand force' underlies not only Israeli military actions but also American performances of military violence in the Middle East. The American journalist who revealed the Abu Ghraib prison scandal, Seymour Hersh, discovered that the use of *sexual* forms of torture in the Bagdad prison arose from a belief among certain American administrators 'that Arabs only understand force, and, two, that the biggest weakness of Arabs is shame and humiliation'. These ideas were informed by an anthropological text called *The Arab Mind* (1973) by Raphael Patai which had become a widely used source of information about Arab society among proponents of the invasion of Iraq in 2003 (see Hersh 2004).

References

Amnesty International (2006) 'Lebanon: deliberate destruction or "collateral damage"? Israeli attacks on civilian infrastructure', 23 August. Online, available at: www.amnesty.org/en/library/asset/MDE18/007/2006/en/dom-MDE180072006en.html (accessed 8 May 2008).

Bayefsky, A. (2006) 'Kofi Annan to Hizbullah's rescue?' *Jerusalem Post*, 8 August. Online, available at: www.jpost.com/servlet/Satellite?cid=1154525833380&pagename =JPost%2FJPArticle%2FPrinter (accessed 8 August 2006).

Benn, A. (2002) 'It's luck there's Saddam', *Haaretz*, 22 August 2002. Online, available at: www.haaretz.com/hasen/pages/ShArt.jhtml?itemNo=200176&contrassID=1&subC ontrassID=1&sbSubContrassID=0&listSrc=Y (accessed 4 June 2008).

Burchill, S. (2006) 'Terrorism and blame', *Australian Financial Review*, 20 October. Online, available at: www.scottburchill.net/terrorismandblame.html (accessed 11 June 2008).

Cambanis, T. (2006) 'For fleeing Lebanese families, road to safety exacts heavy toll', *Boston Globe*, 24 July. Online, available at: www.boston.com/news/world/middleeast/ articles/2006/07/24/for_fleeing_lebanese_families_road_to_safety_exacts_heavy_toll/ (accessed 12 October 2008).

Chafets, Z. (2004) 'Sharon as godfather using Corleone's plan: before you leave, kill your enemies', *Daily News*, 14 March. Online, available at: www.nydailynews.com/ archives/opinions/2004/03/14/2004–03–14_sharon_as__godfather____usin.html (accessed 14 March 2004).

Crooke, A. (2006) 'New orientalism's "barbarians" and "outlaws"', *Daily Star*, 5 September. Online, available at: www.dailystar.com.lb/article.asp?edition_id=1&categ_id=5&article_id=75230 (accessed 5 September 2006).

Erlanger, S. (2006) 'Israel vows to crash militia; group's leader is defiant', *New York Times*, 14 July. Online, available at: www.nytimes.com/2006/07/14/world/middleeast/14cnd-mideast.html (accessed 13 May 2008).

Farrell, S. (2006) 'Our aim is to win – nothing is safe, Israeli chiefs declare', *The Times* 14 July. Online, available at: www.timesonline.co.uk/tol/news/world/article687574.ece (accessed 13 May 2008).

Feldman, A. (2004) 'On cultural anaesthesia: from Desert Storm to Rodney King', in N. Scheper-Hughs and P. Bourgois (eds) *Violence in War and Peace: An Anthology*, Malden: Blackwell.

Fisk, R. (2006) 'How can we stand by and allow this to go on?', *Independent*, 31 July. Online, available at: www.independent.co.uk/opinion/commentators/fisk/robert-fisk-how-can-we-stand-by-and-allow-this-to-go-on-409983.html (accessed 13 May 2008).

Frey, B.S. (2004) *Dealing with Terrorism: Stick or Carrot?*, Cheltenham: Edward Elgar Publishing.

Gavriely-Nuri, D. (2008) 'The "metaphorical annihilation" of the Second Lebanon War (2006) from the Israeli political discourse', *Discourse and Society*, 19: 5–20.

Hamilton, K. (2007) 'Remembering Sabra and Shatila: the silences of Zionist political imaginaries', unpublished thesis, Curtin University of Technology.

Harel, A., Benn, A. and Alon, G. (2006) 'Hezbollah attack/Gov't okays massive strikes on Lebanon; Israel readies for rocket attacks in north', *Haaretz*, 13 July. Online, available at: www.haaretz.com/hasen/pages/ShArt.jhtml?itemNo=737827 (accessed 13 May 2008).

Heinrichs, P. (2006) 'Textbook links US, Israel to "state terrorism"', Melbourne, *Age*, 10 September. Online, available at: www.theage.com.au/news/national/textbook-links-us-israel-to-terrorism/2006/09/09/1157222384098.html?page=fullpage (accessed 11 June).

Hersh, S.M. (2004) 'The gray zone: how a secret Pentagon program came to Abu Ghraib', *New Yorker*, 24 May. Online, available at: www.newyorker.com/archive/2004/05/24/040524fa_fact?currentPage=all (accessed 24 May 2004).

Horovitz, D. (2006) 'Ethical dilemmas for Israel at war', *Jerusalem Post*, 8 August. Online, available at: www.jpost.com/servlet/Satellite?pagename=JPost/JPArticle/ShowFull&cid=1154525826321 (accessed 8 May 2008).

Human Rights Watch (2006) 'The "hoax" that wasn't: the July 23 Qana ambulance attack', December. Online, available: www.hrw.org/backgrounder/mena/qana1206/ (accessed 12 October 2008).

—— (2007) 'Lebanon why they died: civilian casualties in Lebanon during the 2006 war', September. Online, available at: www.hrw.org/reports/2007/lebanon0907/ (accessed 8 May 2008).

—— (2008) 'Flooding south Lebanon: Israel's use of cluster munitions in Lebanon in July and August 2006', February. Online, available at: www.hrw.org/reports/2008/lebanon0208/ (accessed 8 May 2008).

Inbar, E. and Sandler, S. (1993) 'Israel's deterrence strategy revisited', *Security Studies*, 3: 330–8.

Israel Ministry of Foreign Affairs (2007) 'Behind the headlines: the Second Lebanon War: one year later', 12 July. Online, available at: www.mfa.gov.il/MFA/Terrorism+Obstacle+to+Peace/Terrorism+from+Lebanon-+Hizbullah/The%20Second%20

Lebanon%20War%20-%20One%20year%20later%20-%20July%202007 (accessed 24 November 2008).

Jackson, R. (2005) *Writing the War on Terrorism: Language, Politics, and Counter-terrorism*, Manchester: Manchester University Press.

Kapitan, T. (2004) 'Terrorism in the Arab–Israeli conflict', in I. Primoratz (ed.) *Terrorism: The Philosophical Issues*, Houndmills: Palgrave.

Labott, E. (2006) 'Israel authorizes "severe" response to abductions', *CNN*, 13 July. Online, available at: www.edition.cnn.com/2006/WORLD/meast/07/12/mideast/ (accessed 13 May 2008).

Laor, Y. (2008) 'You are terrorists, we are virtuous', in N. Hovespian (ed.) *The War in Lebanon: A Reader*, Massachusetts: Olive Branch Press.

Levy, G. (2006) 'Days of darkness', *Haaretz*, 30 July. Online, available at: www.haaretz.com/hasen/spages/744061.html (accessed 30 July 2006).

Mahdawi, D. (2008) 'Lebanese receive threatening mobile messages from "state of Israel"', *Daily Star*, 18 July. Online, available at: www.dailystar.com.lb/article.asp?edition_ID=1&article_ID=94238&categ_id= (accessed 18 July 2008).

Mairovich, S. (2007) 'Waiting for the next war', *Haaretz*. 4 May. Online, available at: www.haaretz.com/hasen/spages/855681.html (accessed 2 June 2008).

Morag, N. (2006) 'Israel's goals in the present conflict', *Christian Science Monitor*, 20 July. Online, available at: www.csmonitor.com/2006/0720/p09s01-coop.html (accessed 4 June 2008).

Morgan, P.M. (1983) *Deterrence: A Conceptual Analysis*, 2nd edition, Beverly Hills: Sage Publications.

Peled, Y. (2008) 'Illusions of unilateralism dispelled in Israel', in N. Hovespian (ed.) *The War in Lebanon: A Reader*, Massachusetts: Olive Branch Press.

Peri, Y. (2002) 'The Israeli military and Israel's Palestinian policy: from Oslo to the Al Aqsa Intifada', *Peaceworks*, 47.

Primoratz, I. (2004) 'State terrorism and counter-terrorism', in I. Primoratz (ed.) *Terrorism: The Philosophical Issues*, Houndmills: Palgrave Macmillan.

Rapoport, M. (2006a) 'What lies beneath', *Haaretz*, 8 September. Online, available at: www.haaretz.com/hasen/spages/760246.html (accessed 4 June 2008).

—— (2006b) 'IDF commander: we fired more than a million cluster bombs in Lebanon', *Haaretz*, 12 September. Online, available at: www.haaretz.com/hasen/spages/761781.html (accessed 4 June 2008).

Rosenthal, D. (2003) *The Israelis: Ordinary People in an Extraordinary Land*, New York: Free Press.

'Russian defense minister says Hezbollah uses "terrorist methods"' (2006) *Haaretz*, 15 July. Online, available at: www.haaretz.com/hasen/pages/ShArt.jhtml?itemNo=738183&contrassID=1&subContrassID=1 (accessed 15 July 2006).

Schiff, Z. (2006) 'Let's get real', *Haaretz*, 20 October. Online, available at: www.haaretz.com/hasen/spages/777197.html (accessed 4 June 2008).

Shavit, A. (2004) 'Survival of the fittest', *Haaretz*, 9 January. Online, available at: www.haaretz.com/hasen/pages/ShArt.jhtml?itemNo=380986&contrassID=2 (accessed 12 January 2004).

Shohat, O. (2007) 'A war in the summer?', *Haaretz*, 23 April. Online, available at: www.haaretz.co.il/hasen/spages/851488.html (accessed 4 June 2008).

Shultz, R. (1979) 'Coercive force and military strategy: deterrence logic and the cost-benefit model of counterinsurgency warfare', *Western Political Quarterly*, 32: 444–66.

Smiles, S. (2006) 'Ambulance attack evidence stands the test', *Age*, 2 September. Online, available at: www.theage.com.au/news/world/ambulance-attack-evidence-stands-the-test/2006/09/01/1156817099370.html (accessed 12 October 2008).

Soares, J.C.B., Othman, M.C. and Perrakis, S. (2006) *Report of the Commission of Inquiry on Lebanon Pursuant to Human Rights Council Resolution S-2/1* Geneva, 10 November 2006. Online, available at: www.unhcr.org/refworld/docid/45c30b6e0.html (accessed 18 August 2008).

Sofer, R. (2006) 'Olmert: we were attacked by a sovereign country', *Ynetnews*, 12 July. Online, available at: www.ynetnews.com/articles/0,7340,L-3274385,00.html (accessed 13 May 2008).

Wright, R. and Ricks, T.E. (2006) 'Bush supports Israel's move against Hezbollah', *Washington Post*, 19 July. Online, available at: www.washingtonpost.com/wpdyn/content/article/2006/07/18/AR2006071801436_pf.html (accessed 3 February 2008).

Conclusion

Contemporary state terrorism – towards a new research agenda

Richard Jackson

Introduction

In this volume, we have made the argument that '*state* terrorism' is a valid analytical category which can usefully illuminate our understanding of certain forms of political behaviour. In addition, we have provided a theoretical discussion and 11 empirical case studies of contemporary state terrorism as a means of illustrating the concept and exploring the aims, nature, causes, and consequences of this type of political violence. The preceding chapters leave absolutely no doubt that 'states can be terrorists too' and do much to illuminate the nature of state terrorism as a political phenomenon in the contemporary international system.

Despite the transparent and rather axiomatic nature of our primary claims – that there is a category of political behaviour which can best be understood as 'state terrorism' and that there are numerous historical and contemporary examples of such behaviour – the topic remains scandalously understudied as a serious subject of scholarly inquiry within the international relations (IR) and terrorism studies fields. A survey of articles in *Terrorism and Political Violence* and *Studies in Conflict and Terrorism*, for example, the terrorism field's two flagship journals, found that less than two per cent of articles from 1990 to 1999 focused on state terrorism (Silke 2004: 206). This trend remains unchanged since then. Similarly, only 12 of the 768 pages in the *Encyclopaedia of World Terrorism* (1997) examined state terrorism in any form (quoted in Goodin 2006: 55), while the more recent *Dictionary of Terrorism* discusses state terrorism on only eight out of 308 pages (Thakrah 2004). My own analysis shows that scholarly papers on state terrorism make up less than five per cent of the total number of terrorism-related papers presented at the most important international relations conferences in the past two years (Jackson 2008). These findings confirm Schmid and Jongman's broader assessment of the field: 'There is a conspicuous absence of literature that addresses itself to the much more serious problem of state terrorism' (1988: 179–80; see also Walter 1969: 3).

The primary purpose of this final chapter is to briefly take stock of our current knowledge about state terrorism, in part through summarizing some of the most important findings of the chapters in this volume, and then to suggest a few issues and questions which could form the basis of a future research agenda on state terrorism. While there is no longer any doubt of the need to 'bring the state back in' to terrorism studies (Blakeley, 2007), it is important to try to carefully think through some of the most pressing issues and questions, and at the same time, to avoid a few well sign-posted dangers.

The study of state terrorism: a brief assessment

Despite the relative dearth of systematic research on state terrorism described above, we can draw upon a relatively small but important body of research from the past two decades (see for example, Becker 2006; Blakeley 2006; Duvall and Stohl 1988; Grosscup 2006; Gareau 2004; Herman 1982; Sluka 2000; George 1991; Stohl 2006, 1988; Stohl and Lopez 1986, 1984; Stokes 2004), as well as the chapters presented in this volume, to briefly describe some key aspects of the current state of knowledge about the broader subject.

In the first instance, we know from previous studies and the chapters in this volume that the use of state terrorism as a tool of foreign policy or internal governance is not limited by any essential characteristic related to state size or political system. From the world's only remaining superpower to small and impoverished states like Papua New Guinea, and from military dictatorships such as Pakistan to liberal democracies such as Australia and Britain, terrorism has been, and continues to be, employed by almost every kind of state. This is an important observation because it underscores the nature of terrorism as a violent political *strategy* which can be employed by any actor, whether individuals, groups, weak states, strong states and theoretically at least, international organizations. It also suggests that, as with non-state terrorism, each case occurs in a unique context of power capabilities, political interests, culture, and institutional and agential configurations. This, in turn, highlights some of the limitations of applying broad generalizations regarding the nature and causes of state terrorism, and the necessity of retaining a strong sense of context. It also demolishes the popular truism that terrorism is primarily a 'weapon of the weak'; objectively and historically, the powerful have employed terrorism far more frequently than weak actors. Importantly, recognising the heterogeneity of state terrorism also works to deconstruct notions of democratic (and Western) exceptionalism which assume the inherently pacific nature of liberal-democratic states.

At the level of violent political practice, the agents of state terrorism include, first and foremost, individuals and groups acting in their official capacity as representatives of the state, such as military and security personnel, the police, the intelligence services, prison officers and other state employees. Importantly, in a significant number of cases, state terrorism is carried out by state employees acting in an unofficial (but tacitly approved) capacity, such as off-duty police or military personnel. Last, the agents of state terrorism frequently involve a variety of private non-state groups and individuals acting on behalf of the state or with the state's (or actors within the state apparatus') approval, whether tacit or explicit. At the more formal end of the scale, this can include private security actors sub-contracted by the state, such as private military companies (PMCs) and private security companies (PSCs). At the informal end, it includes private militias, death squads, lone assassins, para-military organizations, gangs, mobs, non-state terrorist groups, and the like.

As the chapters in this volume reveal, what we know about the modalities, types, and specific tactics of state terrorism is that they come in a variety of forms. One typology divides state terrorism into limited forms, such as one-off operations designed for a specific outcome, and the more generalized, governance-based or wholesale use of terrorism when a state seeks to intimidate an entire society, large sectors of society, or another state over an extended period of time (see Blakeley 2009).

Limited state terrorism is the rarest form of the phenomenon, and perhaps the least controversial because it most often involves exactly the same actions as those perpetrated by non-state terrorist groups, such as civilian-directed bombings, assassinations, and kidnappings, or direct support for acts of non-state terrorism. Some examples of this form of state terrorism include: the so-called Lavon affair when Israeli agents planted bombs in Cairo; the black-flag operations by the Italian government in the 1980s designed to discredit the leftist movement; the Lockerbie bombing by Libyan agents; the Korean Airline bombing by North Korean agents in 1987; US sponsorship of anti-Castro terrorist attacks; the mining of Nicaraguan ports by US agents; the French bombing of the *Rainbow Warrior* in Auckland harbour; and many others. In some instances, limited state terrorism involves acts of coercive diplomacy, such as threatened or actual military actions against another state, in order to achieve particular policy outcomes, such as the Mayaguez operation against Cambodia in 1975 (Stohl 1988: 174–5). Coercive diplomacy may also take place during war, such as the atomic attacks on Japan and the saturation bombing of German residential areas during the Second World War (Grosscup 2006), the Christmas bombing of Hanoi in 1972, and Israel's attack on Lebanon in 2006 (see Hamilton this volume).

Wholesale state terrorism, on the other hand, is the most common but also the most controversial form of the phenomenon, involving as it does, a range of state actions and actors that usually function collectively to coerce and intimidate a large population. As the chapters in this volume indicate, wholesale state terrorism is widely employed around the world and involves an imaginative array of specific tactics, including: extra-judicial killing and political assassination; kidnapping, extraordinary rendition, disappearances and illegal detention; pogroms and mass killings; torture and prisoner abuse; mass rape and sexual violence; indiscriminate attacks on civilian populations during war or counter-insurgency; using civilians as human shields during military operations; harsh and politicized forms of counter-terrorism; the destruction of people's livelihoods during counter-insurgency operations; collective punishments and revenge attacks; the construction of punitive and brutal forms of incarceration; and many more. As already noted, these actions may be undertaken directly by state agents or indirectly through proxy actors. In practice, they typically involve a mix of state and non-state groups acting in concert, such as the coordinated use of private militia and military forces to attack civilians in Darfur (see Mickler this volume).

In an important insight, Duvall and Stohl have outlined an 'expected utility' model which suggests that states employ terrorism under two broad conditions: (*a*) when they calculate that it will achieve their goals more effectively than other policies – it has lower production costs than the alternatives; and (*b*) when they anticipate that the response costs of using terrorism will be lower than the costs of other strategies (Duvall and Stohl 1988: 253–62). As the chapters in this volume demonstrate, there are a great many contexts in which states have made, and continue to make, exactly these calculations in deciding to employ terrorism in pursuit of specific political or political-economic goals.

In deciding to employ terrorism, the specific aims and goals of states can be conservative or revolutionary, depending upon the circumstances and actors involved. They include, among others: isolating, demoralizing, and governing through fear, individuals and groups who voice opposition under colonialism, dictatorship, military occupation, or post-revolutionary rule; rendering social movements impotent; attempting to gain psychological advantage over an adversary in counter-insurgency, counter-terrorism, and war; securing access to resources; maintaining economic privilege or the enforcement of labour flows; punishment, revenge and the restoration of national pride; population expulsion and ethnic cleansing; the intimidation or deterrence of foreign adversaries; and many others. A key point is that state terrorism has a rational basis, and is sometimes a highly successful policy, at least in the short and medium term, for the elites who enact it (Terry 1980: 99). In Latin America, for example, state terrorism during the Cold War successfully undermined the emergence of a great many progressive and reform-oriented social movements (see Raphael this volume, for example).

A key finding from several chapters in this and other studies, is that states will calculate the potential costs of employing terrorism in relation to the external support they receive from other (usually powerful) states, or alternately, their ability to compensate for any external anticipated or unanticipated costs (see Lasslett this volume). In other words, state terrorism is frequently enabled, at least in part, by the military, economic and diplomatic support, tacit approval or even simply the calculated indifference they receive from influential, international actors. This has also been described as a kind of surrogate state terrorism by great powers (Stohl 1988: 192). Alternately, it can be enabled by the fact that powerful states can absorb or deflect any externally imposed costs of employing terrorism. The international context therefore – the presence of external patrons or the ability to compensate – is an important determinant (enabling cause) of state terrorism.

At the same time, an important internal condition for the decision to employ state terrorism are those situations in which the state or its ruling elite perceive that they are facing a potentially serious challenge to their authority or continued rule. This occurs more often in fragile and institutionally weak states – states that are still trying to consolidate their monopoly on the instruments of violence and their institutional reach, often following periods of revolutionary change or decolonization (Duvall and Stohl 1988: 241–3) – but it can also occur in strong, established states when political leaders perceive that a terrorist movement, for example, poses a serious threat to the stability of the nation. In both cases, the use of exemplary violence against opponents appears as a readily available, psychologically satisfying, and efficient response, certainly in comparison to the much more difficult and uncertain options of political dialogue or social reform. In this sense, state terrorism is in part a reflexive strategy rooted in the accepted doctrines and practices of sovereignty, particularly the notion that the state should have a monopoly on the means of violence and the legitimate right to employ both punitive and defensive violence. Historically, it is only recently that states have begun to accept limits on the forms and types of violence they may employ, and there is still controversy over whether the state can legitimately use 'any means necessary' (including, massive and indiscriminate terror) if it faces a 'supreme emergency' or a direct threat to the continuation of its sovereignty.

In short, what we know about the causes or the 'conditions of possibility' of state terrorism is that there are a series of enabling structures which, in combination with the calculations and decisions of state elites, lead to the practice of state terrorism in a given situation. In other words, it takes both specific enabling structures – internal and external structures, and social/discursive and material structures – and the involvement of active agents – political elites and their agents and supporters – to turn the latent possibility of state terrorism into a form of political practice in a given situation.

Perhaps the most commonly studied aspect of state terrorism relates to its effects and consequences for individuals and communities. There is a wealth of information from human rights organizations, lawyers, criminologists, psychologists and scholars from different disciplines, including those represented in this volume, which document and describe the physical, psychological, cultural and political harm resulting from state terrorism. No one can doubt that state terrorism is immensely destructive to individuals, communities and entire societies, and has a myriad of negative consequences for democratic participation, institutional legitimacy, human rights, human and social well-being, law and order, security, the rule of law, social trust, community cohesion, social capital, the positive functioning of civil society, inter-communal relations, and a great many other aspects of political, social and cultural life (see in particular, Mickler, Murphy, Wardrop, Poynting, McCulloch, Hamilton this volume). On the other hand, relatively undocumented to date are the effects of state terrorism on diplomacy, law, norms, institutions, and the wider processes of international politics, especially when it is perpetrated by the major powers who function as opinion leaders and norm setters (see Stohl 1988: 158).

In the end however, one of the primary problems with much contemporary (and previous) research on state terrorism is that it is, with only a few notable exceptions (see Blakeley 2009), oriented primarily towards the empirical description of state abuses. In fact, we have a great deal of information and a great many descriptive accounts of cases of state terrorism. What are largely missing are theoretically oriented analyses of the processes, causes, outcomes, and termination of state terrorism, and the refinement of concepts and analytical tools for its analysis. Related to this, there is the problem of selective coverage in terms of both cases and types of state terrorism. While some cases of state terrorism have received a great deal of attention from scholars and human rights organizations, many others have been relatively neglected – for the reason that they are taboo cases, such as Israeli and Western state terrorism (see Herring 2008), or they have occurred in countries considered to be peripheral to the priorities of Western societies, such as Papua New Guinea. Similarly, while wholesale state terrorism and so-called state sponsorship of terrorism has received relatively solid coverage, the practices of coercive diplomacy or the use of terrorism during war, has been largely ignored – with only a small number of notable exceptions (see for example, Grosscup 2006; Stohl 1988).

Towards a new research agenda

In its collective aims, this volume represents a call to, first, *broaden* the study of state terrorism beyond the usual focus on the US State Department annual list of 'state sponsors of terrorism' or the typical cases of authoritarian dictatorships, to include a wider set of cases, including Western states, other taboo cases such as Israel and China, states in regions considered peripheral, and historical cases, including the colonial period. Broadening the study of state terrorism also means attempting to go beyond the description of comprehensive, governance-based terrorism to include the examination of state terrorism within the practices of international politics, such coercive diplomacy and state terrorism in war. Second, this volume represents a call to *deepen* the study of state terrorism beyond the all-too-common empirical description of cases. We see an urgent need to develop and apply sophisticated theories, approaches, and concepts for understanding the nature, aims, causes, consequences, and termination of such forms of state-based violence. Deepening research on state terrorism also entails the application of a broader range of disciplinary and methodological approaches beyond IR and terrorism studies, including post-positive, reflectivist approaches. Last, we would argue for the retention of *emancipatory praxis* as the normative heart of the research enterprise and the articulation of a rigorous and clear ethical framework which links research and practice in the organization of political opposition to oppressive forms of state violence and terrorism.

Beyond these broad appeals, however, and choosing from an almost infinite set of possible subjects, we want to suggest that the following questions and issues could provide a useful starting point for developing a new research agenda for the study of state terrorism. We recognize that some of these subjects are already being researched in cognate fields and disciplines; however, we see important benefits in bringing these studies more firmly within the ambit of terrorism studies and its key priorities and concerns.

First, there is a clear need for a more thorough and systematic examination of the discourses and representational practices of state terrorism and the ontological-discursive foundations – the ideological, conceptual and institutional underpinnings – which make it possible. This entails, among other things, an examination of elite discourses on violence and the discursive foundations and practices of state violence and sovereignty itself. In a related sense, it also includes an examination of the discursive practices of the politically influential terrorism studies and IR fields (see Jackson 2008), in which the exclusion of state terrorism as a legitimate focus of research functions to reinforce the belief that states cannot and do not practise 'terrorism' – which in turn, functions as a form of legitimation for state violence and is therefore one of its conditions of possibility.

Second, as mentioned above, we would argue for a greater priority to be accorded to the theoretical and conceptual aspects of state terrorism. In particular, further development of the highly contested and frequently imprecise definition of state terrorism is crucial, especially if we are to develop a transparent, operational definition which could then be employed in the construction of a major database (see below), or in expanded numbers of empirical case studies. Other analytical concepts and typologies are also needed for the examination of the modalities, contexts, causes, outcomes and ending of domestic state terrorism, as well as the types, modalities and causes of state terrorism as a form of diplomatic behaviour and state terrorism during war. Once we have better developed analytical frameworks, these will then need to be carefully operationalized when and as they are needed for empirical research.

Third, as alluded to earlier, rigorous and detailed new research on a series of neglected cases and topics is urgently required, including a whole series of what we would refer to as taboo cases, which currently includes: Israeli state terrorism against the Palestinian territories and its surrounding neighbours in the form of occupational governance practices, counter-terrorism, and counter-insurgency, and coercive diplomacy and war (see Nasr, Hamilton this volume); Western state terrorism during the colonial, Cold War and post-Cold War periods, including for example, British actions in Africa, Asia and Northern Ireland, US actions in Latin America (see Raphael this volume), French actions in Indochina and Africa, Spanish actions during its 'dirty war' with ETA, and many other cases; China's actions in Tibet and elsewhere; Russia's actions in Chechnya, Georgia, and its 'near abroad'; and state terrorism within a number of key Western allies such as Kuwait (see Mason this volume), Pakistan (see Murphy and Tamana this volume), India (see Murphy this volume), Saudi Arabia, Egypt, and others.

Further research which adopts a conscious focus on state *terrorism* is also needed on the nature and modalities of historical cases, such as the use of terrorism during colonization and colonial rule, and the numerous cases of populist, rightist and communist dictatorships of the past two centuries, some of which, such as many past (and ongoing) dictatorships in small African states for example, remain entirely unknown and unstudied within the field. Although some of these cases will have been examined in the context of post-colonial, historical, and area studies, they have rarely to our knowledge been examined through the prism of terrorism studies, applying its key concepts and perspectives. Last, there is a real need for further research on cases of state terrorism that remain largely peripheral to the primary concerns of Western scholarship, primarily because they occur in developing regions like Africa and the Pacific (see Wardrop, Lasslett this volume). According to yearly human rights reports, acts of state terrorism occur with regular frequency across the peripheral regions of the world, but they are rarely examined as such within the scholarly journals and conferences of terrorism studies or IR.

Fourth, directly related to the need for specific, new empirical research, we would strongly argue for the prioritization of an ambitious, large-scale, authoritative dataset on state terrorism comparable to the recognized and widely used databases on non-state terrorism. Although it would necessarily be a partial accounting due to the sheer number of cases of state terrorism over the past few hundred years, and due to the difficulties of verifying information about events which states do not always want the outside world to know about, we believe that if it was systematically and rigorously constructed over the next few years, it could nonetheless provide a tremendous resource for researchers and over time would contain sufficient data for important kinds of comparative statistical analyses. In fact, there exists a modest database called the *Political Terror Scale* which 'measures levels of political violence and terror that a country experiences in a particular year based on a 5-level "terror scale"', and which covers the period from 1976–2007 (see Political Terror Scale website www.politicalterror-scale.org/). This type of effort could be built upon in a more systematic and ambitious project. The fact is that reliable data is widely available from human rights reports, lawyers, anthropologists, historians, the media, and elsewhere; it only requires a modest amount of funding and research assistance to translate this information into systematized data. Such a project, if it was done consistently and in a transparent manner, could potentially also have some normative value, as states would be unable to deny their involvement in acts of terrorism and could conceivably be forced to change their behaviour – notwithstanding the depressing track record of most states in response to such revelations.

Fifth, a consequence of the call for more empirical research is the need for the further exploration and development of research practices and ethics in this extremely difficult and potentially dangerous area. New scholars, in particular, need thorough preparation and instruction on how to go about researching state terrorism practically and the specific ethical and political challenges facing researchers in this area. It is an unfortunate reality that openly researching certain cases of state terrorism today, including the state terrorism of Israel, China, the United States, and others, can sometimes result in intimidation and harassment, public accusation in the media, travel restrictions, threats to one's career, and worse – as some of the contributors to this volume can personally attest. Scholars entering the field need to be prepared for such eventualities and academic and legal processes need to be developed across universities and professional associations to protect researcher independence and well-being, especially in the case of early career scholars without tenure. There are obviously particular problems related to field research within states who actively practise terrorism which anthropologists and other kinds of participant-oriented researchers have begun to discuss (see Sluka 2000).

Sixth, we see the need for more in-depth research into the causes of state terrorism – the reasons why elites choose to employ it at particular moments and the specific contexts within which it occurs and is made possible. In this regard, we see real value in applying Duvall and Stohl's elegant model of the causes of state terrorism (Duvall and Stohl 1988: 253–62) to large numbers of empirical cases in order to work out exactly what internal and external conditions lead political elites to calculate that state terrorism will be more or less efficient than other policy options and result in fewer costs. The chapters in this volume and other studies suggest that the processes of state consolidation following revolution or decolonization, perceived social crisis, insurgency, counter-terrorism, and war provide particularly potent contexts in which elites are tempted to employ terrorism. However, given that these conditions do not always result in state terrorism, further research is needed to determine the precise circumstances and reasons why elites make such terrible choices across different cases.

It also seems clear that for strong, mature (usually Western) states, situations of diplomatic conflict, economic imperialism, and (publicly perceived) serious internal threats are also state terrorism-provoking conditions. Again however, not all strong states engage in coercive diplomacy or political-economic forms of state terrorism, suggesting the need for further research on the exact conditions and processes under which the elites of strong states choose to employ terrorism. The reasons why Western elites in particular sometimes employ state terrorism are genuinely puzzling and in need of systematic research, in part because of their normal sensitivity to public scrutiny and the human rights-based political systems they operate within. This question could do with in-depth and extremely careful interview and archival research of former leaders and their aides to try to decipher their perceptions and calculations at the time of the terrorism policy, assuming of course, their cooperation with such sensitive questioning.

Seventh, we see a real need to prioritize the examination of the many cases of state terrorism being enacted within the broader practices of the global war on terror (see Poynting, McCulloch this volume). Human rights organizations, legal experts and scholars have provided clear indications that the war on terrorism is both leading to specific cases of state terrorism, such as the widespread use of torture, rendition, and disproportionate forms of counter-terrorism, and providing governments around the world with the public justification to engage in repression and terrorism against internal opponents. Documenting and analysing these abuses is important for the reasons of ensuring that important information is not lost to later attempts by governments to destroy their records of involvement, such as the CIA admission in March 2009 that they had already destroyed 92 interview tapes which most likely provided evidence of torture (BBC 2009), and for applying pressure on governments now to end ongoing abuses. In particular, there is an urgent need to examine what appear to be obvious but neglected cases of state terrorism, such the widespread operation of Western trained and equipped death squads in Iraq, the practice of kidnapping and 'disappearing' suspected militants after capture in Pakistan, Afghanistan, the Horn of

Africa, and elsewhere, and the targeted killing of terrorist suspects in a number of different regions.

Finally, there is a pressing need for further research on how state terrorism ends. While there is a growing literature on the different processes and conditions by which non-state terrorism is ended, we are not aware of any specific research which explores exactly how, why, and under what conditions political elites end their policies of state terrorism and how the practices of state terrorism are then expunged from state institutions. There are, of course, important studies on truth and reconciliation processes following civil war or transitions from authoritarian rule, but such research tends to focus on the aftermath of state violence more broadly and not necessarily on state terrorism or the specific reasons for its termination. Researching this question would have both analytical and normative value; understanding how state terrorism ends – whether it is the result of internal calculations or pressures from external actors, for example – could prove vital to devising strategies for activists seeking to end or prevent state terrorism in particular cases.

Of course, these are only a few possible suggestions for a new research agenda on state terrorism; there are many others which we are not able to elaborate on, such as: the linkages and interdependencies between state and non-state terrorism; the relationship between state terrorism and structural violence, such as inequality and discrimination; the growing privatization of state terrorism in terms of the employment of private security and military companies; forms of social response and resistance to state terrorism, including the effectiveness of non-violence and peace education; the meaning of emancipation in the context of state terrorism; and others. Our hope is that as more and more scholars begin to engage with this important project, new questions and ideas will emerge to add to this list.

Conclusion

Although state violence and repression have long been studied in cognate fields such as law, history, political science, criminology, and sociology, among others, research on state *terrorism* which deliberately utilizes the concepts, theories, methods, and insights of the well-established and rapidly growing terrorism studies field is still relatively rare. We have tried to argue in this volume that the study of state terrorism is both intellectually valid and illuminating of political behaviour, and should command a higher priority in the research activities of IR and terrorism scholars than it presently does. We have also suggested a preliminary list of topics and questions which could form the basis of a future research agenda for the still nascent but visibly growing sub-field of state terrorism research (see Blakeley 2009; Stokes and Raphael forthcoming). Notwithstanding our call to expand and deepen the study of state terrorism, and to prioritize some key questions, there are a number of well-posted dangers from the broader field of terrorism studies (see Jackson *et al.* 2009: 232–6) which we would do well to avoid.

First, we must remain sensitive to the inherent and often serious problems and challenges surrounding the employment of the ontologically unstable term 'terrorism' as a key part of our research agenda. 'Terrorism', whether state or non-state, is not an objective, empirically identifiable phenomenon in which the terroristic qualities are inherent to the violent act; rather, it is a socially constructed, historically contingent category of human behaviour that is dependent upon circumstance, context, and intention. Most often, the term is deployed as a derogatory label against one's enemies. Although the observed regularities in state violence may be analytically and normatively usefully described as 'state terrorism' at the present moment, we must remain sensitive to those circumstances in which the term 'terrorism' is not necessarily helpful or productive and to the possibility that in the future it may have to give way to other, more productive labels and concepts.

Second, and perhaps most importantly, we must avoid the temptation to engage in polemics and politically biased analyses, especially the kind which view all state violence as inherently terroristic or which single out particular cases for unrelenting condemnation. Accusations of political bias and unfair treatment are already common strategies employed against state terrorism researchers and human rights activists; in some cases, they are entirely justified. These cases damage the credibility of research on the subject. Such accusations are best met with an uncompromising commitment to the highest standards of scholarship, consistency towards all cases of state terrorism, and complete transparency regarding our definitions, criteria, and approaches. In this regard, an authoritative dataset describing all the cases of state terrorism we can find, backed up by source evidence, and published in the public domain would be tremendously useful. In short, we suggest that scholars of state terrorism aim to be continually reflexive and use the term judiciously and with real sensitivity to its inherent instability and to the social and political consequences of its usage.

Last, there is a danger of marginalization and irrelevancy in the competition for both the funding which will sustain our research, and political influence, whether we are aiming for input into the policy process or civil society-based activism. Avoiding both of these outcomes will depend greatly on the nature of our research – its rigour, transparency, the terms in which it is expressed, and the purposes to which it is put – and our willingness to engage with some of the key issues and concerns of the broader terrorism studies field. On the latter issue, we see real value in exploring the ways in which studies on state terrorism can add value to the study of non-state terrorism. It seems clear that state and non-state terrorism are linked, and in some real-world cases, they feed off each other in violent cycles. However, a stronger case needs to be made that studying state and non-state forms of the phenomenon together is a useful way forward. In the end, there is little to be gained, we feel, in bifurcating the terrorism studies field into state/non-state and critical/orthodox sections. Such an outcome can best be avoided through respectful dialogue and debate. In addition to our broader aims, we hope that this volume will go some way towards opening up new kinds of questions and provoking new debates on this critical issue within the wider field.

References

BBC (2009) 'CIA Destroyed 92 Interview Tapes', 2 March. Online, available at: http://news.bbc.co.uk/2/hi/americas/7919579.stm (accessed 2 March 2009).

Becker, T. (2006) *Terrorism and the State: Rethinking the Rules of State Responsibility*, Oxford: Hart Publishing.

Blakeley, R. (2006) 'Still Training to Torture? US Training of Military Forces from Latin America', *Third World Quarterly*, 27 (8): 1439–61.

—— (2007) 'Bringing the State back into Terrorism Studies', *European Political Science*, 6 (3): 228–35.

—— (2009) *State Terrorism and Neoliberalism: The North in the South*, Abingdon: Routledge.

Duvall, R., and Stohl, M. (1988) 'Governance by Terror', in M. Stohl (ed.) *The Politics of Terrorism*, 3rd edition, New York: Marce Dekker.

Gareau, F. (2004) *State Terrorism and the United States: From Counterinsurgency to the War on Terrorism*, London: Zed Books.

George, A. (ed.) (1991) *Western State Terrorism*, Cambridge: Polity Press.

Goodin, R. (2006) *What's Wrong with Terrorism?* Cambridge: Polity Press.

Grosscup, B. (2006) *Strategic Terror: The Politics and Ethics of Aerial Bombardment*, London: Zed Books.

Herman, E. (1982) *The Real Terror Network: Terrorism in Fact and Propaganda*, South End Press.

Herring, E. (2008) 'Critical Terrorism Studies: An Activist Scholar Perspective', *Critical Studies on Terrorism*, 1 (2): 197–212.

Jackson, R. (2008) 'The Ghosts of State Terror: Knowledge, Politics and Terrorism Studies', *Critical Studies on Terrorism*, 1 (3): 377–92.

Jackson, R., M. Breen Smyth and J. Gunning, (eds) (2009) *Critical Terrorism Studies: A New Research Agenda*, Abingdon: Routledge.

Schmid, A., and Jongman, A. (1988) *Political Terrorism: A New Guide to Actors, Authors, Concepts, Databases, Theories and Literature*, Oxford: North Holland.

Silke, A. (2004) 'The Road Less Travelled', in A. Silke, (ed.) *Research on Terrorism: Trends, Achievements and Failures*, London: Frank Cass.

Sluka, J. (ed.) (2000) *Death Squad: An Anthropology of State Terror*, University of Pennsylvania Press.

Stohl, M. (1988) 'States, Terrorism and State Terrorism: The Role of the Superpowers', in R. Slater and M. Stohl (eds) *Current Perspectives on International Terrorism*, Macmillan.

—— (2006) The State as Terrorist: Insights and Implications', *Democracy and Security*, 2: 1–25.

Stohl, M., and Lopez, G. (eds) (1984) *The State as Terrorist: The Dynamics of Governmental Violence and Repression*, Westport: Greenwood Press.

—— (1986) 'Government Violence and Repression: An Agenda for Research', in Bernard Johnpoll (ed.) *Contributions in Political Science*, New York: Greenwood.

Stokes, D. (2004) *America's Other War: Terrorizing Colombia*, London: Zed Books.

Stokes, D., and S. Raphael (forthcoming) *Transnational Empire, Oil and Human Rights: Understanding US Intervention in the Age of Terror*, Baltimore: Johns Hopkins University Press.

Terry, J. (1980) 'State Terrorism: A Juridical Examination in Terms of Existing International Law', *Journal of Palestine Studies*, 10 (1): 94–117.

Thakrah, J. (2004) *Dictionary of Terrorism*, 2nd edition, London: Routledge.

Walter, E.V. (1969) *Terror and Resistance*, New York: Oxford University Press.

Index

Lightning Source UK Ltd.
Milton Keynes UK
UKOW021426270112

186196UK00002B/19/P

9 780415 664479